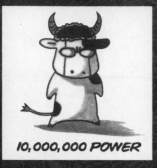

10,000,000 POWER

What do I most look forward to when creating manga? Why, doing the bonus pages, of course! I wish I could just do a whole 180 pages of nothing but bonus pages!

—*Hiromu Arakawa, 2003*

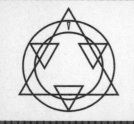

Born in Hokkaido (northern Japan), Hiromu Arakawa first attracted national attention in 1999 with her award-winning manga **Stray Dog**. Her series **Fullmetal Alchemist** debuted in 2001 in Square Enix's monthly manga anthology **Shonen Gangan**.

FULLMETAL ALCHEMIST
VOL. 4

VIZ Media Edition

Story and Art by Hiromu Arakawa

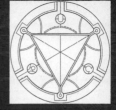

Translation/Akira Watanabe
English Adaptation/Jake Forbes
Touch-up Art & Lettering/Wayne Truman
Design/Amy Martin
Editor/Jason Thompson
Series Consultant/Egan Loo

Hagane no RenkinJutsushi vol. 4 © 2003 Hiromu Arakawa/SQUARE ENIX. First published in Japan in 2003 by SQUARE ENIX CO., LTD. English translation rights arranged with SQUARE ENIX CO., LTD. and VIZ Media, LLC.

The stories, characters and incidents mentioned in this publication are entirely fictional.

Printed in the U.S.A.

Published by VIZ Media, LLC
P.O. Box 77010
San Francisco, CA 94107

14
First printing, October 2005
Fourteenth printing, June 2016

www.viz.com

鋼の錬金術師

FULLMETAL ALCHEMIST

4

荒川弘

HIROMU ARAKAWA

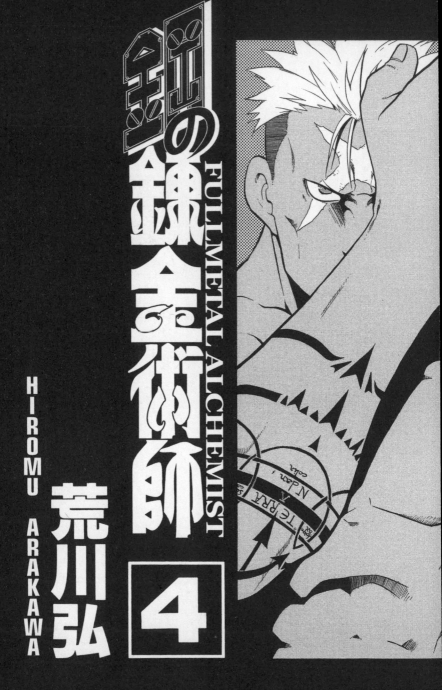

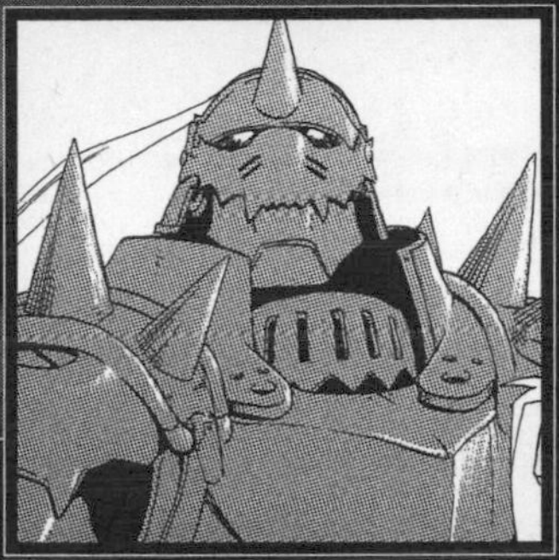

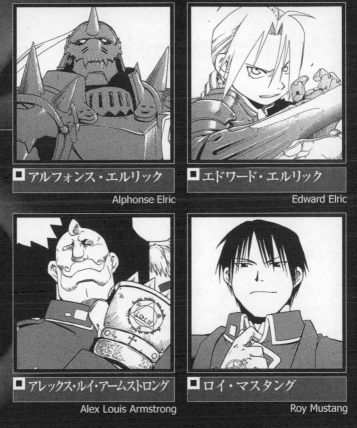

アルフォンス・エルリック

Alphonse Elric

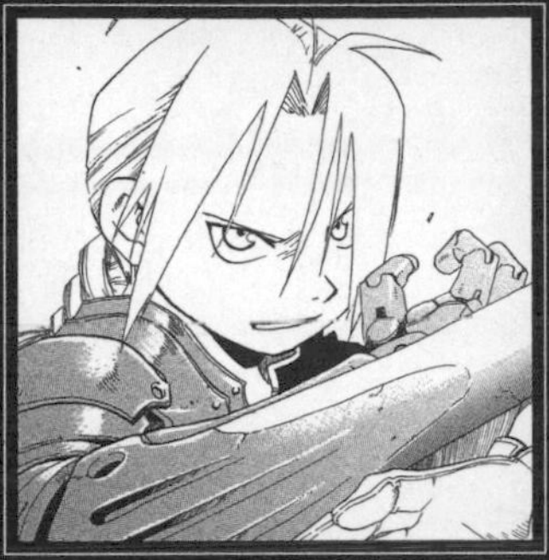

エドワード・エルリック

Edward Elric

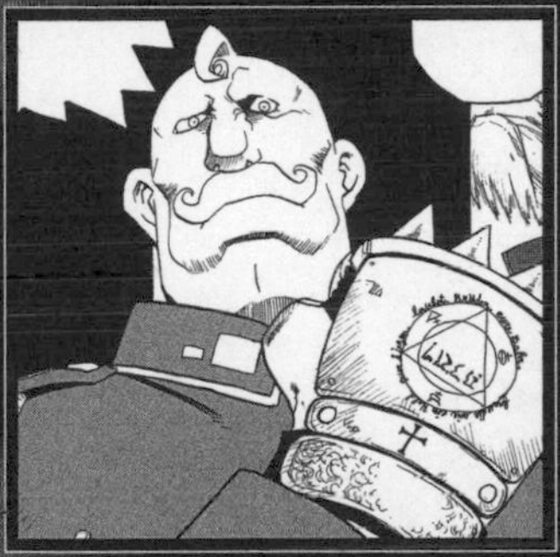

アレックス・ルイ・アームストロング

Alex Louis Armstrong

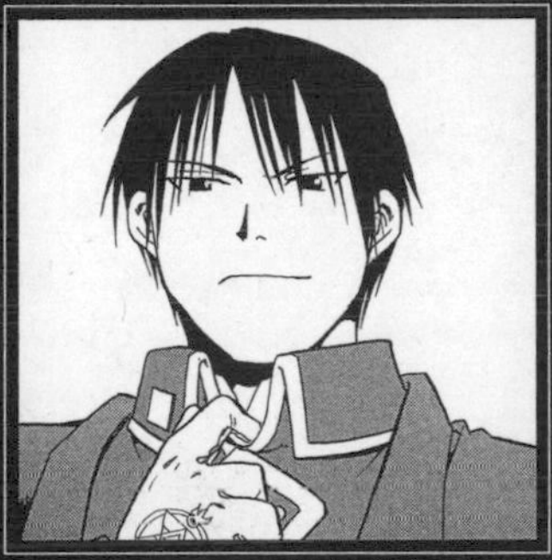

ロイ・マスタング

Roy Mustang

OUTLINE
FULLMETAL ALCHEMIST

Using a forbidden alchemical ritual, the Elric brothers attempted to bring their dead mother back to life. But the ritual went wrong, consuming Edward Elric's leg and Alphonse Elric's entire body. At the cost of his arm, Edward was able to graft his brother's soul into a suit of armor. Equipped with mechanical "auto-mail" to replace his missing limbs, Edward becomes a state alchemist, serving the military on deadly missions. Now, the two brothers roam the world in search of a way to regain what they have lost…

In search of the Philosopher's Stone, the Elric brothers break into a top-secret government laboratory. Within, they find evidence of horrible experiments, guarded by two killers whose souls are housed in suits of armor, like Alphonse. But just when the killers are about to explain everything, the "clean-up crew" arrives…

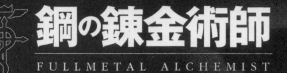

鋼の錬金術師
FULLMETAL ALCHEMIST

CHARACTERS
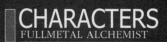
FULLMETAL ALCHEMIST

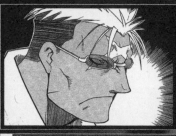

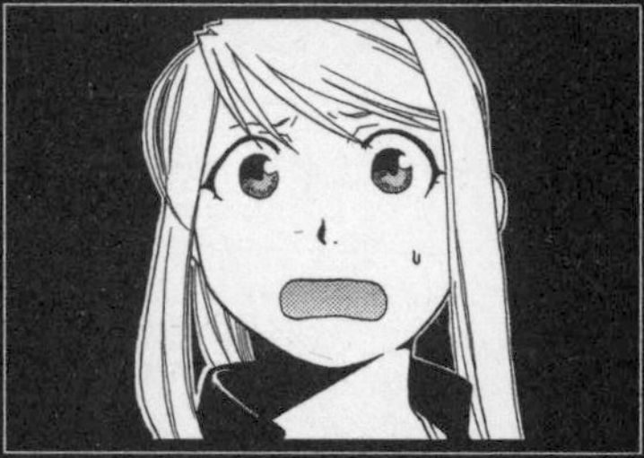

□ ウィンリィ・ロックベル

Winry Rockbell

□ 傷の男（スカー）

Scar

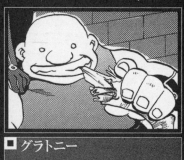

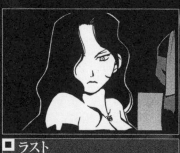

□ グラトニー

Gluttony

□ ラスト

Lust

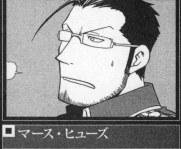

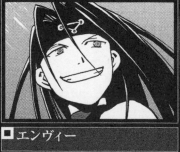

□ マース・ヒューズ

Maes Hughes

□ エンヴィー

Envy

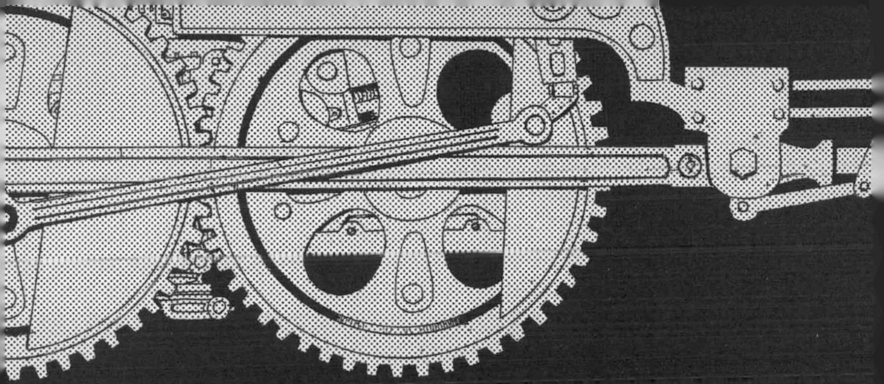

CONTENTS

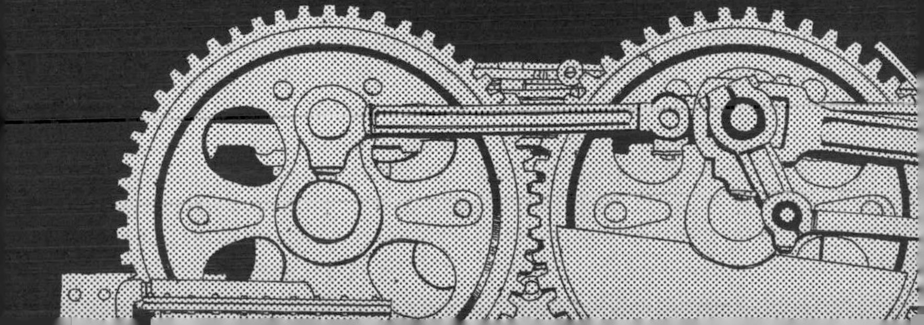

Chapter 13: Fullmetal Body

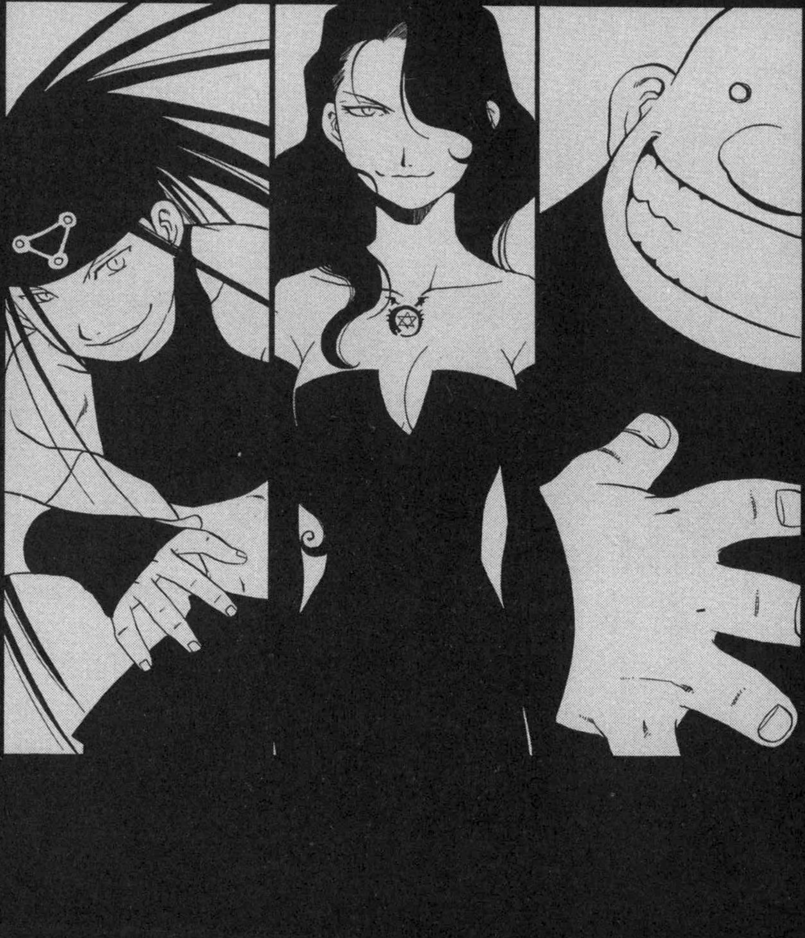

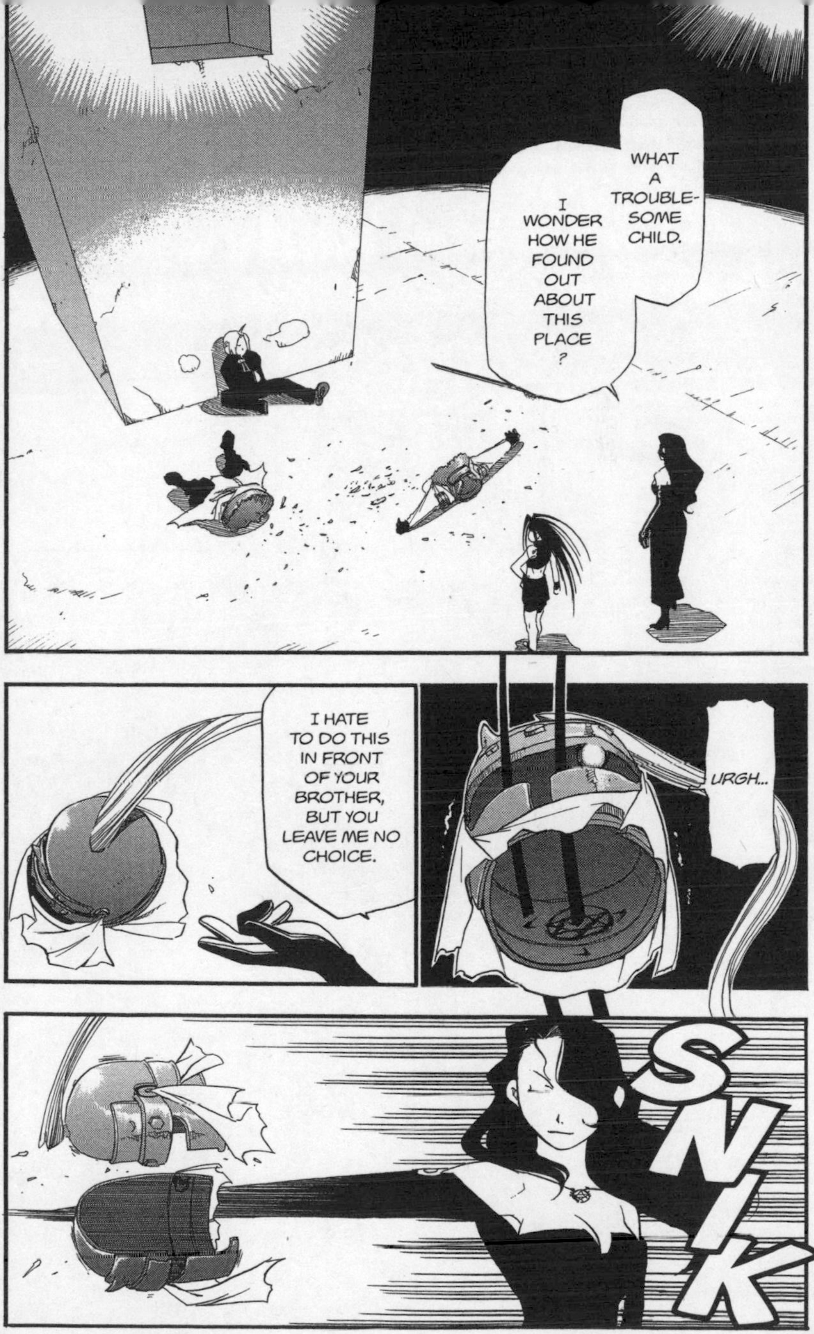
WHAT A TROUBLE-SOME CHILD.
I WONDER HOW HE FOUND OUT ABOUT THIS PLACE?
URGH...
I HATE TO DO THIS IN FRONT OF YOUR BROTHER, BUT YOU LEAVE ME NO CHOICE.
SNIK

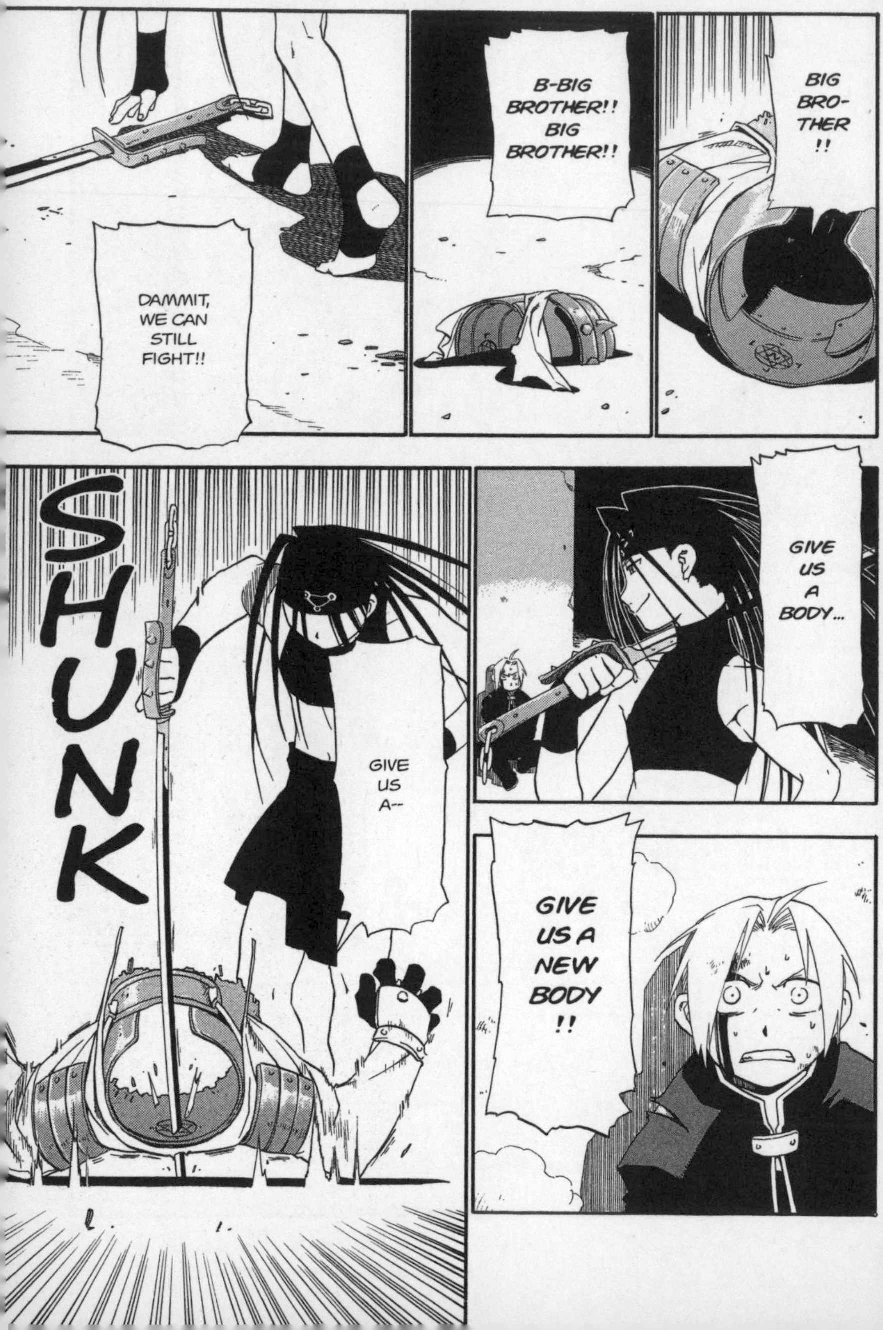

BIG BRO-THER !!
B-BIG BROTHER!! BIG BROTHER!!
DAMMIT, WE CAN STILL FIGHT!!
GIVE US A BODY...
GIVE US A NEW BODY !!
GIVE US A--
SHUNK

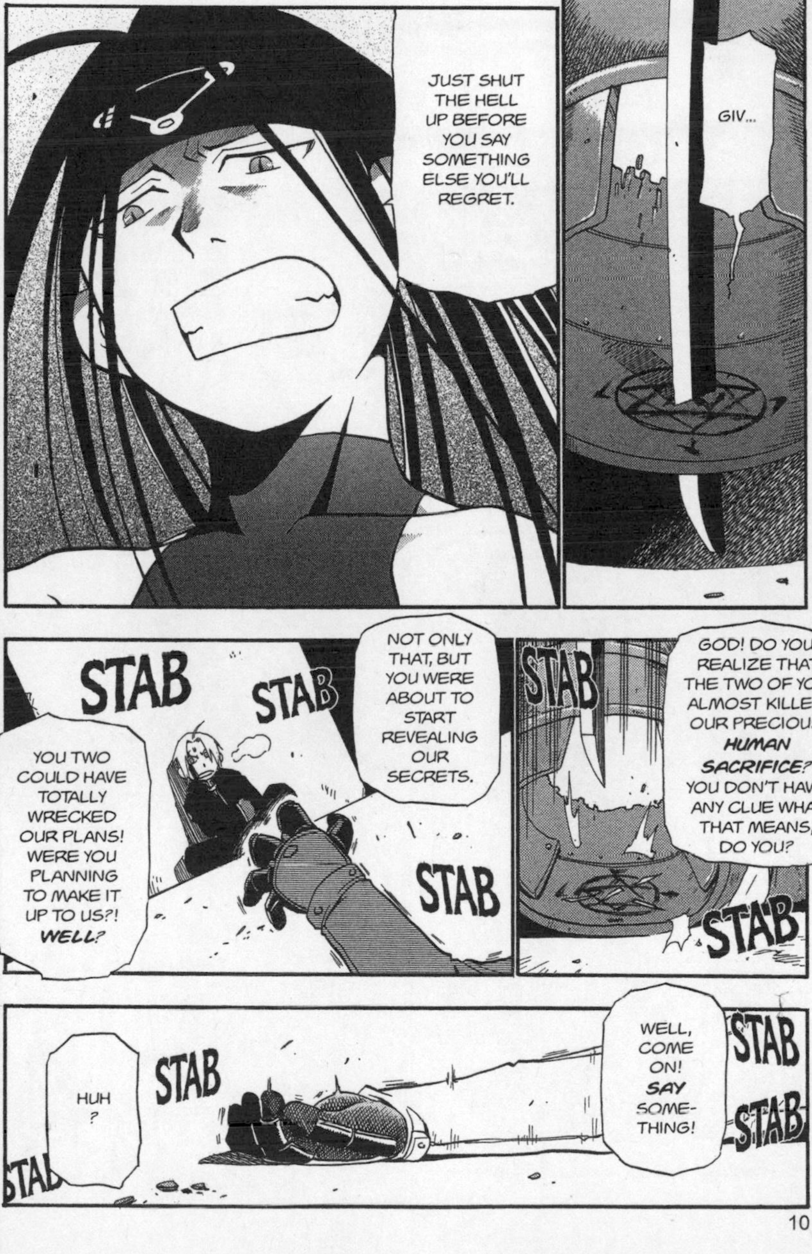
GIV...
JUST SHUT THE HELL UP BEFORE YOU SAY SOMETHING ELSE YOU'LL REGRET.
GOD! DO YOU REALIZE THAT THE TWO OF YOU ALMOST KILLED OUR PRECIOUS *HUMAN SACRIFICE?* YOU DON'T HAVE ANY CLUE WHAT THAT MEANS, DO YOU?
STAB
STAB
NOT ONLY THAT, BUT YOU WERE ABOUT TO START REVEALING OUR SECRETS.
STAB
STAB
YOU TWO COULD HAVE TOTALLY WRECKED OUR PLANS! WERE YOU PLANNING TO MAKE IT UP TO US?! *WELL?*
STAB
WELL, COME ON! *SAY* SOME-THING!
STAB
STAB
STAB
HUH ?
STAB

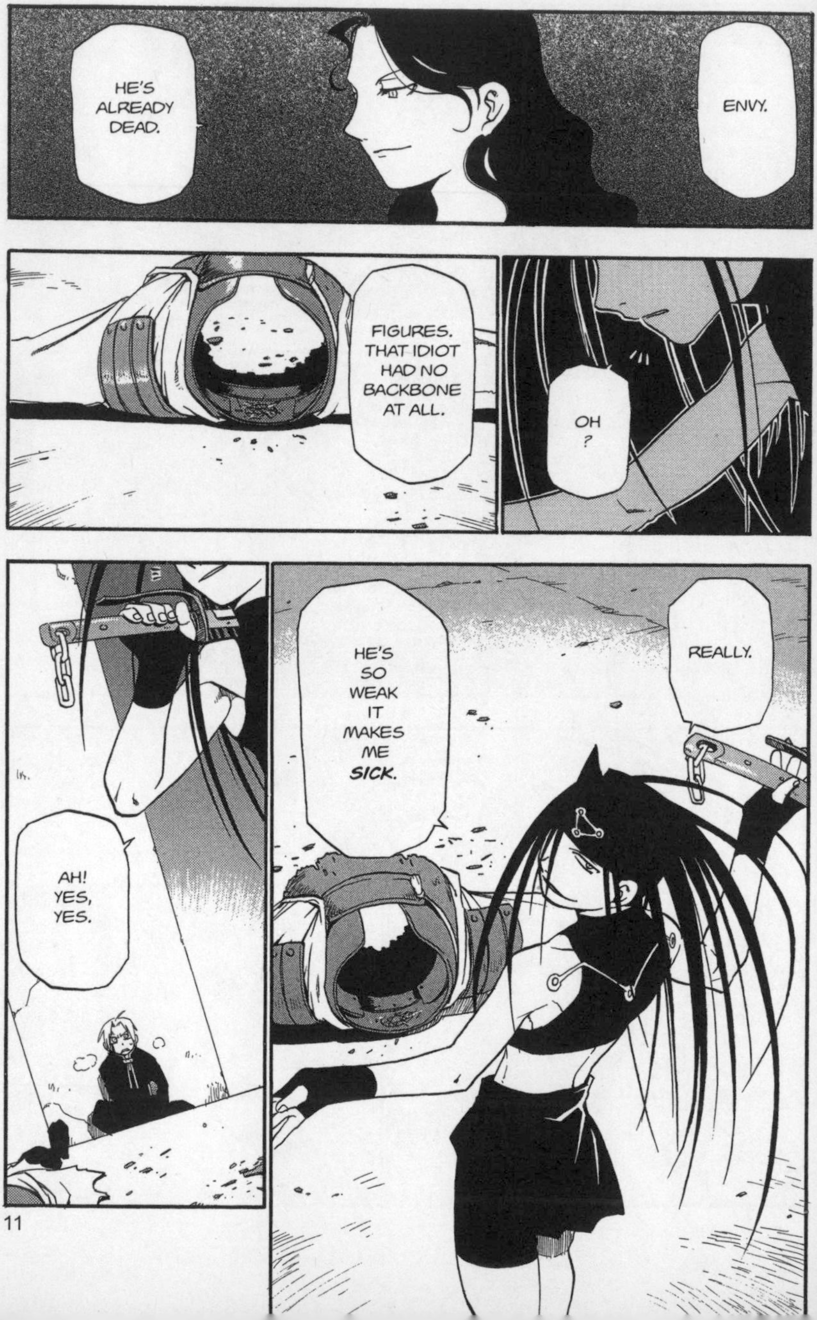
ENVY.
HE'S ALREADY DEAD.
OH ?
FIGURES. THAT IDIOT HAD NO BACKBONE AT ALL.
REALLY.
HE'S SO WEAK IT MAKES ME SICK.
AH! YES, YES.

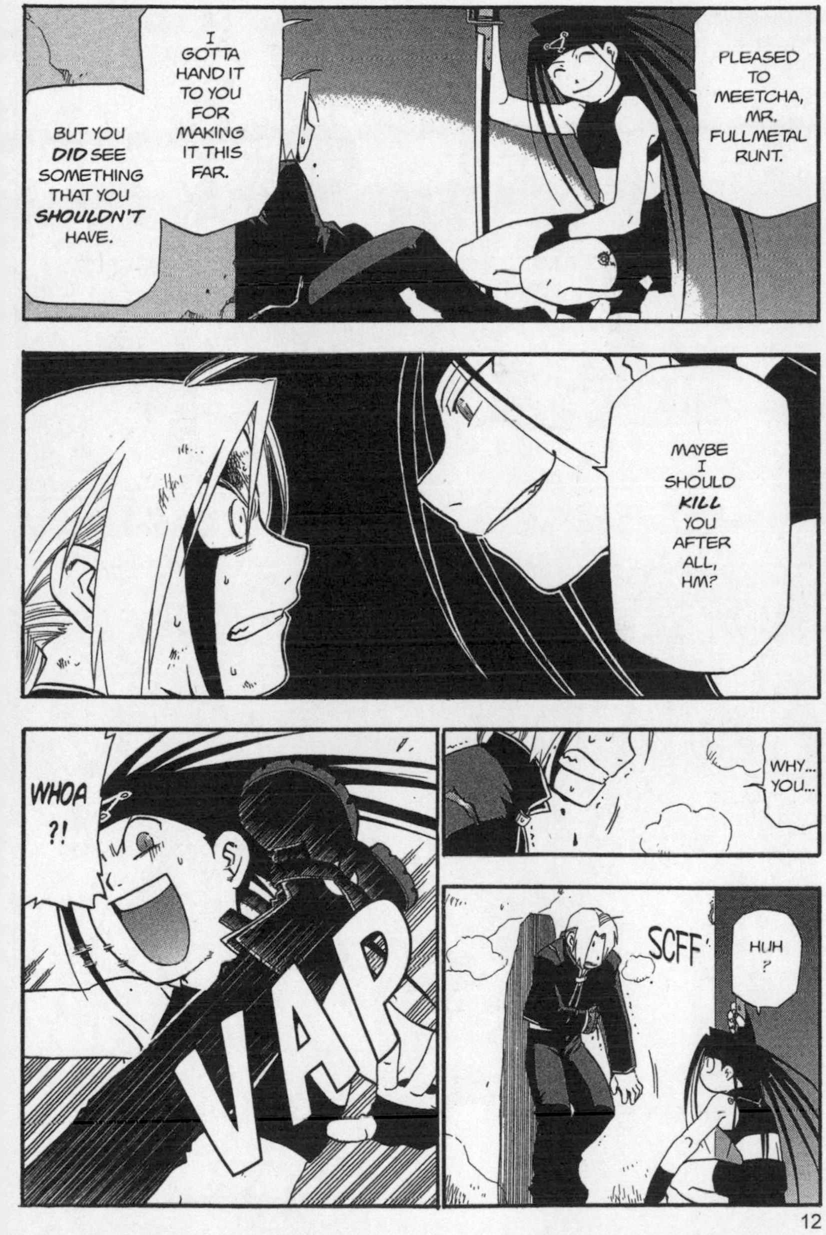
PLEASED TO MEETCHA, MR. FULLMETAL RUNT.
I GOTTA HAND IT TO YOU FOR MAKING IT THIS FAR.
BUT YOU **DID** SEE SOMETHING THAT YOU **SHOULDN'T** HAVE.
MAYBE I SHOULD **KILL** YOU AFTER ALL, HM?
WHY... YOU...
HUH ?
SCFF
WHOA ?!
VAP

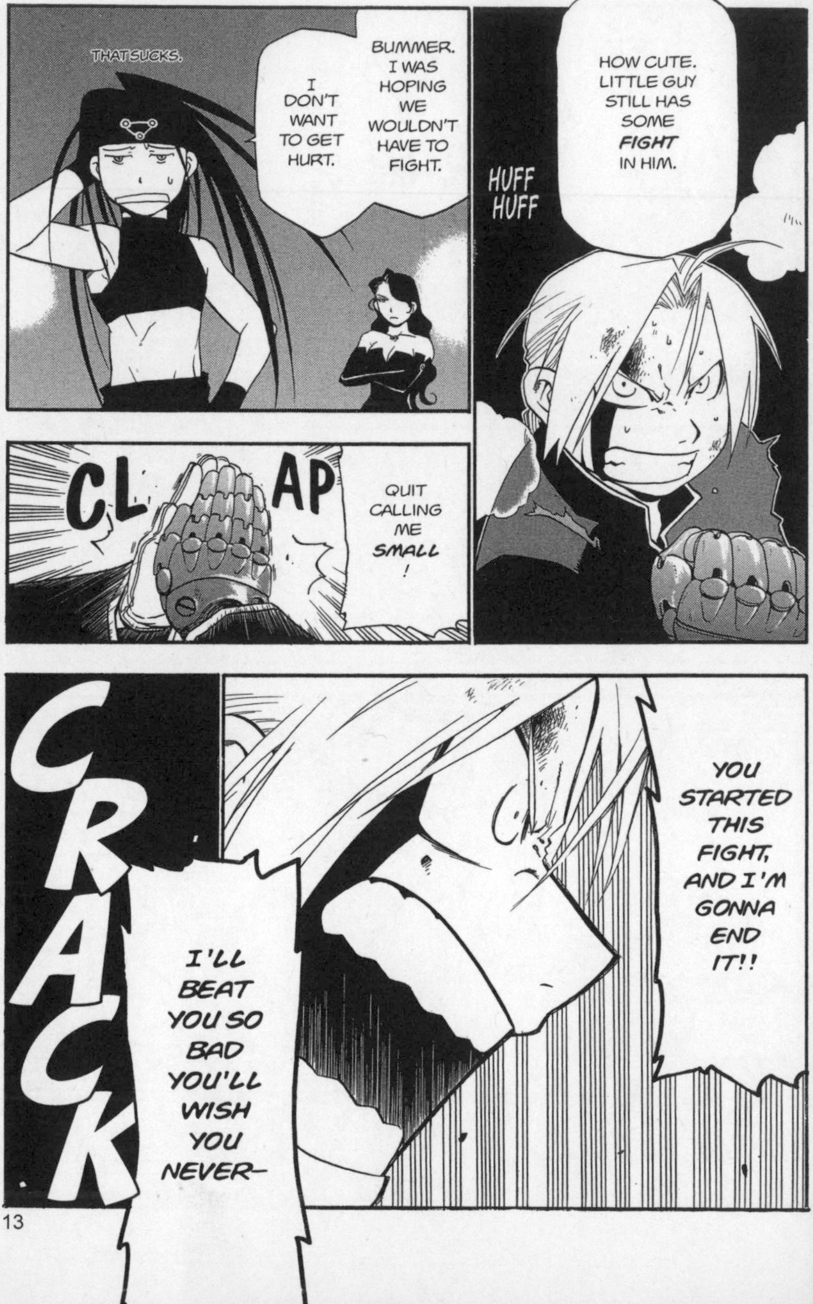
HOW CUTE. LITTLE GUY STILL HAS SOME FIGHT IN HIM.
HUFF HUFF
BUMMER. I WAS HOPING WE WOULDN'T HAVE TO FIGHT.
I DON'T WANT TO GET HURT.
THAT SUCKS.
QUIT CALLING ME SMALL!
CLAP
YOU STARTED THIS FIGHT, AND I'M GONNA END IT!!
I'LL BEAT YOU SO BAD YOU'LL WISH YOU NEVER—
CRACK

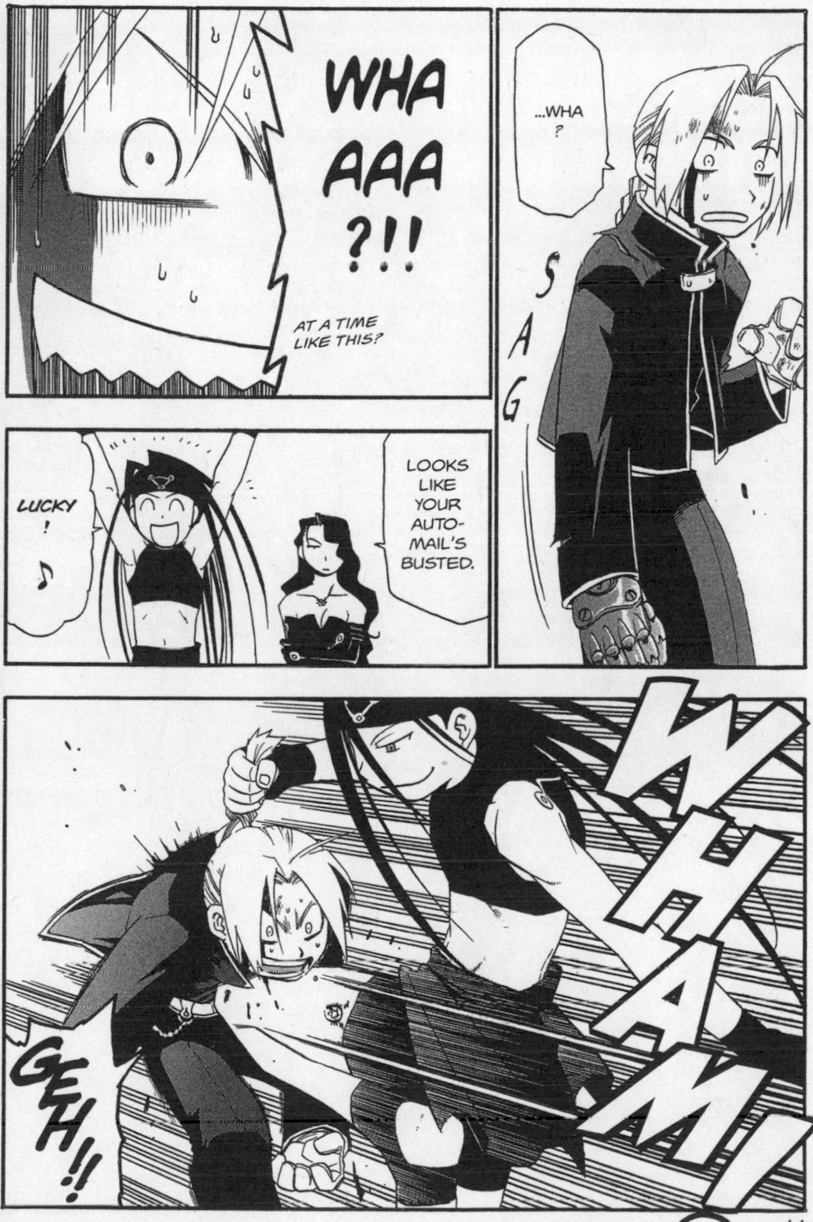
...WHA ?
SAG
WHA AAA ?!!
AT A TIME LIKE THIS?
LOOKS LIKE YOUR AUTO-MAIL'S BUSTED.
LUCKY! ♪
WHAM!
GEH!!

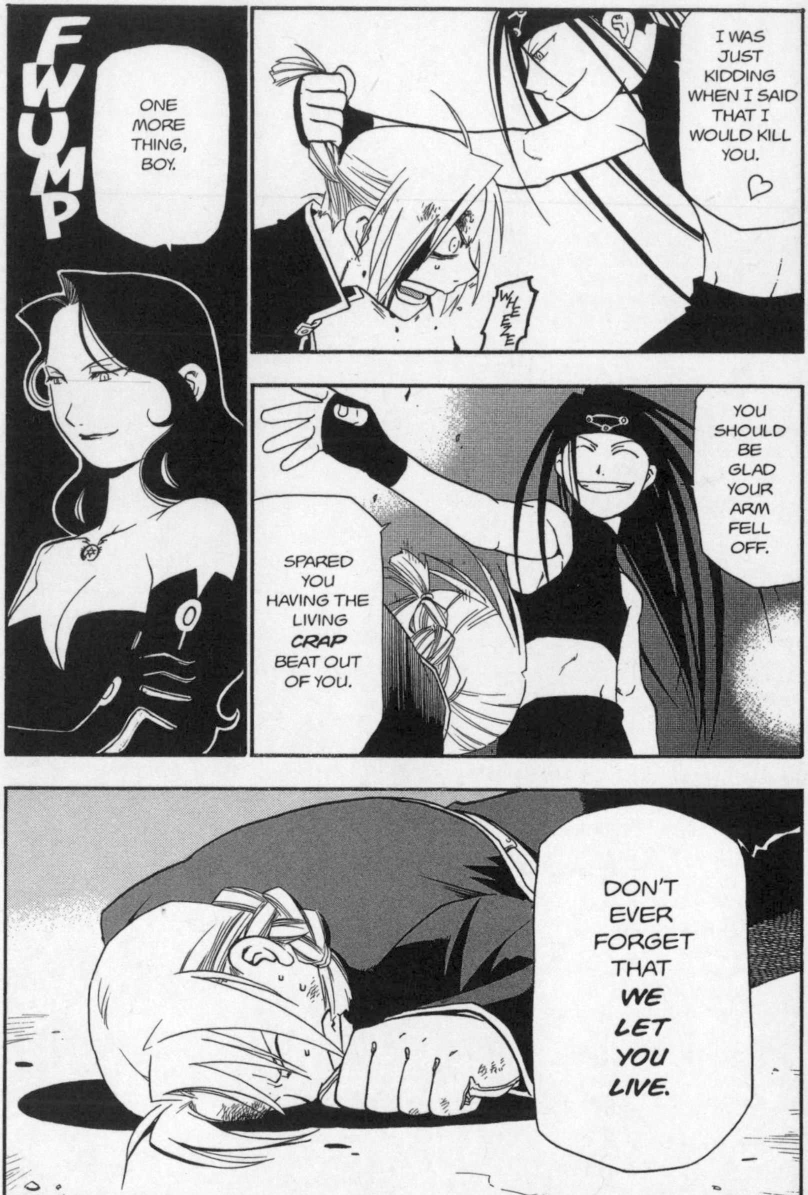
I WAS JUST KIDDING WHEN I SAID THAT I WOULD KILL YOU. ♡
WHEEZE
YOU SHOULD BE GLAD YOUR ARM FELL OFF.
SPARED YOU HAVING THE LIVING *CRAP* BEAT OUT OF YOU.
FWUMP
ONE MORE THING, BOY.
DON'T EVER FORGET THAT *WE LET YOU LIVE.*

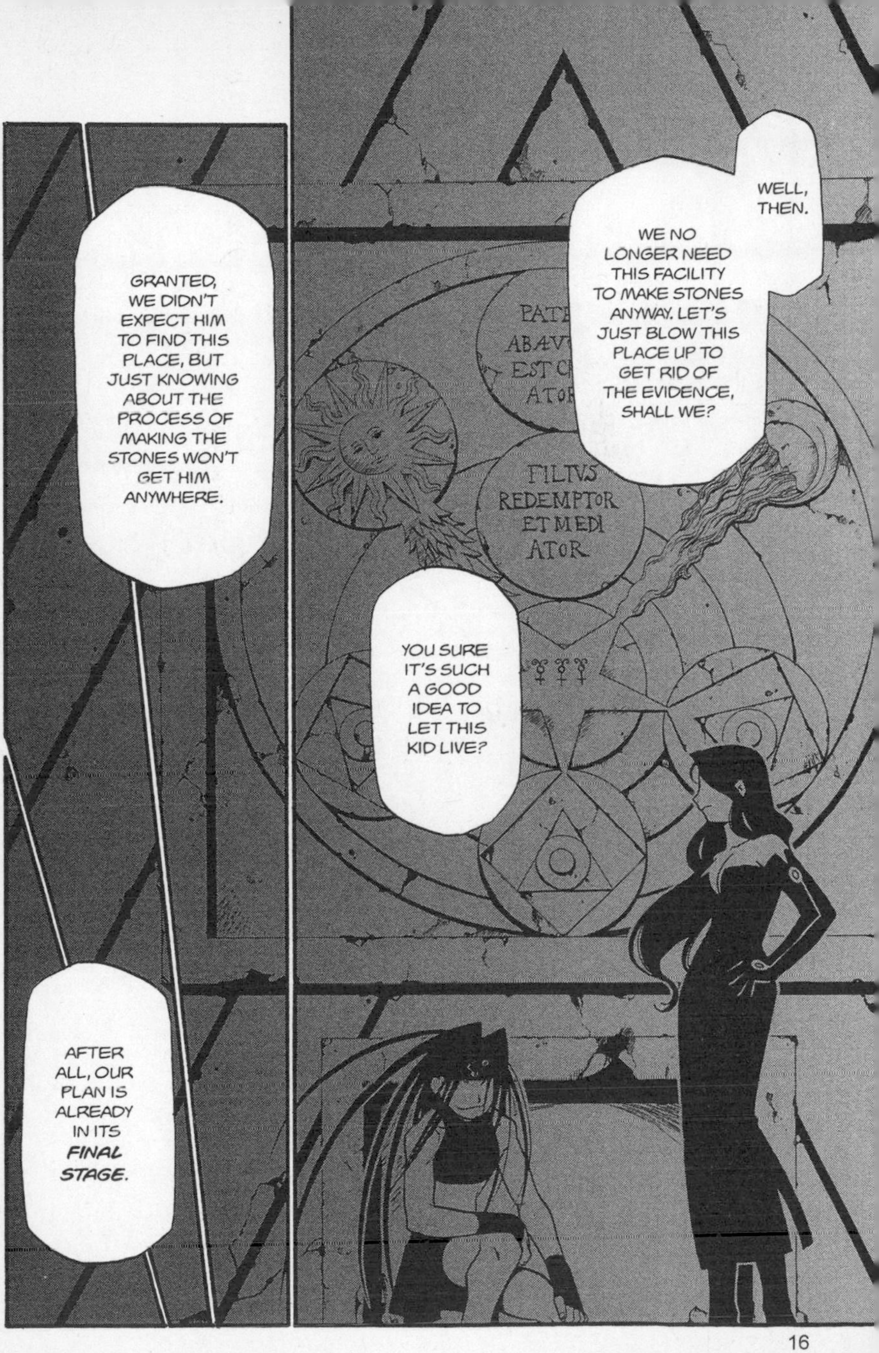
WELL, THEN.
WE NO LONGER NEED THIS FACILITY TO MAKE STONES ANYWAY. LET'S JUST BLOW THIS PLACE UP TO GET RID OF THE EVIDENCE, SHALL WE?
FILIVS REDEMPTOR ET MEDI ATOR
YOU SURE IT'S SUCH A GOOD IDEA TO LET THIS KID LIVE?
GRANTED, WE DIDN'T EXPECT HIM TO FIND THIS PLACE, BUT JUST KNOWING ABOUT THE PROCESS OF MAKING THE STONES WON'T GET HIM ANYWHERE.
AFTER ALL, OUR PLAN IS ALREADY IN ITS *FINAL STAGE*.

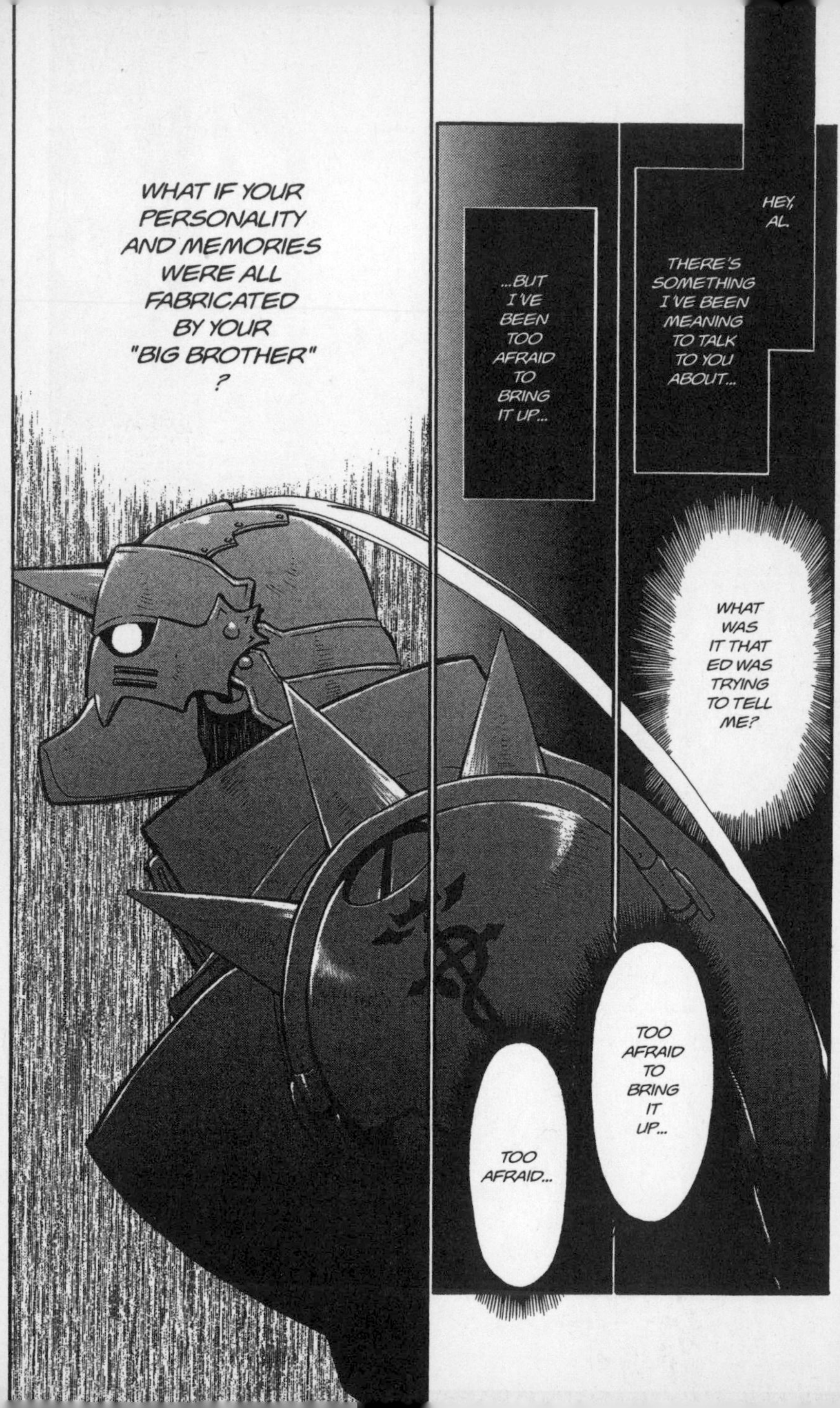
HEY, AL.
THERE'S SOMETHING I'VE BEEN MEANING TO TALK TO YOU ABOUT...
...BUT I'VE BEEN TOO AFRAID TO BRING IT UP...
WHAT WAS IT THAT ED WAS TRYING TO TELL ME?
TOO AFRAID TO BRING IT UP...
TOO AFRAID...
WHAT IF YOUR PERSONALITY AND MEMORIES WERE ALL FABRICATED BY YOUR "BIG BROTHER"?

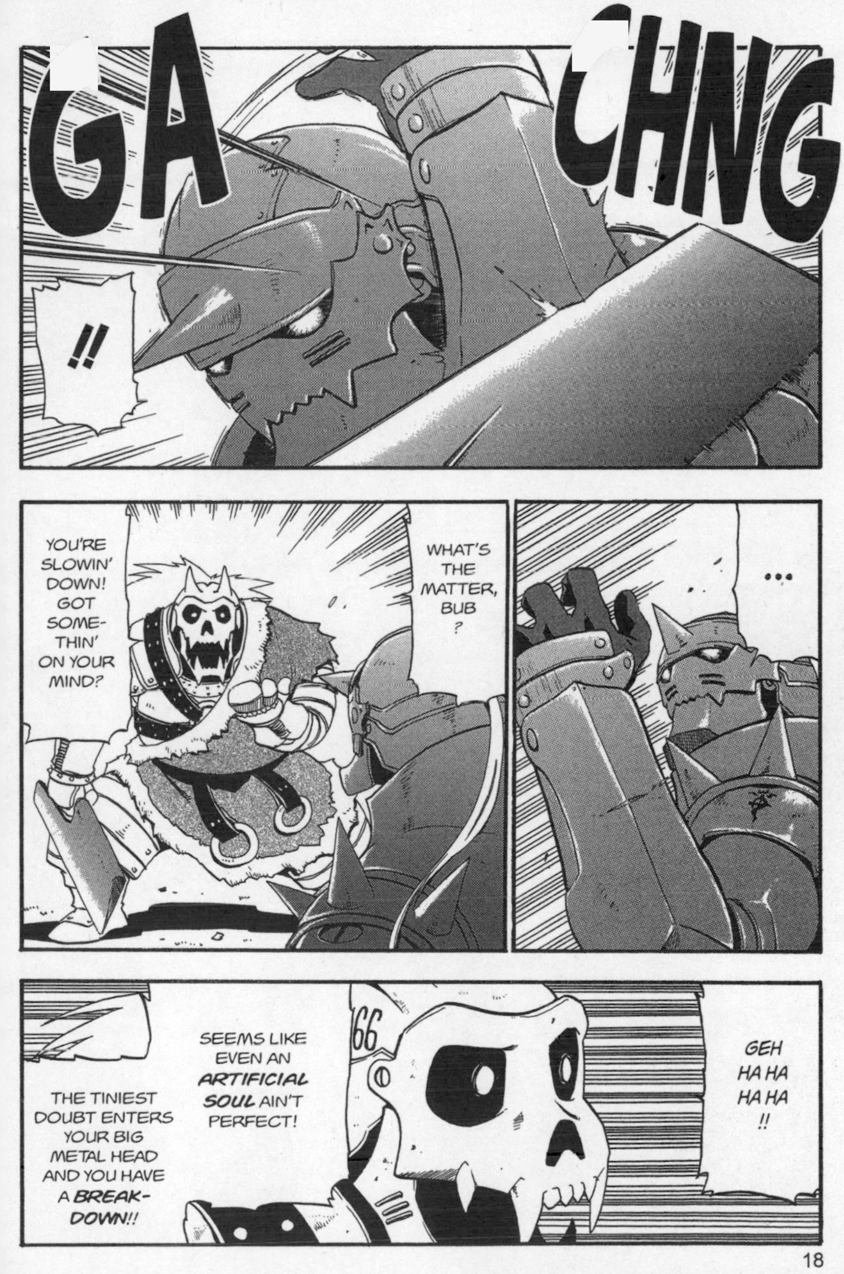
GA CHNG
!!
...
WHAT'S THE MATTER, BUB?
YOU'RE SLOWIN' DOWN! GOT SOMETHIN' ON YOUR MIND?
GEH HA HA HA HA!!
SEEMS LIKE EVEN AN ARTIFICIAL SOUL AIN'T PERFECT!
THE TINIEST DOUBT ENTERS YOUR BIG METAL HEAD AND YOU HAVE A BREAK-DOWN!!

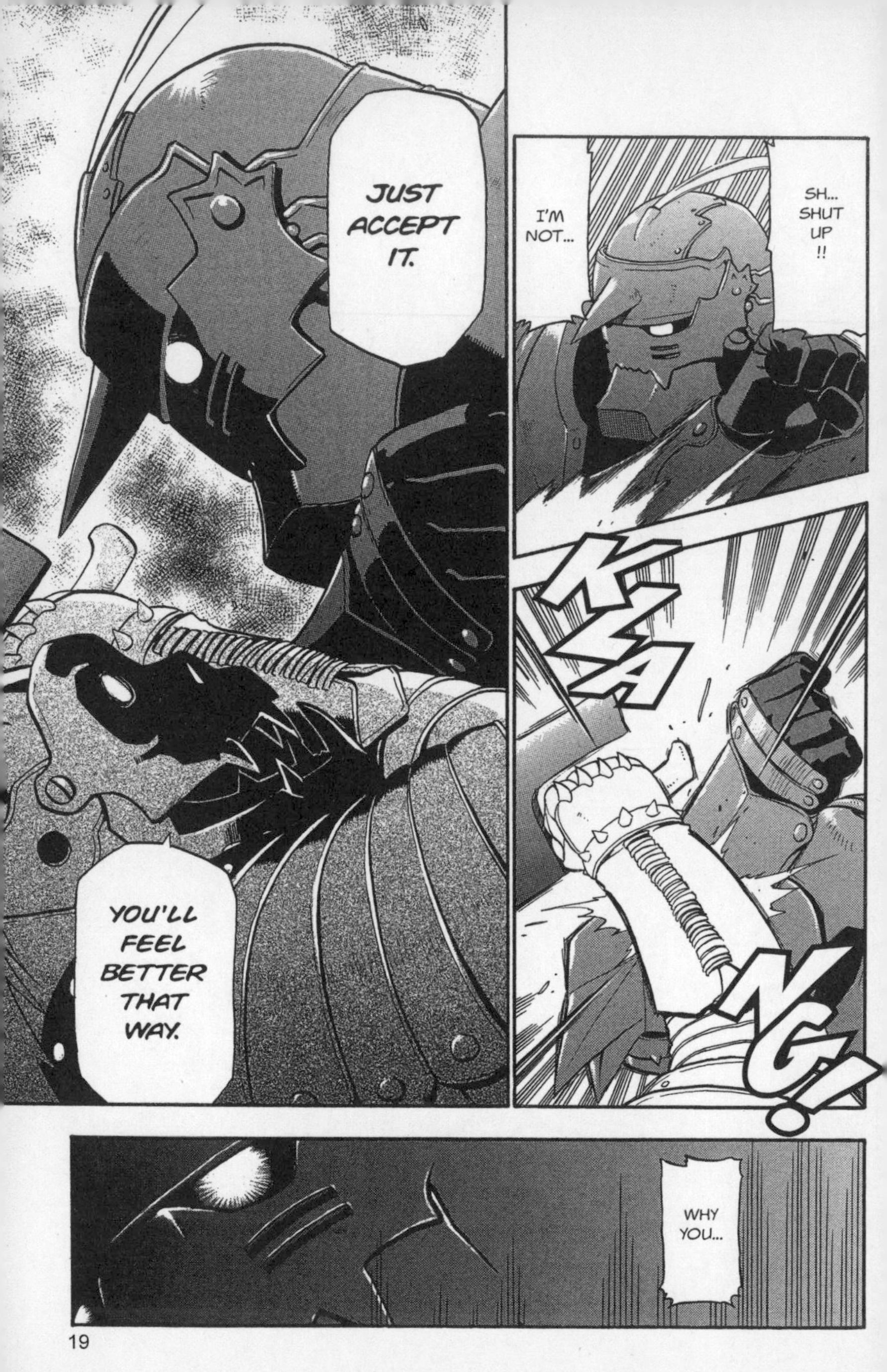
SH... SHUT UP !!
I'M NOT...
KA
NG!!
JUST ACCEPT IT.
YOU'LL FEEL BETTER THAT WAY.
WHY YOU...

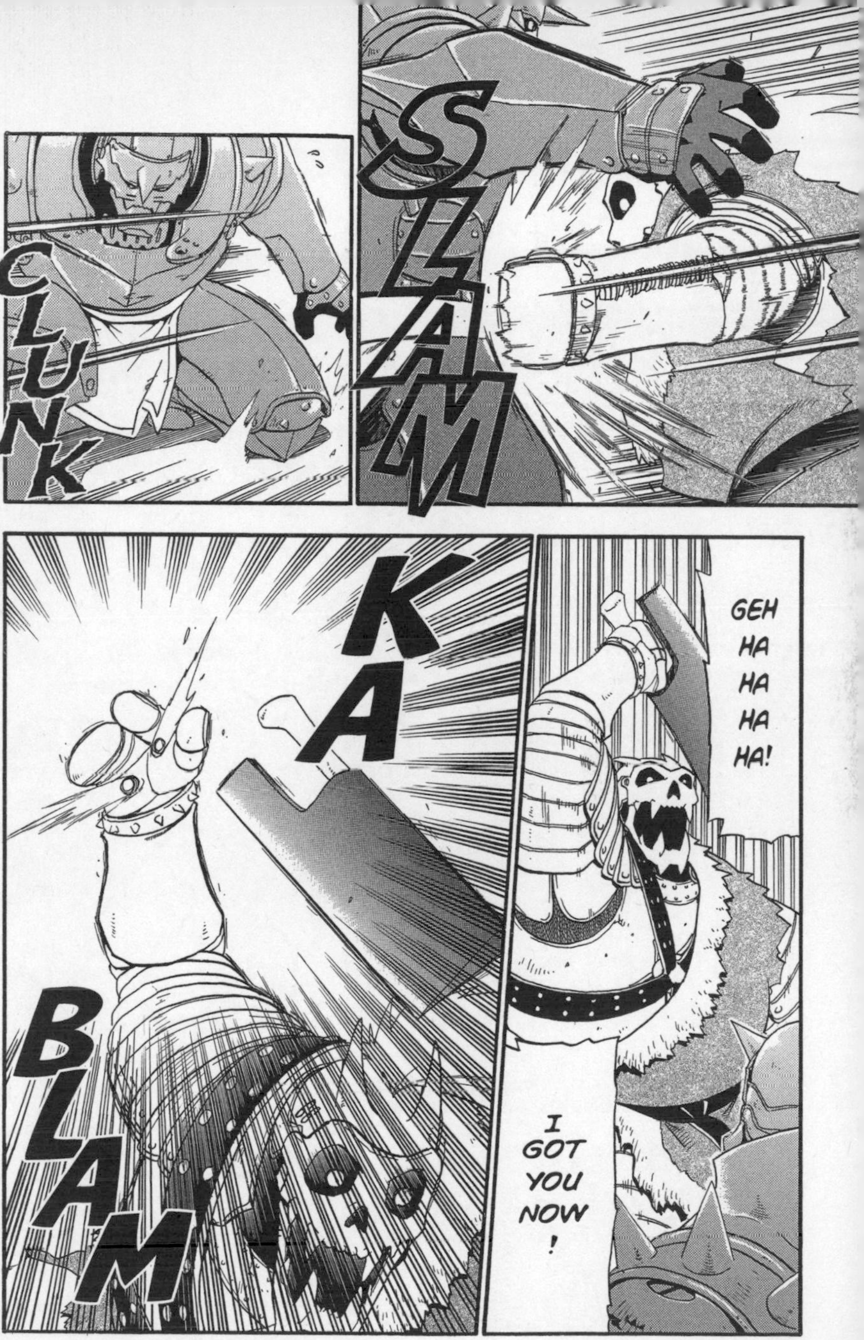

SLAM
CLUNK
GEH HA HA HA HA!
I GOT YOU NOW!
KA
BLAM

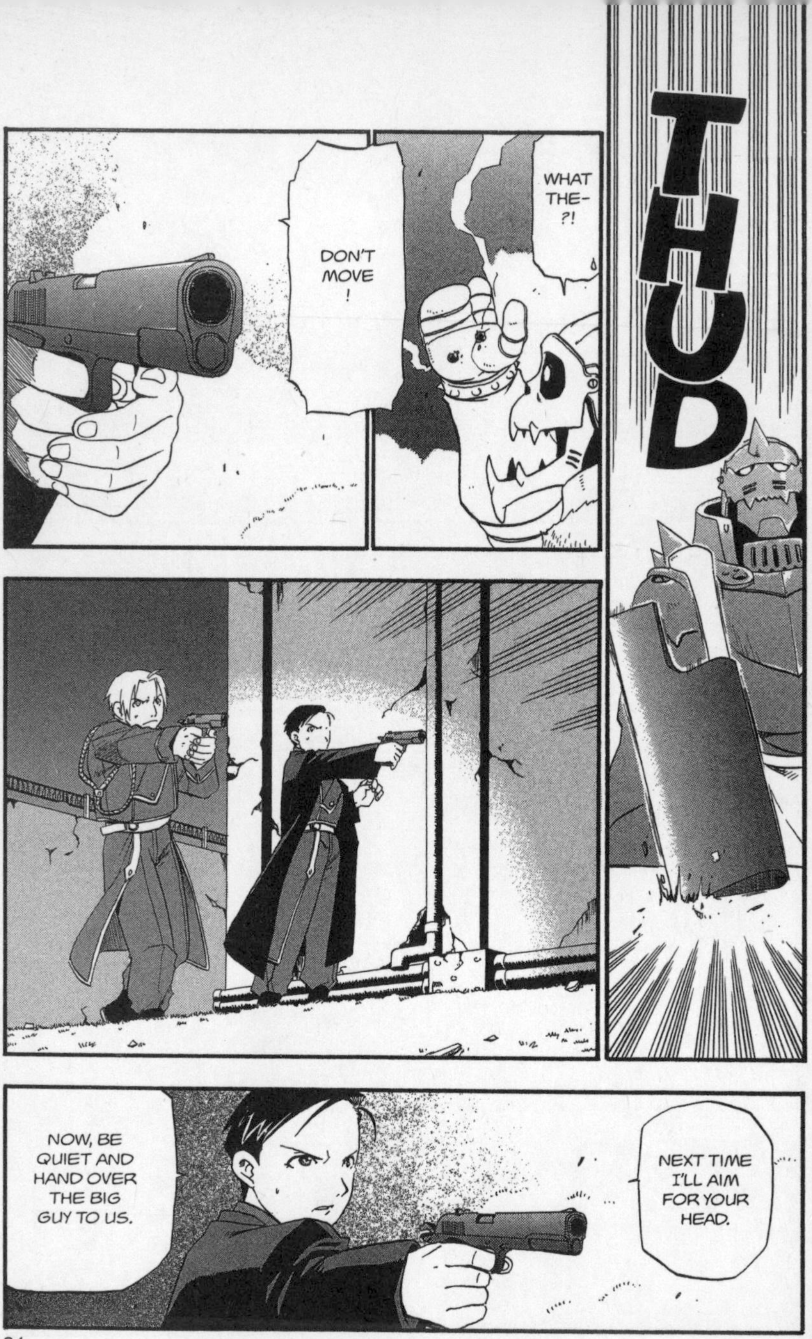
THUD
WHAT THE-?!
DON'T MOVE!
NEXT TIME I'LL AIM FOR YOUR HEAD.
NOW, BE QUIET AND HAND OVER THE BIG GUY TO US.

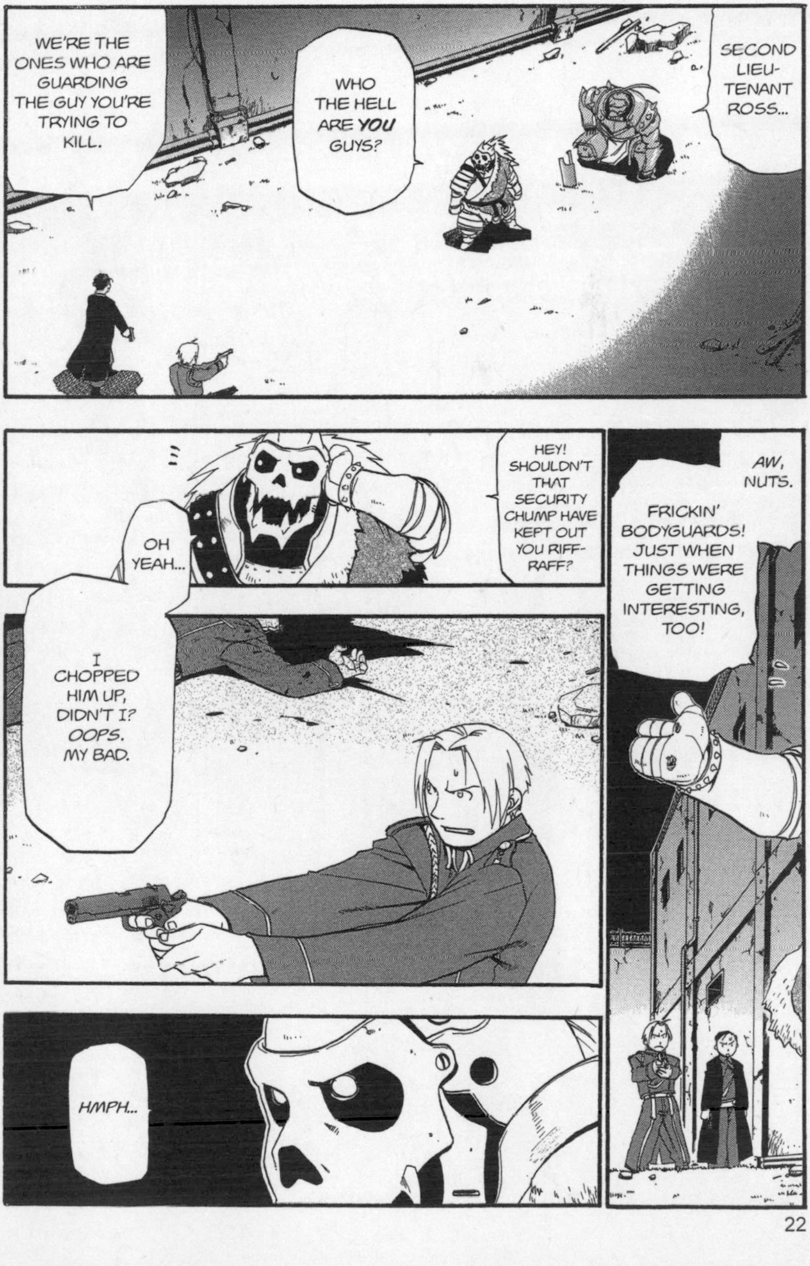
SECOND LIEU-TENANT ROSS...
WHO THE HELL ARE *YOU* GUYS?
WE'RE THE ONES WHO ARE GUARDING THE GUY YOU'RE TRYING TO KILL.
AW, NUTS.
FRICKIN' BODYGUARDS! JUST WHEN THINGS WERE GETTING INTERESTING, TOO!
HEY! SHOULDN'T THAT SECURITY CHUMP HAVE KEPT OUT YOU RIFF-RAFF?
OH YEAH...
I CHOPPED HIM UP, DIDN'T I? *OOPS.* MY BAD.
HMPH...

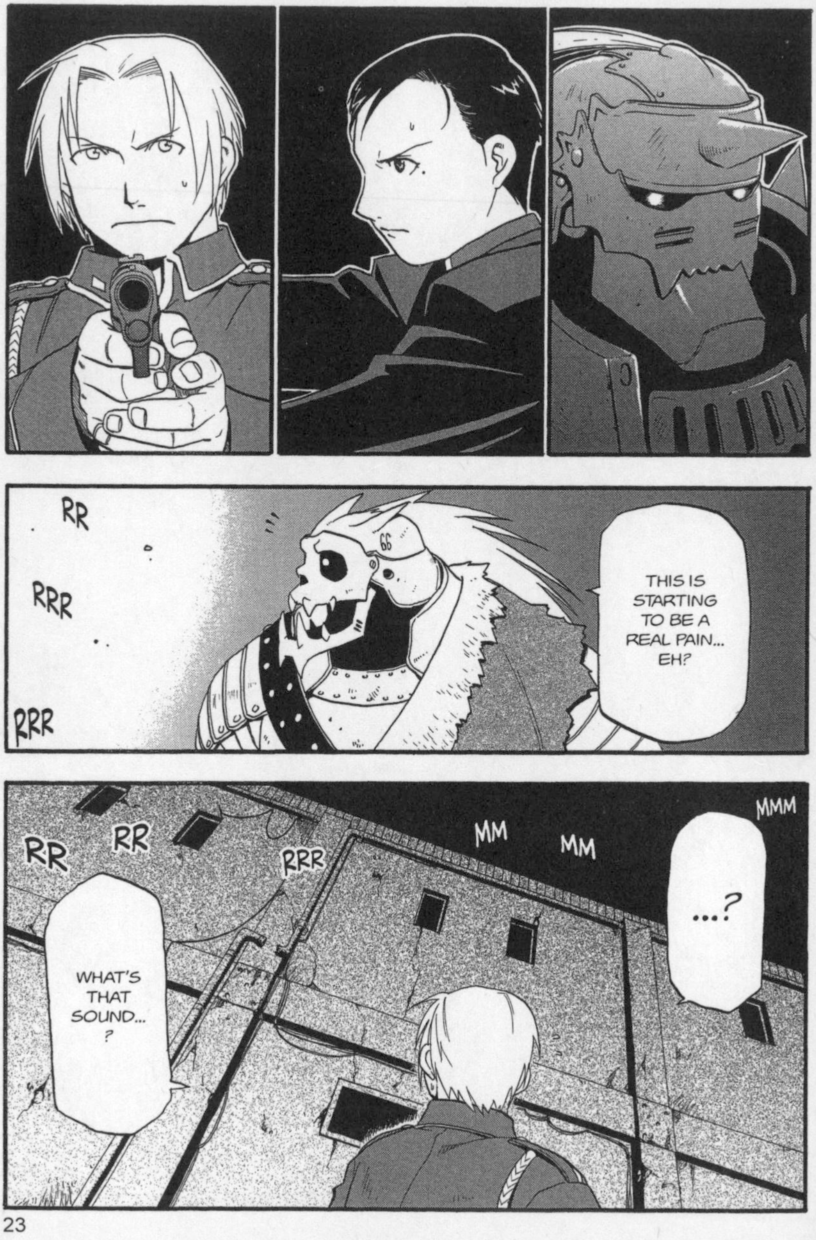
THIS IS STARTING TO BE A REAL PAIN... EH?
RR
RRR
RRR
MMM
MM
MM
...?
RRR
RR
RR
WHAT'S THAT SOUND... ?

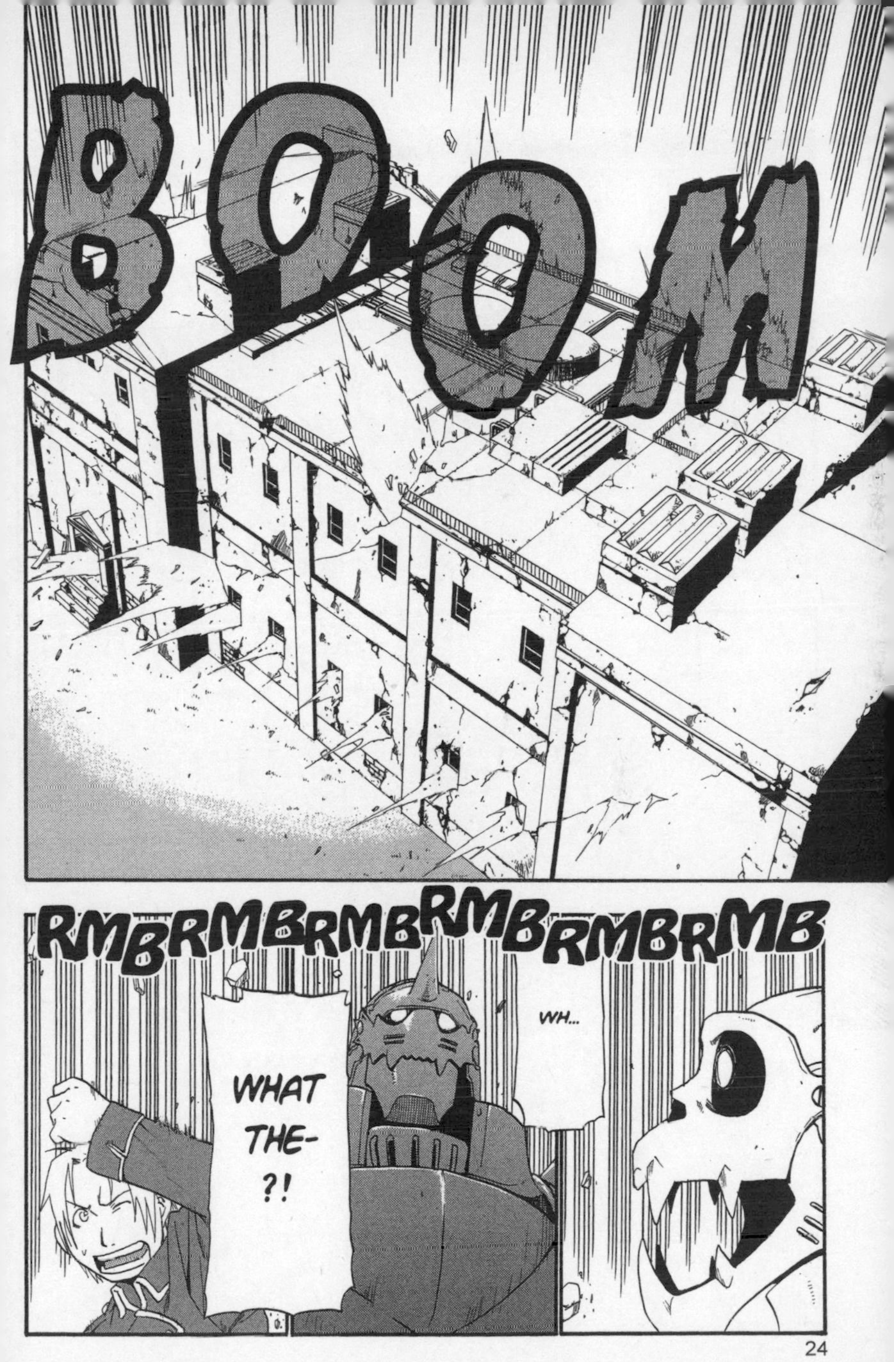
BOOM
RMBRMBRMBRMBRMBRMBRMB
WH...
WHAT THE-?!

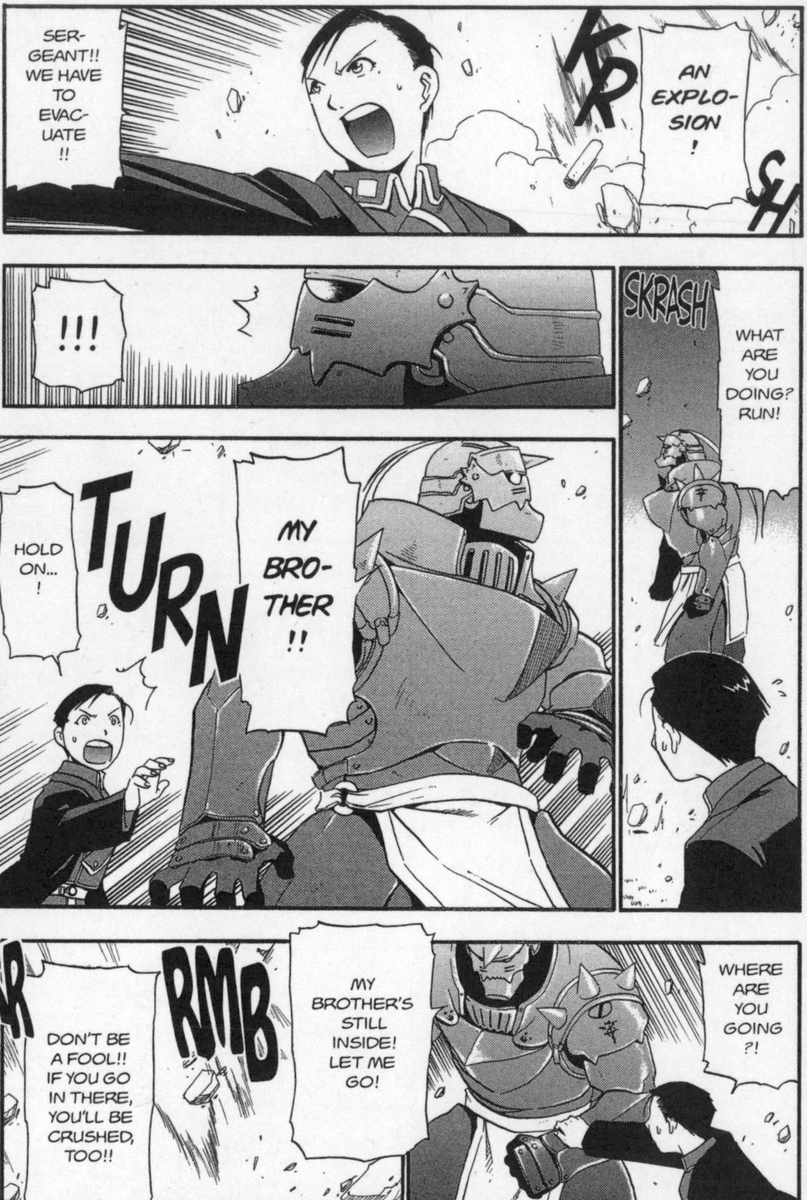
KR
AN EXPLOSION!
SH
SERGEANT!! WE HAVE TO EVACUATE!!
SKRASH
WHAT ARE YOU DOING? RUN!
!!!
MY BROTHER!!
TURN
HOLD ON...!
WHERE ARE YOU GOING?!
MY BROTHER'S STILL INSIDE! LET ME GO!
RR
RMB
DON'T BE A FOOL!! IF YOU GO IN THERE, YOU'LL BE CRUSHED, TOO!!

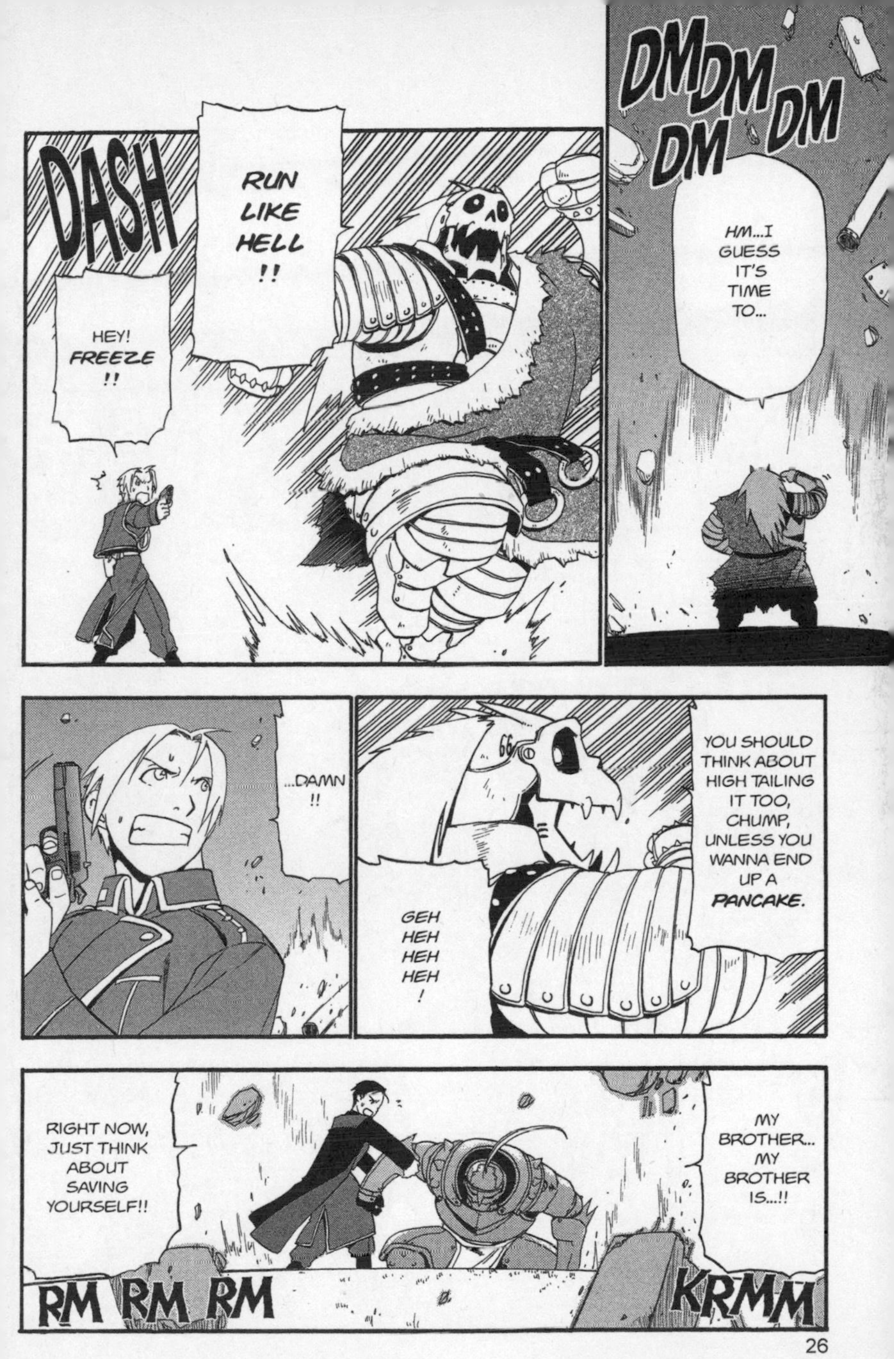
DM DM DM DM DM
HM...I GUESS IT'S TIME TO...
RUN LIKE HELL !!
DASH
HEY! FREEZE !!
YOU SHOULD THINK ABOUT HIGH TAILING IT TOO, CHUMP, UNLESS YOU WANNA END UP A PANCAKE.
GEH HEH HEH HEH !
...DAMN !!
MY BROTHER... MY BROTHER IS...!!
RIGHT NOW, JUST THINK ABOUT SAVING YOURSELF!!
KRMM
RM RM RM

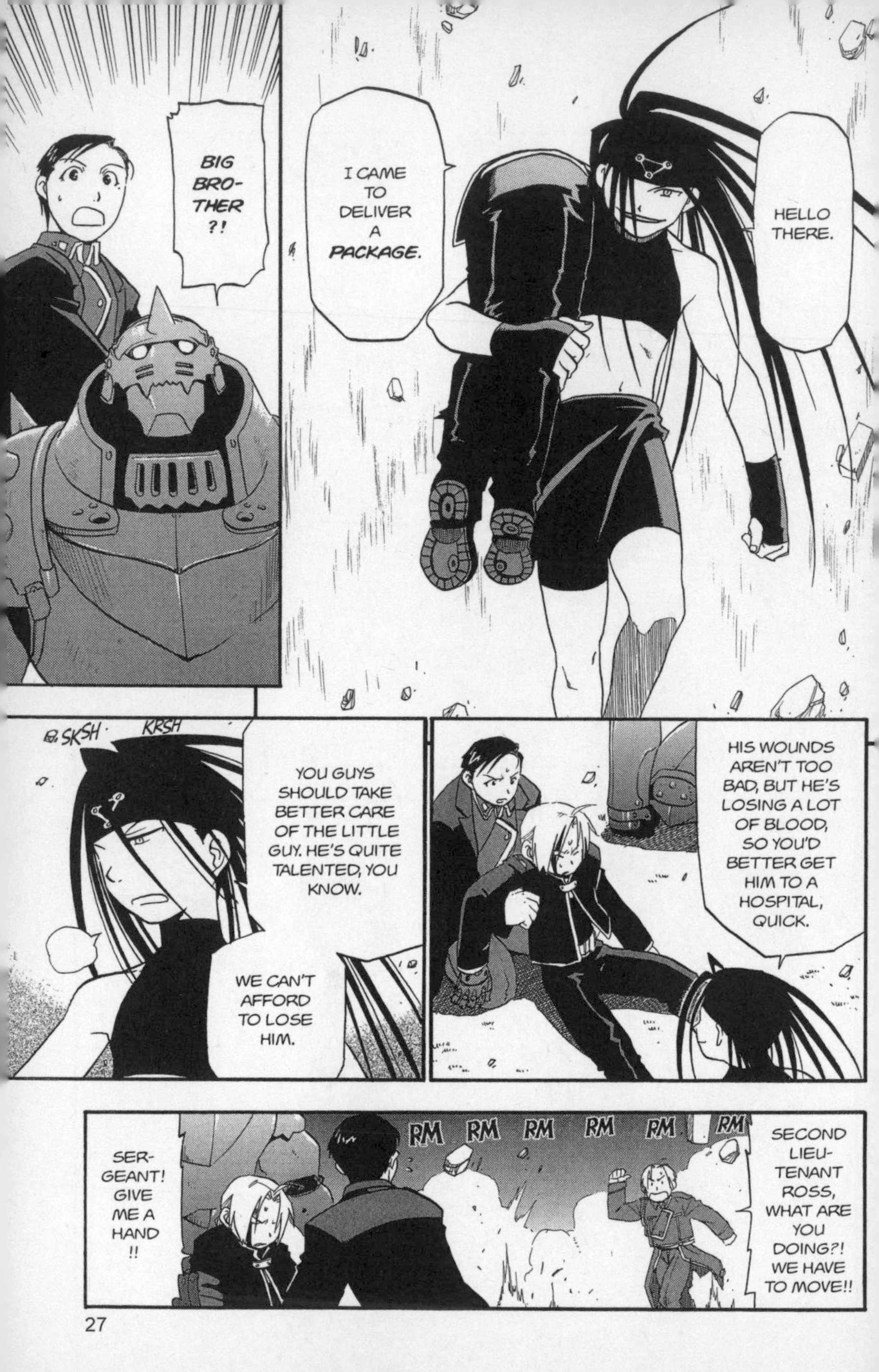
HELLO THERE.
I CAME TO DELIVER A PACKAGE.
BIG BROTHER?!
HIS WOUNDS AREN'T TOO BAD, BUT HE'S LOSING A LOT OF BLOOD, SO YOU'D BETTER GET HIM TO A HOSPITAL, QUICK.
KRSH
SKSH
YOU GUYS SHOULD TAKE BETTER CARE OF THE LITTLE GUY. HE'S QUITE TALENTED, YOU KNOW.
WE CAN'T AFFORD TO LOSE HIM.
SECOND LIEUTENANT ROSS, WHAT ARE YOU DOING?! WE HAVE TO MOVE!!
RM RM RM RM RM RM
SERGEANT! GIVE ME A HAND!!

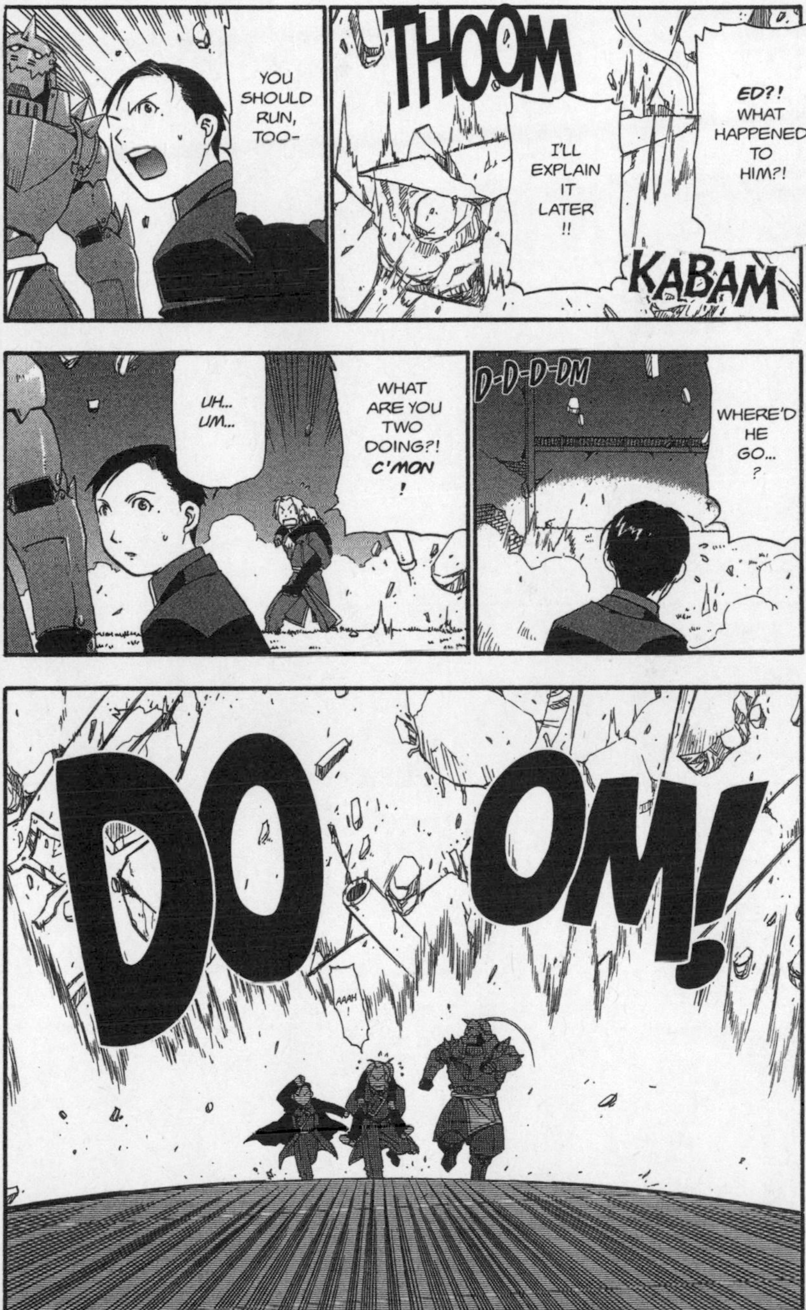
ED?! WHAT HAPPENED TO HIM?!
THOOM
I'LL EXPLAIN IT LATER !!
KABAM
YOU SHOULD RUN, TOO-
WHERE'D HE GO...?
D-D-D-DM
WHAT ARE YOU TWO DOING?! C'MON!
UH... UM...
DOOM!
AAAH

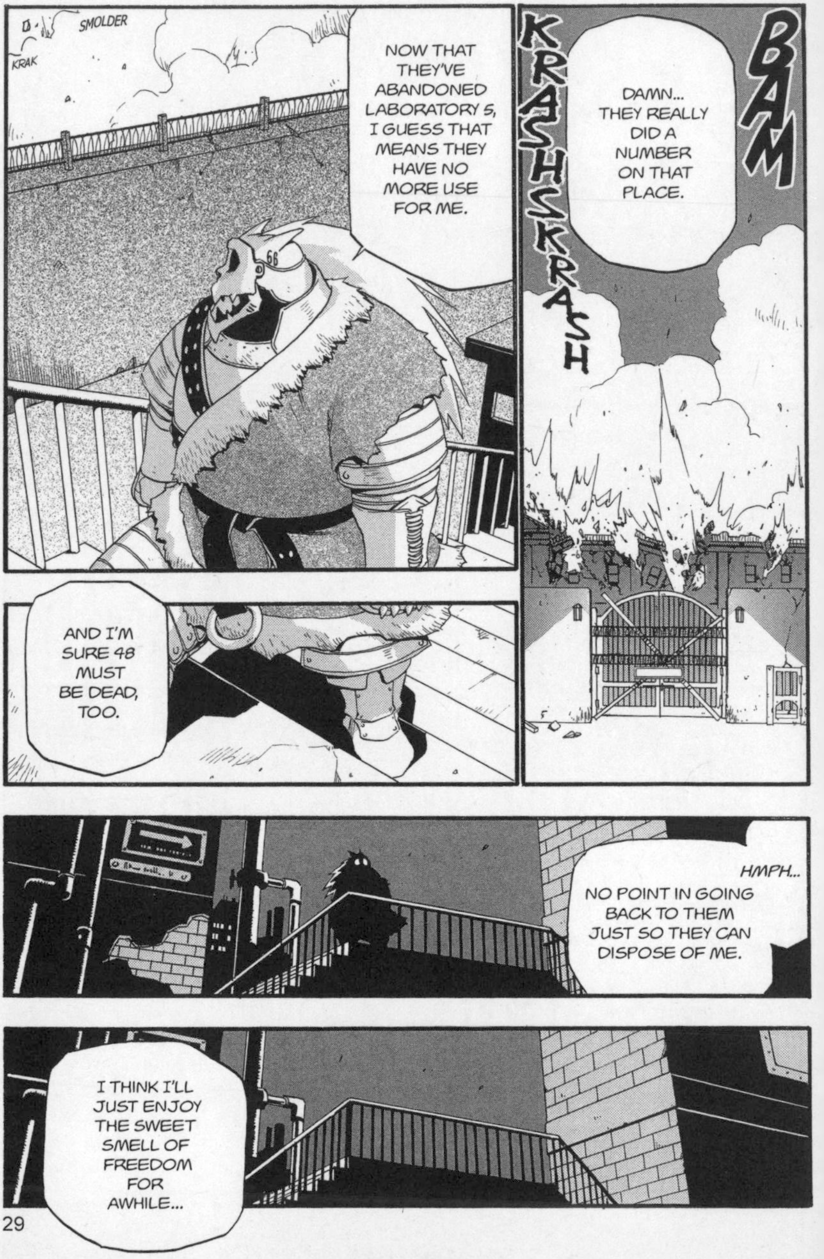
BAM
KRASHSKRASH
DAMN... THEY REALLY DID A NUMBER ON THAT PLACE.
SMOLDER
KRAK
NOW THAT THEY'VE ABANDONED LABORATORY 5, I GUESS THAT MEANS THEY HAVE NO MORE USE FOR ME.
AND I'M SURE 48 MUST BE DEAD, TOO.
HMPH... NO POINT IN GOING BACK TO THEM JUST SO THEY CAN DISPOSE OF ME.
I THINK I'LL JUST ENJOY THE SWEET SMELL OF FREEDOM FOR AWHILE...

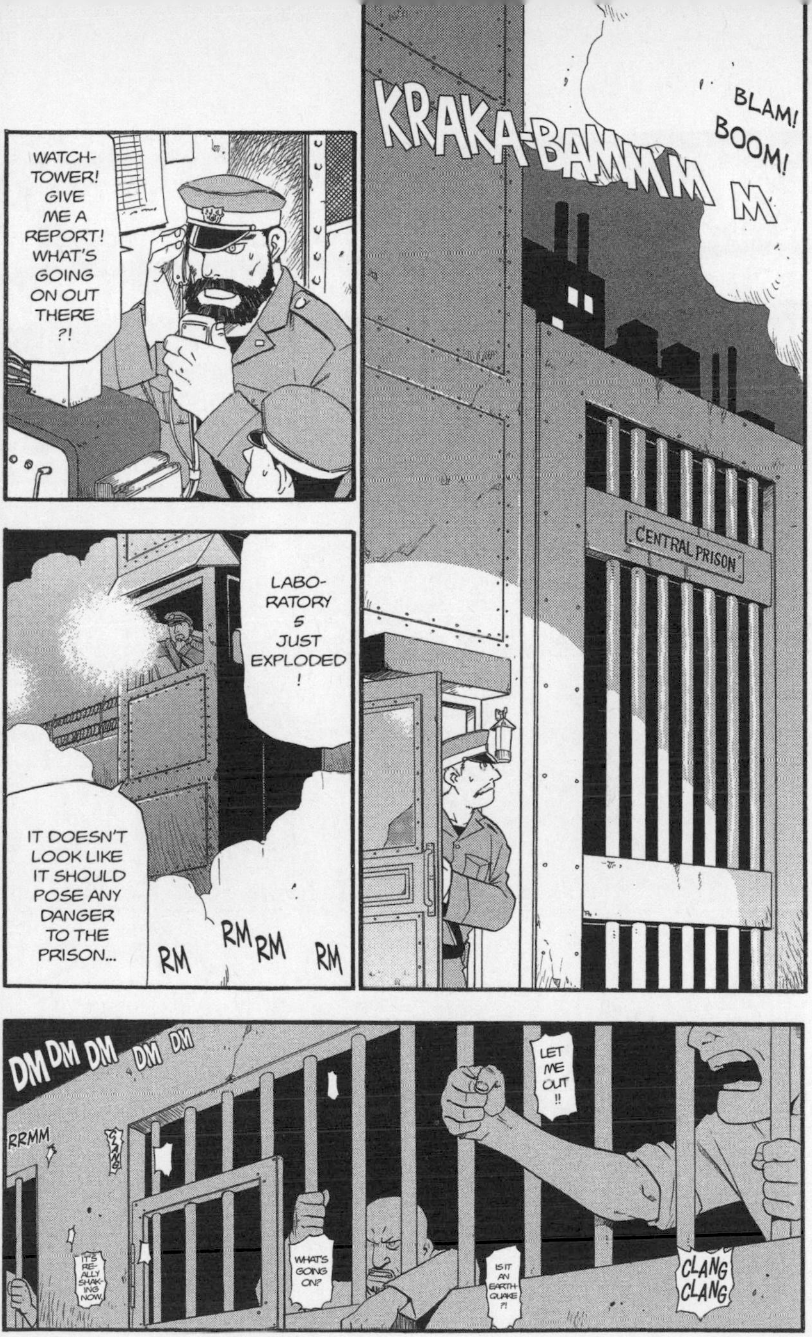

BLAM!
BOOM!
KRAKA-BAMMM M M
CENTRAL PRISON
WATCHTOWER! GIVE ME A REPORT! WHAT'S GOING ON OUT THERE?!
LABORATORY 5 JUST EXPLODED!
IT DOESN'T LOOK LIKE IT SHOULD POSE ANY DANGER TO THE PRISON...
RM RM RM RM
LET ME OUT!!
CLANG CLANG
IS IT AN EARTHQUAKE?!
WHAT'S GOING ON?
IT'S REALLY SHAKING NOW.
CLANG
RRMM
DM DM DM DM DM

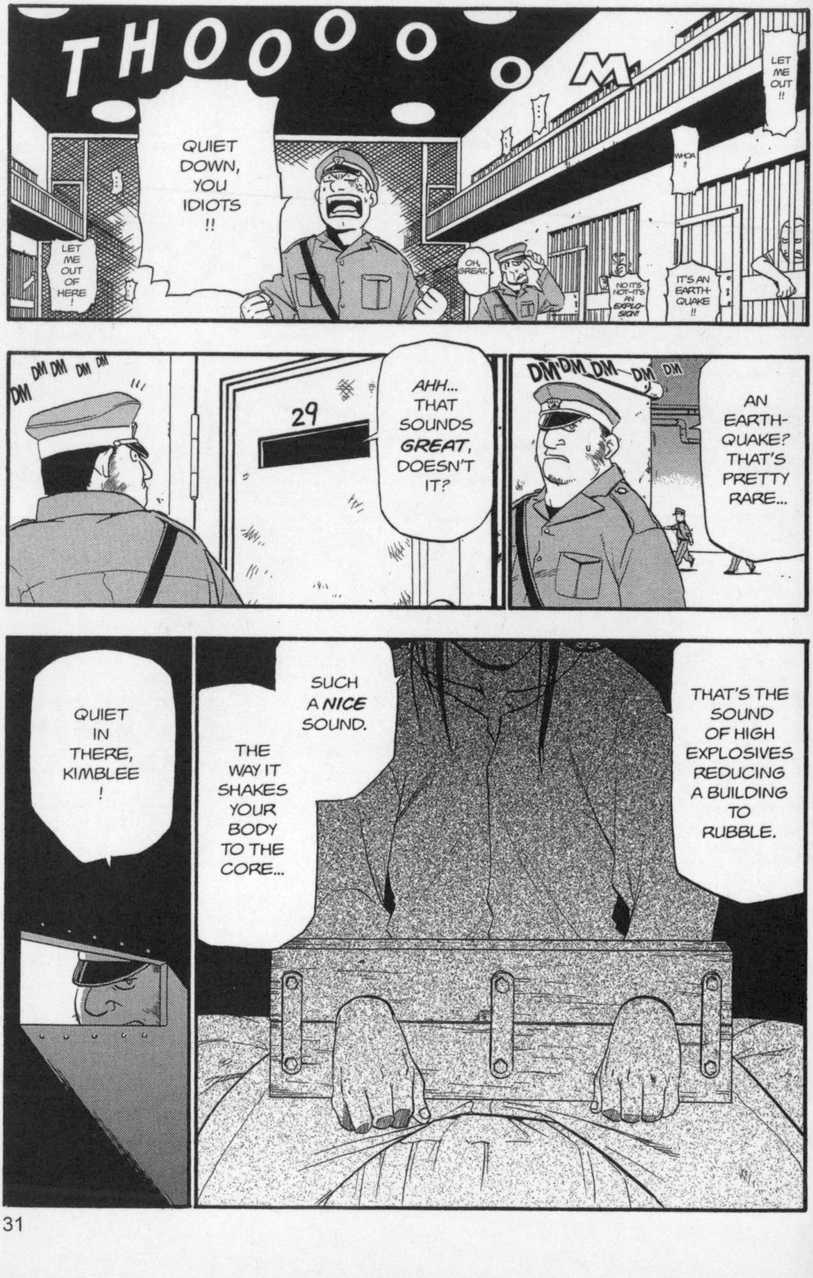
THOOOOOOM
LET ME OUT !!
WHOA !!
IT'S AN EARTHQUAKE !!
NO IT'S NOT—IT'S AN EXPLOSION!
OH, GREAT.
QUIET DOWN, YOU IDIOTS !!
LET ME OUT OF HERE !
DM DM DM DM DM
AN EARTHQUAKE? THAT'S PRETTY RARE...
AHH... THAT SOUNDS GREAT, DOESN'T IT?
DM DM DM DM DM
THAT'S THE SOUND OF HIGH EXPLOSIVES REDUCING A BUILDING TO RUBBLE.
SUCH A NICE SOUND.
THE WAY IT SHAKES YOUR BODY TO THE CORE...
QUIET IN THERE, KIMBLEE !

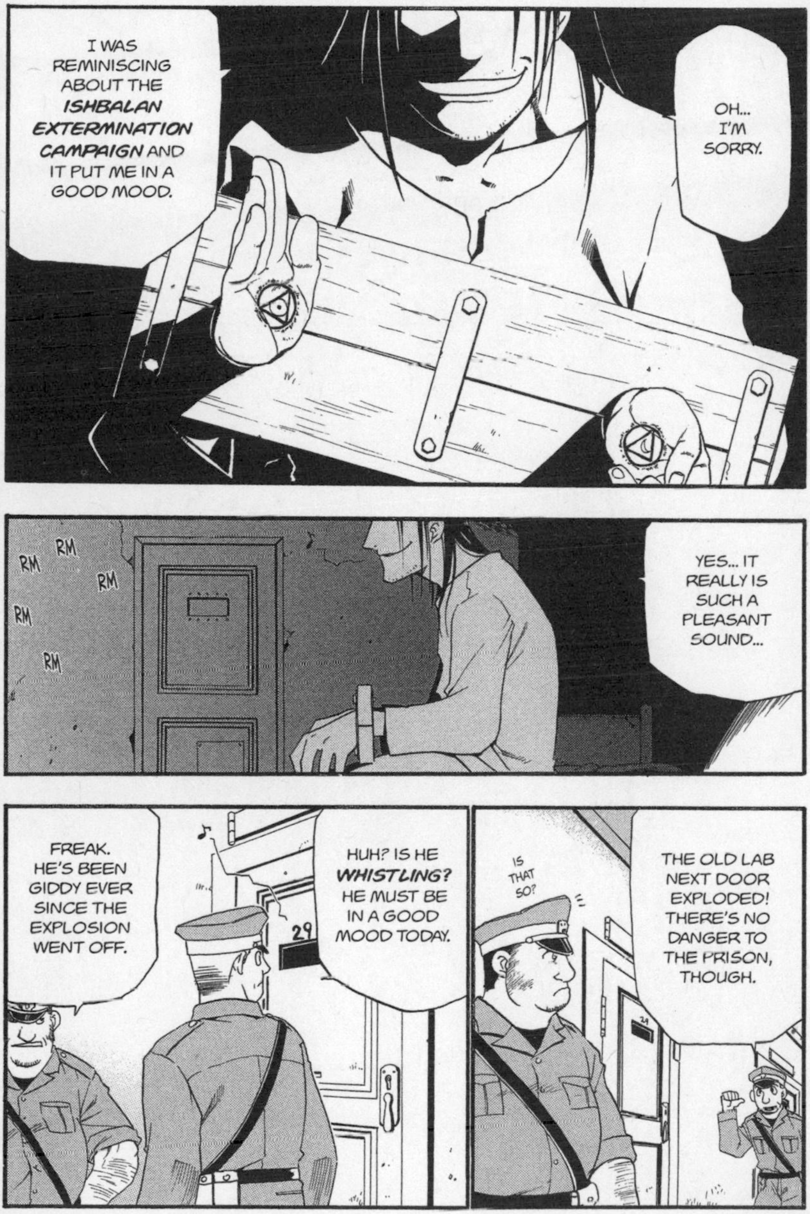
OH... I'M SORRY.
I WAS REMINISCING ABOUT THE ISHBALAN EXTERMINATION CAMPAIGN AND IT PUT ME IN A GOOD MOOD.
YES... IT REALLY IS SUCH A PLEASANT SOUND...
RM RM RM RM RM
THE OLD LAB NEXT DOOR EXPLODED! THERE'S NO DANGER TO THE PRISON, THOUGH.
IS THAT SO?
HUH? IS HE WHISTLING? HE MUST BE IN A GOOD MOOD TODAY.
FREAK. HE'S BEEN GIDDY EVER SINCE THE EXPLOSION WENT OFF.

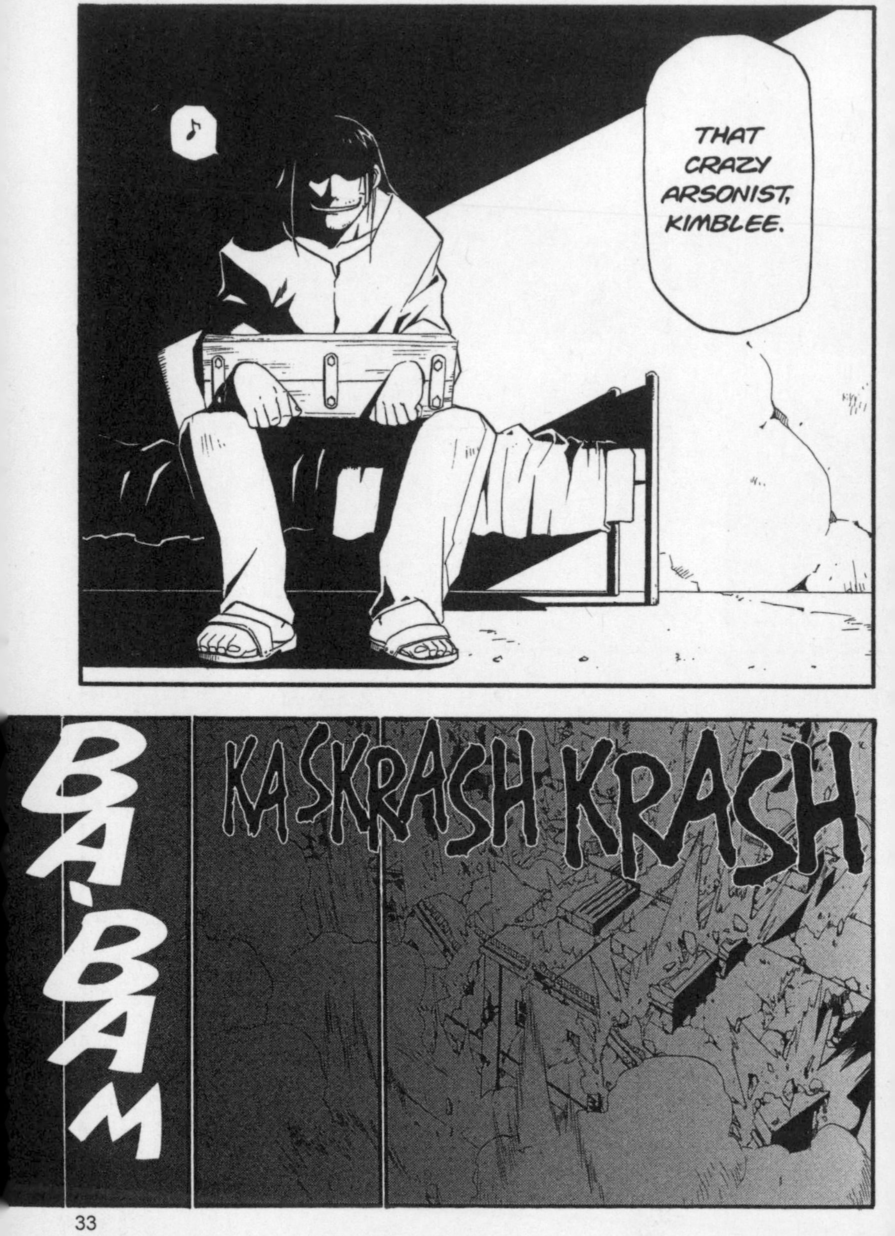
♪
THAT CRAZY ARSONIST, KIMBLEE.
KA SKRASH KRASH
BA-BAM

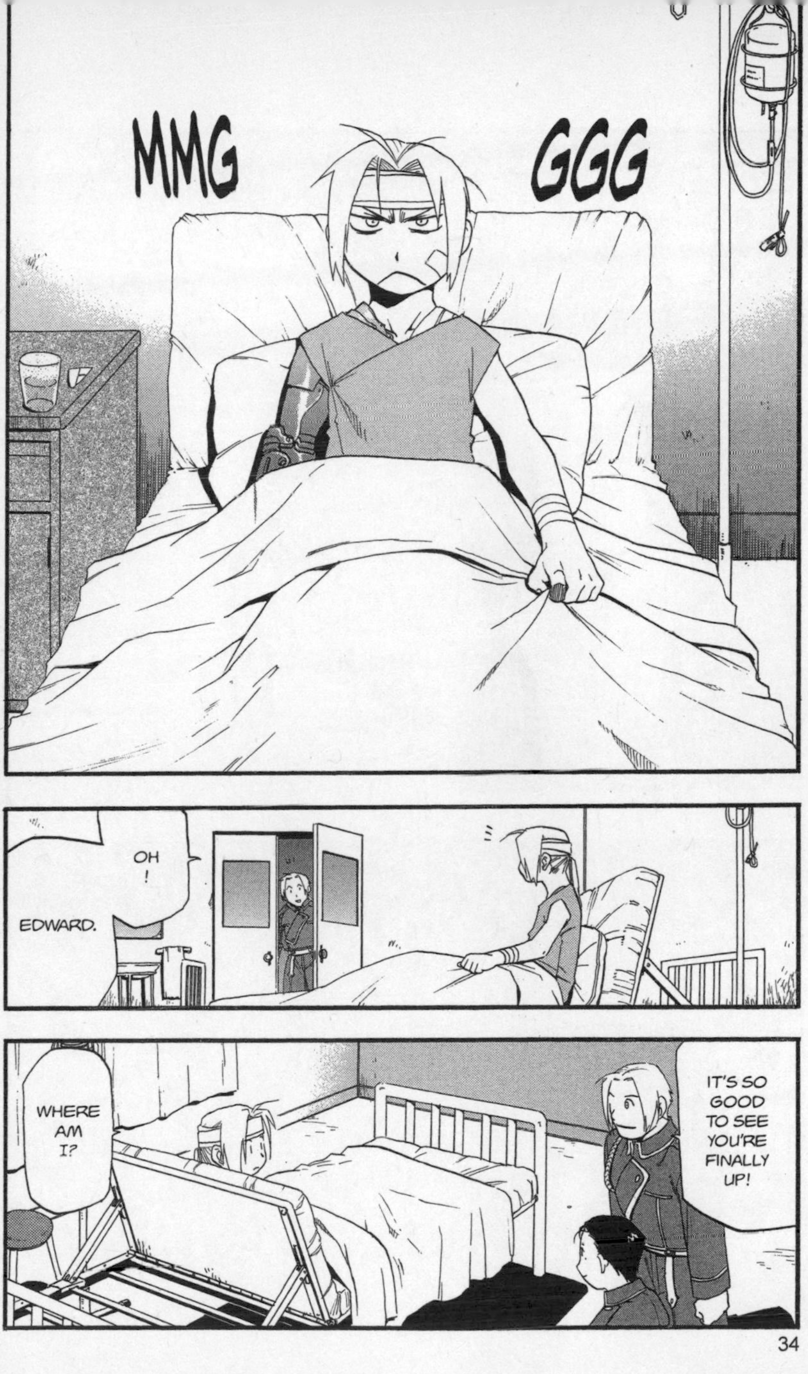
MMG GGG
OH!
EDWARD.
IT'S SO GOOD TO SEE YOU'RE FINALLY UP!
WHERE AM I?

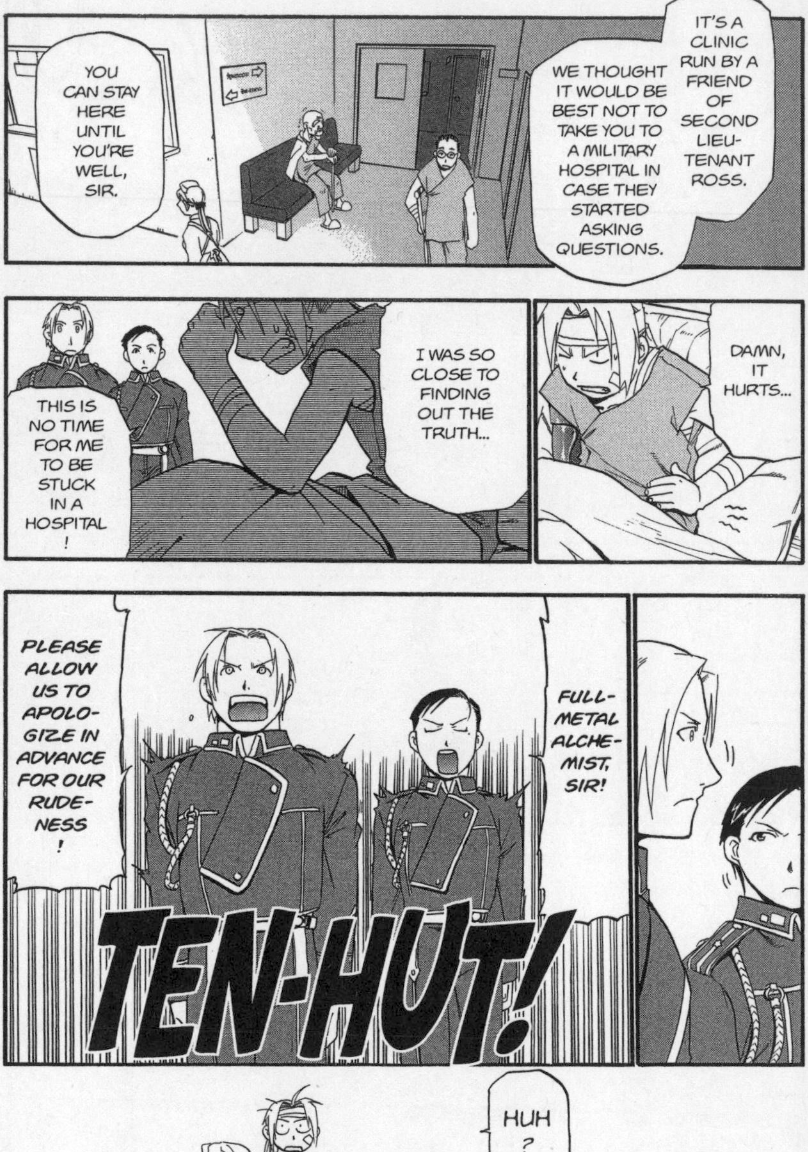
IT'S A CLINIC RUN BY A FRIEND OF SECOND LIEU-TENANT ROSS.
WE THOUGHT IT WOULD BE BEST NOT TO TAKE YOU TO A MILITARY HOSPITAL IN CASE THEY STARTED ASKING QUESTIONS.
YOU CAN STAY HERE UNTIL YOU'RE WELL, SIR.
DAMN, IT HURTS...
I WAS SO CLOSE TO FINDING OUT THE TRUTH...
THIS IS NO TIME FOR ME TO BE STUCK IN A HOSPITAL!
FULL-METAL ALCHE-MIST, SIR!
PLEASE ALLOW US TO APOLO-GIZE IN ADVANCE FOR OUR RUDE-NESS!
TEN-HUT!
HUH?

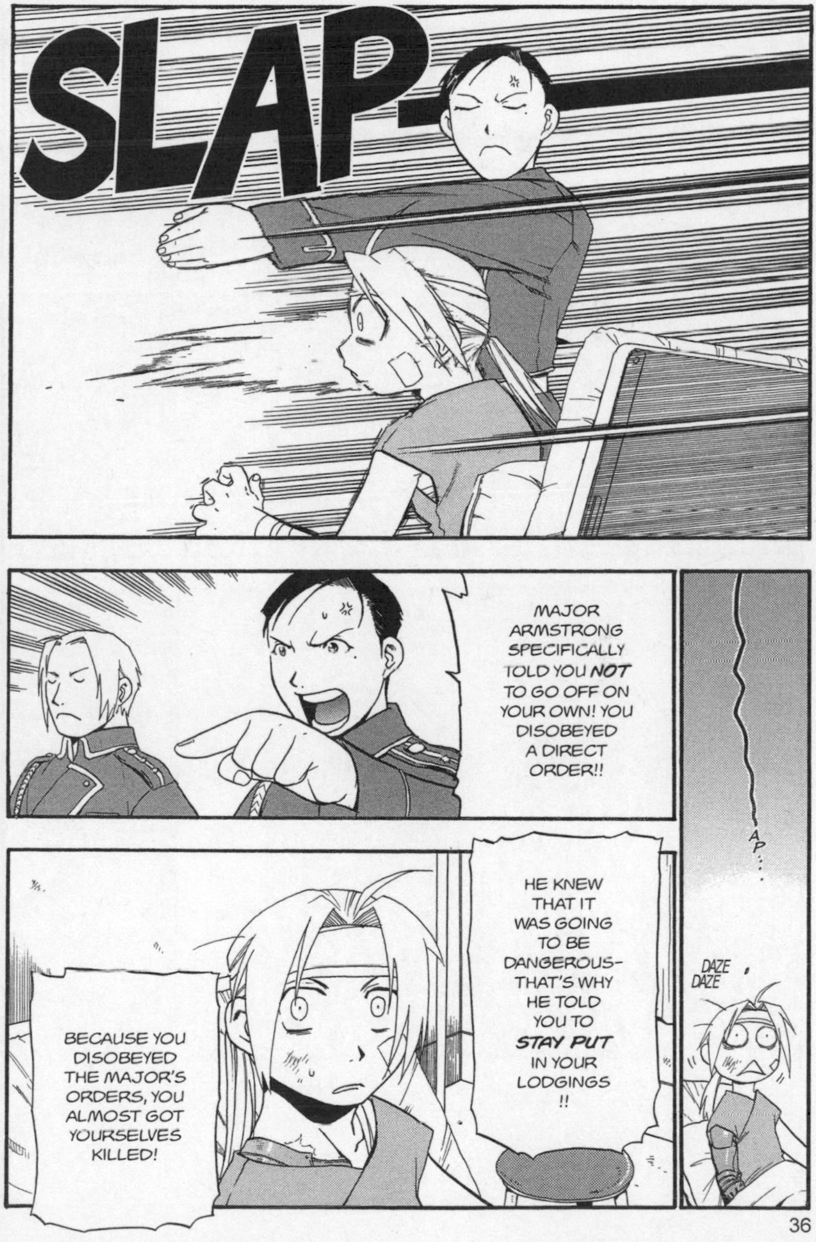
SLAP-
AP...
DAZE DAZE
MAJOR ARMSTRONG SPECIFICALLY TOLD YOU **NOT** TO GO OFF ON YOUR OWN! YOU DISOBEYED A DIRECT ORDER!!
HE KNEW THAT IT WAS GOING TO BE DANGEROUS- THAT'S WHY HE TOLD YOU TO **STAY PUT** IN YOUR LODGINGS !!
BECAUSE YOU DISOBEYED THE MAJOR'S ORDERS, YOU ALMOST GOT YOURSELVES KILLED!

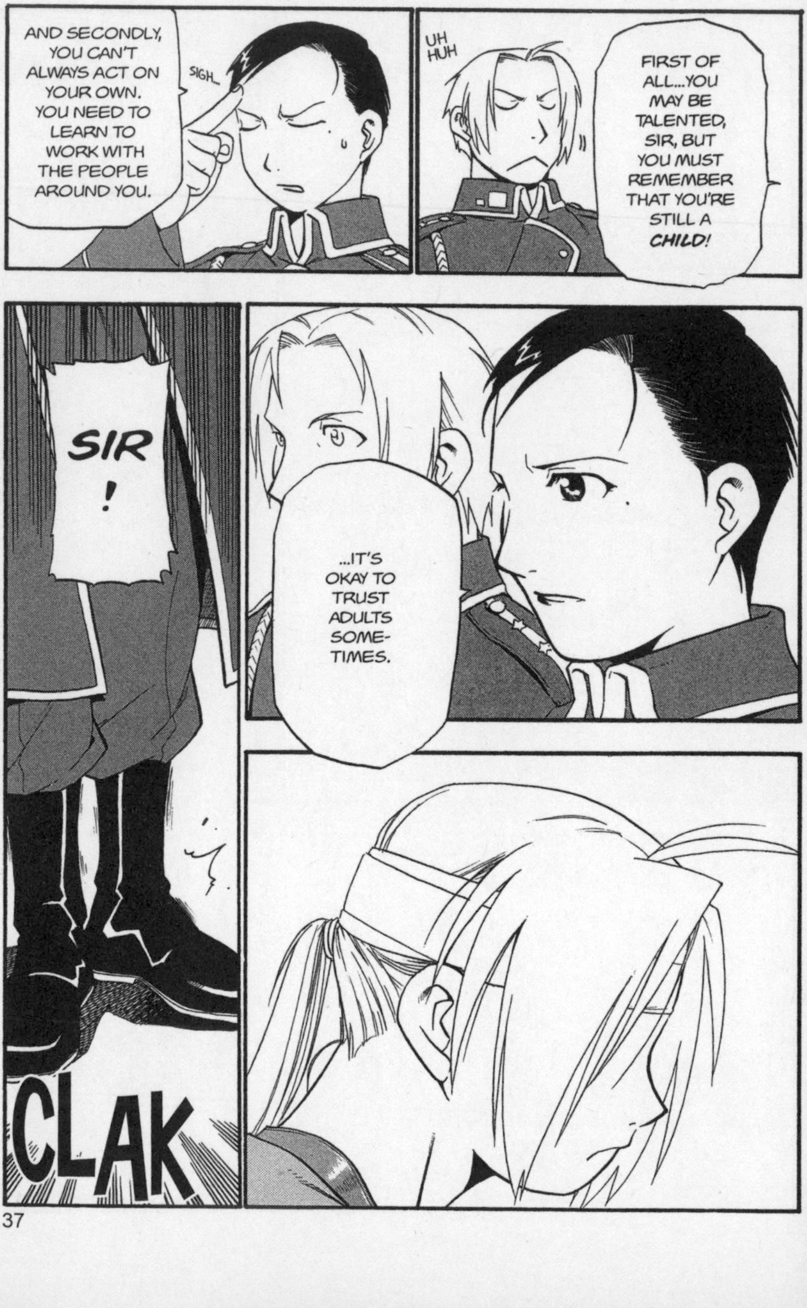
FIRST OF ALL...YOU MAY BE TALENTED, SIR, BUT YOU MUST REMEMBER THAT YOU'RE STILL A CHILD!
UH HUH
SIGH..
AND SECONDLY, YOU CAN'T ALWAYS ACT ON YOUR OWN. YOU NEED TO LEARN TO WORK WITH THE PEOPLE AROUND YOU.
...IT'S OKAY TO TRUST ADULTS SOME-TIMES.
SIR !
CLAK

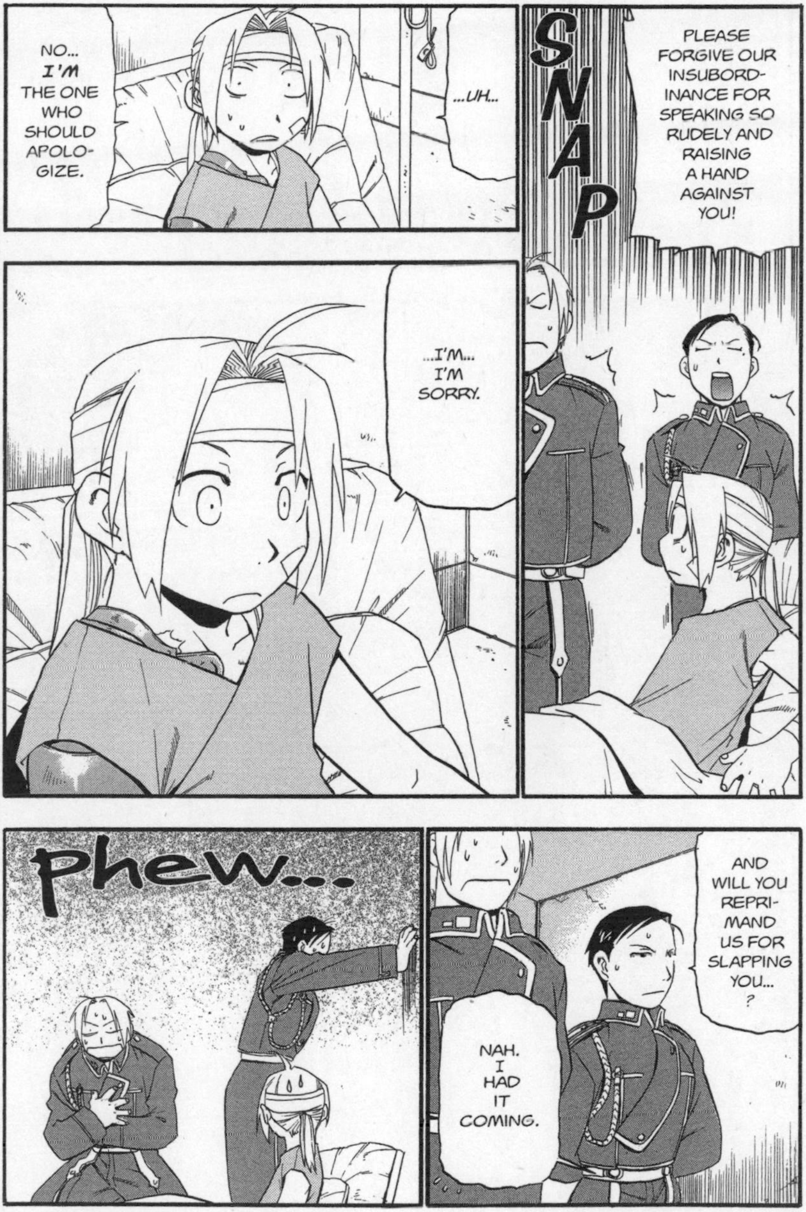
SNAP
PLEASE FORGIVE OUR INSUBORDINANCE FOR SPEAKING SO RUDELY AND RAISING A HAND AGAINST YOU!
...UH...
NO... I'M THE ONE WHO SHOULD APOLOGIZE.
...I'M... I'M SORRY.
AND WILL YOU REPRIMAND US FOR SLAPPING YOU...?
NAH. I HAD IT COMING.
Phew...

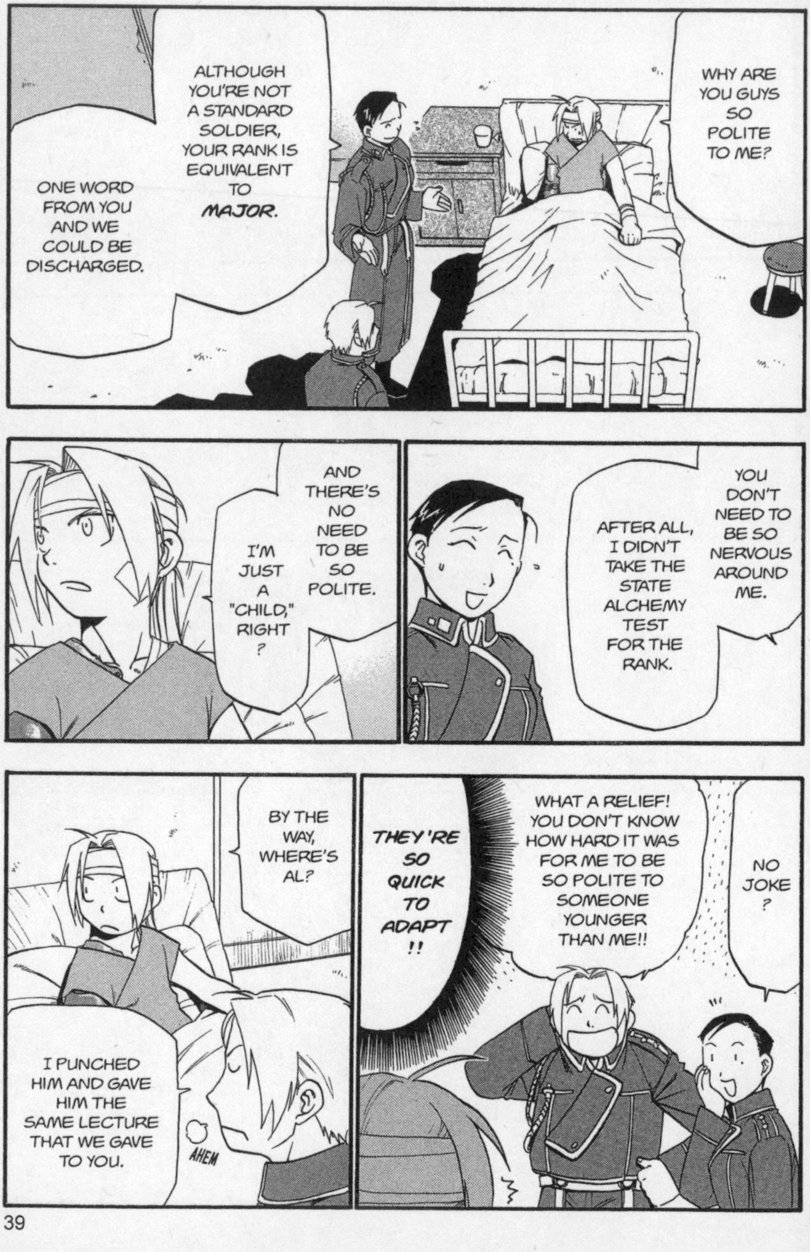
WHY ARE YOU GUYS SO POLITE TO ME?
ALTHOUGH YOU'RE NOT A STANDARD SOLDIER, YOUR RANK IS EQUIVALENT TO *MAJOR.*
ONE WORD FROM YOU AND WE COULD BE DISCHARGED.
YOU DON'T NEED TO BE SO NERVOUS AROUND ME.
AFTER ALL, I DIDN'T TAKE THE STATE ALCHEMY TEST FOR THE RANK.
AND THERE'S NO NEED TO BE SO POLITE.
I'M JUST A "CHILD," RIGHT?
NO JOKE?
WHAT A RELIEF! YOU DON'T KNOW HOW HARD IT WAS FOR ME TO BE SO POLITE TO SOMEONE YOUNGER THAN ME!!
THEY'RE SO QUICK TO ADAPT!!
BY THE WAY, WHERE'S AL?
I PUNCHED HIM AND GAVE HIM THE SAME LECTURE THAT WE GAVE TO YOU.
AHEM

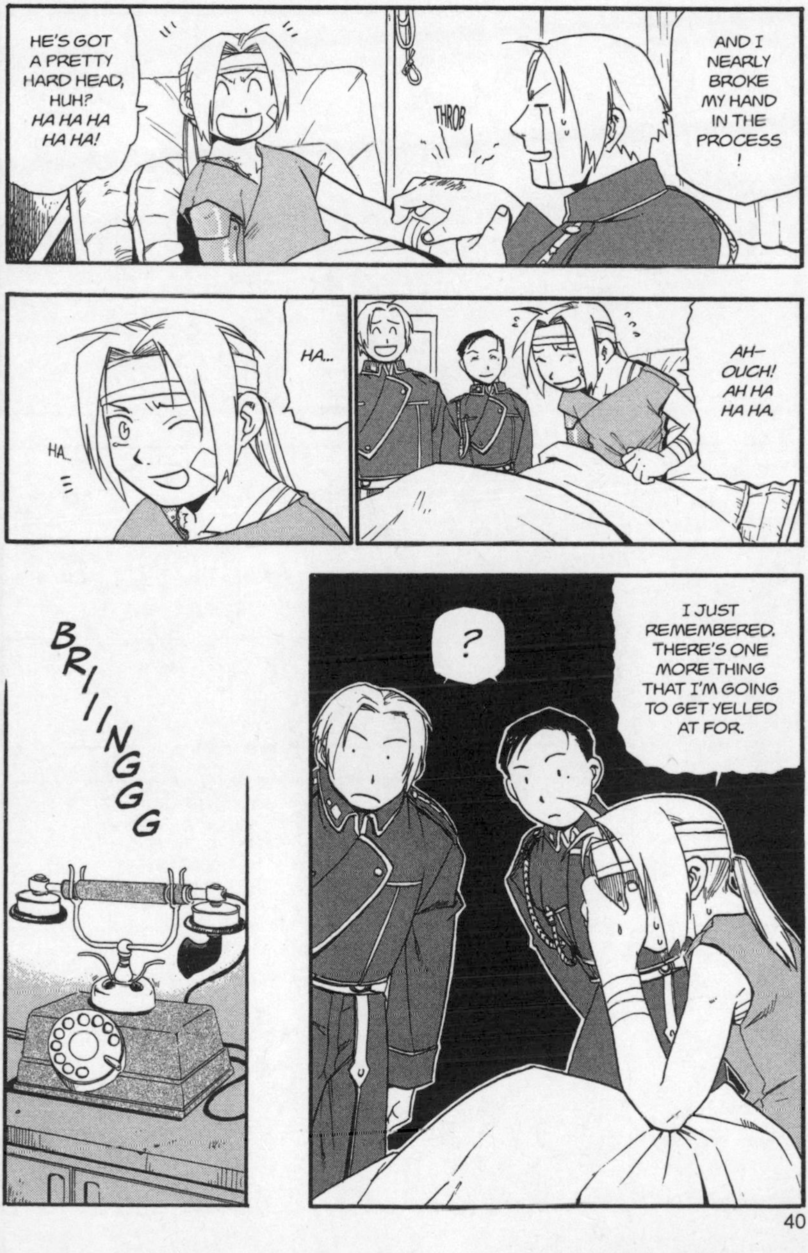
AND I NEARLY BROKE MY HAND IN THE PROCESS!
THROB
HE'S GOT A PRETTY HARD HEAD, HUH? HA HA HA HA HA!
AH— OUCH! AH HA HA HA.
HA...
HA..
I JUST REMEMBERED. THERE'S ONE MORE THING THAT I'M GOING TO GET YELLED AT FOR.
?
BRIIINGGG

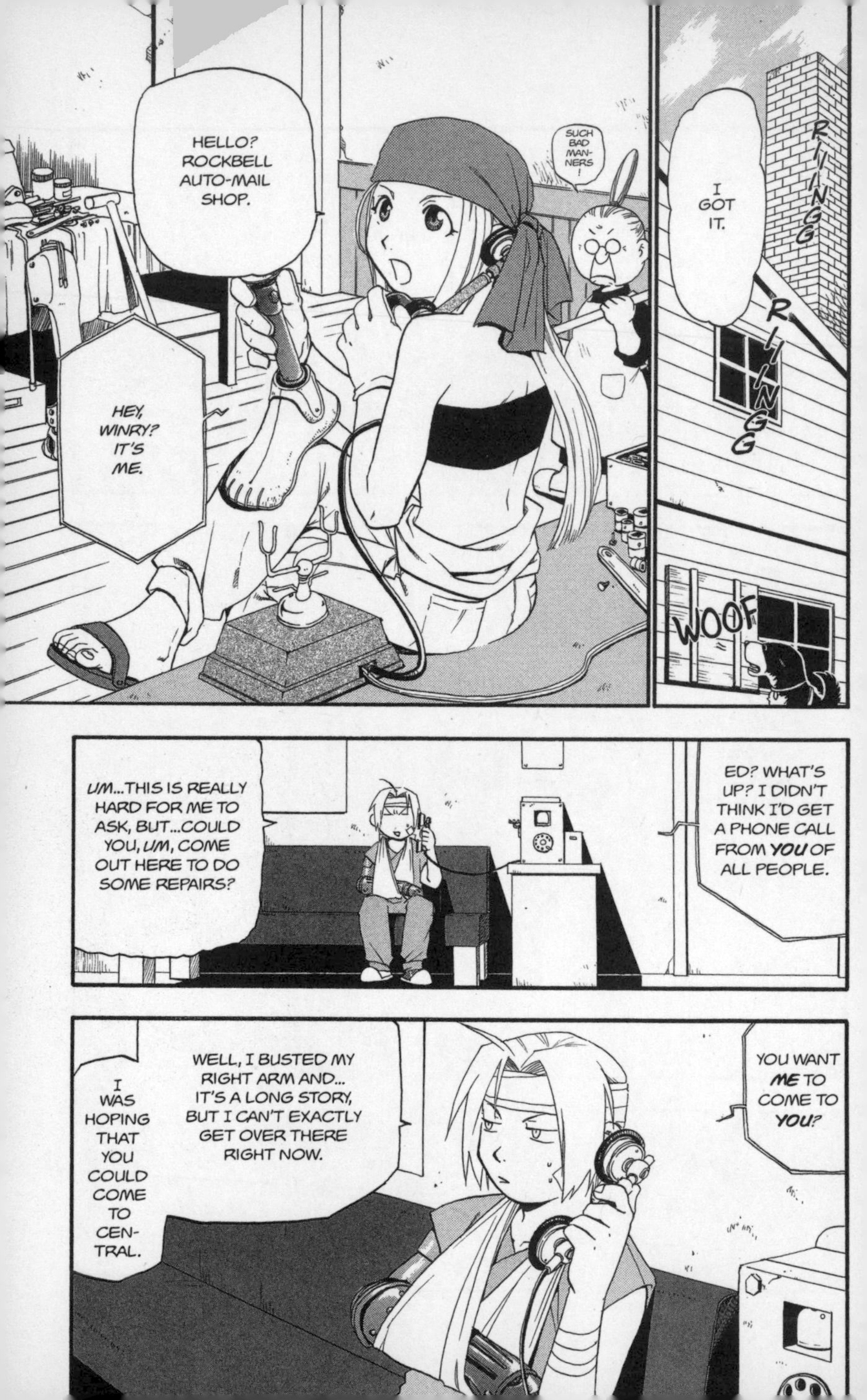
RIIINGG
I GOT IT.
RIIINGG
WOOF
SUCH BAD MAN-NERS!
HELLO? ROCKBELL AUTO-MAIL SHOP.
HEY, WINRY? IT'S ME.
ED? WHAT'S UP? I DIDN'T THINK I'D GET A PHONE CALL FROM *YOU* OF ALL PEOPLE.
UM...THIS IS REALLY HARD FOR ME TO ASK, BUT...COULD YOU, *UM*, COME OUT HERE TO DO SOME REPAIRS?
YOU WANT *ME* TO COME TO *YOU*?
WELL, I BUSTED MY RIGHT ARM AND... IT'S A LONG STORY, BUT I CAN'T EXACTLY GET OVER THERE RIGHT NOW.
I WAS HOPING THAT YOU COULD COME TO CEN-TRAL.

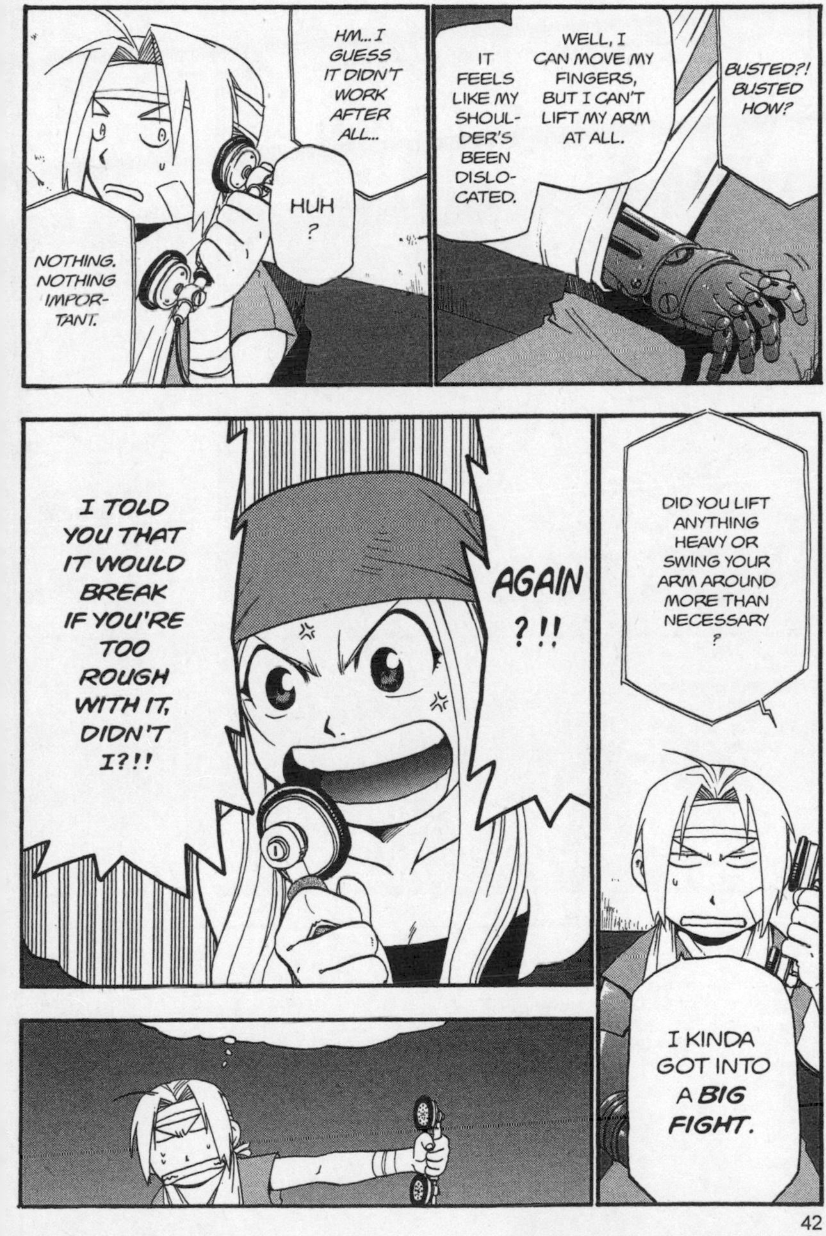
BUSTED?! BUSTED HOW?
WELL, I CAN MOVE MY FINGERS, BUT I CAN'T LIFT MY ARM AT ALL.
IT FEELS LIKE MY SHOUL-DER'S BEEN DISLO-CATED.
HM...I GUESS IT DIDN'T WORK AFTER ALL...
HUH?
NOTHING. NOTHING IMPOR-TANT.
DID YOU LIFT ANYTHING HEAVY OR SWING YOUR ARM AROUND MORE THAN NECESSARY?
I KINDA GOT INTO A **BIG FIGHT**.
AGAIN?!!
I TOLD YOU THAT IT WOULD BREAK IF YOU'RE TOO ROUGH WITH IT, DIDN'T I?!!

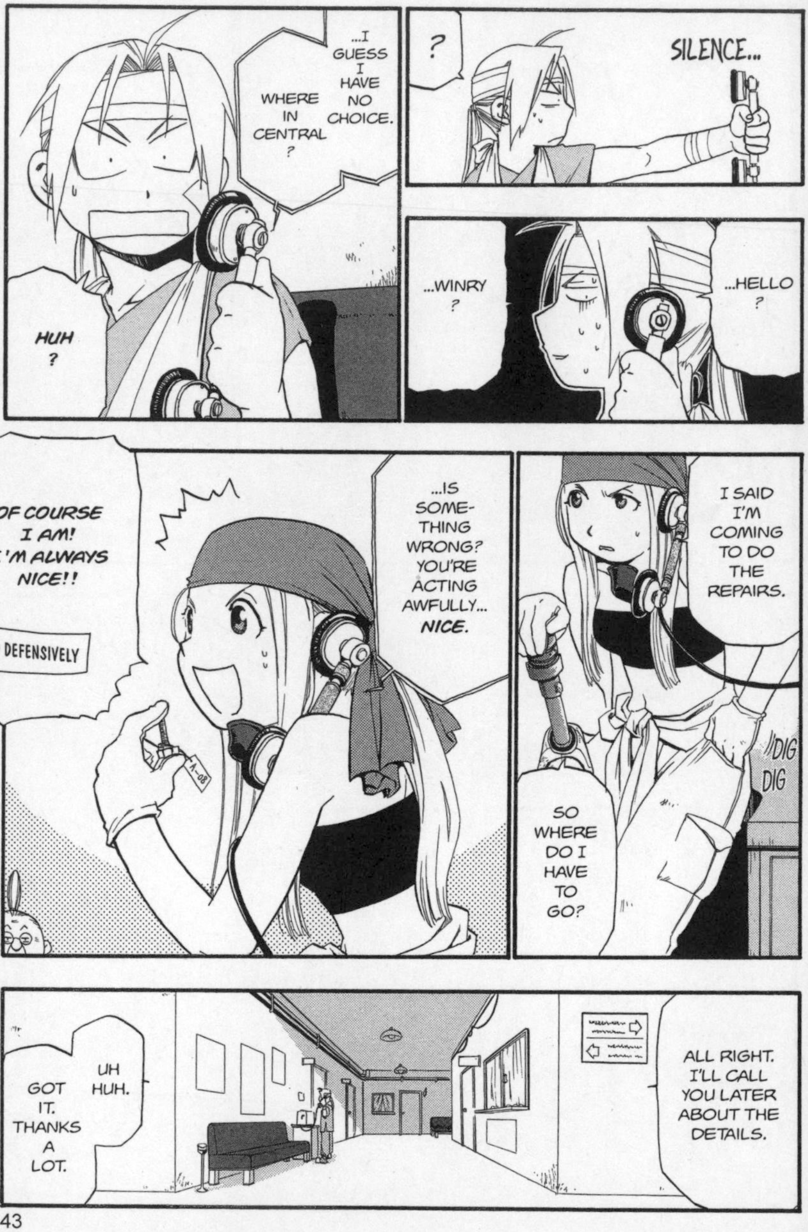
SILENCE...
?
...HELLO ?
...WINRY ?
...I GUESS I HAVE NO CHOICE.
WHERE IN CENTRAL ?
HUH ?
I SAID I'M COMING TO DO THE REPAIRS.
DIG DIG
SO WHERE DO I HAVE TO GO?
...IS SOME-THING WRONG? YOU'RE ACTING AWFULLY... NICE.
OF COURSE I AM! I'M ALWAYS NICE!!
SAID DEFENSIVELY
ALL RIGHT. I'LL CALL YOU LATER ABOUT THE DETAILS.
UH HUH.
GOT IT. THANKS A LOT.

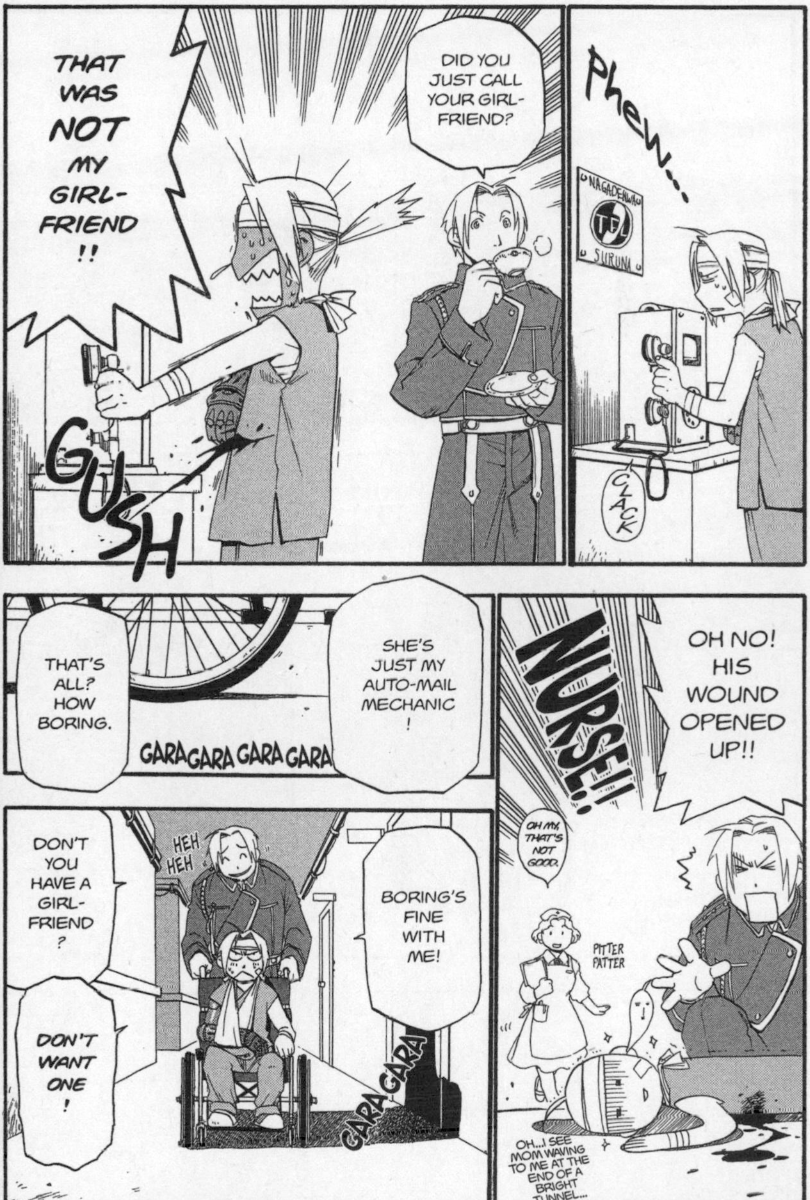
Phew...
NAGADENWA
TEL
SURUNA
CLACK
DID YOU JUST CALL YOUR GIRL-FRIEND?
THAT WAS NOT MY GIRL-FRIEND!!
GUSH
OH NO! HIS WOUND OPENED UP!!
NURSE!!
OH MY, THAT'S NOT GOOD.
PITTER PATTER
OH...I SEE MOM WAVING TO ME AT THE END OF A BRIGHT TUNNEL...
SHE'S JUST MY AUTO-MAIL MECHANIC!
THAT'S ALL? HOW BORING.
GARAGARA GARAGARA
BORING'S FINE WITH ME!
HEH HEH
DON'T YOU HAVE A GIRL-FRIEND?
DON'T WANT ONE!
GARAGARA

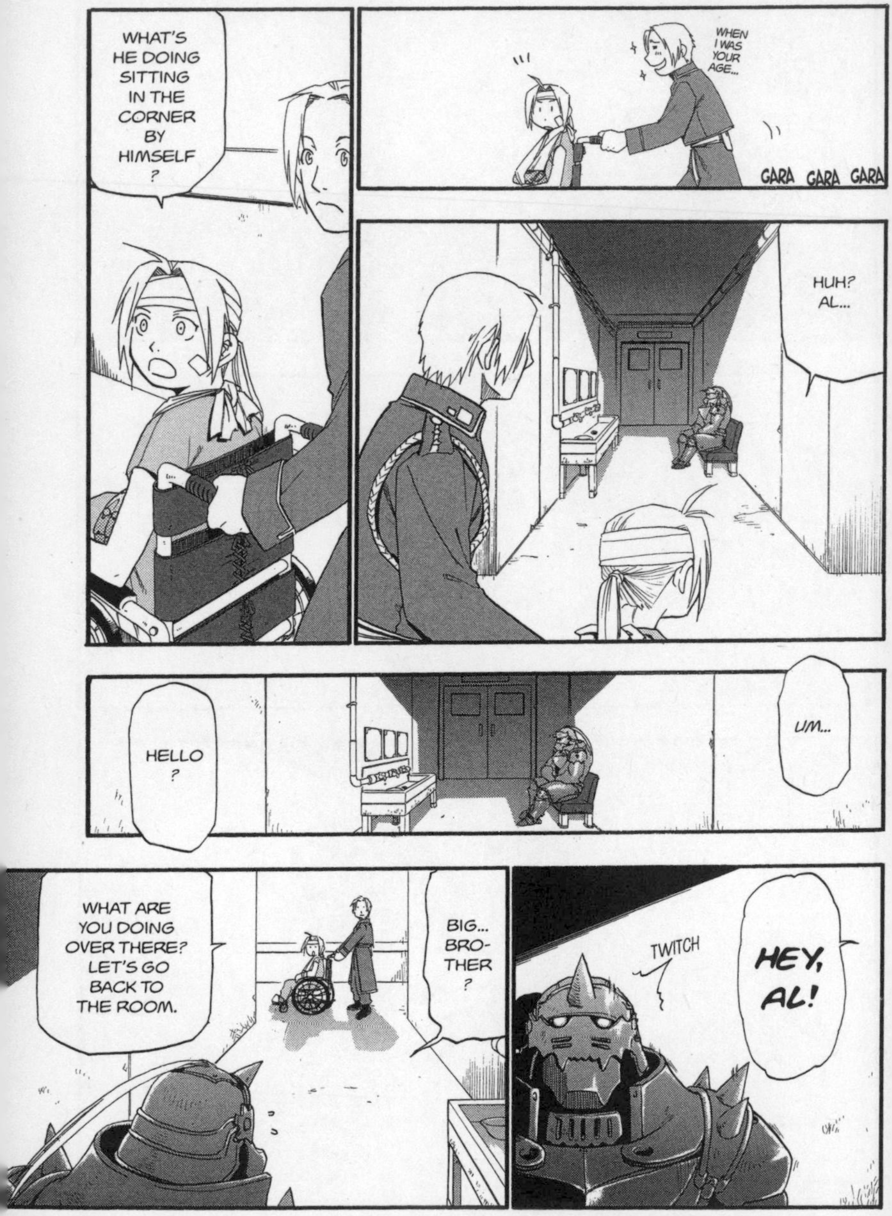
WHEN I WAS YOUR AGE...
GARA GARA GARA
HUH? AL...
WHAT'S HE DOING SITTING IN THE CORNER BY HIMSELF?
UM...
HELLO?
HEY, AL!
TWITCH
BIG... BRO-THER?
WHAT ARE YOU DOING OVER THERE? LET'S GO BACK TO THE ROOM.

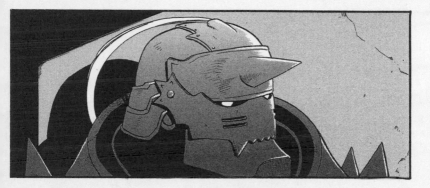

YOU OKAY ?
TURN
... IT'S... IT'S NOTHING.
I'LL BE RIGHT THERE.
?
SEE YOU BACK THERE, THEN.

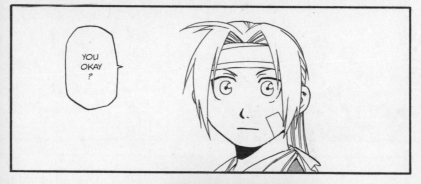

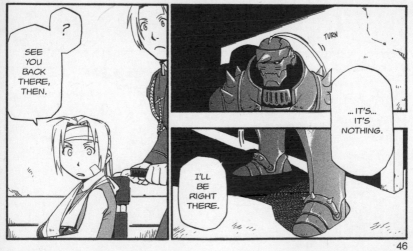

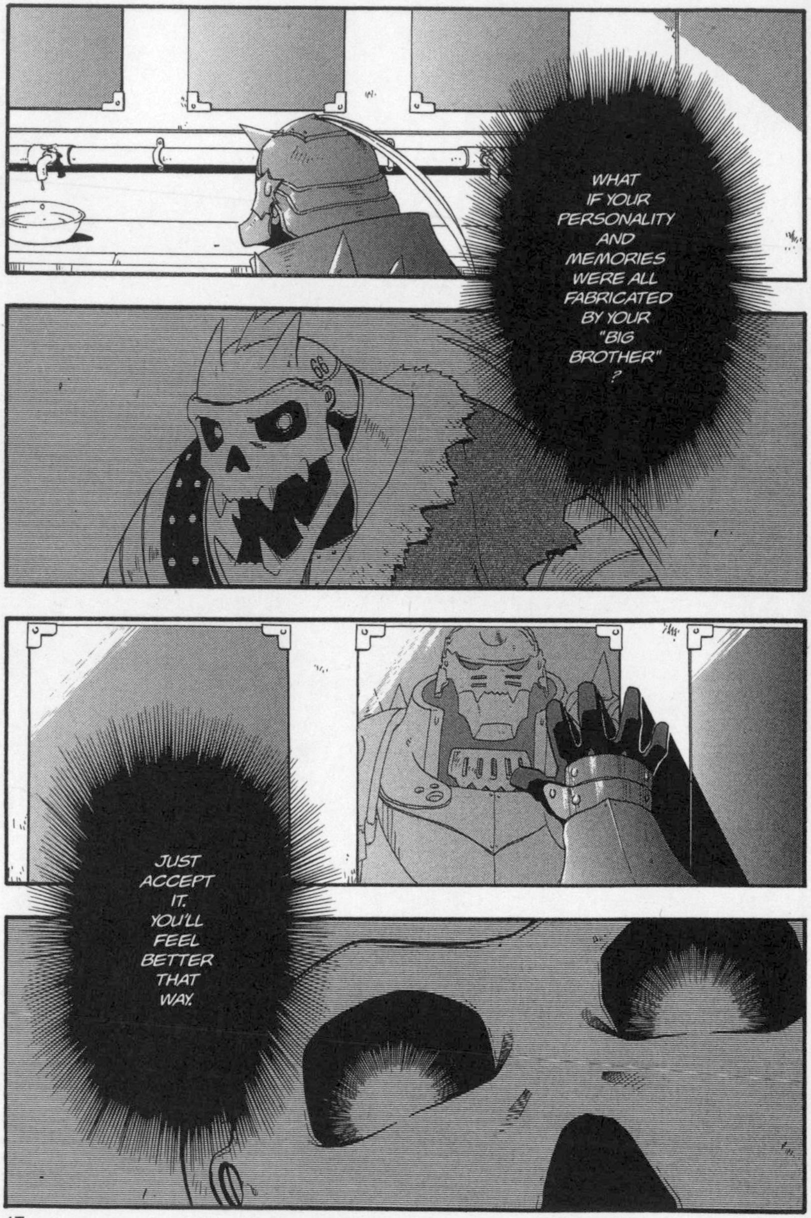
WHAT IF YOUR PERSONALITY AND MEMORIES WERE ALL FABRICATED BY YOUR "BIG BROTHER" ?
JUST ACCEPT IT. YOU'LL FEEL BETTER THAT WAY.

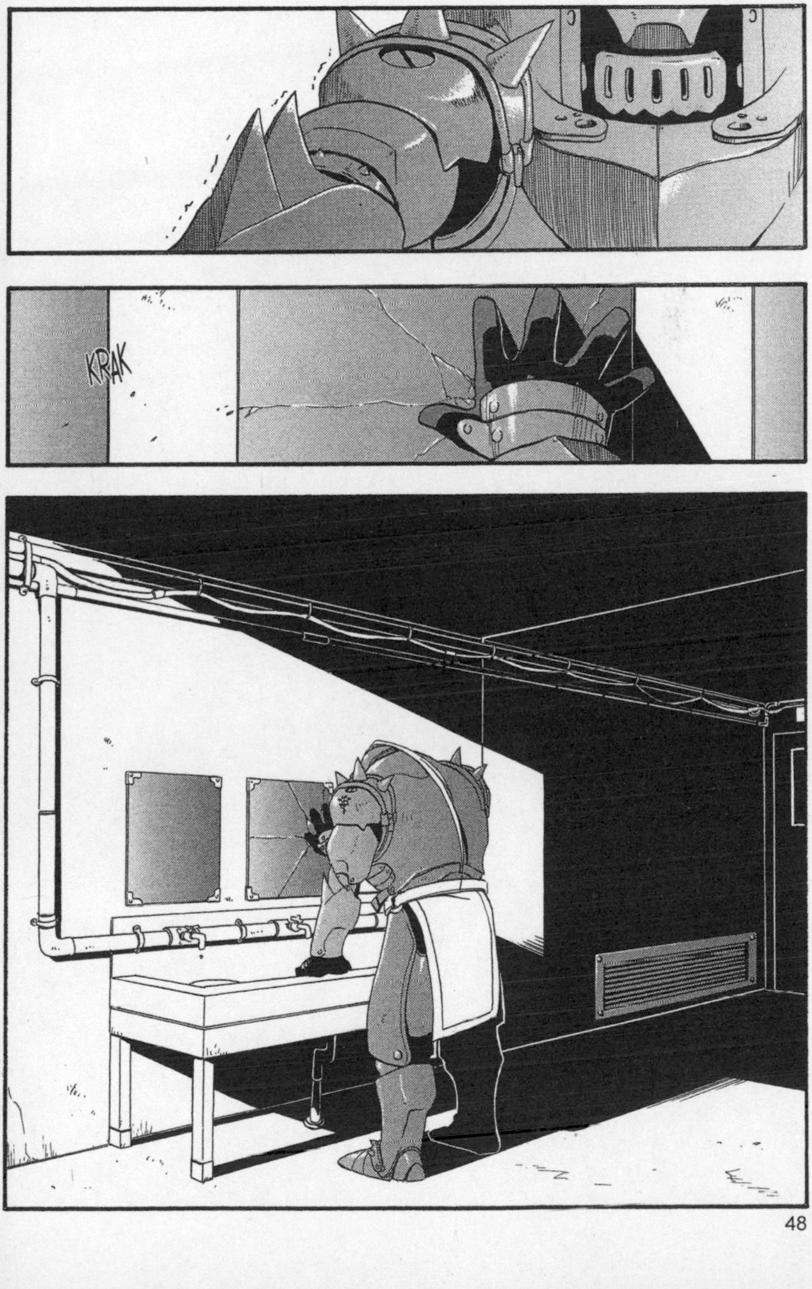
KRAK

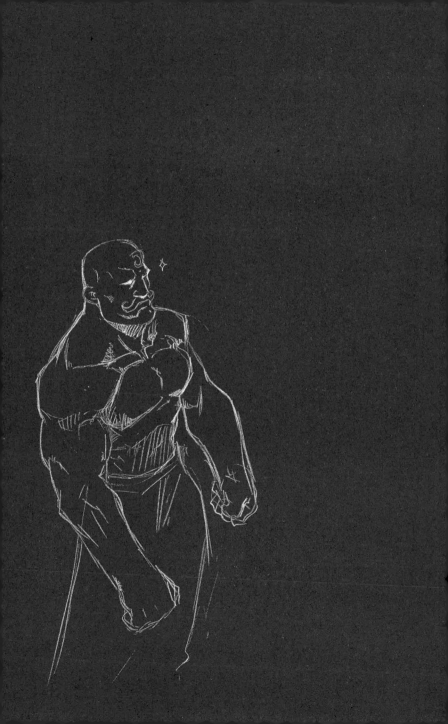

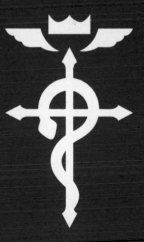

FULLMETAL
ALCHEMIST

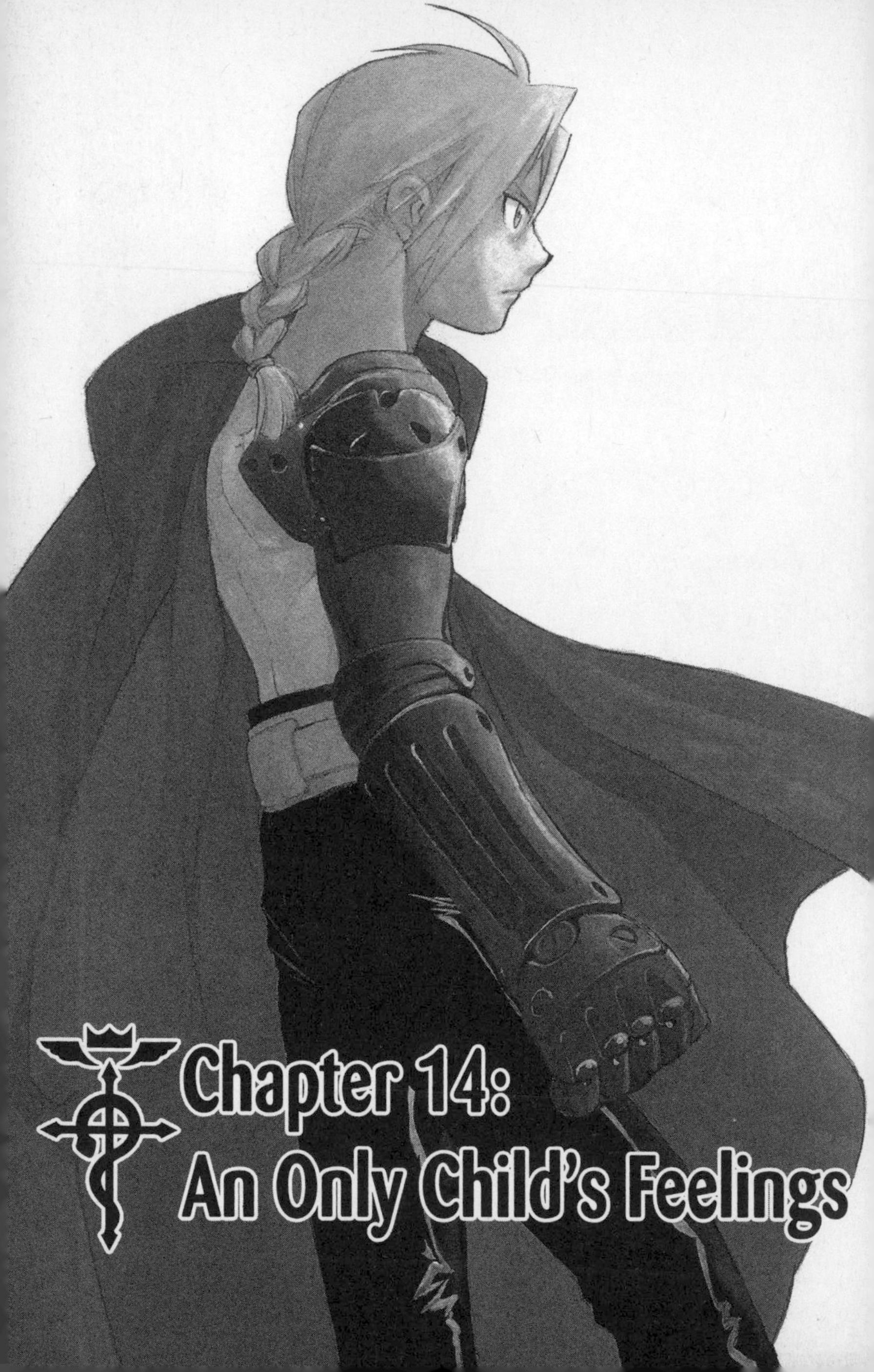

Chapter 14: An Only Child's Feelings

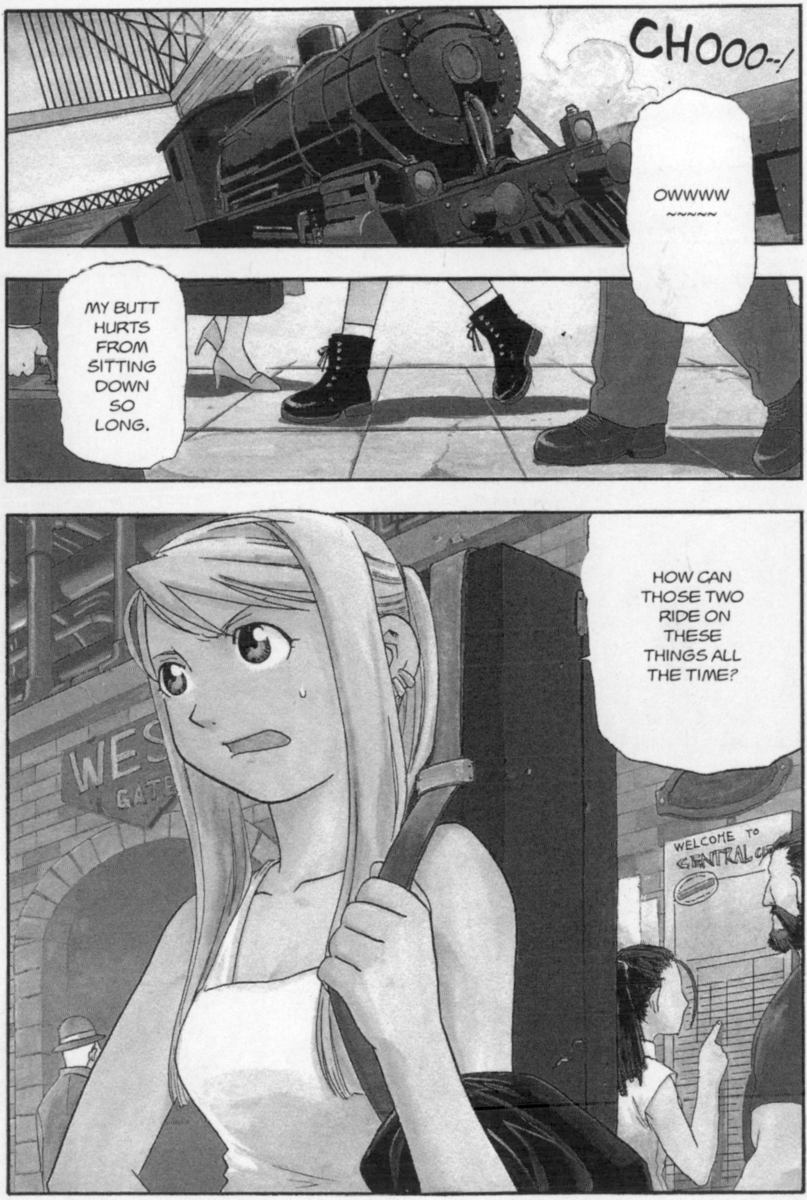
CHOOO--!
OWWWW ~~~~~
MY BUTT HURTS FROM SITTING DOWN SO LONG.
HOW CAN THOSE TWO RIDE ON THESE THINGS ALL THE TIME?
WELCOME TO

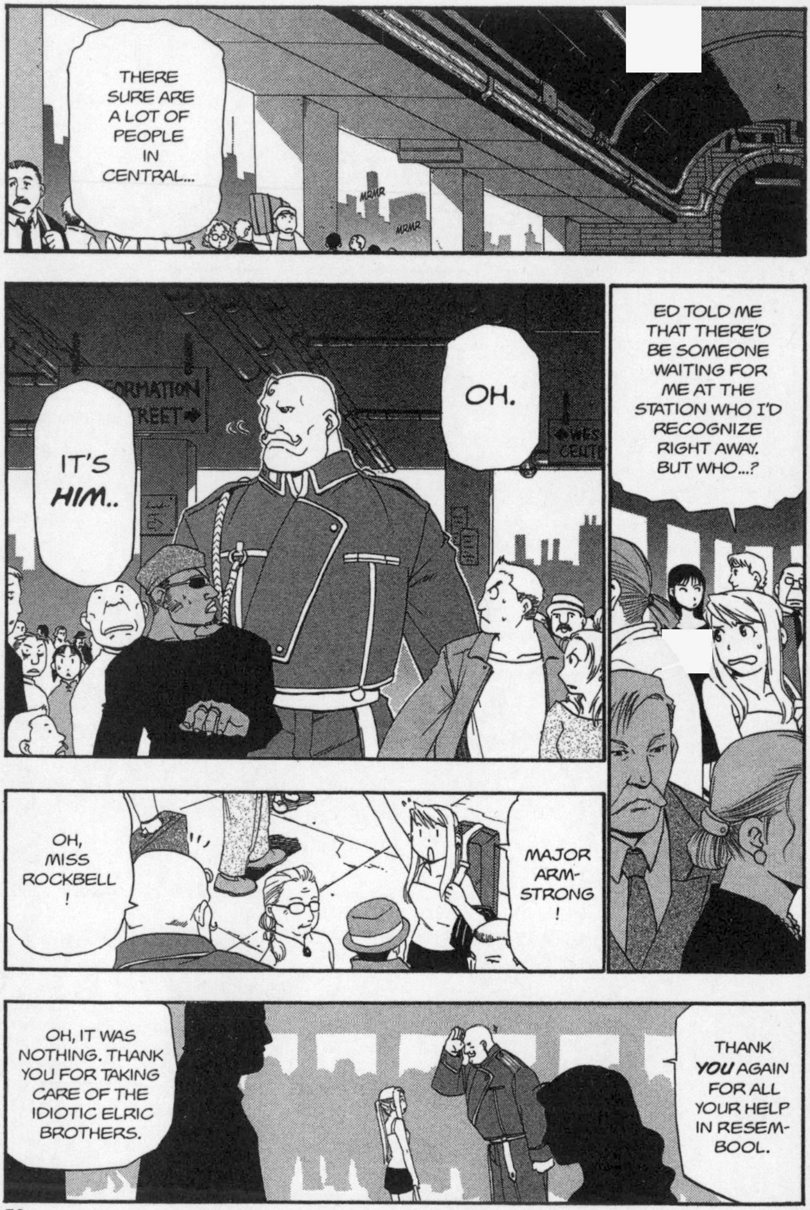
THERE SURE ARE A LOT OF PEOPLE IN CENTRAL...
MRMR
MRMR
ED TOLD ME THAT THERE'D BE SOMEONE WAITING FOR ME AT THE STATION WHO I'D RECOGNIZE RIGHT AWAY. BUT WHO...?
OH.
IT'S **HIM**..
MAJOR ARM-STRONG!
OH, MISS ROCKBELL!
THANK **YOU** AGAIN FOR ALL YOUR HELP IN RESEM-BOOL.
OH, IT WAS NOTHING. THANK YOU FOR TAKING CARE OF THE IDIOTIC ELRIC BROTHERS.

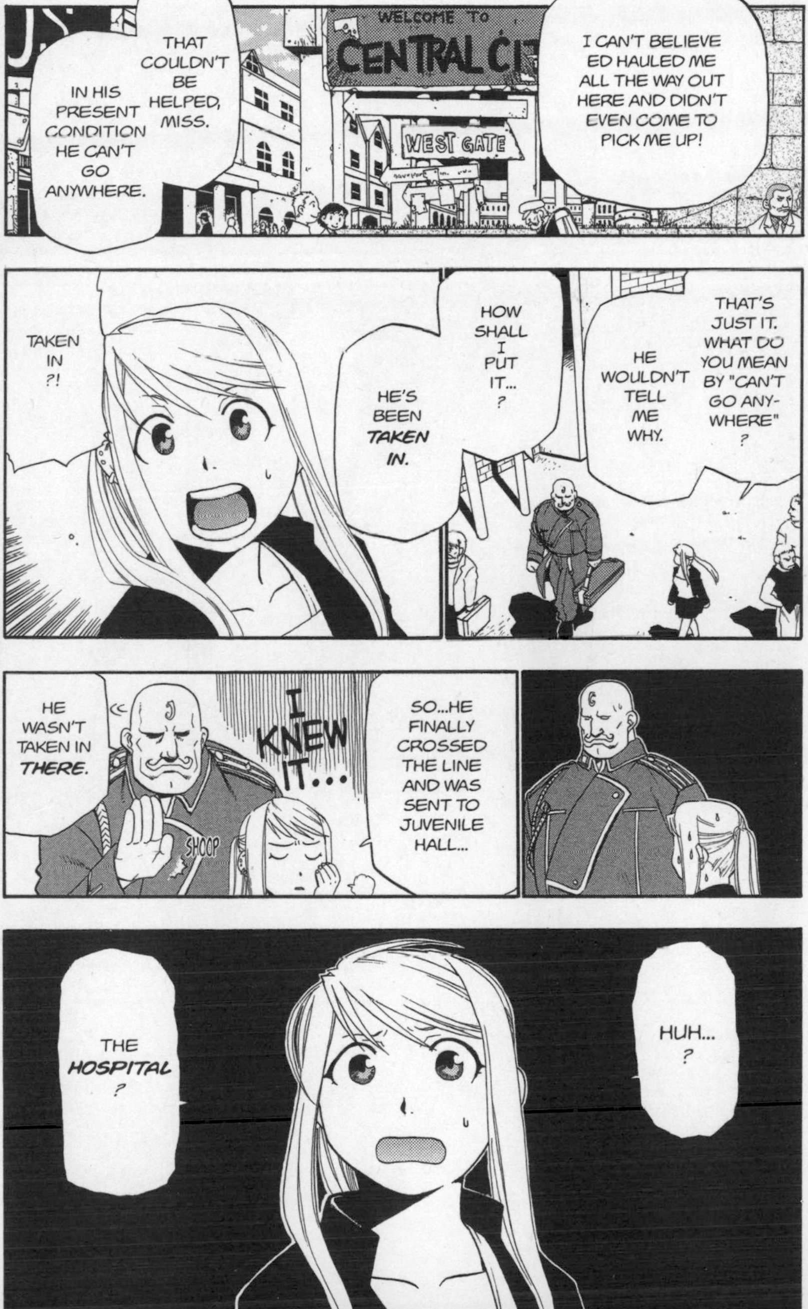
WELCOME TO
CENTRAL CI
WEST GATE
I CAN'T BELIEVE ED HAULED ME ALL THE WAY OUT HERE AND DIDN'T EVEN COME TO PICK ME UP!
THAT COULDN'T BE HELPED, MISS.
IN HIS PRESENT CONDITION HE CAN'T GO ANYWHERE.
THAT'S JUST IT. WHAT DO YOU MEAN BY "CAN'T GO ANYWHERE"?
HE WOULDN'T TELL ME WHY.
HOW SHALL I PUT IT...?
HE'S BEEN *TAKEN IN.*
TAKEN IN?!
SO...HE FINALLY CROSSED THE LINE AND WAS SENT TO JUVENILE HALL...
I KNEW IT...
HE WASN'T TAKEN IN *THERE.*
SHOOP
HUH...?
THE *HOSPITAL*?

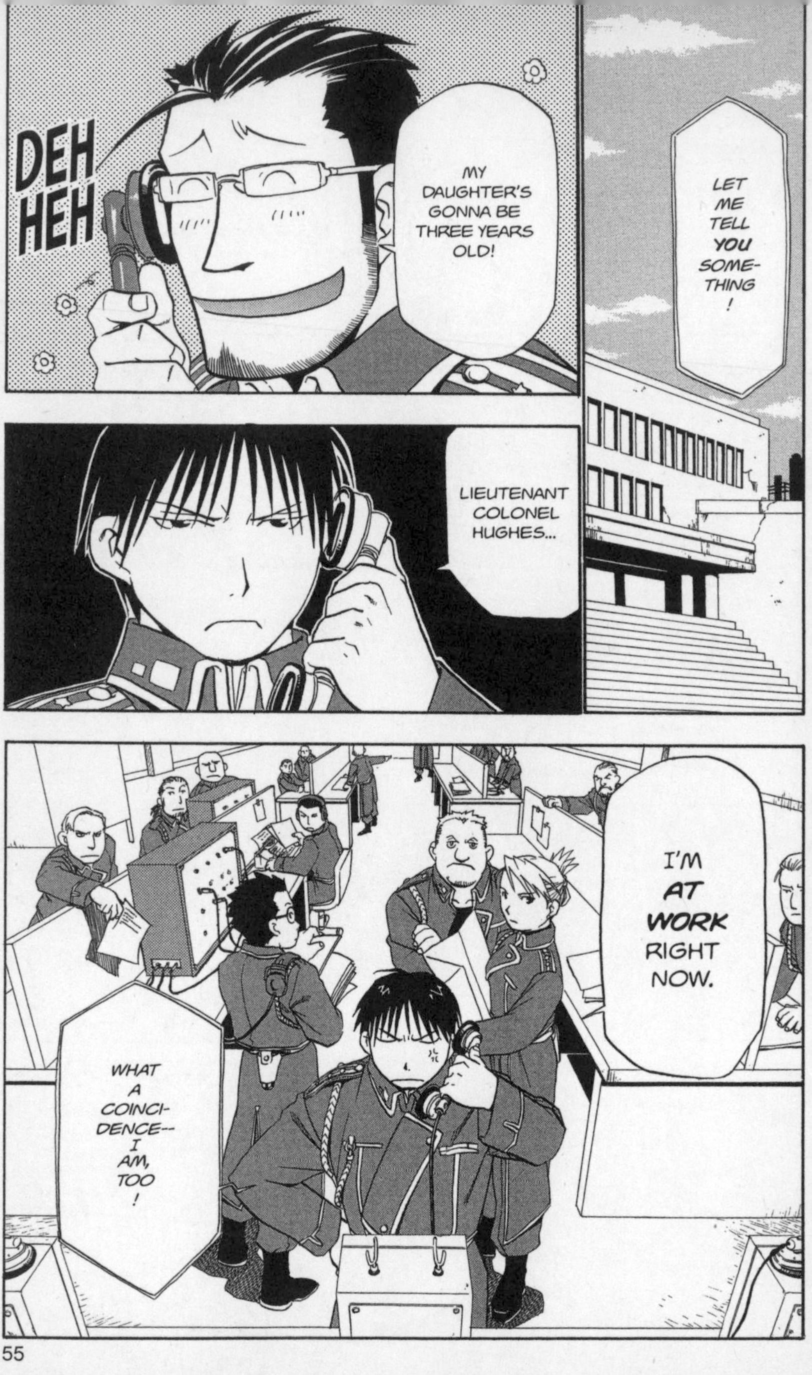
LET ME TELL YOU SOMETHING!
DEH HEH
MY DAUGHTER'S GONNA BE THREE YEARS OLD!
LIEUTENANT COLONEL HUGHES...
I'M AT WORK RIGHT NOW.
WHAT A COINCIDENCE--I AM, TOO!

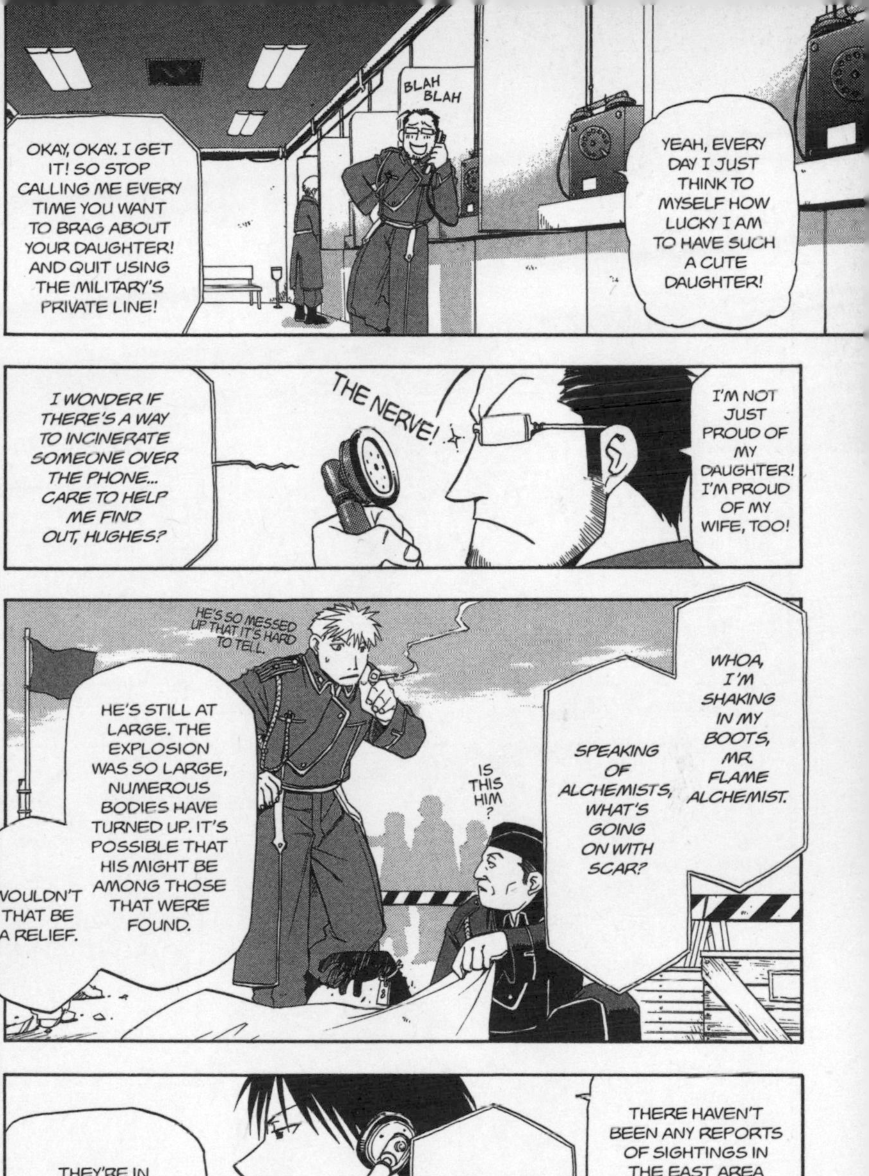
YEAH, EVERY DAY I JUST THINK TO MYSELF HOW LUCKY I AM TO HAVE SUCH A CUTE DAUGHTER!
BLAH BLAH
OKAY, OKAY. I GET IT! SO STOP CALLING ME EVERY TIME YOU WANT TO BRAG ABOUT YOUR DAUGHTER! AND QUIT USING THE MILITARY'S PRIVATE LINE!
I'M NOT JUST PROUD OF MY DAUGHTER! I'M PROUD OF MY WIFE, TOO!
THE NERVE!
I WONDER IF THERE'S A WAY TO INCINERATE SOMEONE OVER THE PHONE... CARE TO HELP ME FIND OUT, HUGHES?
WHOA, I'M SHAKING IN MY BOOTS, MR. FLAME ALCHEMIST.
SPEAKING OF ALCHEMISTS, WHAT'S GOING ON WITH SCAR?
IS THIS HIM?
HE'S SO MESSED UP THAT IT'S HARD TO TELL.
HE'S STILL AT LARGE. THE EXPLOSION WAS SO LARGE, NUMEROUS BODIES HAVE TURNED UP. IT'S POSSIBLE THAT HIS MIGHT BE AMONG THOSE THAT WERE FOUND.
WOULDN'T THAT BE A RELIEF.
THERE HAVEN'T BEEN ANY REPORTS OF SIGHTINGS IN THE EAST AREA SINCE THE INCIDENT, SO THE MAJORITY OPINION IS THAT HE'S DEAD.
SO, WILL THE ELRIC BROTHERS' GUARDS BE DISMISSED?
THEY'RE IN CENTRAL. I'LL LEAVE IT TO WHOEVER'S IN CHARGE THERE TO DECIDE.

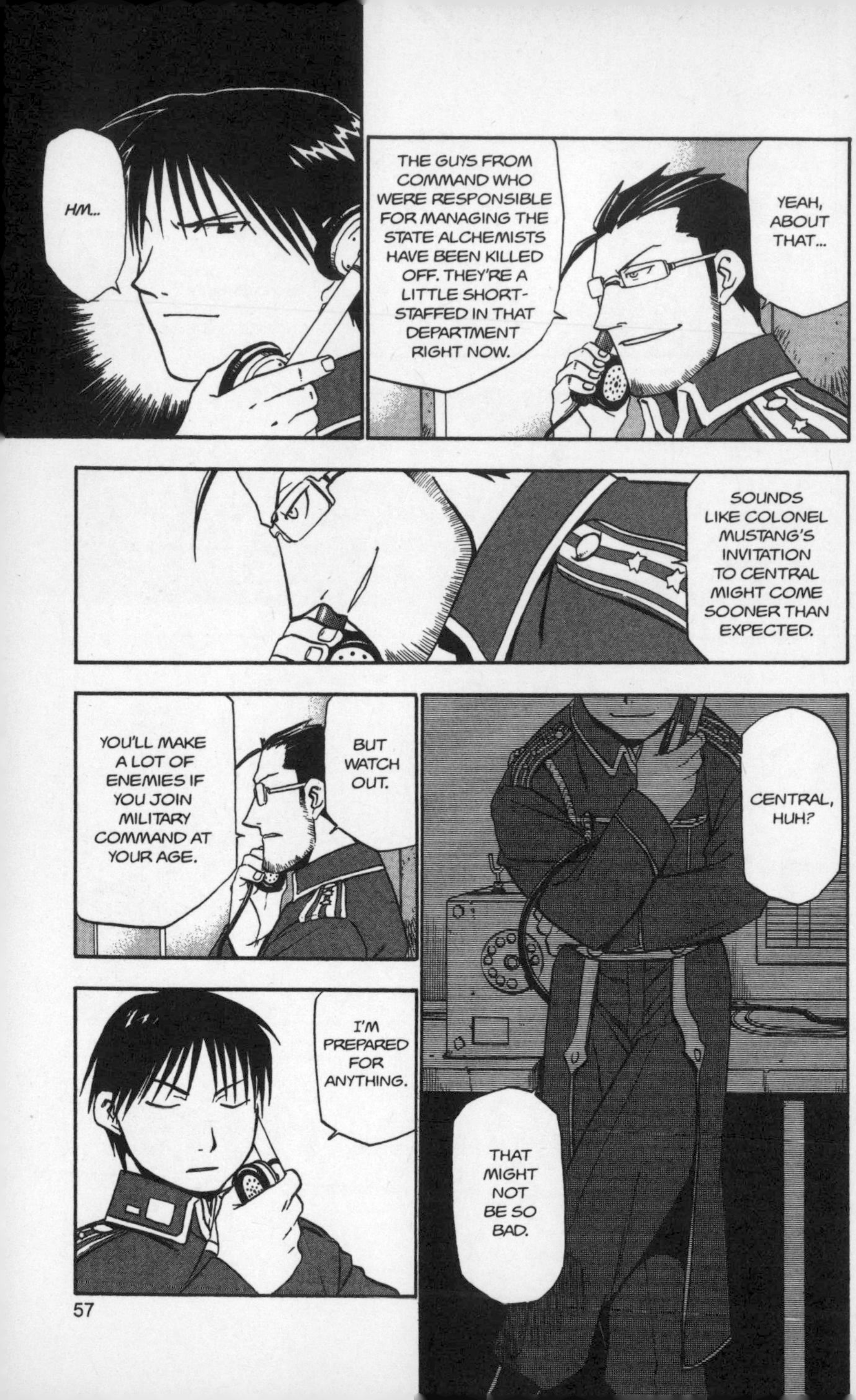
YEAH, ABOUT THAT...
THE GUYS FROM COMMAND WHO WERE RESPONSIBLE FOR MANAGING THE STATE ALCHEMISTS HAVE BEEN KILLED OFF. THEY'RE A LITTLE SHORT-STAFFED IN THAT DEPARTMENT RIGHT NOW.
HM..
SOUNDS LIKE COLONEL MUSTANG'S INVITATION TO CENTRAL MIGHT COME SOONER THAN EXPECTED.
CENTRAL, HUH?
THAT MIGHT NOT BE SO BAD.
BUT WATCH OUT.
YOU'LL MAKE A LOT OF ENEMIES IF YOU JOIN MILITARY COMMAND AT YOUR AGE.
I'M PREPARED FOR ANYTHING.

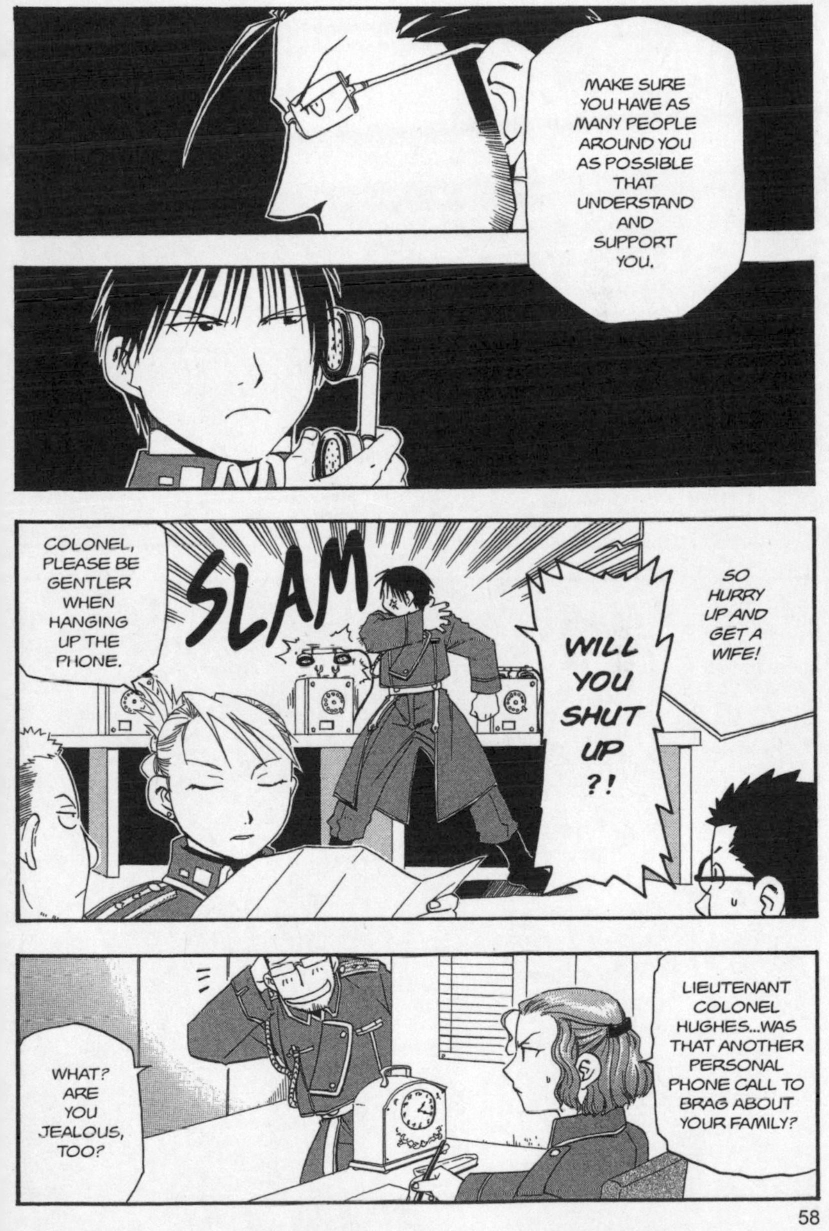
MAKE SURE YOU HAVE AS MANY PEOPLE AROUND YOU AS POSSIBLE THAT UNDERSTAND AND SUPPORT YOU.
SO HURRY UP AND GET A WIFE!
WILL YOU SHUT UP ?!
SLAM
COLONEL, PLEASE BE GENTLER WHEN HANGING UP THE PHONE.
LIEUTENANT COLONEL HUGHES...WAS THAT ANOTHER PERSONAL PHONE CALL TO BRAG ABOUT YOUR FAMILY?
WHAT? ARE YOU JEALOUS, TOO?

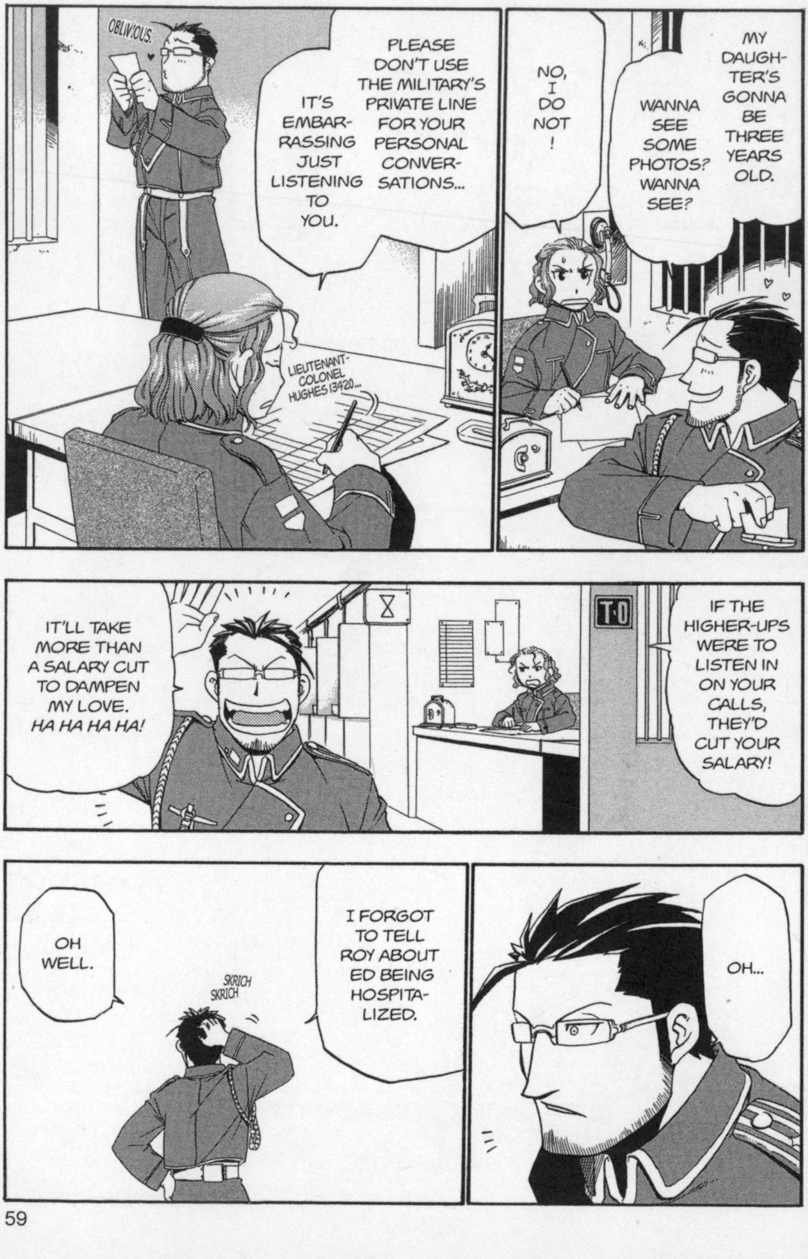
MY DAUGHTER'S GONNA BE THREE YEARS OLD.
WANNA SEE SOME PHOTOS? WANNA SEE?
NO, I DO NOT!
PLEASE DON'T USE THE MILITARY'S PRIVATE LINE FOR YOUR PERSONAL CONVERSATIONS...
IT'S EMBARRASSING JUST LISTENING TO YOU.
OBLIVIOUS.
LIEUTENANT-COLONEL HUGHES 13420...
IF THE HIGHER-UPS WERE TO LISTEN IN ON YOUR CALLS, THEY'D CUT YOUR SALARY!
IT'LL TAKE MORE THAN A SALARY CUT TO DAMPEN MY LOVE. HA HA HA HA!
OH...
I FORGOT TO TELL ROY ABOUT ED BEING HOSPITALIZED.
SKRICH SKRICH
OH WELL.

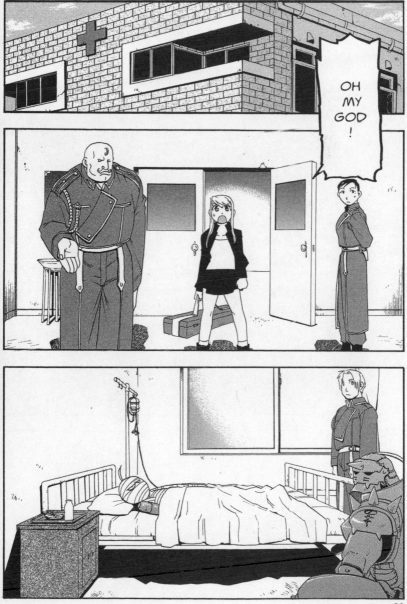

OH
MY
GOD
!

60

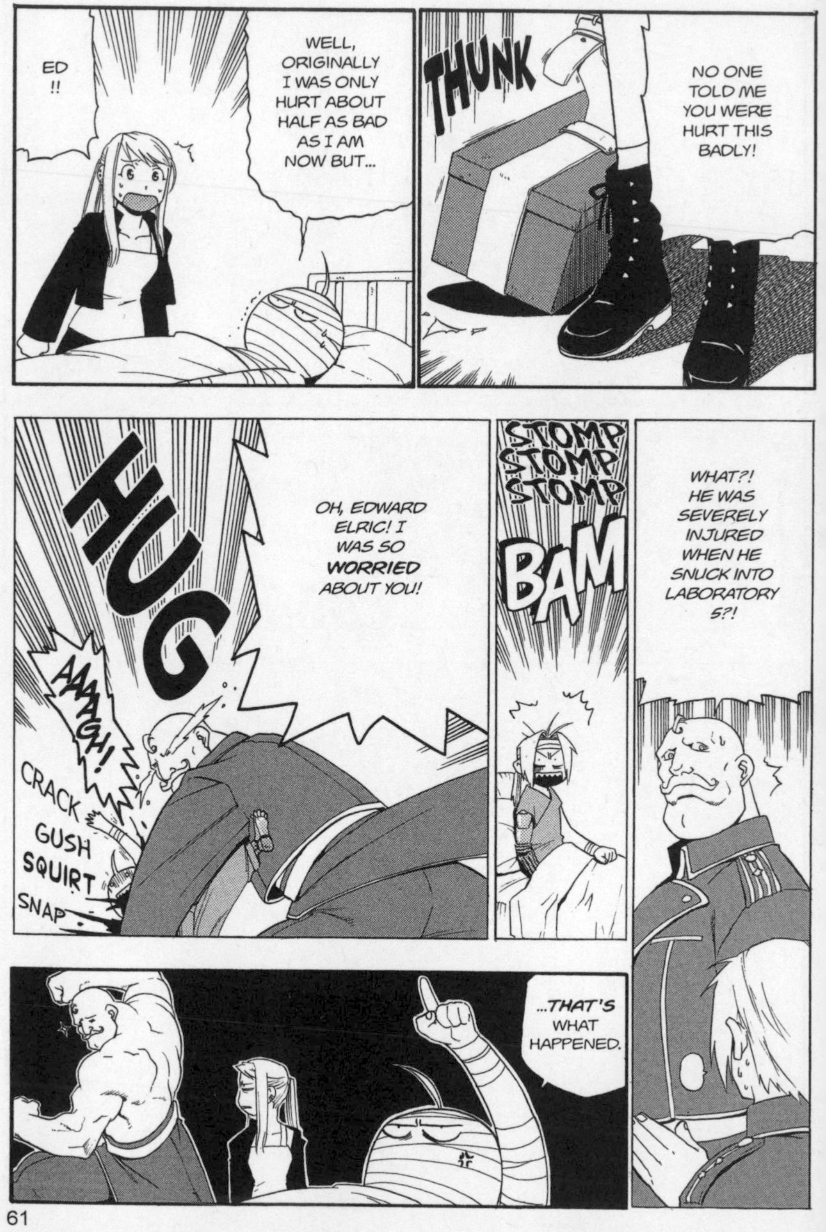
THUNK
NO ONE TOLD ME YOU WERE HURT THIS BADLY!
ED !!
WELL, ORIGINALLY I WAS ONLY HURT ABOUT HALF AS BAD AS I AM NOW BUT...
WHAT?! HE WAS SEVERELY INJURED WHEN HE SNUCK INTO LABORATORY 5?!
STOMP STOMP STOMP
BAM
OH, EDWARD ELRIC! I WAS SO WORRIED ABOUT YOU!
HUG
AAAAGH!
CRACK
GUSH
SQUIRT
SNAP
...THAT'S WHAT HAPPENED.

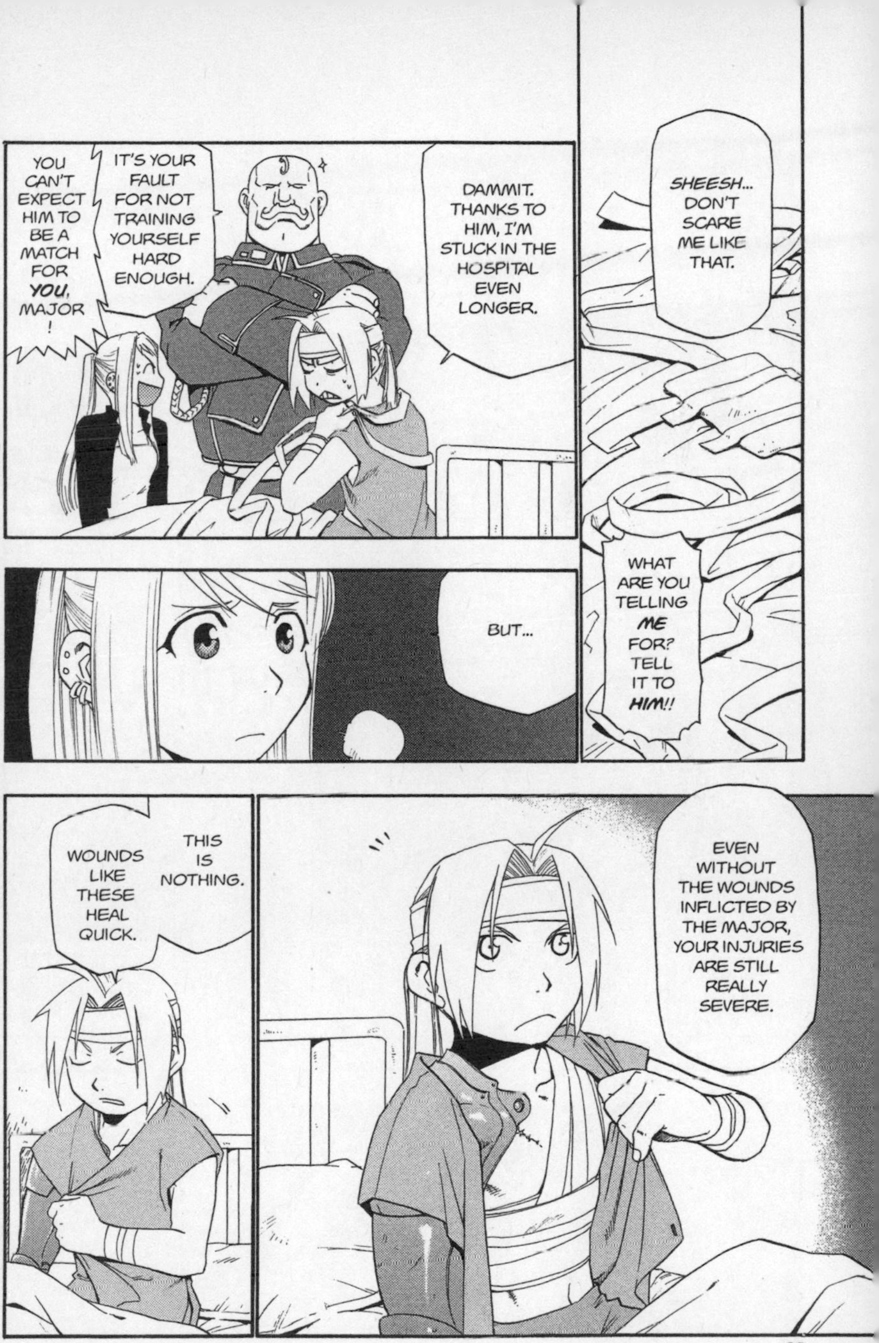
SHEESH... DON'T SCARE ME LIKE THAT.
WHAT ARE YOU TELLING ME FOR? TELL IT TO HIM!!
DAMMIT. THANKS TO HIM, I'M STUCK IN THE HOSPITAL EVEN LONGER.
IT'S YOUR FAULT FOR NOT TRAINING YOURSELF HARD ENOUGH.
YOU CAN'T EXPECT HIM TO BE A MATCH FOR YOU, MAJOR!
BUT...
EVEN WITHOUT THE WOUNDS INFLICTED BY THE MAJOR, YOUR INJURIES ARE STILL REALLY SEVERE.
THIS IS NOTHING.
WOUNDS LIKE THESE HEAL QUICK.

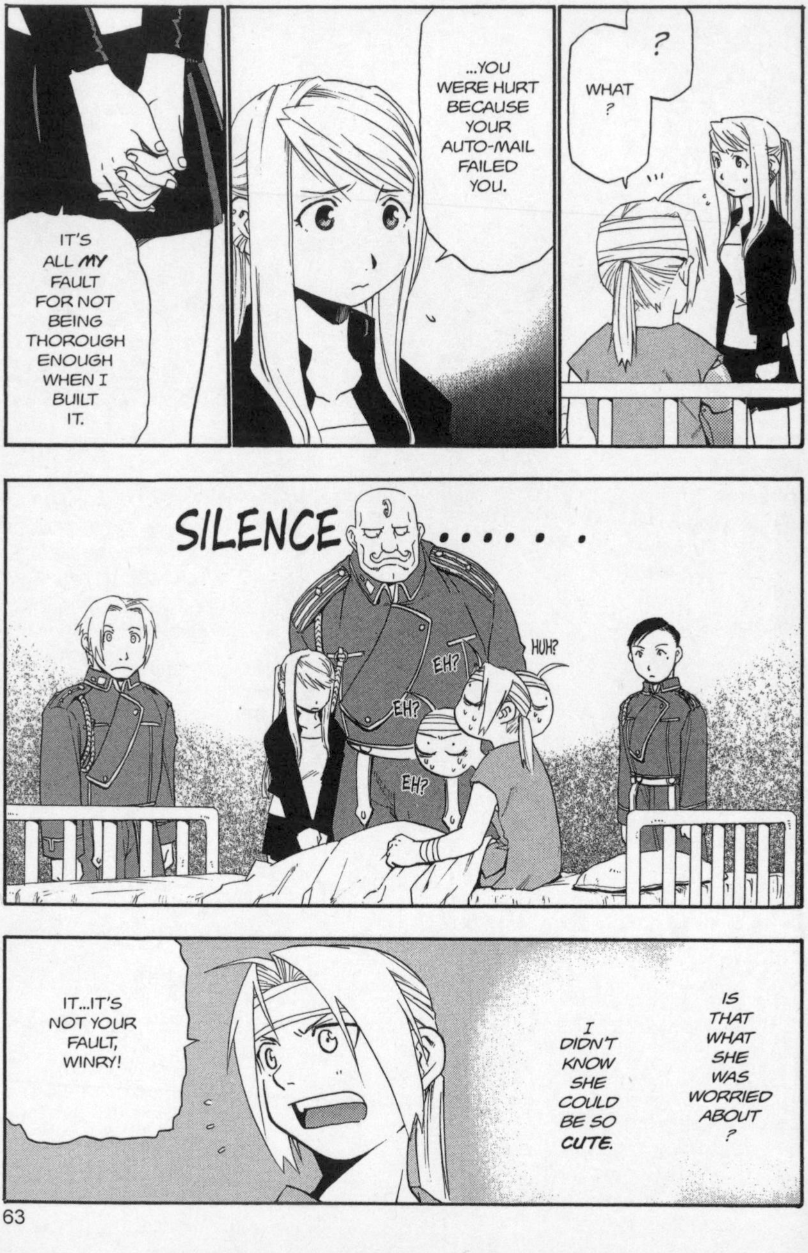
?
WHAT ?
...YOU WERE HURT BECAUSE YOUR AUTO-MAIL FAILED YOU.
IT'S ALL MY FAULT FOR NOT BEING THOROUGH ENOUGH WHEN I BUILT IT.
SILENCE......
HUH?
EH?
EH?
EH?
IS THAT WHAT SHE WAS WORRIED ABOUT ?
I DIDN'T KNOW SHE COULD BE SO CUTE.
IT...IT'S NOT YOUR FAULT, WINRY!

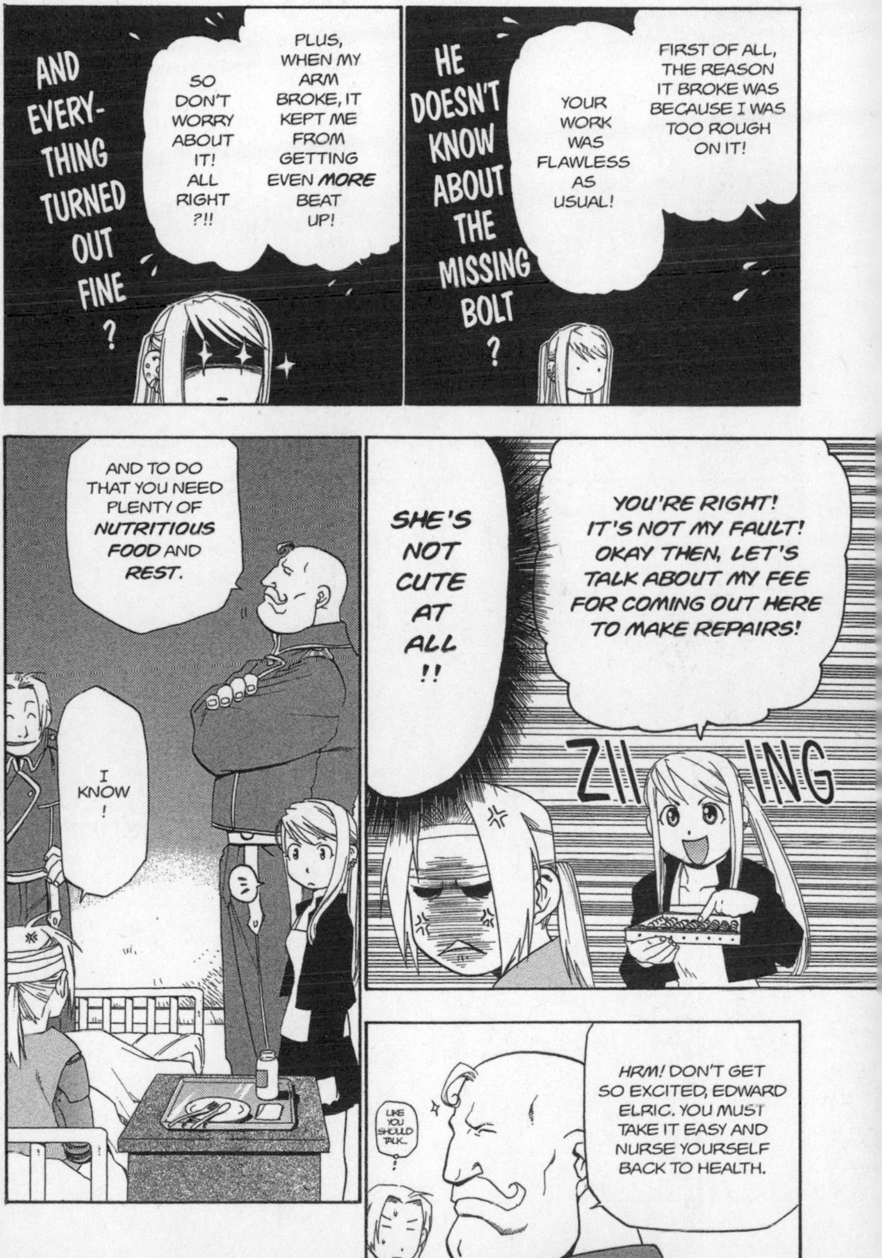
FIRST OF ALL, THE REASON IT BROKE WAS BECAUSE I WAS TOO ROUGH ON IT!
YOUR WORK WAS FLAWLESS AS USUAL!
HE DOESN'T KNOW ABOUT THE MISSING BOLT?
PLUS, WHEN MY ARM BROKE, IT KEPT ME FROM GETTING EVEN MORE BEAT UP!
SO DON'T WORRY ABOUT IT! ALL RIGHT?!!
AND EVERYTHING TURNED OUT FINE?
YOU'RE RIGHT! IT'S NOT MY FAULT! OKAY THEN, LET'S TALK ABOUT MY FEE FOR COMING OUT HERE TO MAKE REPAIRS!
SHE'S NOT CUTE AT ALL!!
ZI ING
HRM! DON'T GET SO EXCITED, EDWARD ELRIC. YOU MUST TAKE IT EASY AND NURSE YOURSELF BACK TO HEALTH.
LIKE YOU SHOULD TALK..
AND TO DO THAT YOU NEED PLENTY OF NUTRITIOUS FOOD AND REST.
I KNOW!

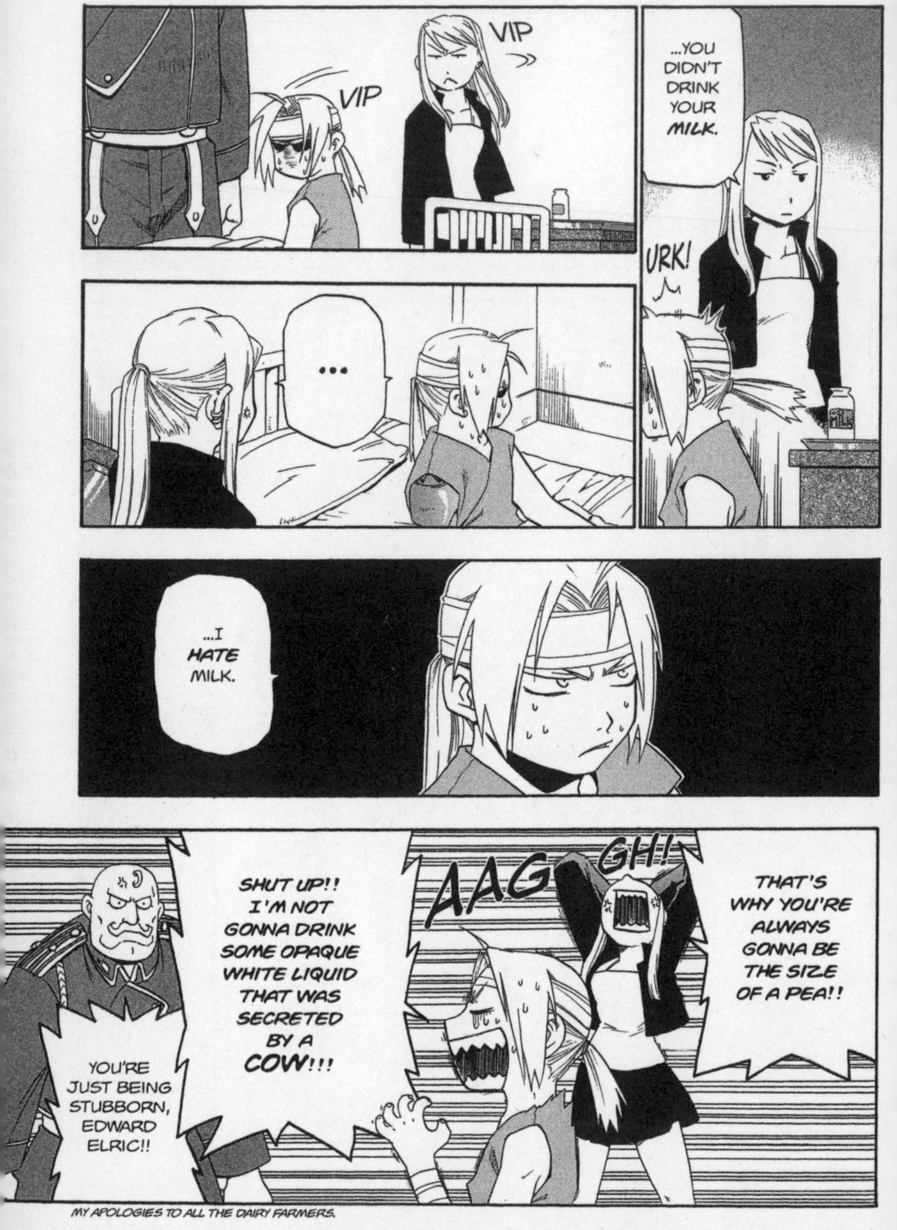
...YOU DIDN'T DRINK YOUR MILK.
URK!
VIP
VIP
...
...I HATE MILK.
THAT'S WHY YOU'RE ALWAYS GONNA BE THE SIZE OF A PEA!!
AAGGH!
SHUT UP!! I'M NOT GONNA DRINK SOME OPAQUE WHITE LIQUID THAT WAS SECRETED BY A COW!!!
YOU'RE JUST BEING STUBBORN, EDWARD ELRIC!!

MY APOLOGIES TO ALL THE DAIRY FARMERS.

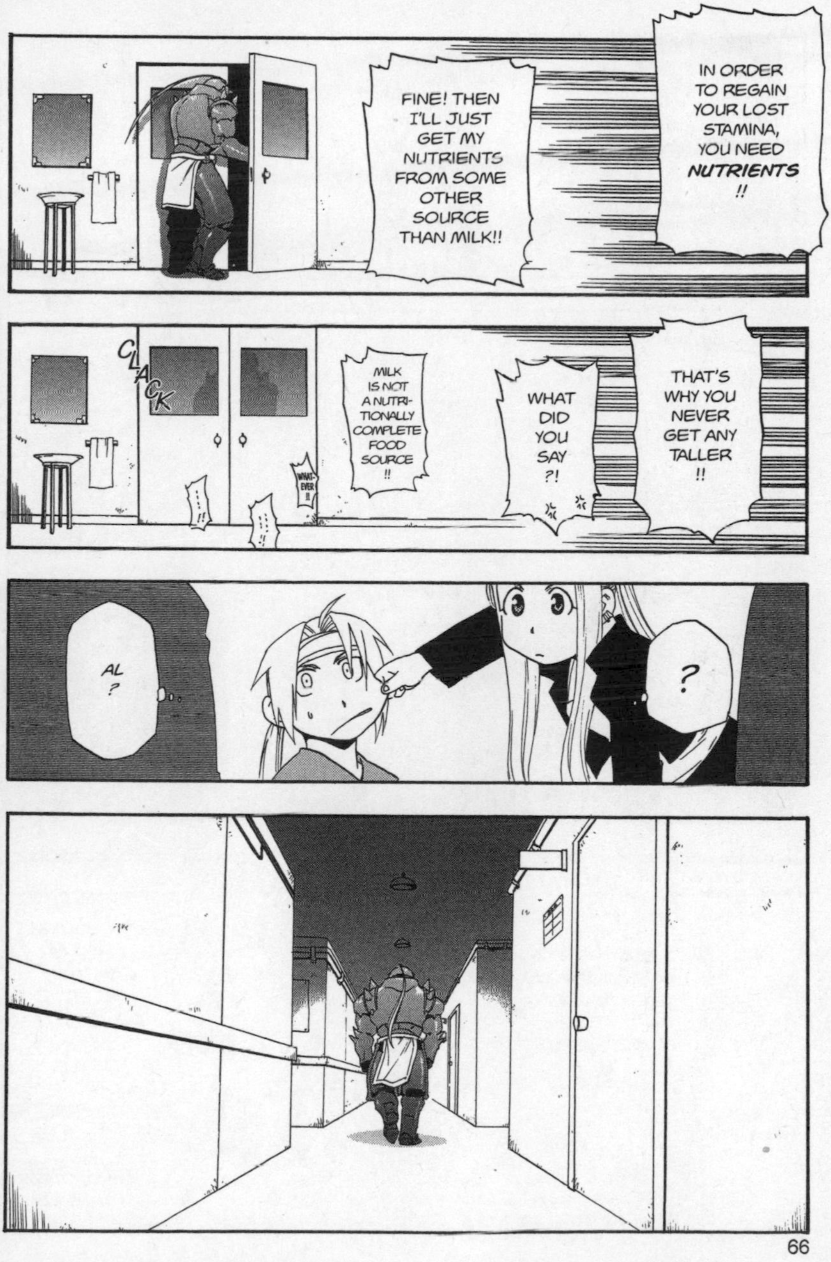
IN ORDER TO REGAIN YOUR LOST STAMINA, YOU NEED **NUTRIENTS** !!
FINE! THEN I'LL JUST GET MY NUTRIENTS FROM SOME OTHER SOURCE THAN MILK!!
THAT'S WHY YOU NEVER GET ANY TALLER !!
WHAT DID YOU SAY ?!
MILK IS NOT A NUTRITIONALLY COMPLETE FOOD SOURCE !!
WHATEVER !!
CLACK
?
AL ?

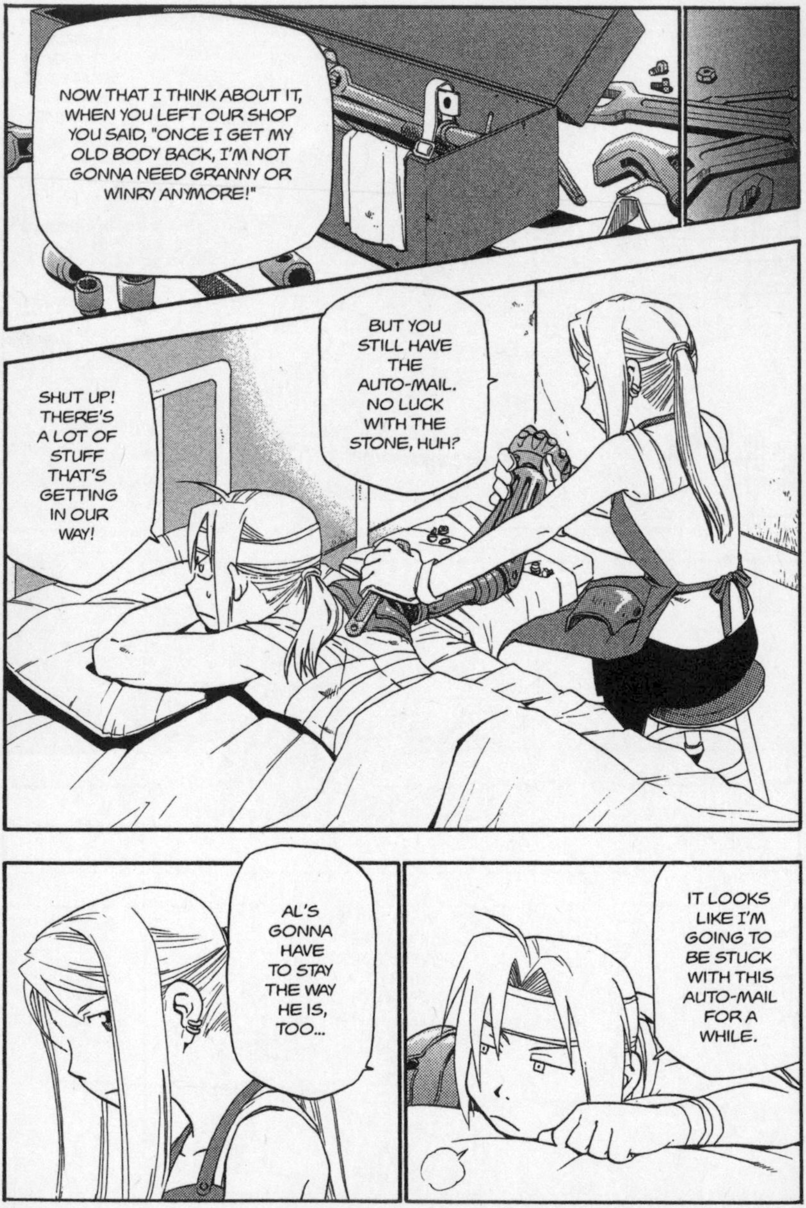
NOW THAT I THINK ABOUT IT, WHEN YOU LEFT OUR SHOP YOU SAID, "ONCE I GET MY OLD BODY BACK, I'M NOT GONNA NEED GRANNY OR WINRY ANYMORE!"
BUT YOU STILL HAVE THE AUTO-MAIL. NO LUCK WITH THE STONE, HUH?
SHUT UP! THERE'S A LOT OF STUFF THAT'S GETTING IN OUR WAY!
IT LOOKS LIKE I'M GOING TO BE STUCK WITH THIS AUTO-MAIL FOR A WHILE.
AL'S GONNA HAVE TO STAY THE WAY HE IS, TOO...

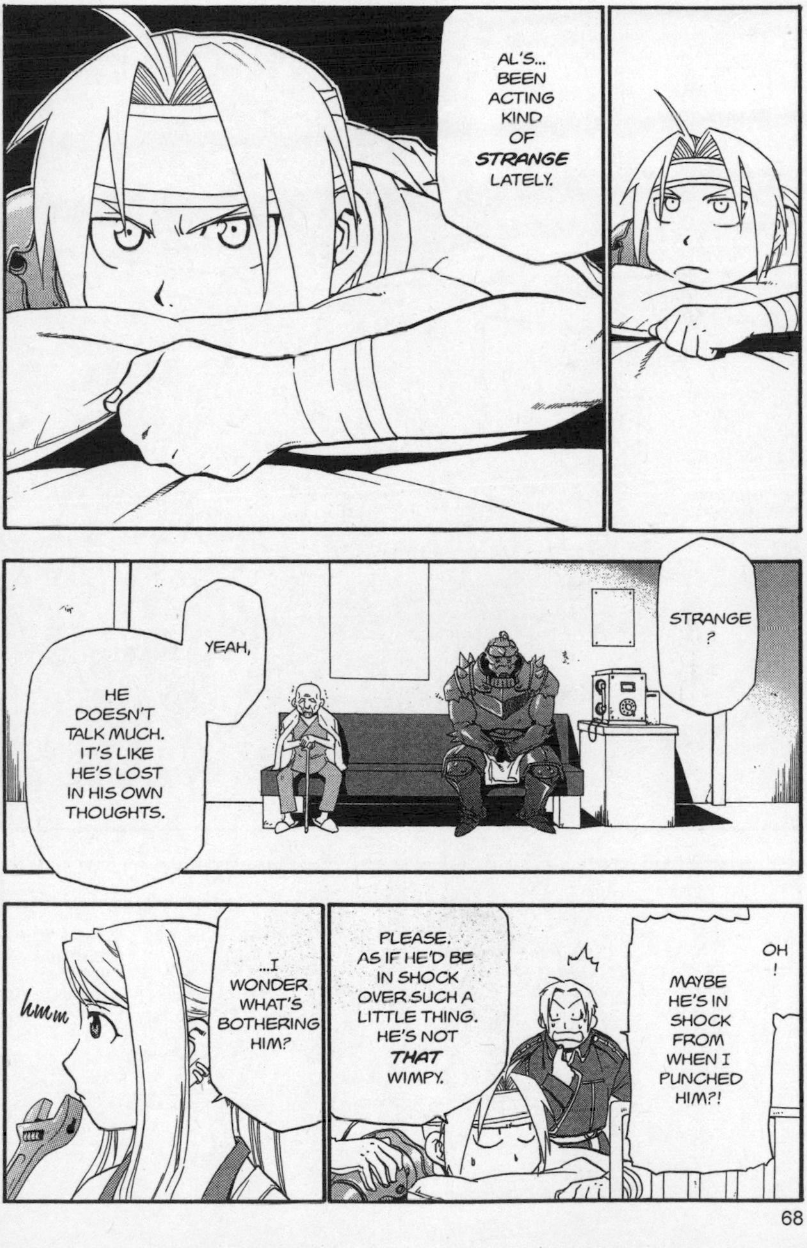
AL'S... BEEN ACTING KIND OF *STRANGE* LATELY.
STRANGE?
YEAH,
HE DOESN'T TALK MUCH. IT'S LIKE HE'S LOST IN HIS OWN THOUGHTS.
OH!
MAYBE HE'S IN SHOCK FROM WHEN I PUNCHED HIM?!
PLEASE. AS IF HE'D BE IN SHOCK OVER SUCH A LITTLE THING. HE'S NOT *THAT* WIMPY.
hmm
...I WONDER WHAT'S BOTHERING HIM?

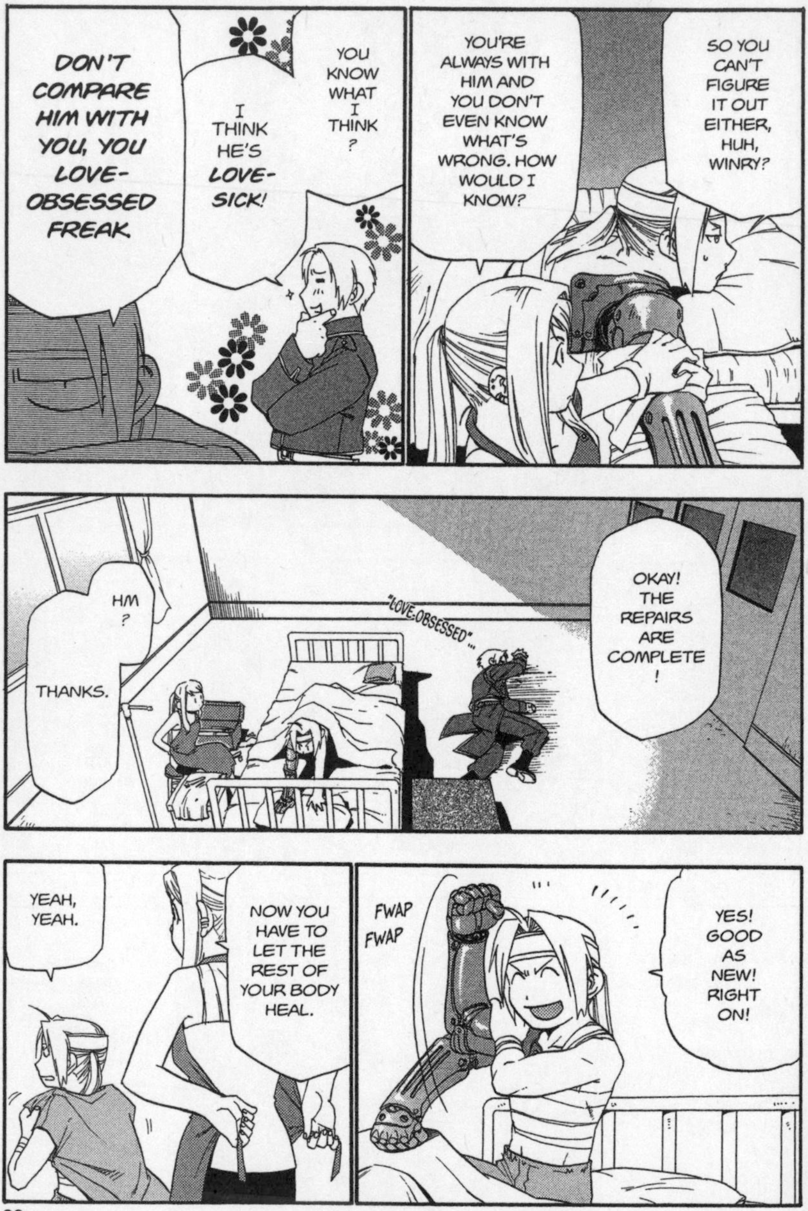
SO YOU CAN'T FIGURE IT OUT EITHER, HUH, WINRY?
YOU'RE ALWAYS WITH HIM AND YOU DON'T EVEN KNOW WHAT'S WRONG. HOW WOULD I KNOW?
YOU KNOW WHAT I THINK?
I THINK HE'S LOVE-SICK!
DON'T COMPARE HIM WITH YOU, YOU LOVE-OBSESSED FREAK.
OKAY! THE REPAIRS ARE COMPLETE!
"LOVE-OBSESSED"...
HM?
THANKS.
YES! GOOD AS NEW! RIGHT ON!
FWAP FWAP
NOW YOU HAVE TO LET THE REST OF YOUR BODY HEAL.
YEAH, YEAH.

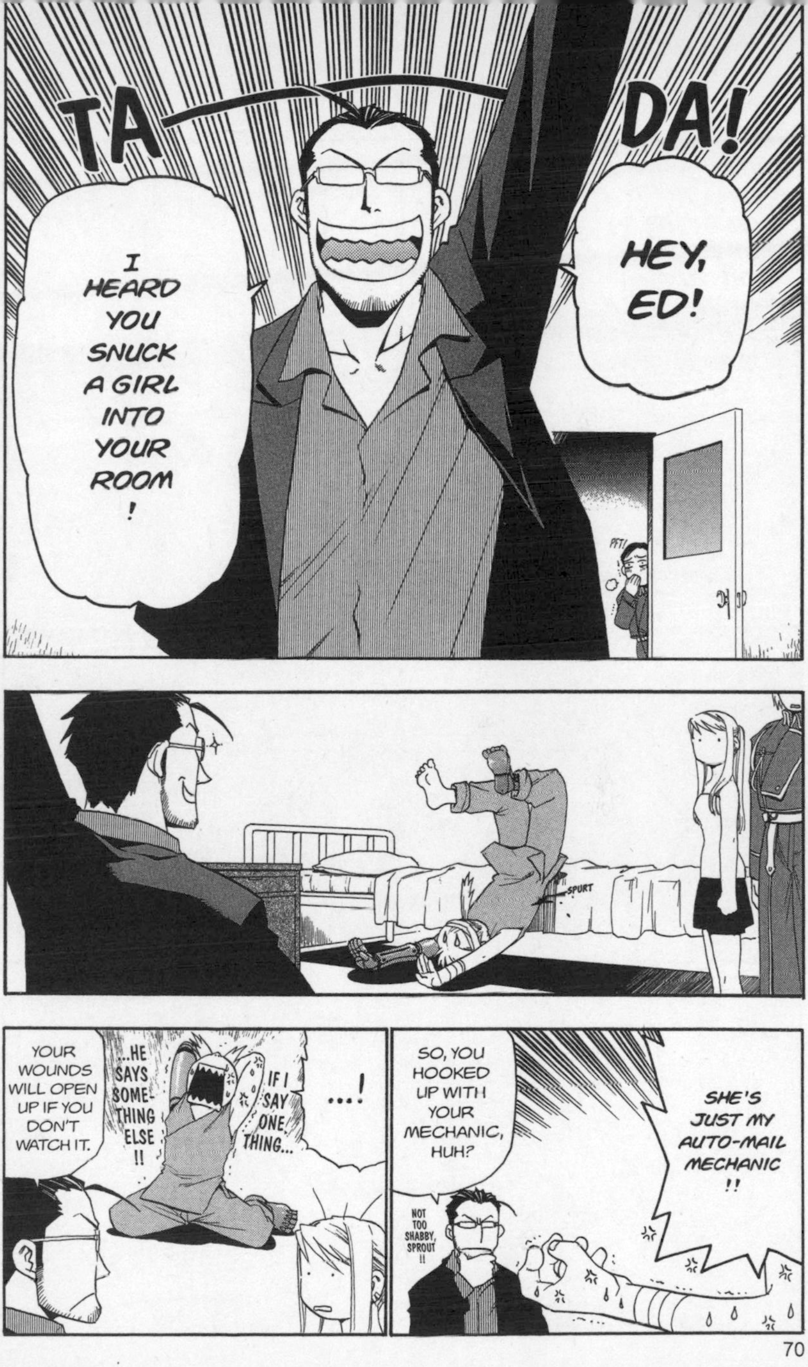

TA—DA!
HEY, ED!
I HEARD YOU SNUCK A GIRL INTO YOUR ROOM!
PFFT!
SPURT
SHE'S JUST MY AUTO-MAIL MECHANIC!!
SO, YOU HOOKED UP WITH YOUR MECHANIC, HUH?
NOT TOO SHABBY, SPROUT!!
...!
IF I SAY ONE THING...
...HE SAYS SOMETHING ELSE!!
YOUR WOUNDS WILL OPEN UP IF YOU DON'T WATCH IT.

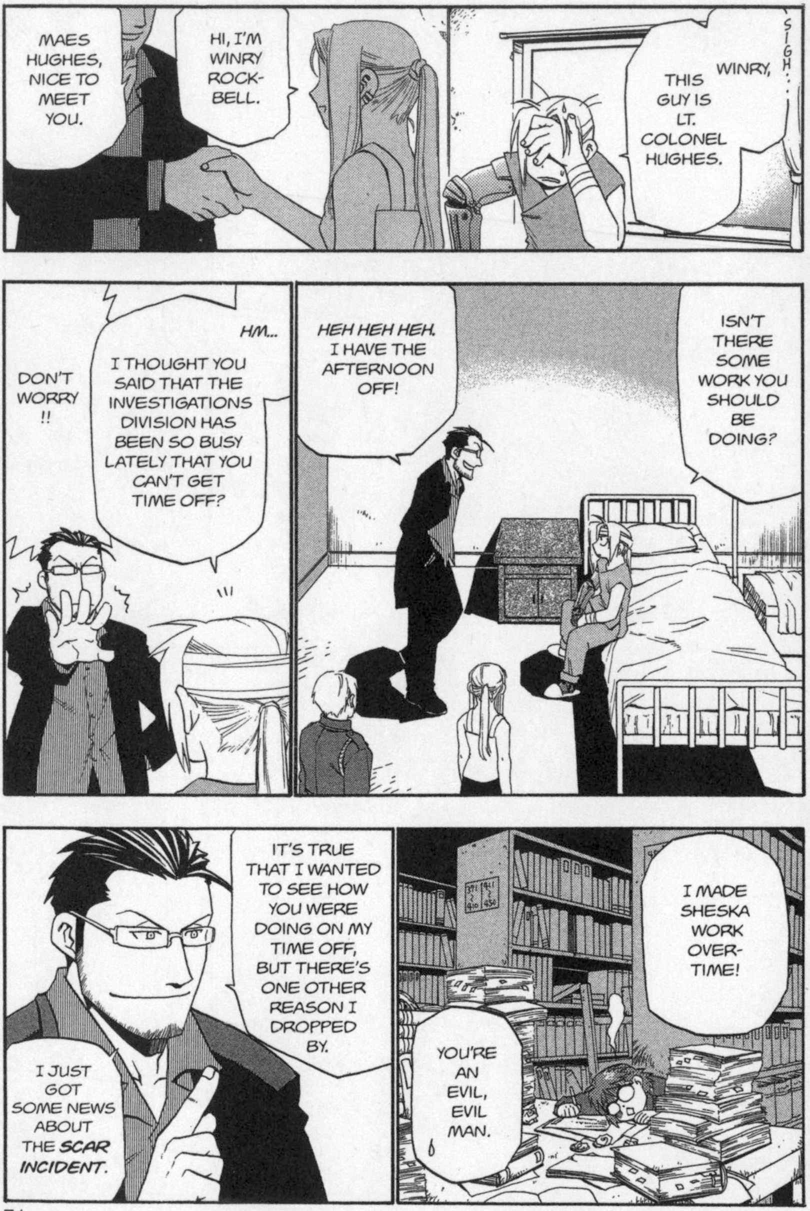
SIGH...
WINRY, THIS GUY IS LT. COLONEL HUGHES.
HI, I'M WINRY ROCK-BELL.
MAES HUGHES, NICE TO MEET YOU.
ISN'T THERE SOME WORK YOU SHOULD BE DOING?
HEH HEH HEH. I HAVE THE AFTERNOON OFF!
HM...
I THOUGHT YOU SAID THAT THE INVESTIGATIONS DIVISION HAS BEEN SO BUSY LATELY THAT YOU CAN'T GET TIME OFF?
DON'T WORRY !!
I MADE SHESKA WORK OVER-TIME!
YOU'RE AN EVIL, EVIL MAN.
IT'S TRUE THAT I WANTED TO SEE HOW YOU WERE DOING ON MY TIME OFF, BUT THERE'S ONE OTHER REASON I DROPPED BY.
I JUST GOT SOME NEWS ABOUT THE ***SCAR INCIDENT***.

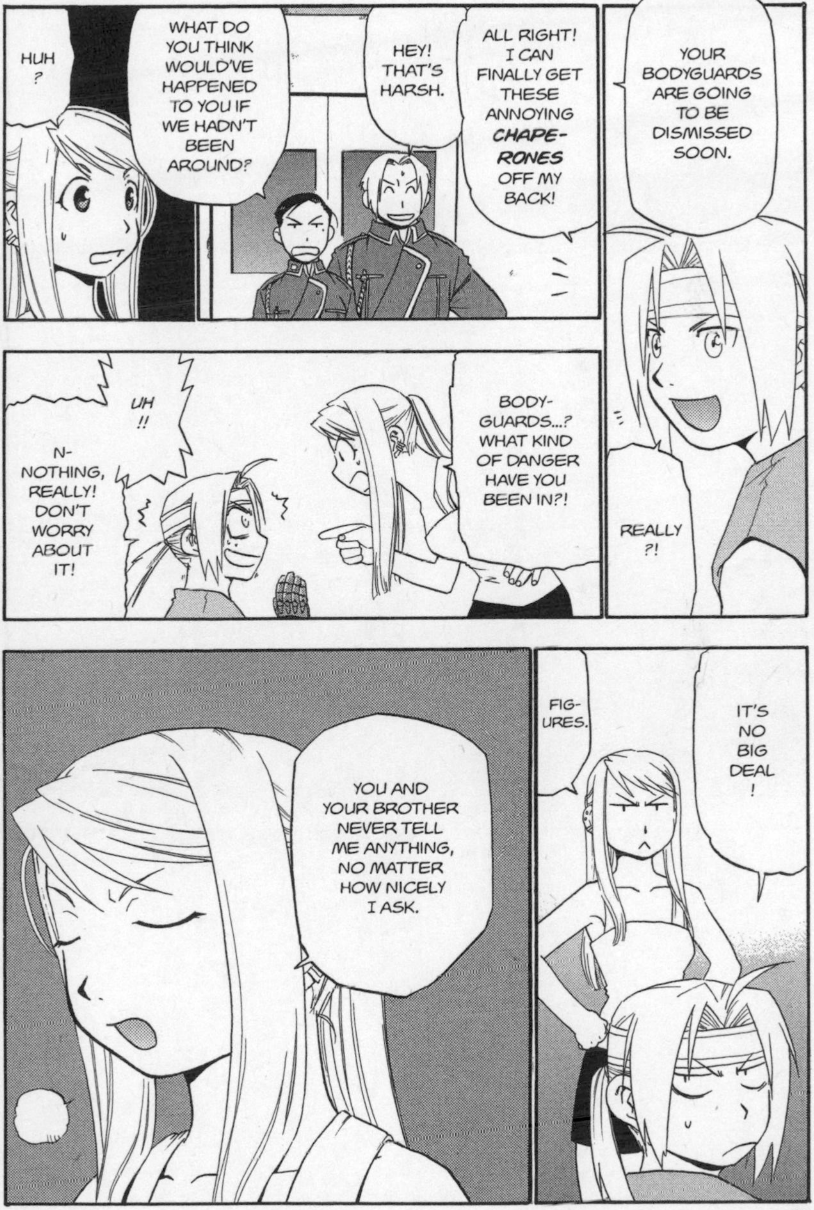
YOUR BODYGUARDS ARE GOING TO BE DISMISSED SOON.
REALLY ?!
ALL RIGHT! I CAN FINALLY GET THESE ANNOYING **CHAPE-RONES** OFF MY BACK!
HEY! THAT'S HARSH.
WHAT DO YOU THINK WOULD'VE HAPPENED TO YOU IF WE HADN'T BEEN AROUND?
HUH ?
BODY-GUARDS...? WHAT KIND OF DANGER HAVE YOU BEEN IN?!
UH !!
N-NOTHING, REALLY! DON'T WORRY ABOUT IT!
IT'S NO BIG DEAL !
FIG-URES.
YOU AND YOUR BROTHER NEVER TELL ME ANYTHING, NO MATTER HOW NICELY I ASK.

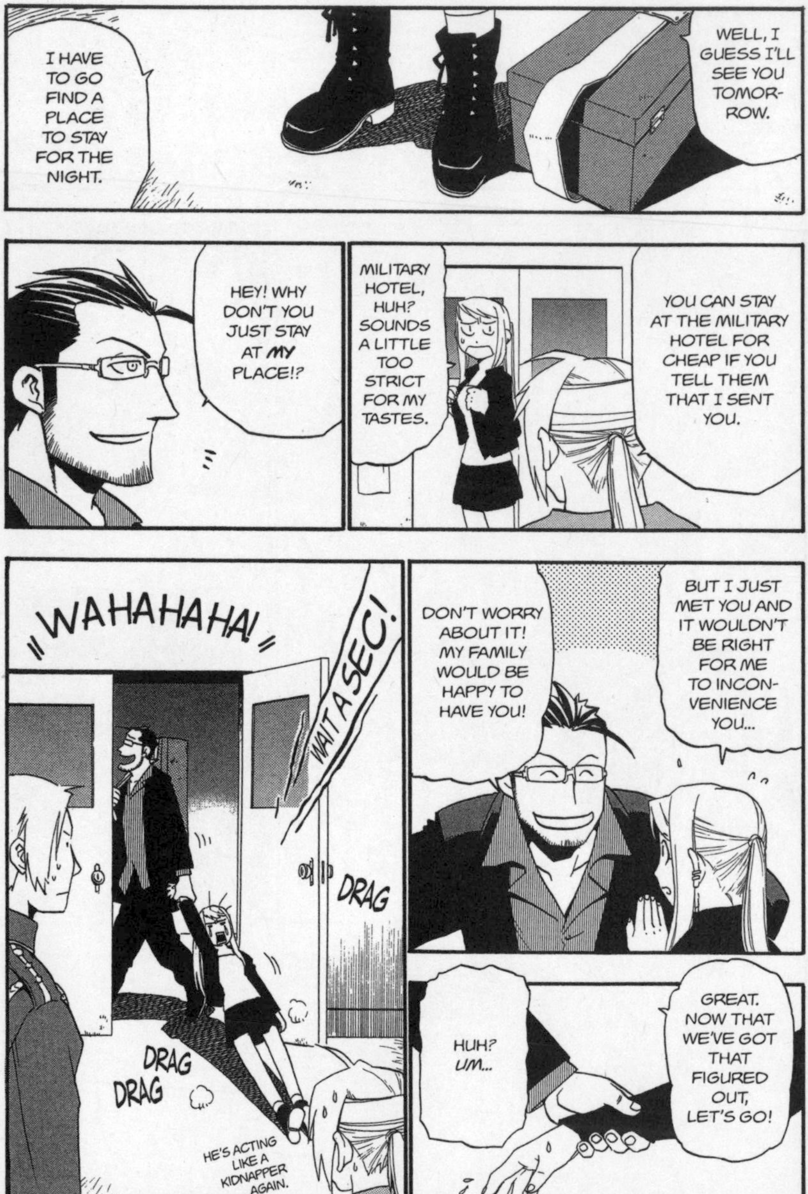
WELL, I GUESS I'LL SEE YOU TOMORROW.
I HAVE TO GO FIND A PLACE TO STAY FOR THE NIGHT.
YOU CAN STAY AT THE MILITARY HOTEL FOR CHEAP IF YOU TELL THEM THAT I SENT YOU.
MILITARY HOTEL, HUH? SOUNDS A LITTLE TOO STRICT FOR MY TASTES.
HEY! WHY DON'T YOU JUST STAY AT MY PLACE!?
BUT I JUST MET YOU AND IT WOULDN'T BE RIGHT FOR ME TO INCONVENIENCE YOU...
DON'T WORRY ABOUT IT! MY FAMILY WOULD BE HAPPY TO HAVE YOU!
GREAT. NOW THAT WE'VE GOT THAT FIGURED OUT, LET'S GO!
HUH? UM...
WAIT A SEC!
WAHAHAHA!
DRAG
DRAG DRAG
HE'S ACTING LIKE A KIDNAPPER AGAIN.

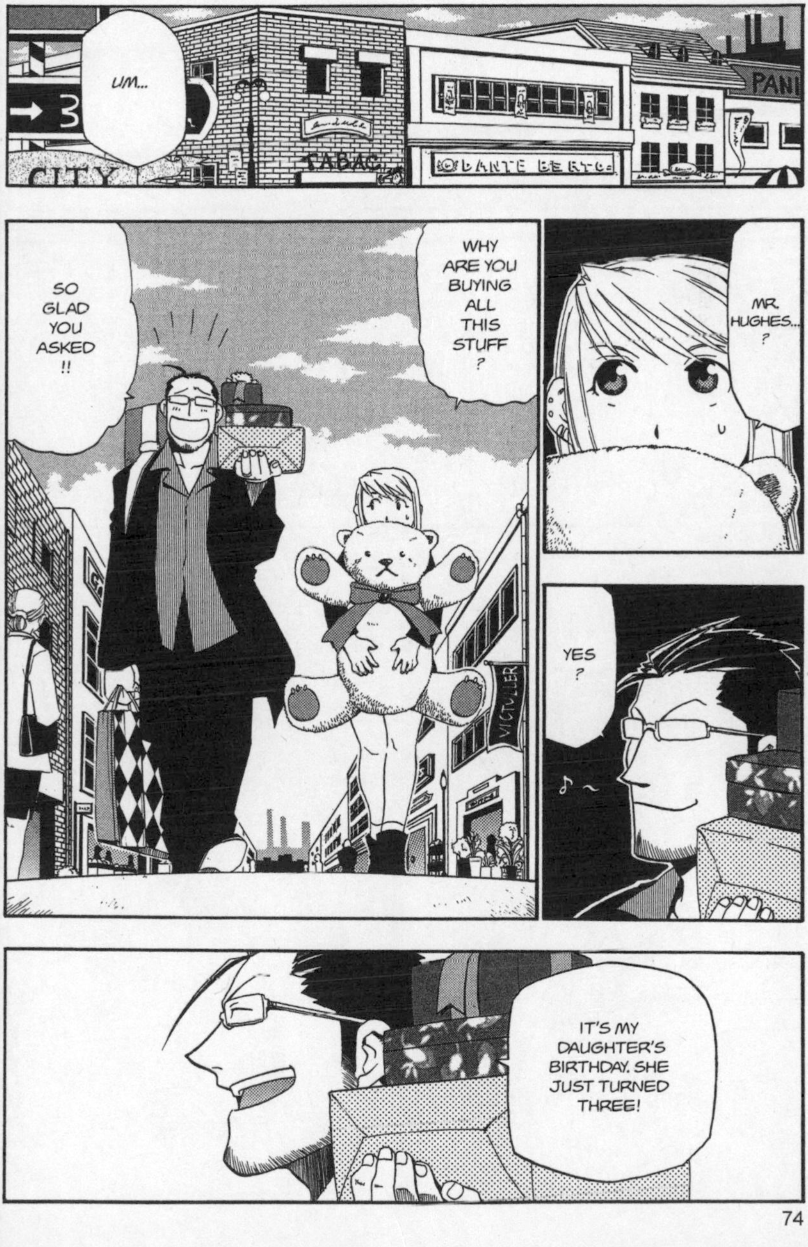
UM...
CITY
TABAC
DANTE BERTO.
PANI
MR. HUGHES...?
YES?
♪~
WHY ARE YOU BUYING ALL THIS STUFF?
SO GLAD YOU ASKED!!
VICTULLER
IT'S MY DAUGHTER'S BIRTHDAY. SHE JUST TURNED THREE!

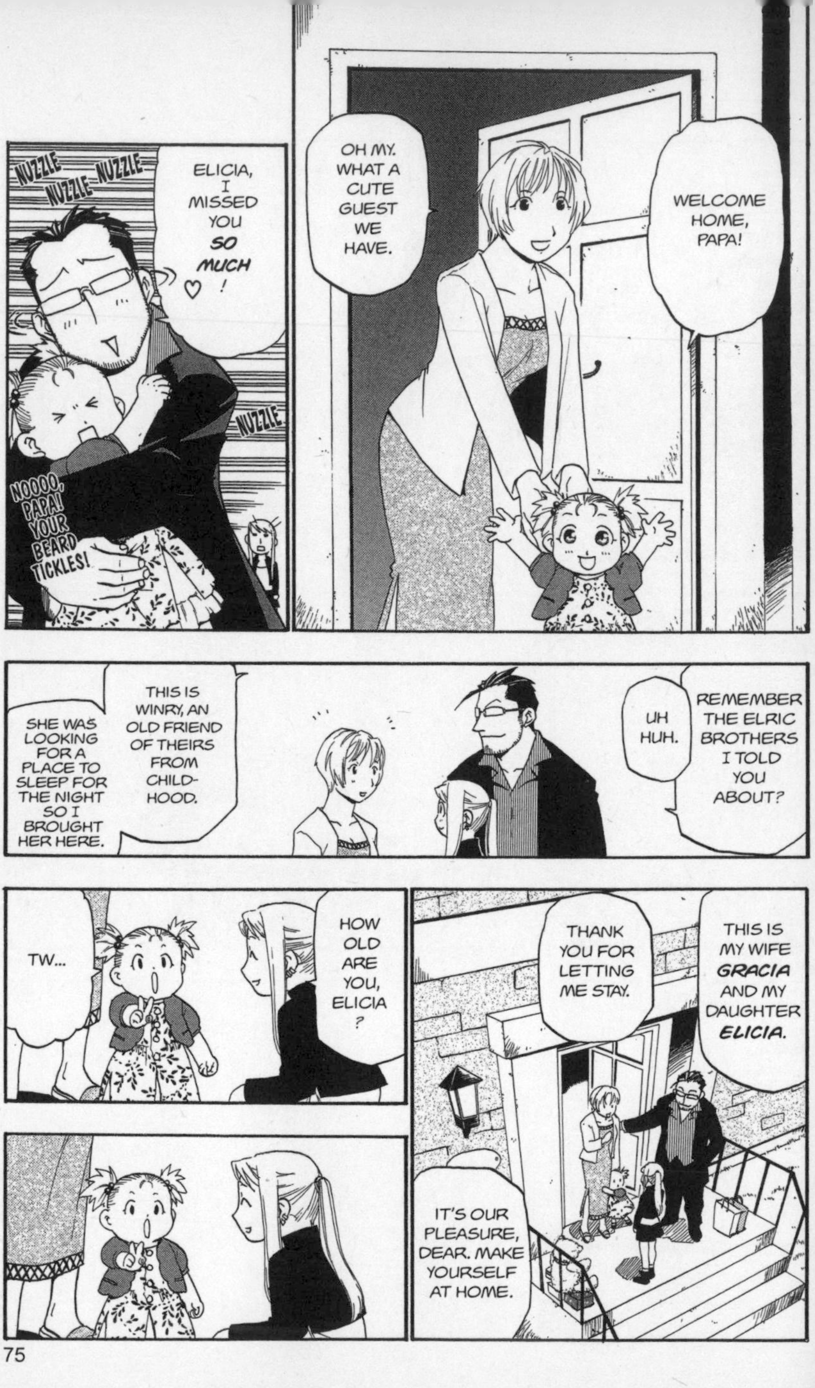
WELCOME HOME, PAPA!
OH MY. WHAT A CUTE GUEST WE HAVE.
NUZZLE NUZZLE NUZZLE
ELICIA, I MISSED YOU SO MUCH ♡!
NUZZLE
NOOOO, PAPA! YOUR BEARD TICKLES!
REMEMBER THE ELRIC BROTHERS I TOLD YOU ABOUT?
UH HUH.
THIS IS WINRY, AN OLD FRIEND OF THEIRS FROM CHILDHOOD.
SHE WAS LOOKING FOR A PLACE TO SLEEP FOR THE NIGHT SO I BROUGHT HER HERE.
THIS IS MY WIFE GRACIA AND MY DAUGHTER ELICIA.
THANK YOU FOR LETTING ME STAY.
IT'S OUR PLEASURE, DEAR. MAKE YOURSELF AT HOME.
HOW OLD ARE YOU, ELICIA?
TW...

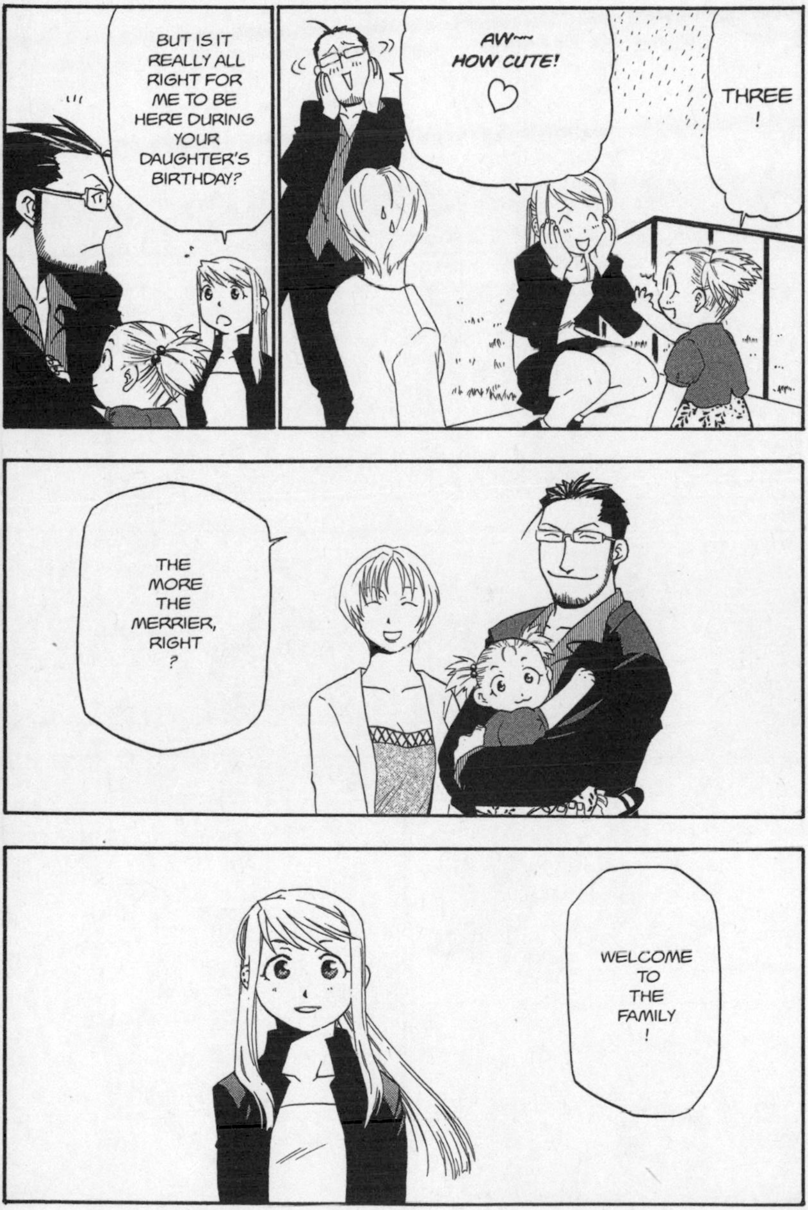
THREE!
AW~~ HOW CUTE! ♡
BUT IS IT REALLY ALL RIGHT FOR ME TO BE HERE DURING YOUR DAUGHTER'S BIRTHDAY?
THE MORE THE MERRIER, RIGHT?
WELCOME TO THE FAMILY!

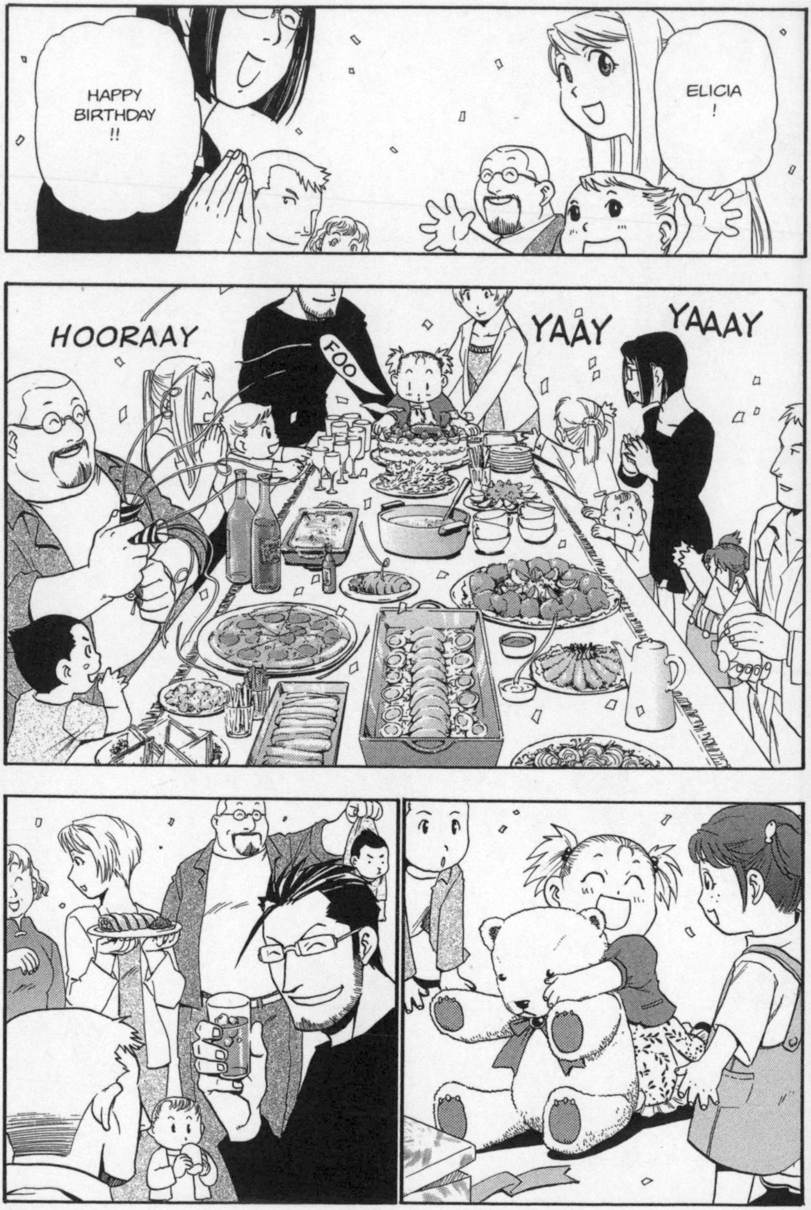
ELICIA !
HAPPY BIRTHDAY !!
YAAAY
YAAY
FOO
HOORAAY

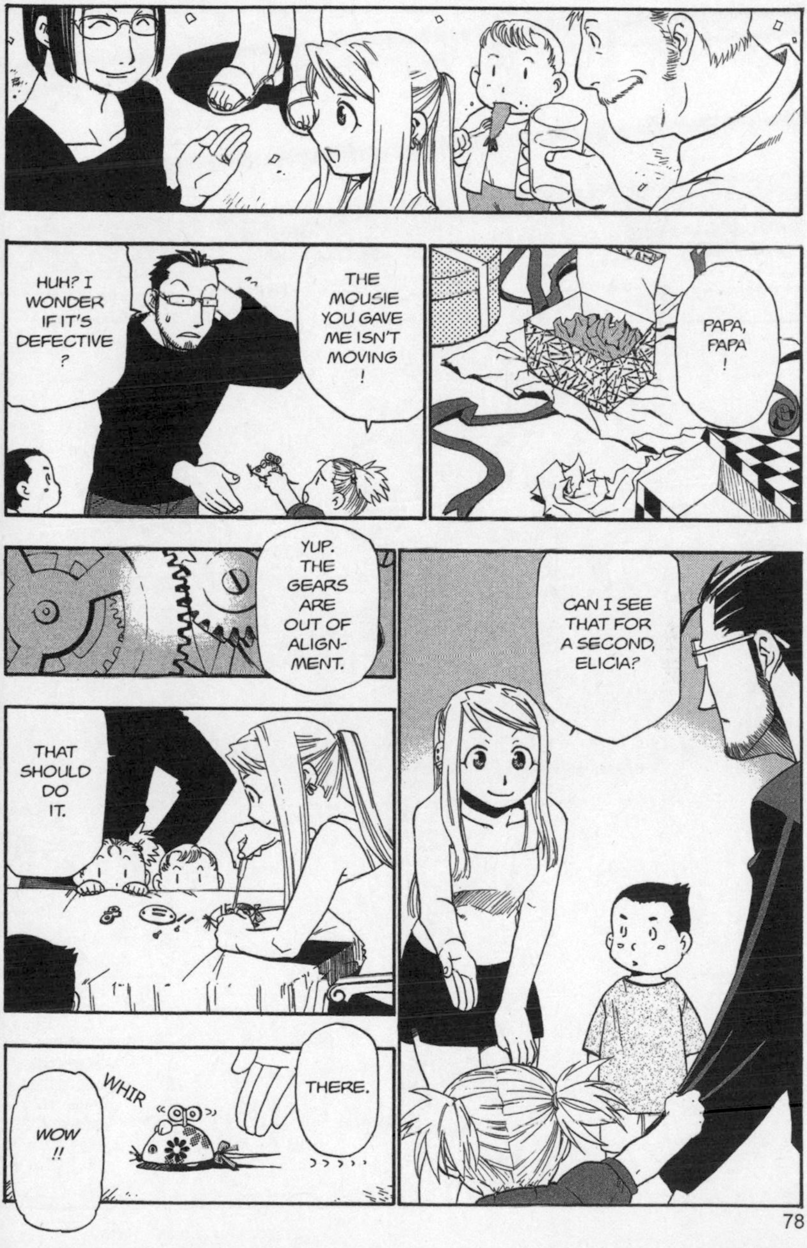
PAPA, PAPA!
THE MOUSIE YOU GAVE ME ISN'T MOVING!
HUH? I WONDER IF IT'S DEFECTIVE?
CAN I SEE THAT FOR A SECOND, ELICIA?
YUP. THE GEARS ARE OUT OF ALIGNMENT.
THAT SHOULD DO IT.
THERE.
WHIR
WOW!!

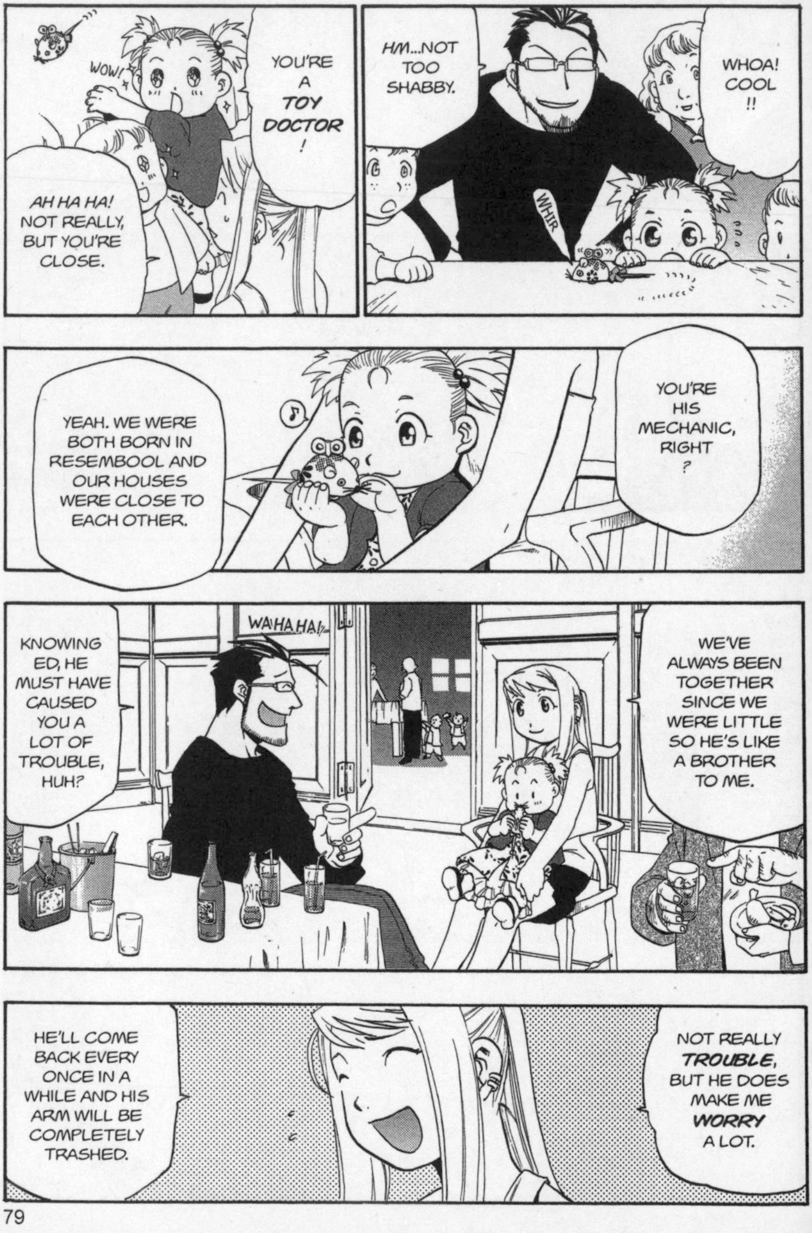
WHOA! COOL!!
HM...NOT TOO SHABBY.
WHIR
WOW!
YOU'RE A TOY DOCTOR!
AH HA HA! NOT REALLY, BUT YOU'RE CLOSE.
YOU'RE HIS MECHANIC, RIGHT?
YEAH. WE WERE BOTH BORN IN RESEMBOOL AND OUR HOUSES WERE CLOSE TO EACH OTHER.
WE'VE ALWAYS BEEN TOGETHER SINCE WE WERE LITTLE SO HE'S LIKE A BROTHER TO ME.
WAHAHA!
KNOWING ED, HE MUST HAVE CAUSED YOU A LOT OF TROUBLE, HUH?
NOT REALLY TROUBLE, BUT HE DOES MAKE ME WORRY A LOT.
HE'LL COME BACK EVERY ONCE IN A WHILE AND HIS ARM WILL BE COMPLETELY TRASHED.

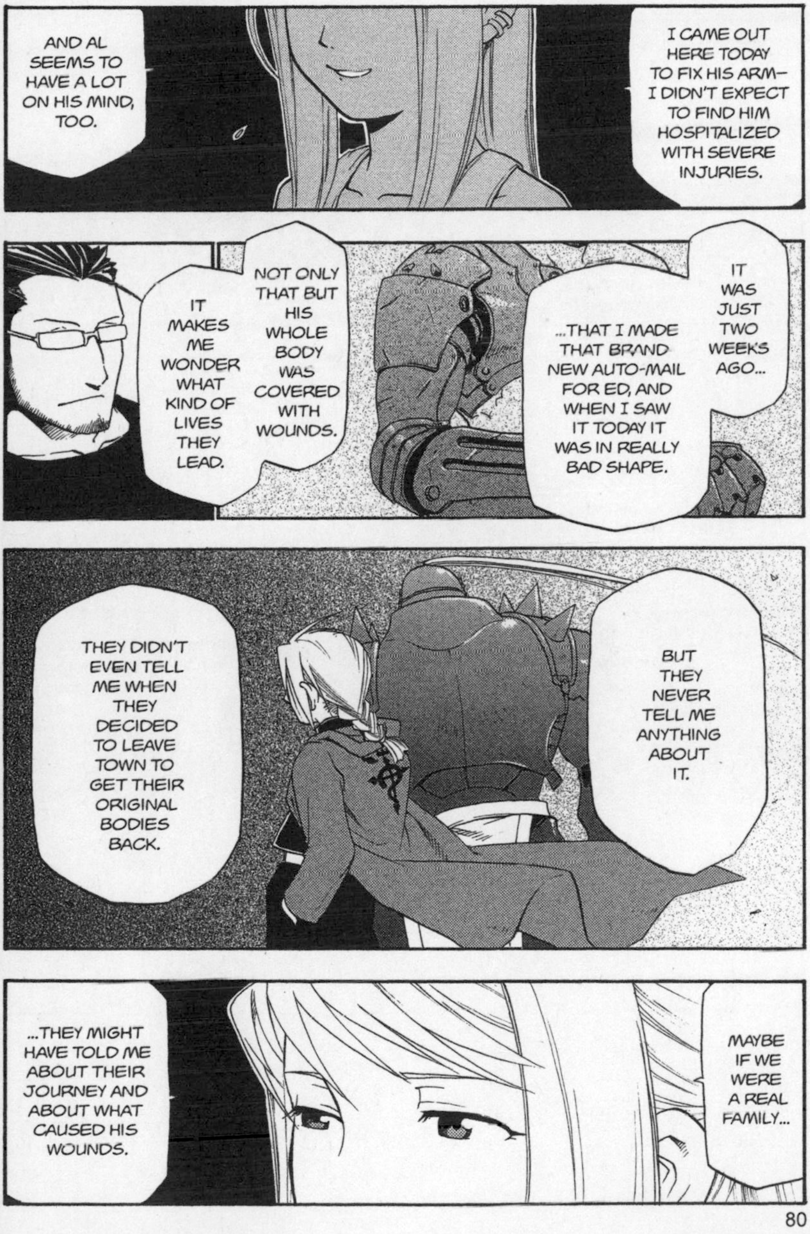
I CAME OUT HERE TODAY TO FIX HIS ARM—I DIDN'T EXPECT TO FIND HIM HOSPITALIZED WITH SEVERE INJURIES.
AND AL SEEMS TO HAVE A LOT ON HIS MIND, TOO.
IT WAS JUST TWO WEEKS AGO...
...THAT I MADE THAT BRAND NEW AUTO-MAIL FOR ED, AND WHEN I SAW IT TODAY IT WAS IN REALLY BAD SHAPE.
NOT ONLY THAT BUT HIS WHOLE BODY WAS COVERED WITH WOUNDS.
IT MAKES ME WONDER WHAT KIND OF LIVES THEY LEAD.
BUT THEY NEVER TELL ME ANYTHING ABOUT IT.
THEY DIDN'T EVEN TELL ME WHEN THEY DECIDED TO LEAVE TOWN TO GET THEIR ORIGINAL BODIES BACK.
MAYBE IF WE WERE A REAL FAMILY...
...THEY MIGHT HAVE TOLD ME ABOUT THEIR JOURNEY AND ABOUT WHAT CAUSED HIS WOUNDS.

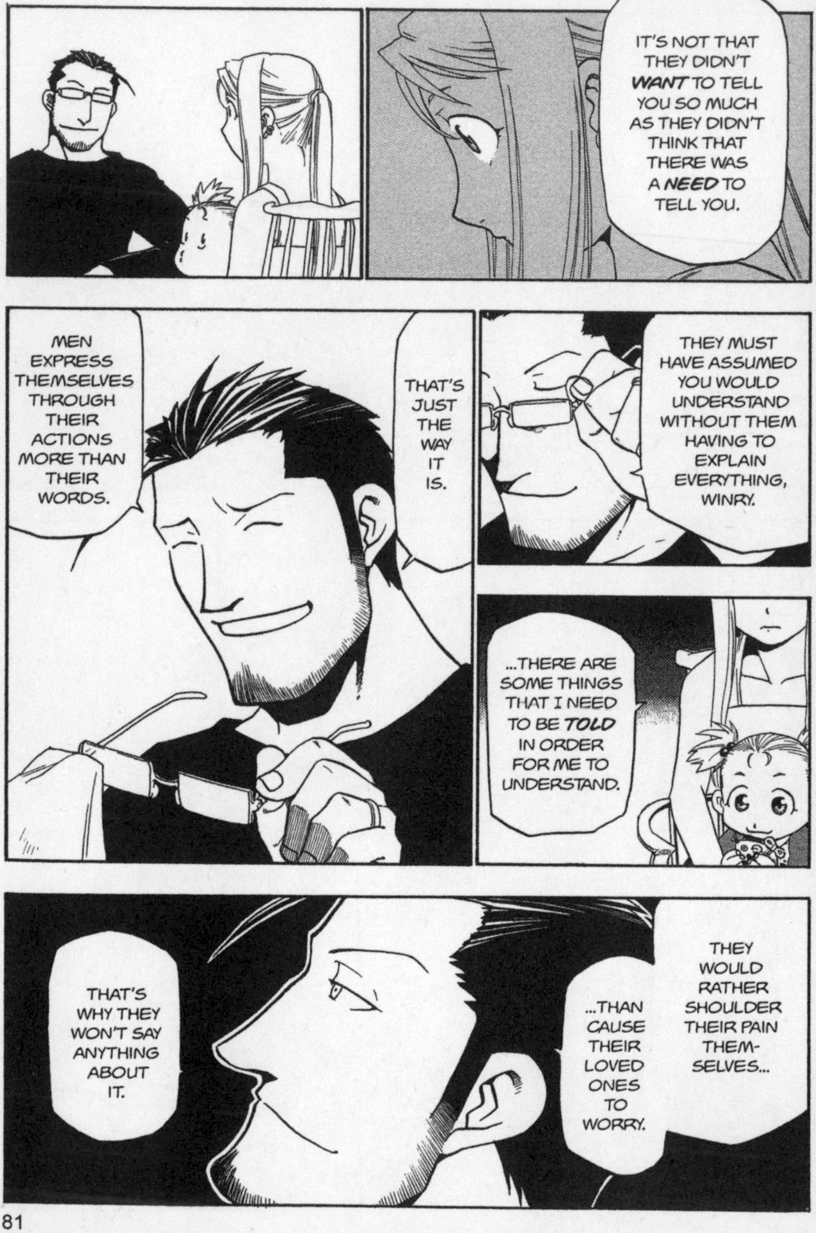
IT'S NOT THAT THEY DIDN'T ***WANT*** TO TELL YOU SO MUCH AS THEY DIDN'T THINK THAT THERE WAS A ***NEED*** TO TELL YOU.
THEY MUST HAVE ASSUMED YOU WOULD UNDERSTAND WITHOUT THEM HAVING TO EXPLAIN EVERYTHING, WINRY.
...THERE ARE SOME THINGS THAT I NEED TO BE ***TOLD*** IN ORDER FOR ME TO UNDERSTAND.
THAT'S JUST THE WAY IT IS.
MEN EXPRESS THEMSELVES THROUGH THEIR ACTIONS MORE THAN THEIR WORDS.
THEY WOULD RATHER SHOULDER THEIR PAIN THEM-SELVES...
...THAN CAUSE THEIR LOVED ONES TO WORRY.
THAT'S WHY THEY WON'T SAY ANYTHING ABOUT IT.

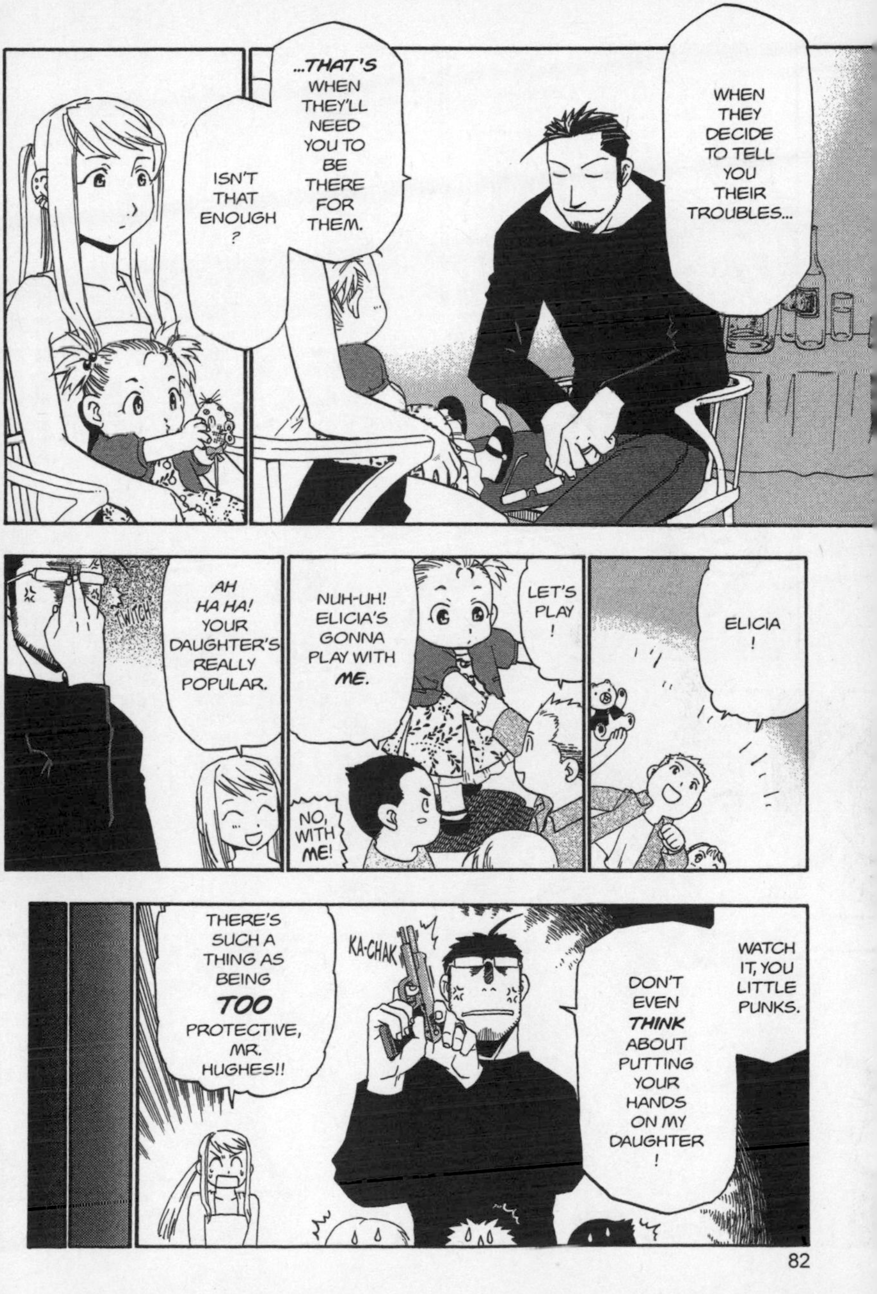
WHEN THEY DECIDE TO TELL YOU THEIR TROUBLES...
...THAT'S WHEN THEY'LL NEED YOU TO BE THERE FOR THEM.
ISN'T THAT ENOUGH ?
ELICIA !
LET'S PLAY !
NUH-UH! ELICIA'S GONNA PLAY WITH ME.
NO, WITH ME!
TWITCH
AH HA HA! YOUR DAUGHTER'S REALLY POPULAR.
WATCH IT, YOU LITTLE PUNKS.
DON'T EVEN THINK ABOUT PUTTING YOUR HANDS ON MY DAUGHTER !
KA-CHAK
THERE'S SUCH A THING AS BEING TOO PROTECTIVE, MR. HUGHES!!

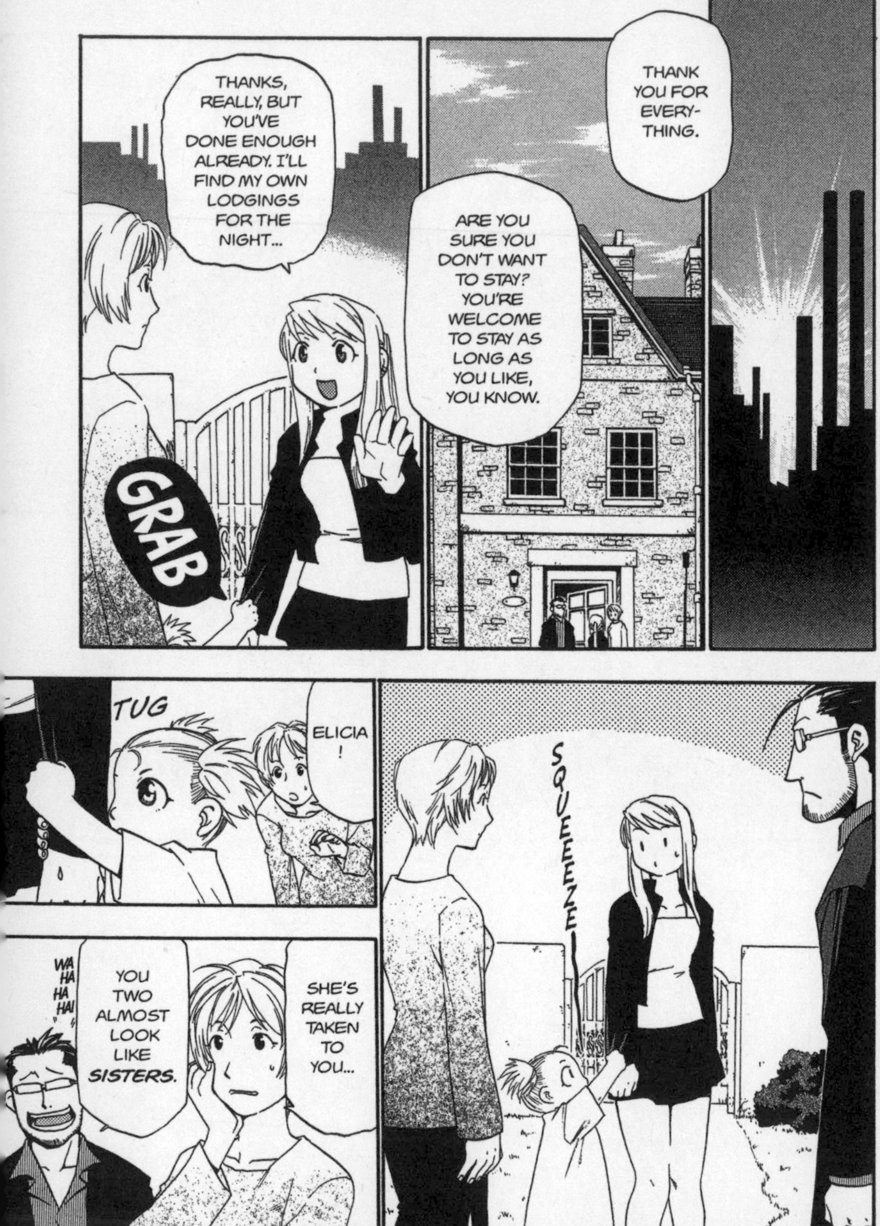
THANK YOU FOR EVERY-THING.
ARE YOU SURE YOU DON'T WANT TO STAY? YOU'RE WELCOME TO STAY AS LONG AS YOU LIKE, YOU KNOW.
THANKS, REALLY, BUT YOU'VE DONE ENOUGH ALREADY. I'LL FIND MY OWN LODGINGS FOR THE NIGHT...
GRAB
SQUEEEEZE!
TUG
ELICIA!
SHE'S REALLY TAKEN TO YOU...
YOU TWO ALMOST LOOK LIKE *SISTERS*.
WA HA HA HA!

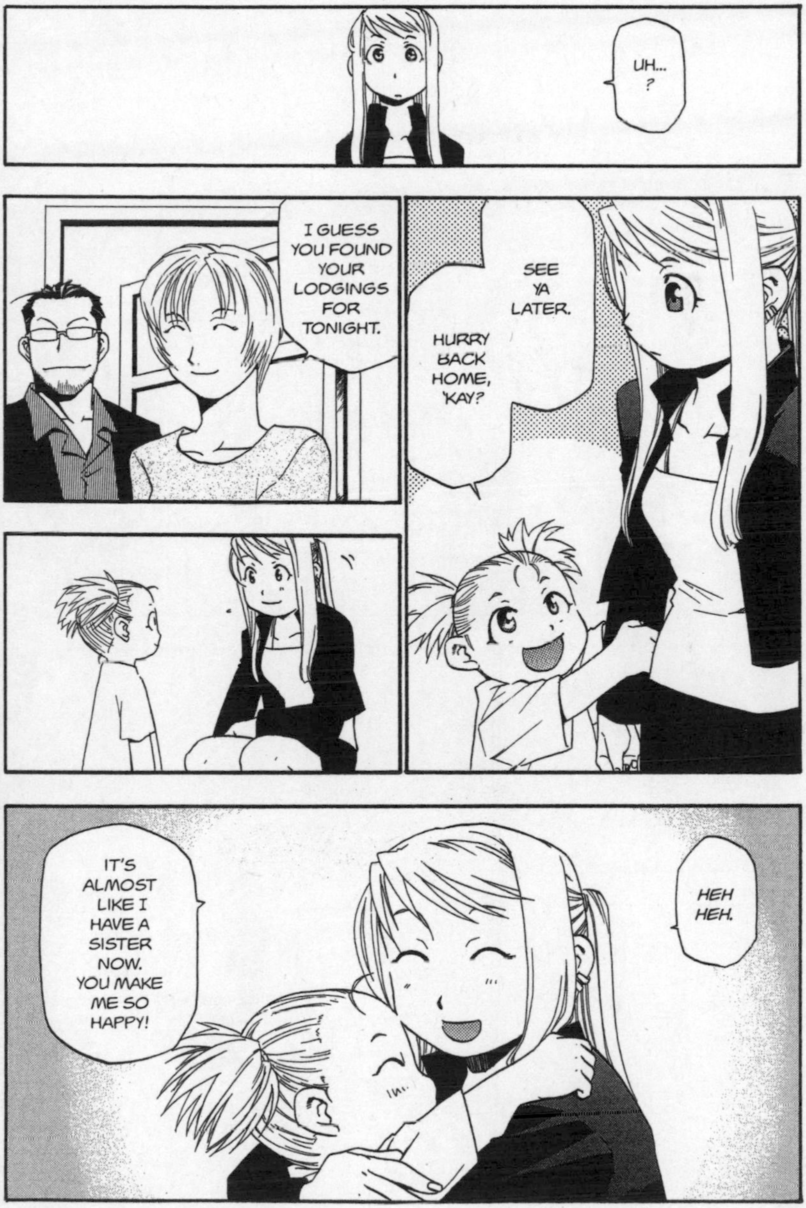
UH... ?
SEE YA LATER.
HURRY BACK HOME, 'KAY?
I GUESS YOU FOUND YOUR LODGINGS FOR TONIGHT.
HEH HEH.
IT'S ALMOST LIKE I HAVE A SISTER NOW. YOU MAKE ME SO HAPPY!

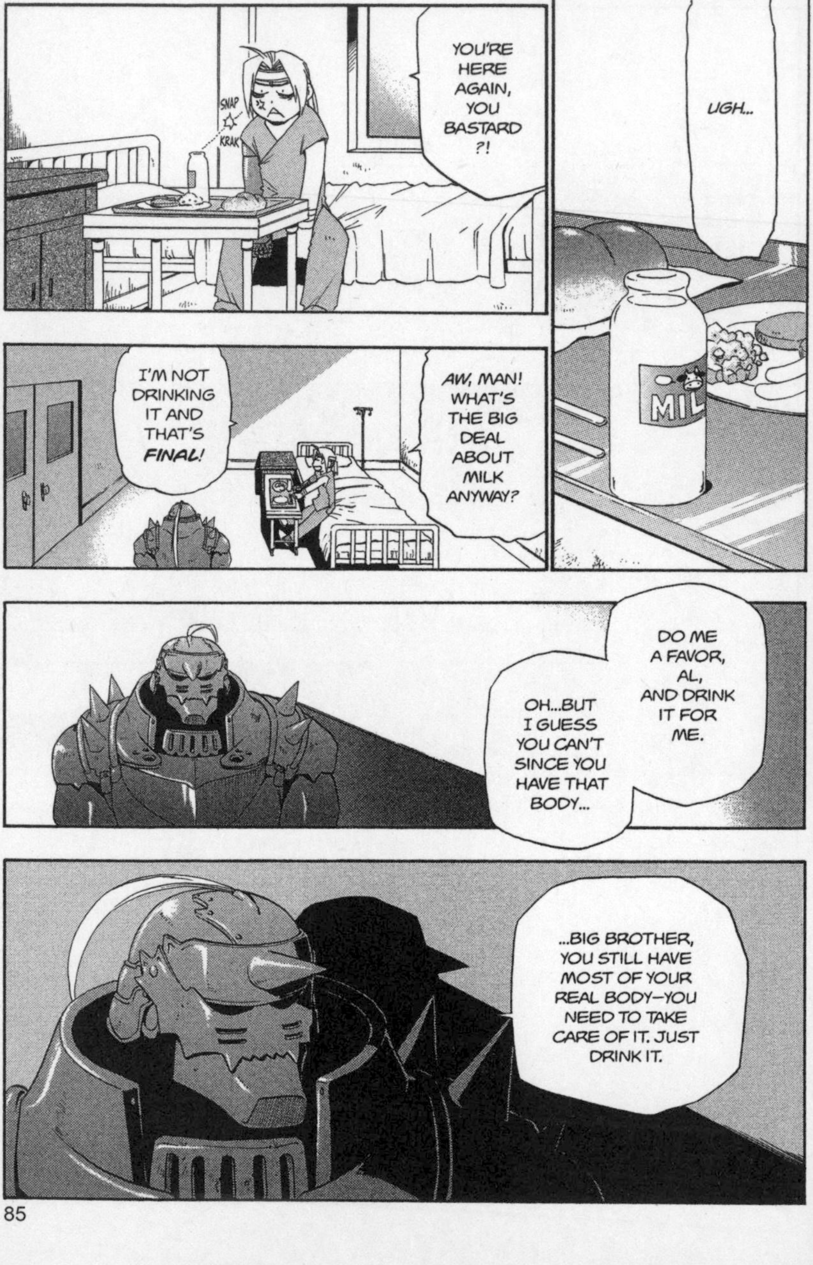
UGH...
YOU'RE HERE AGAIN, YOU BASTARD ?!
SNAP
KRAK
AW, MAN! WHAT'S THE BIG DEAL ABOUT MILK ANYWAY?
I'M NOT DRINKING IT AND THAT'S *FINAL*!
MILK
DO ME A FAVOR, AL, AND DRINK IT FOR ME.
OH...BUT I GUESS YOU CAN'T SINCE YOU HAVE THAT BODY...
...BIG BROTHER, YOU STILL HAVE MOST OF YOUR REAL BODY—YOU NEED TO TAKE CARE OF IT. JUST DRINK IT.

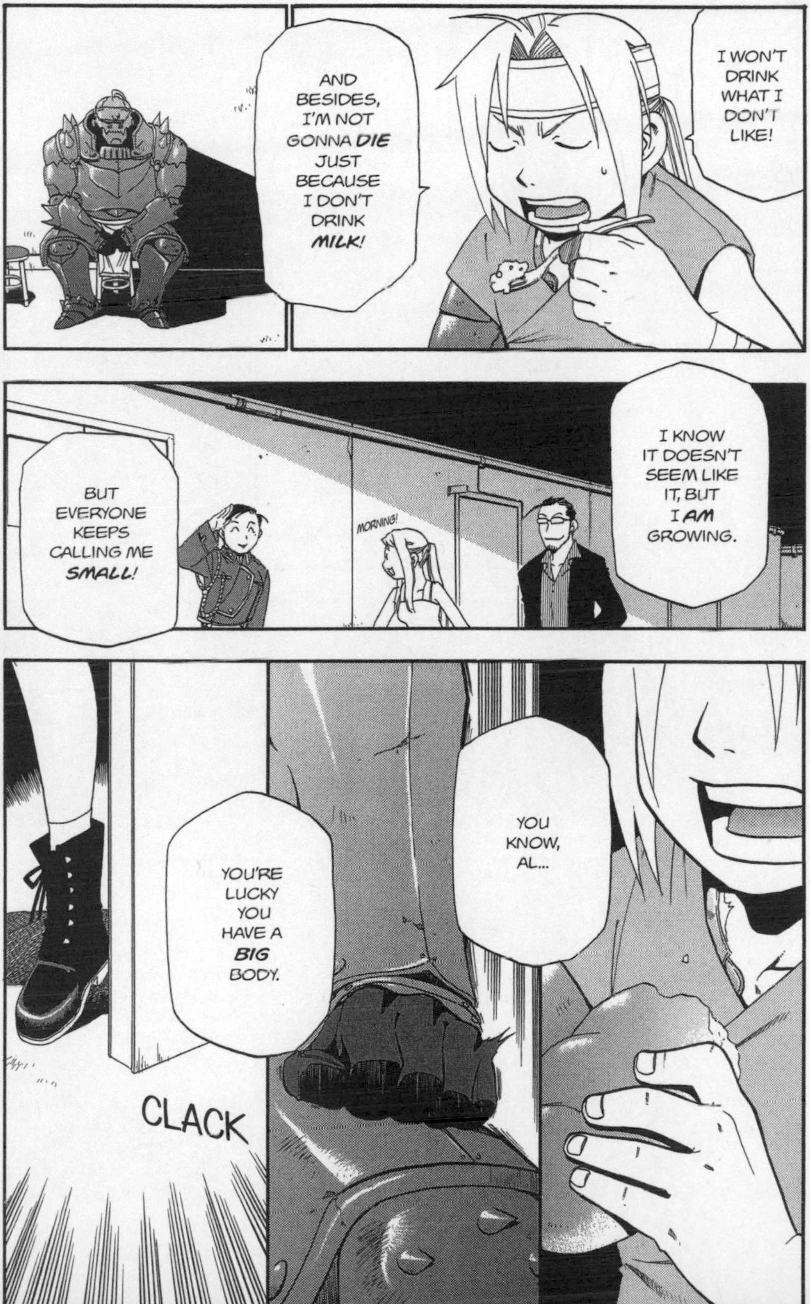
I WON'T DRINK WHAT I DON'T LIKE!
AND BESIDES, I'M NOT GONNA ***DIE*** JUST BECAUSE I DON'T DRINK ***MILK***!
I KNOW IT DOESN'T SEEM LIKE IT, BUT I ***AM*** GROWING.
MORNING!
BUT EVERYONE KEEPS CALLING ME ***SMALL***!
YOU KNOW, AL...
YOU'RE LUCKY YOU HAVE A ***BIG*** BODY.
CLACK

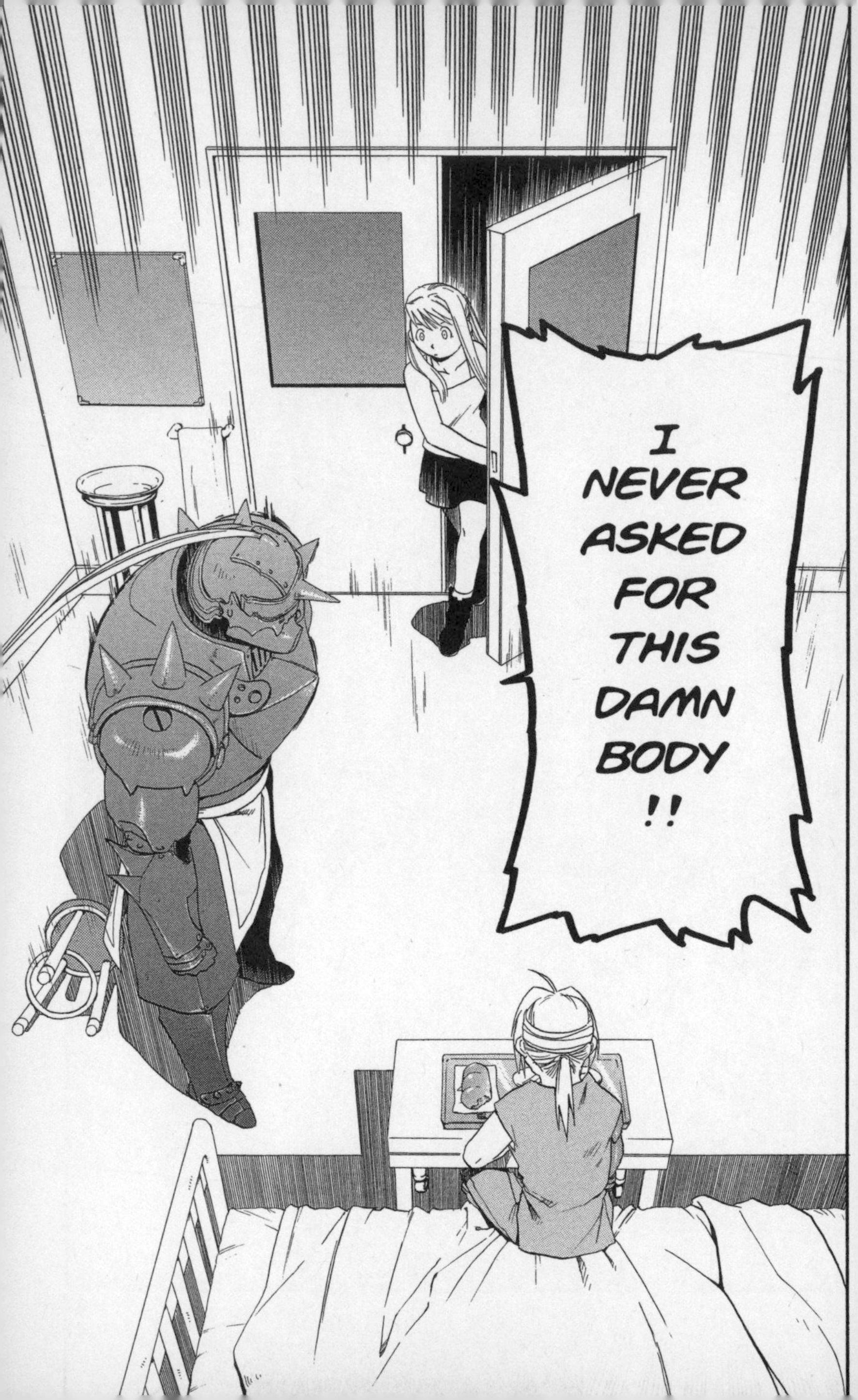
I NEVER ASKED FOR THIS DAMN BODY !!

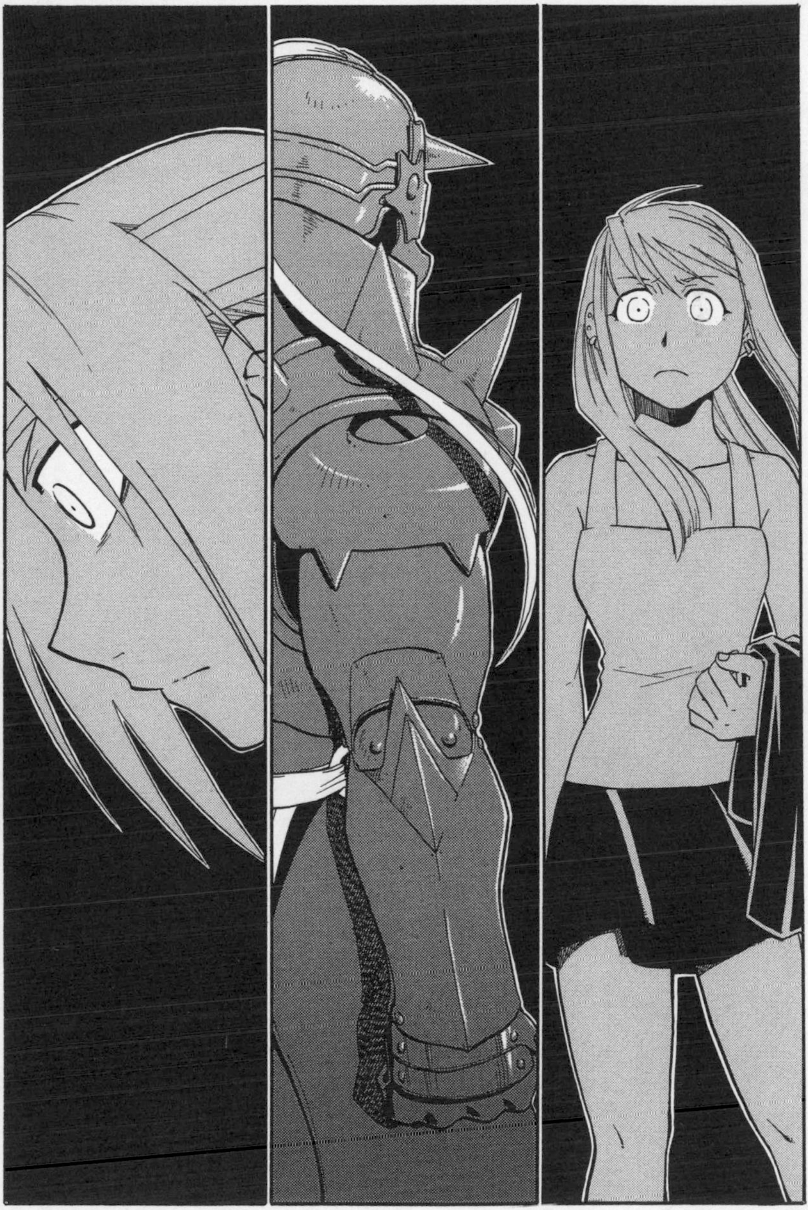

Chapter 15: Fullmetal Heart

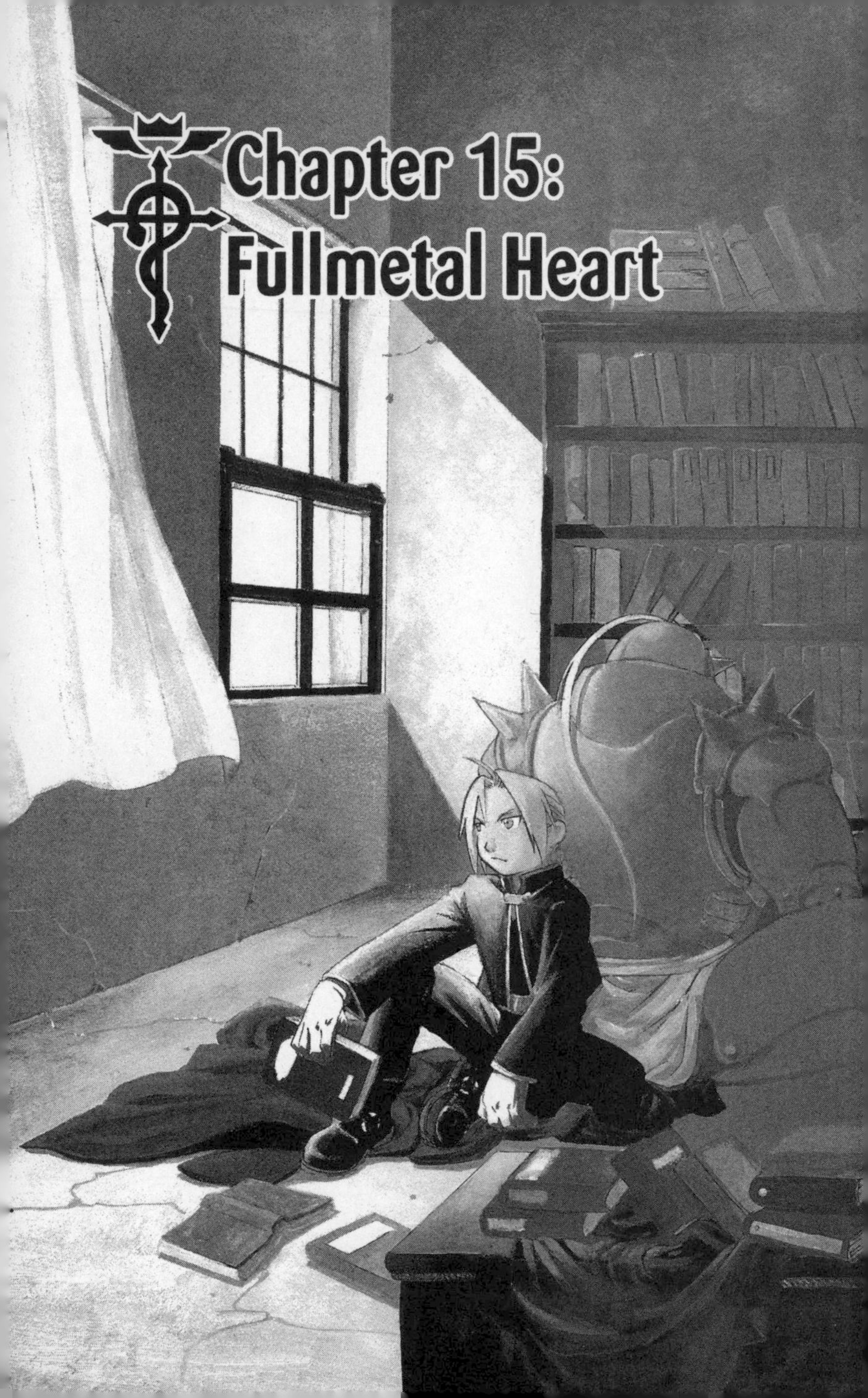

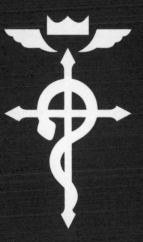

FULLMETAL
ALCHEMIST

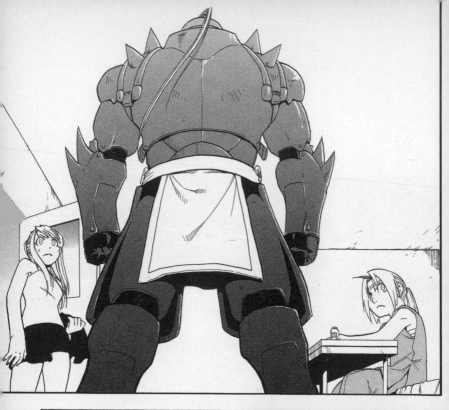

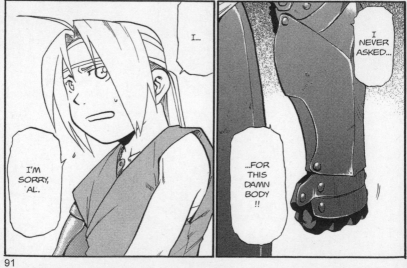

I...

I'M SORRY, AL.

I NEVER ASKED...

...FOR THIS DAMN BODY!!

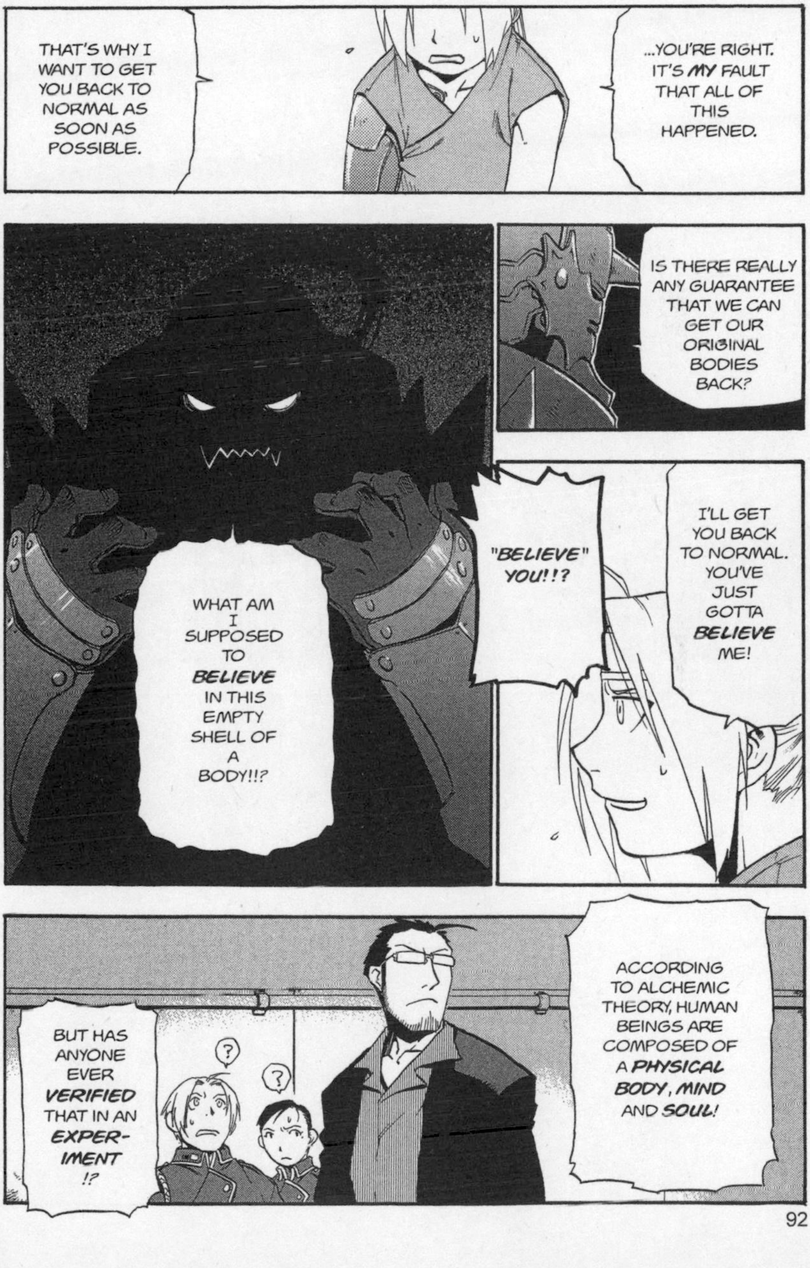
...YOU'RE RIGHT. IT'S MY FAULT THAT ALL OF THIS HAPPENED.
THAT'S WHY I WANT TO GET YOU BACK TO NORMAL AS SOON AS POSSIBLE.
IS THERE REALLY ANY GUARANTEE THAT WE CAN GET OUR ORIGINAL BODIES BACK?
I'LL GET YOU BACK TO NORMAL. YOU'VE JUST GOTTA BELIEVE ME!
"BELIEVE" YOU!!?
WHAT AM I SUPPOSED TO BELIEVE IN THIS EMPTY SHELL OF A BODY!!?
ACCORDING TO ALCHEMIC THEORY, HUMAN BEINGS ARE COMPOSED OF A PHYSICAL BODY, MIND AND SOUL!
?
?
BUT HAS ANYONE EVER VERIFIED THAT IN AN EXPERIMENT !?

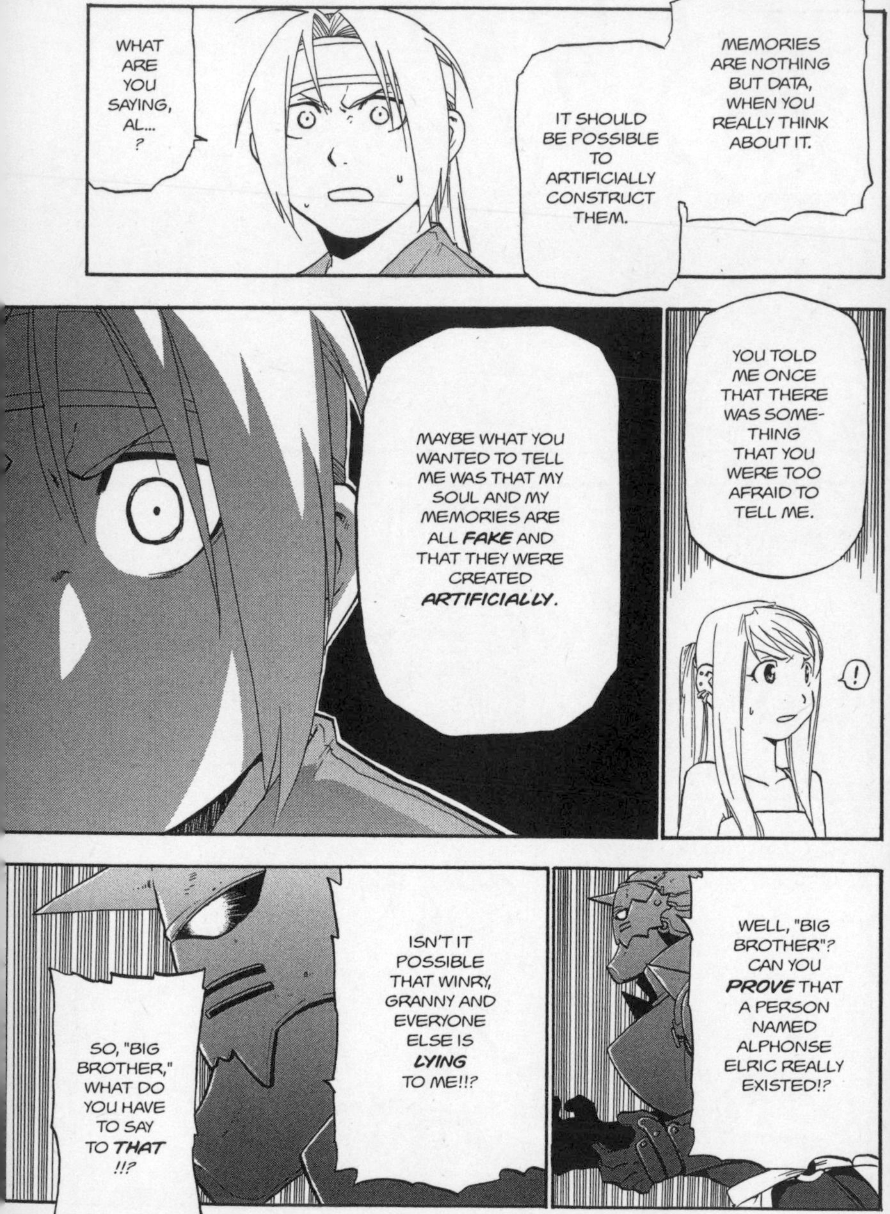
MEMORIES ARE NOTHING BUT DATA, WHEN YOU REALLY THINK ABOUT IT.
IT SHOULD BE POSSIBLE TO ARTIFICIALLY CONSTRUCT THEM.
WHAT ARE YOU SAYING, AL...?
YOU TOLD ME ONCE THAT THERE WAS SOME-THING THAT YOU WERE TOO AFRAID TO TELL ME.
!
MAYBE WHAT YOU WANTED TO TELL ME WAS THAT MY SOUL AND MY MEMORIES ARE ALL **FAKE** AND THAT THEY WERE CREATED **ARTIFICIALLY**.
WELL, "BIG BROTHER"? CAN YOU **PROVE** THAT A PERSON NAMED ALPHONSE ELRIC REALLY EXISTED!?
ISN'T IT POSSIBLE THAT WINRY, GRANNY AND EVERYONE ELSE IS **LYING** TO ME!!?
SO, "BIG BROTHER," WHAT DO YOU HAVE TO SAY TO **THAT** !!?

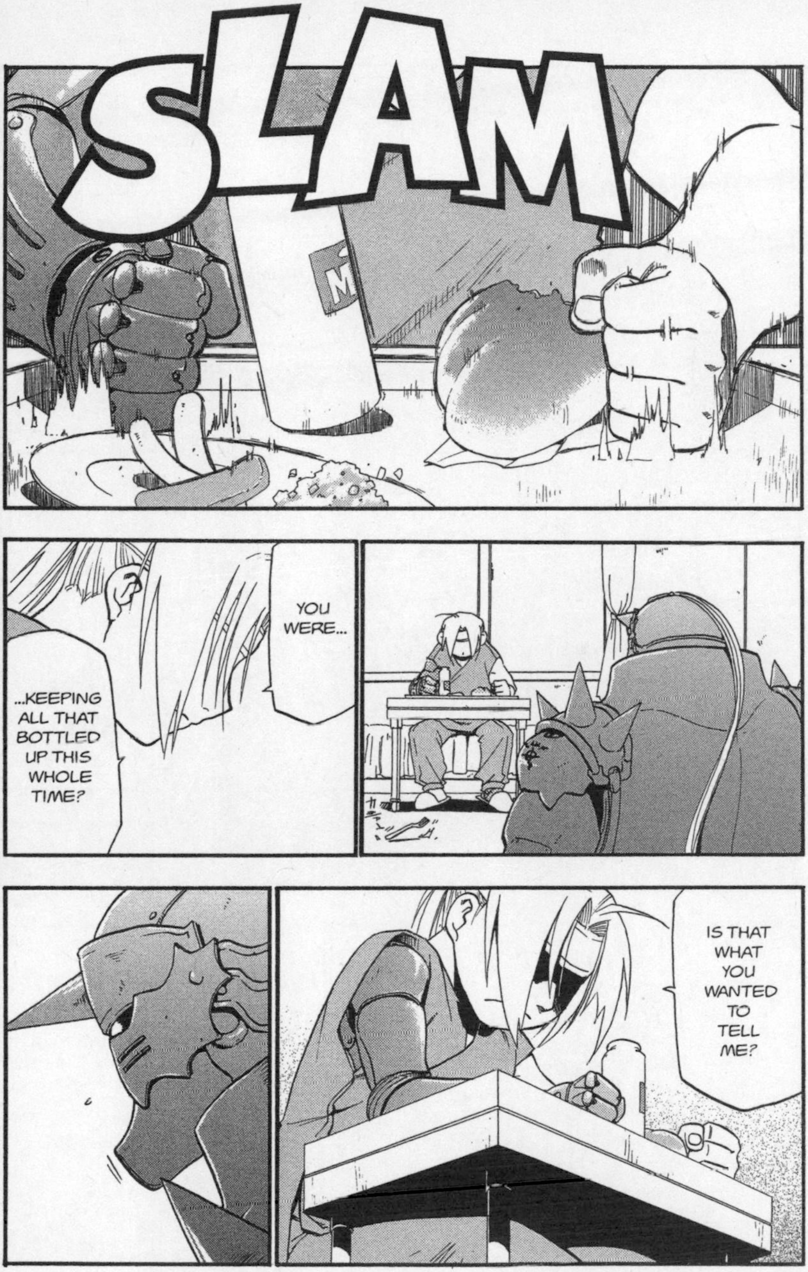
SLAM
YOU WERE...
...KEEPING ALL THAT BOTTLED UP THIS WHOLE TIME?
IS THAT WHAT YOU WANTED TO TELL ME?

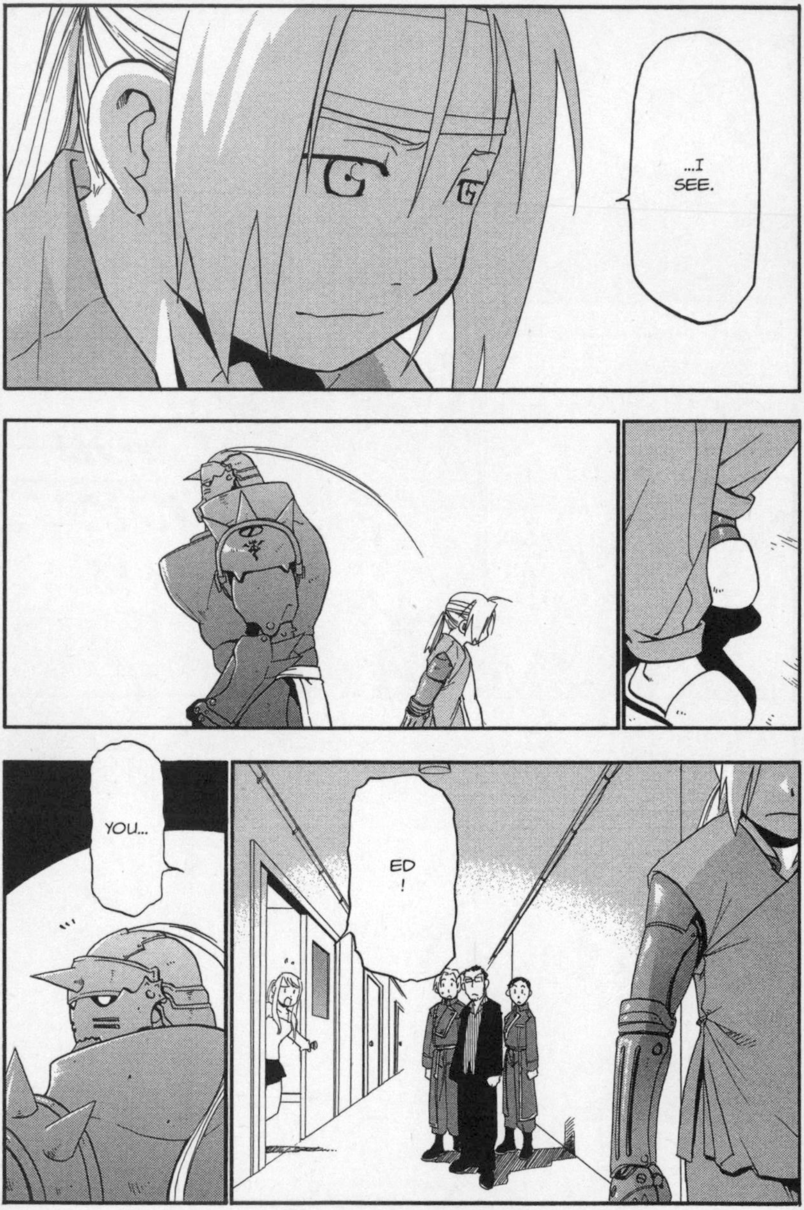
...I SEE.
ED!
YOU...

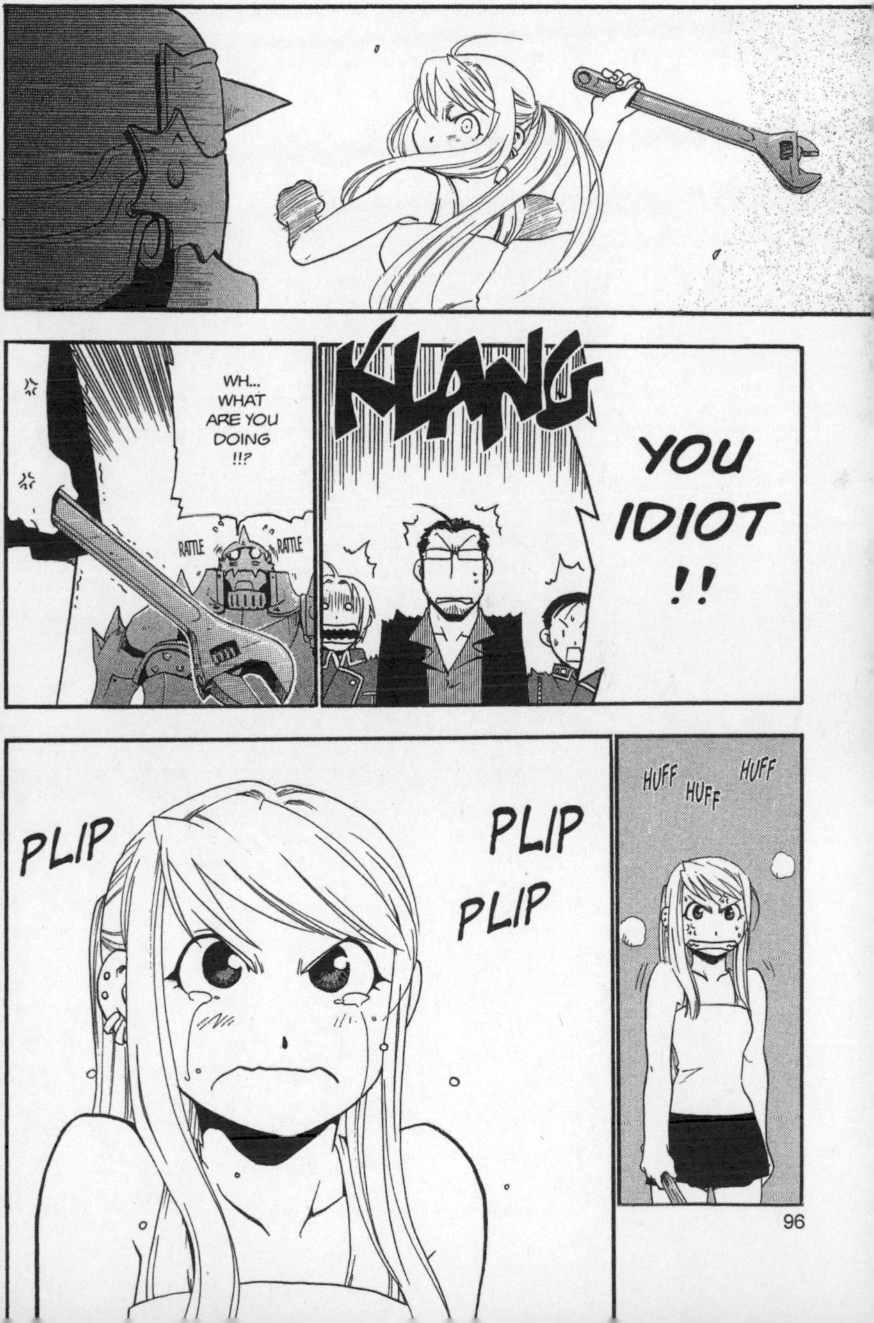
KLANG
YOU IDIOT !!
WH... WHAT ARE YOU DOING !!?
RATTLE RATTLE
HUFF HUFF HUFF
PLIP PLIP PLIP

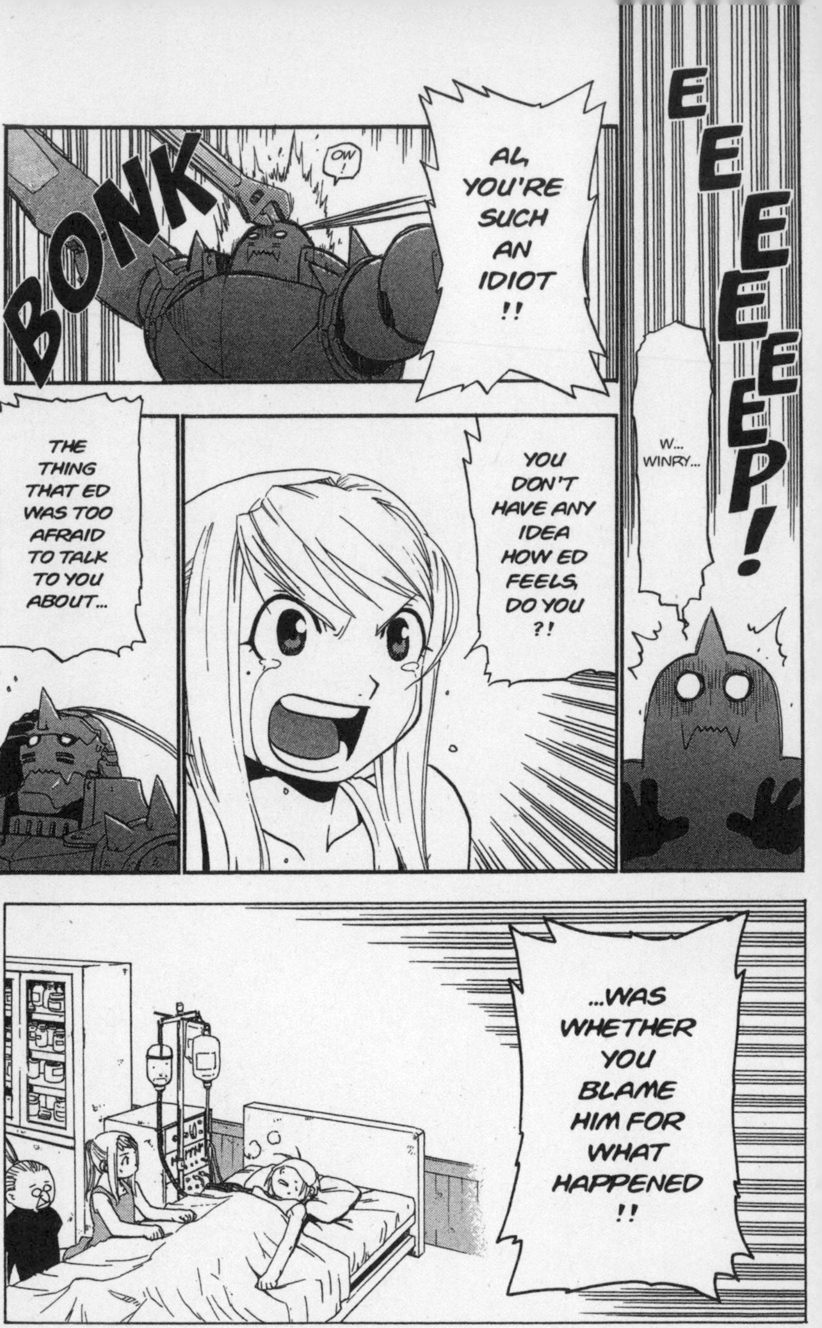
EEEEEEP!
W... WINRY...
AL, YOU'RE SUCH AN IDIOT!!
BONK
OW!
YOU DON'T HAVE ANY IDEA HOW ED FEELS, DO YOU?!
THE THING THAT ED WAS TOO AFRAID TO TALK TO YOU ABOUT...
...WAS WHETHER YOU BLAME HIM FOR WHAT HAPPENED!!

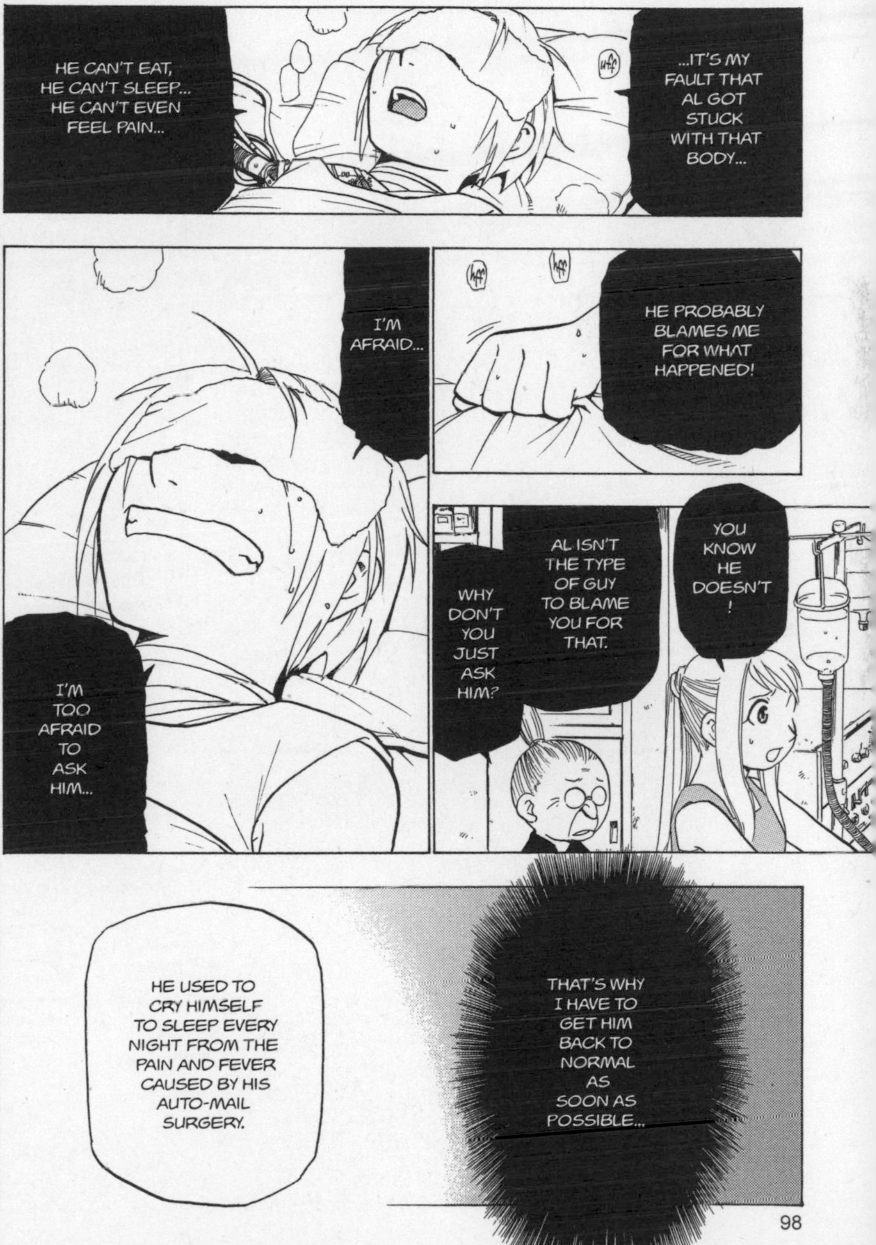
uff
...IT'S MY FAULT THAT AL GOT STUCK WITH THAT BODY...
HE CAN'T EAT, HE CAN'T SLEEP... HE CAN'T EVEN FEEL PAIN...
hff
hff
HE PROBABLY BLAMES ME FOR WHAT HAPPENED!
YOU KNOW HE DOESN'T!
AL ISN'T THE TYPE OF GUY TO BLAME YOU FOR THAT.
WHY DON'T YOU JUST ASK HIM?
I'M AFRAID...
I'M TOO AFRAID TO ASK HIM...
THAT'S WHY I HAVE TO GET HIM BACK TO NORMAL AS SOON AS POSSIBLE...
HE USED TO CRY HIMSELF TO SLEEP EVERY NIGHT FROM THE PAIN AND FEVER CAUSED BY HIS AUTO-MAIL SURGERY.

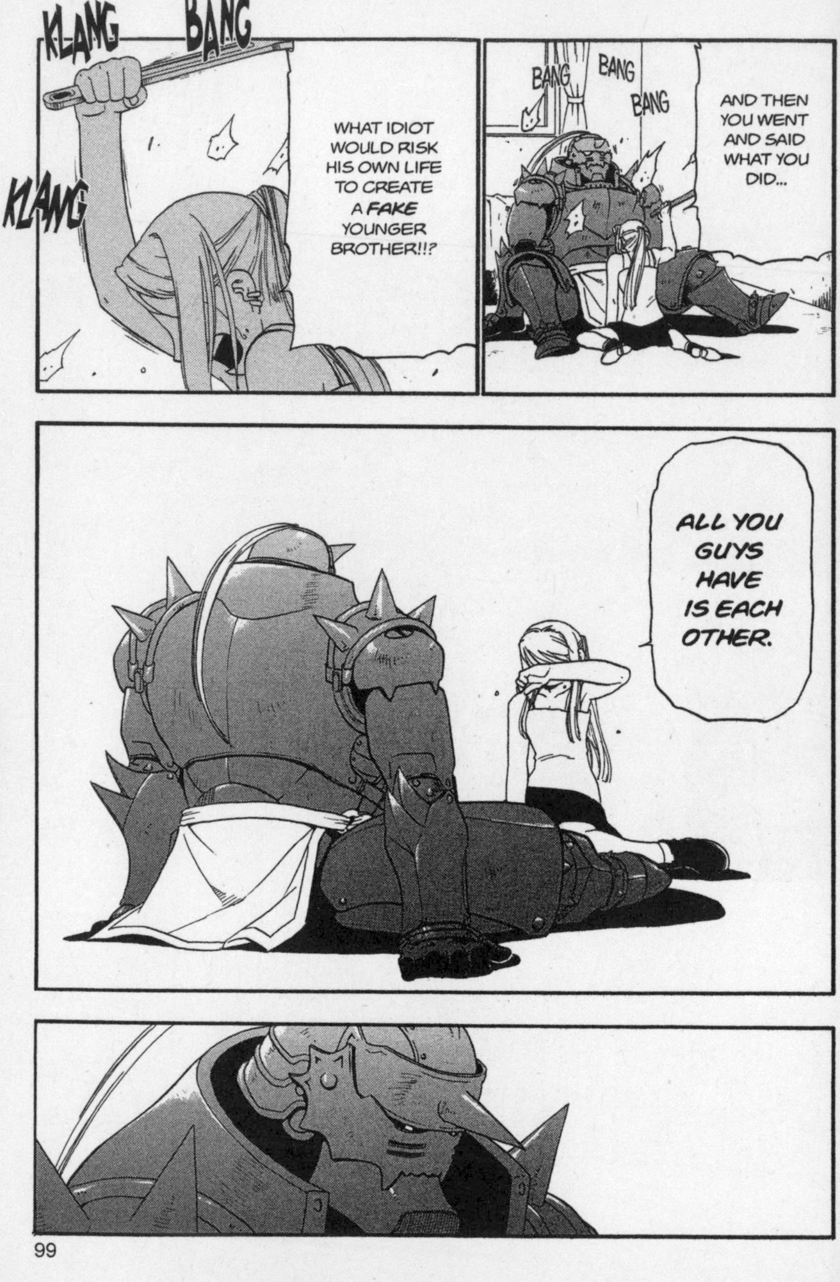
BANG
BANG
BANG
AND THEN YOU WENT AND SAID WHAT YOU DID...
KLANG
BANG
KLANG
WHAT IDIOT WOULD RISK HIS OWN LIFE TO CREATE A **FAKE** YOUNGER BROTHER!!?
ALL YOU GUYS HAVE IS EACH OTHER.

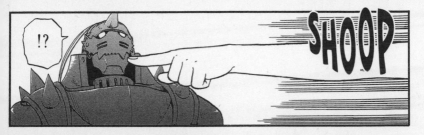

!?

SHOOP

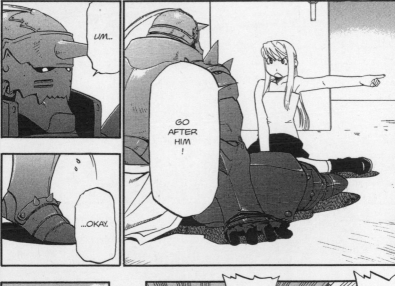

UM...

GO AFTER HIM!

...OKAY.

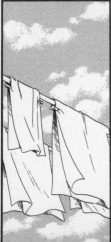

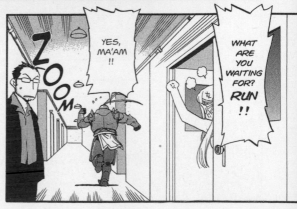

ZOOM

YES, MA'AM!!

WHAT ARE YOU WAITING FOR? RUN!!

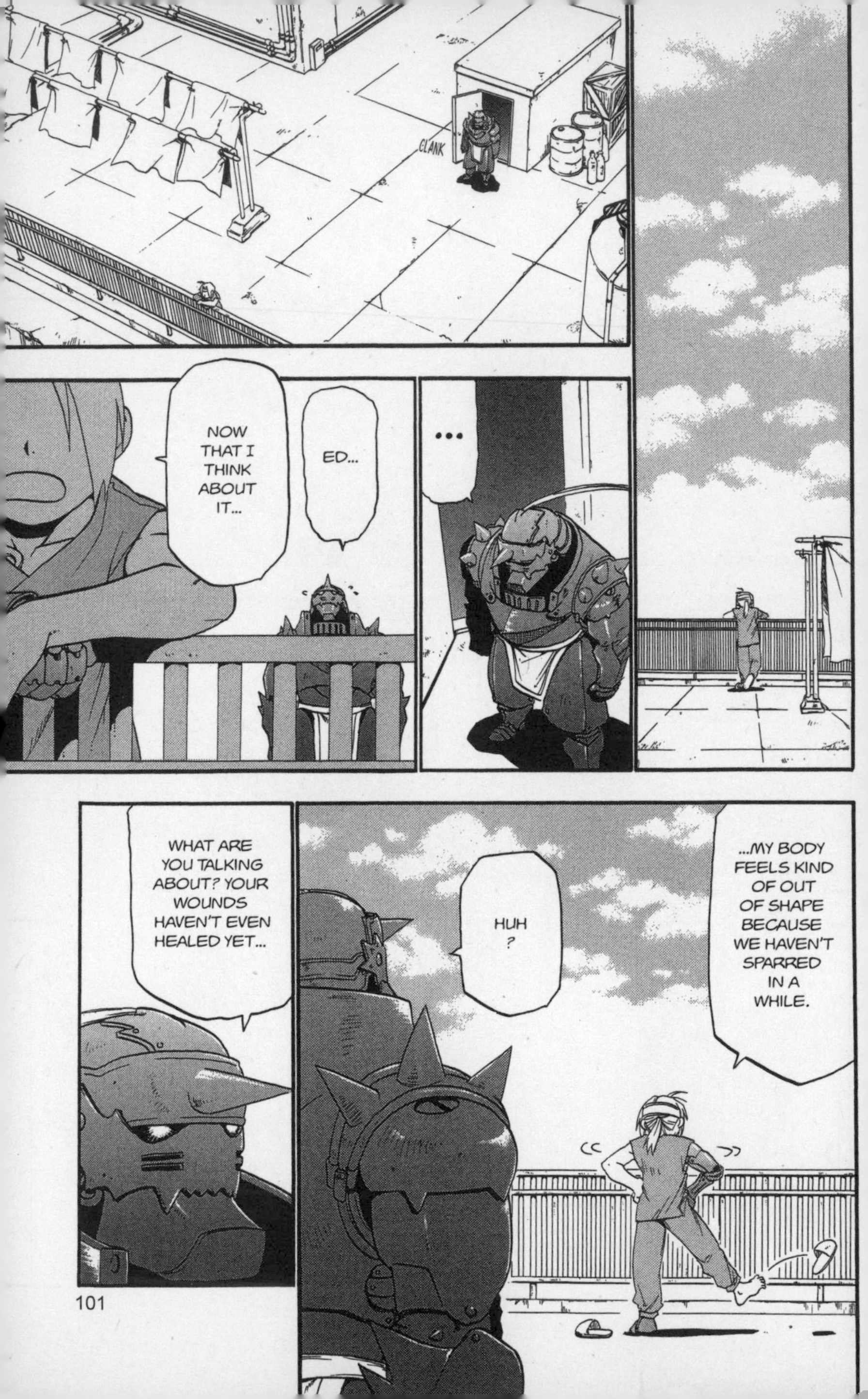
CLANK
...
ED...
NOW THAT I THINK ABOUT IT...
...MY BODY FEELS KIND OF OUT OF SHAPE BECAUSE WE HAVEN'T SPARRED IN A WHILE.
HUH?
WHAT ARE YOU TALKING ABOUT? YOUR WOUNDS HAVEN'T EVEN HEALED YET...

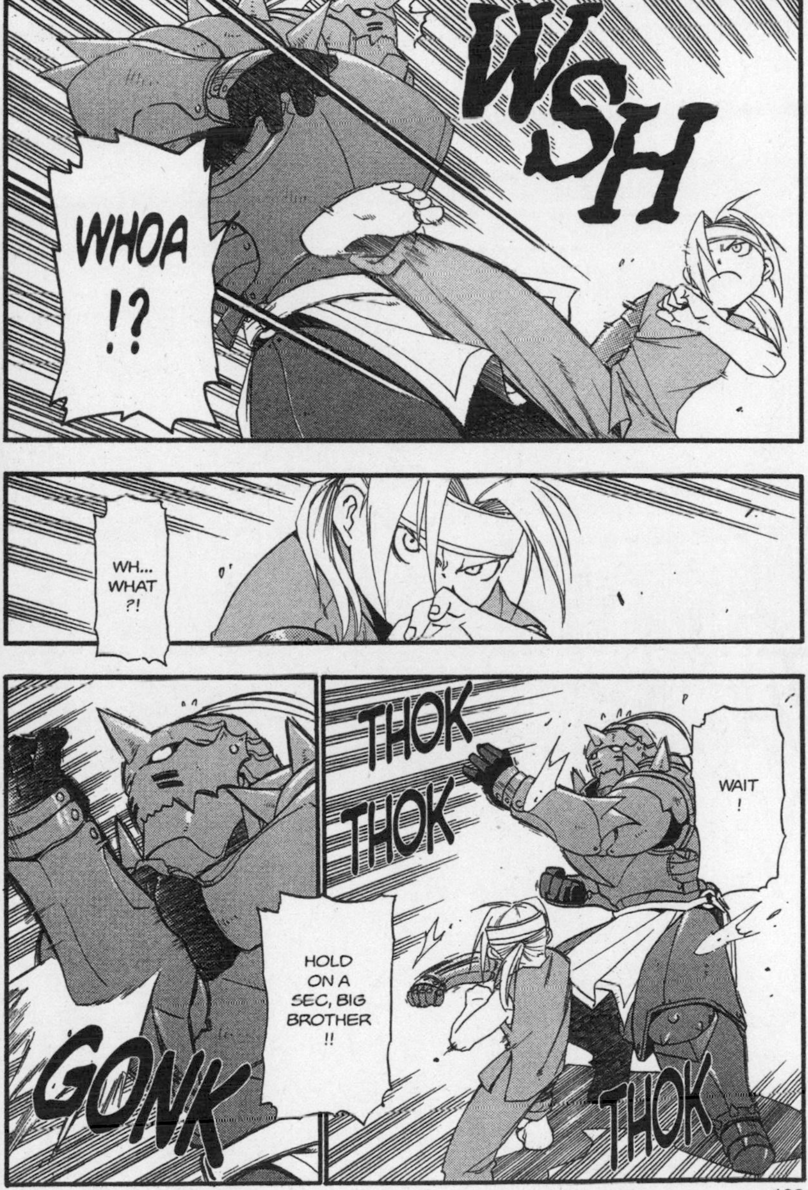
WSH
WHOA !?
WH... WHAT ?!
WAIT !
THOK
THOK
HOLD ON A SEC, BIG BROTHER !!
THOK
GONK

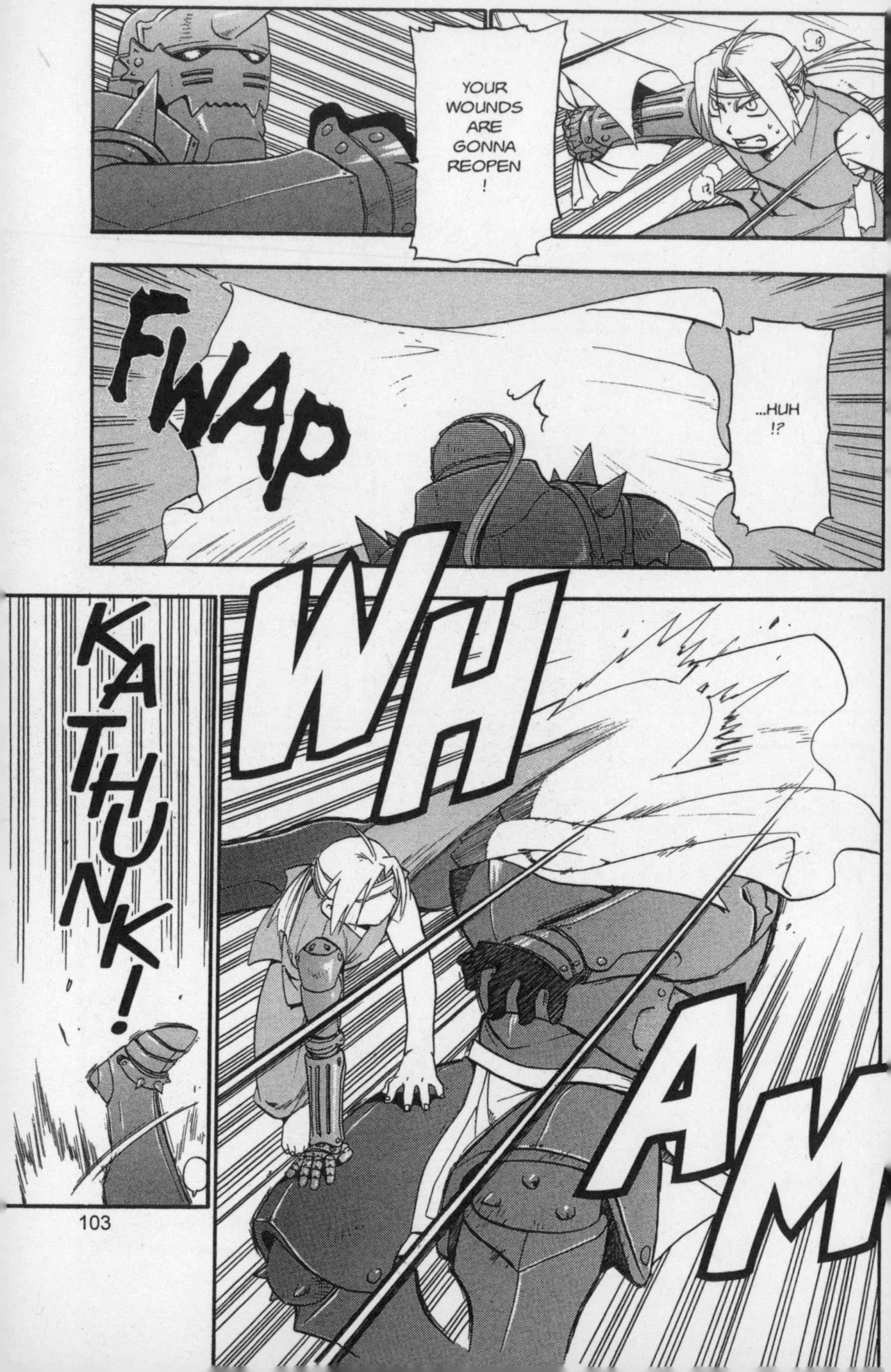
YOUR WOUNDS ARE GONNA REOPEN!
FWAP
...HUH !?
WH
AM
KATHUNK!

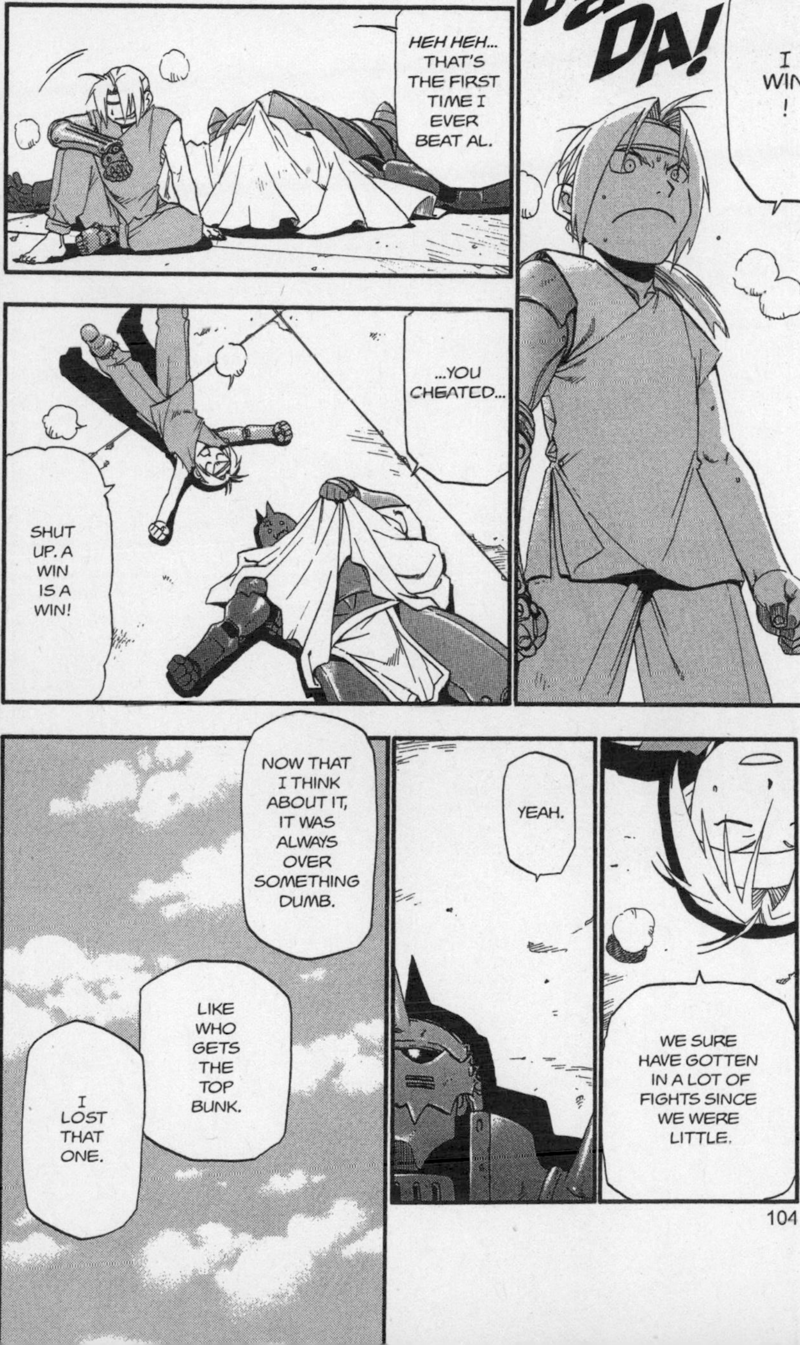
ta-DA!
I WIN!
HEH HEH... THAT'S THE FIRST TIME I EVER BEAT AL.
...YOU CHEATED...
SHUT UP. A WIN IS A WIN!
WE SURE HAVE GOTTEN IN A LOT OF FIGHTS SINCE WE WERE LITTLE.
YEAH.
NOW THAT I THINK ABOUT IT, IT WAS ALWAYS OVER SOMETHING DUMB.
LIKE WHO GETS THE TOP BUNK.
I LOST THAT ONE.

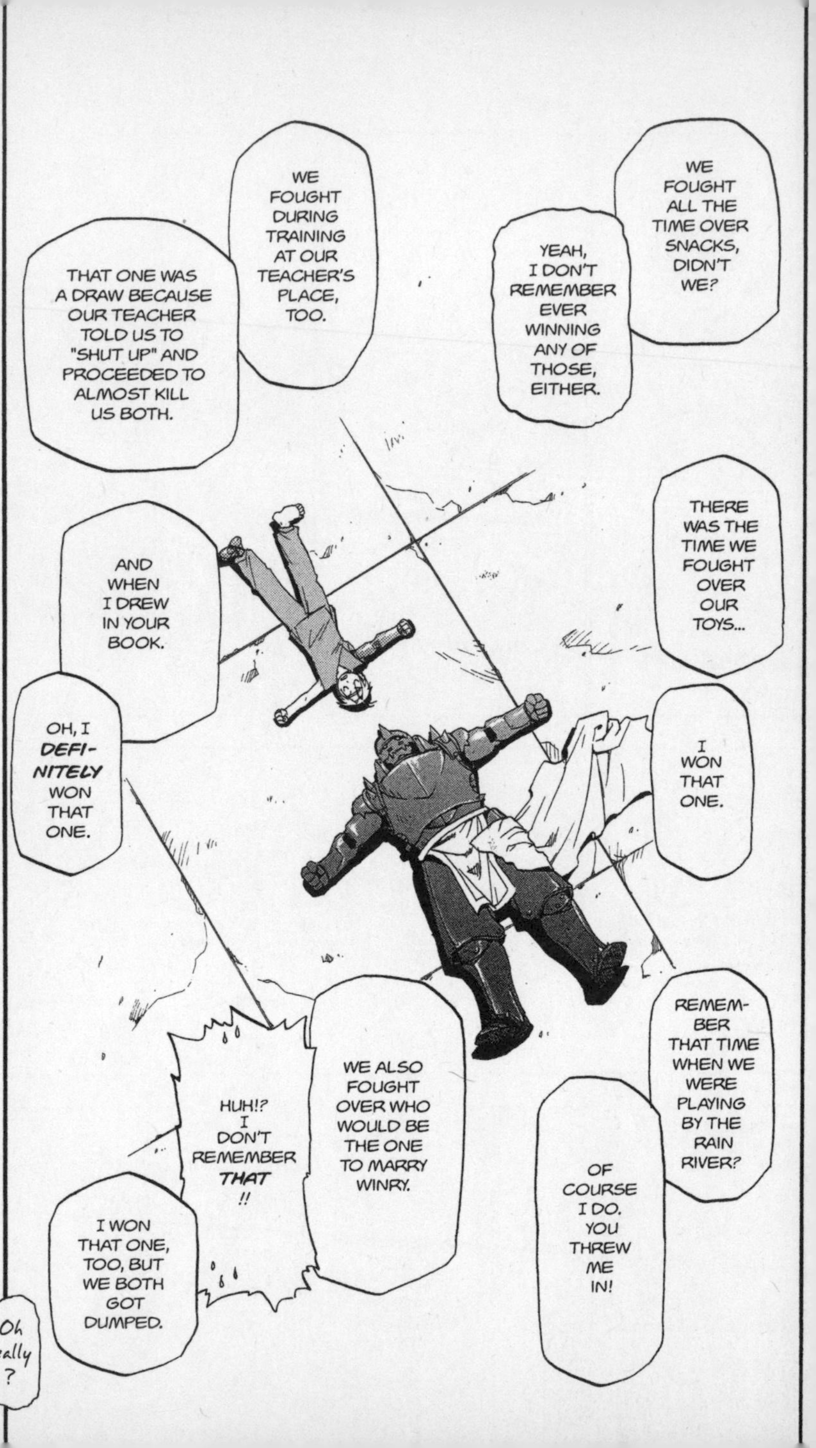
WE FOUGHT ALL THE TIME OVER SNACKS, DIDN'T WE?
YEAH, I DON'T REMEMBER EVER WINNING ANY OF THOSE, EITHER.
WE FOUGHT DURING TRAINING AT OUR TEACHER'S PLACE, TOO.
THAT ONE WAS A DRAW BECAUSE OUR TEACHER TOLD US TO "SHUT UP" AND PROCEEDED TO ALMOST KILL US BOTH.
THERE WAS THE TIME WE FOUGHT OVER OUR TOYS...
I WON THAT ONE.
AND WHEN I DREW IN YOUR BOOK.
OH, I *DEFINITELY* WON THAT ONE.
REMEMBER THAT TIME WHEN WE WERE PLAYING BY THE RAIN RIVER?
OF COURSE I DO. YOU THREW ME IN!
WE ALSO FOUGHT OVER WHO WOULD BE THE ONE TO MARRY WINRY.
HUH!? I DON'T REMEMBER *THAT*!!
I WON THAT ONE, TOO, BUT WE BOTH GOT DUMPED.
Oh really?

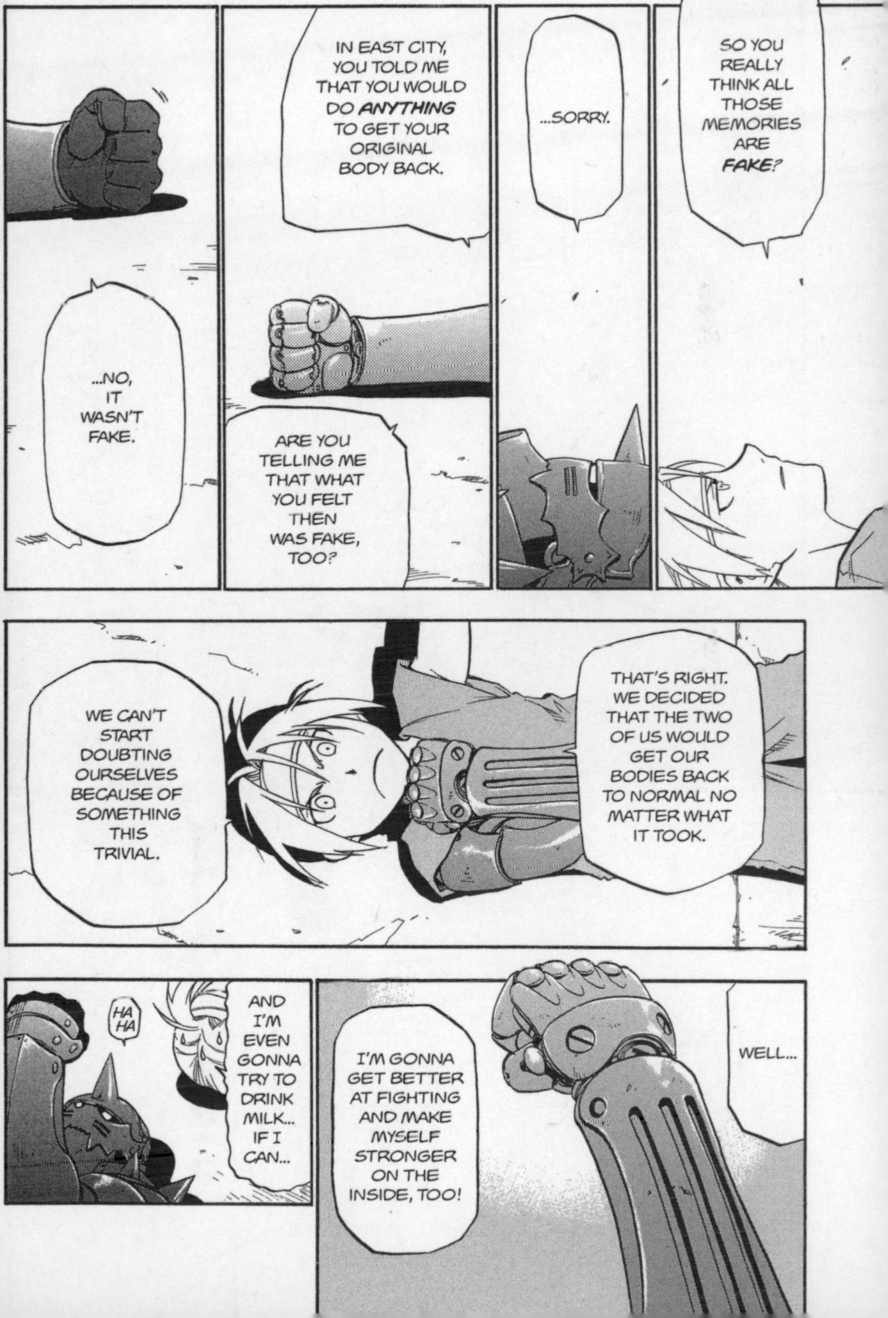
SO YOU REALLY THINK ALL THOSE MEMORIES ARE *FAKE*?
...SORRY.
IN EAST CITY, YOU TOLD ME THAT YOU WOULD DO *ANYTHING* TO GET YOUR ORIGINAL BODY BACK.
ARE YOU TELLING ME THAT WHAT YOU FELT THEN WAS FAKE, TOO?
...NO, IT WASN'T FAKE.
THAT'S RIGHT. WE DECIDED THAT THE TWO OF US WOULD GET OUR BODIES BACK TO NORMAL NO MATTER WHAT IT TOOK.
WE CAN'T START DOUBTING OURSELVES BECAUSE OF SOMETHING THIS TRIVIAL.
WELL...
I'M GONNA GET BETTER AT FIGHTING AND MAKE MYSELF STRONGER ON THE INSIDE, TOO!
AND I'M EVEN GONNA TRY TO DRINK MILK... IF I CAN...
HA HA

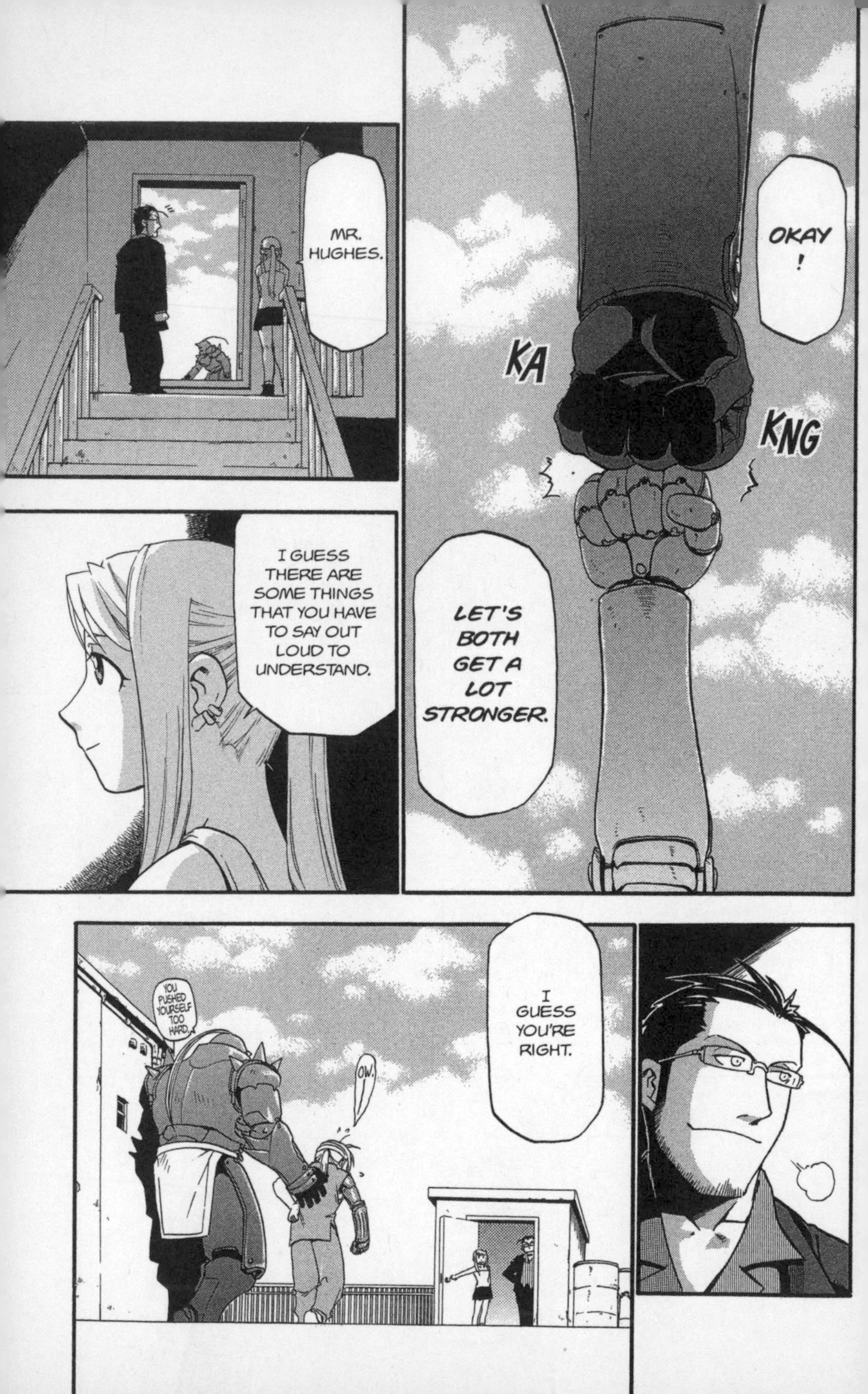
OKAY!
KA
KNG
LET'S BOTH GET A LOT STRONGER.
MR. HUGHES.
I GUESS THERE ARE SOME THINGS THAT YOU HAVE TO SAY OUT LOUD TO UNDERSTAND.
I GUESS YOU'RE RIGHT.
OW.
YOU PUSHED YOURSELF TOO HARD.

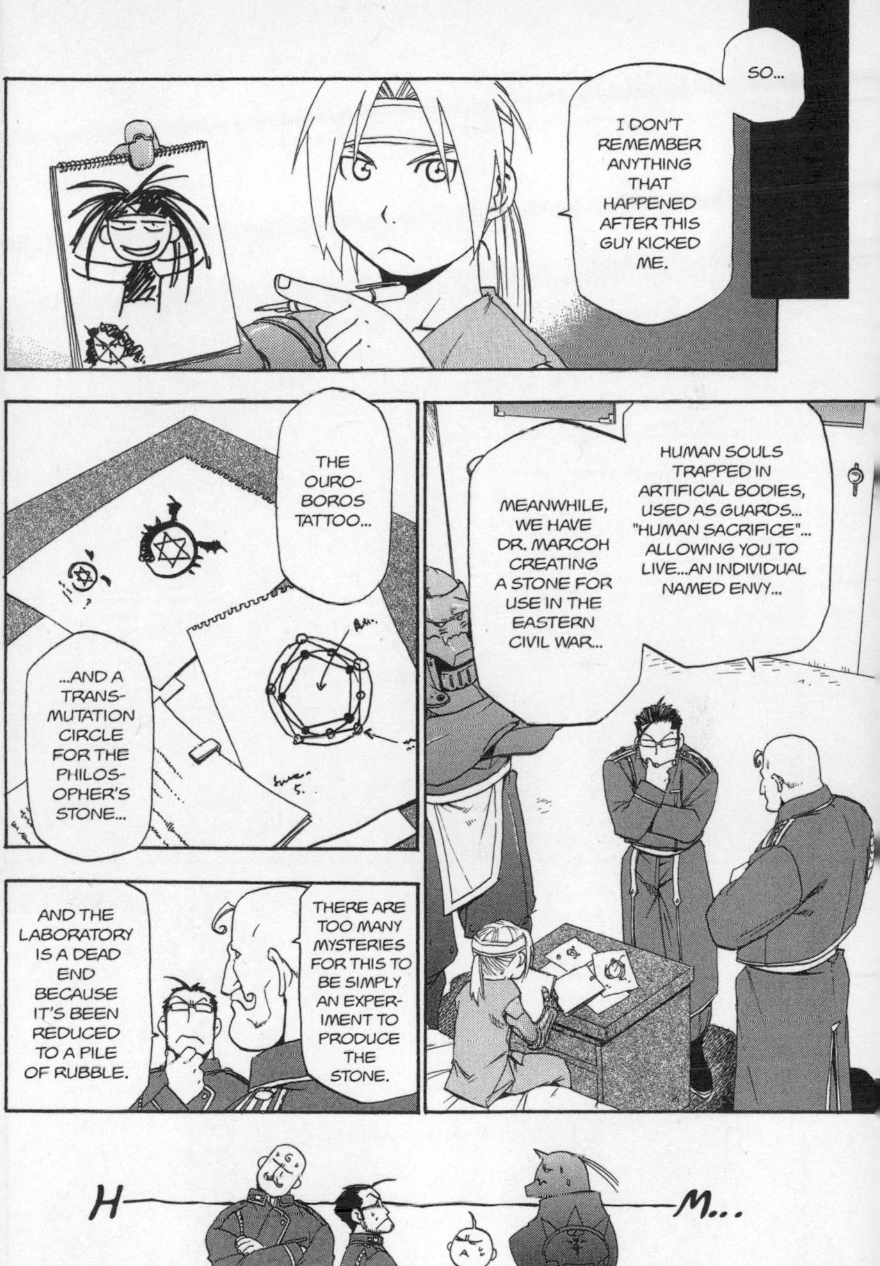
SO...
I DON'T REMEMBER ANYTHING THAT HAPPENED AFTER THIS GUY KICKED ME.
HUMAN SOULS TRAPPED IN ARTIFICIAL BODIES, USED AS GUARDS... "HUMAN SACRIFICE"... ALLOWING YOU TO LIVE...AN INDIVIDUAL NAMED ENVY...
MEANWHILE, WE HAVE DR. MARCOH CREATING A STONE FOR USE IN THE EASTERN CIVIL WAR...
THE OURO-BOROS TATTOO...
...AND A TRANS-MUTATION CIRCLE FOR THE PHILOS-OPHER'S STONE...
THERE ARE TOO MANY MYSTERIES FOR THIS TO BE SIMPLY AN EXPER-IMENT TO PRODUCE THE STONE.
AND THE LABORATORY IS A DEAD END BECAUSE IT'S BEEN REDUCED TO A PILE OF RUBBLE.
H——M...

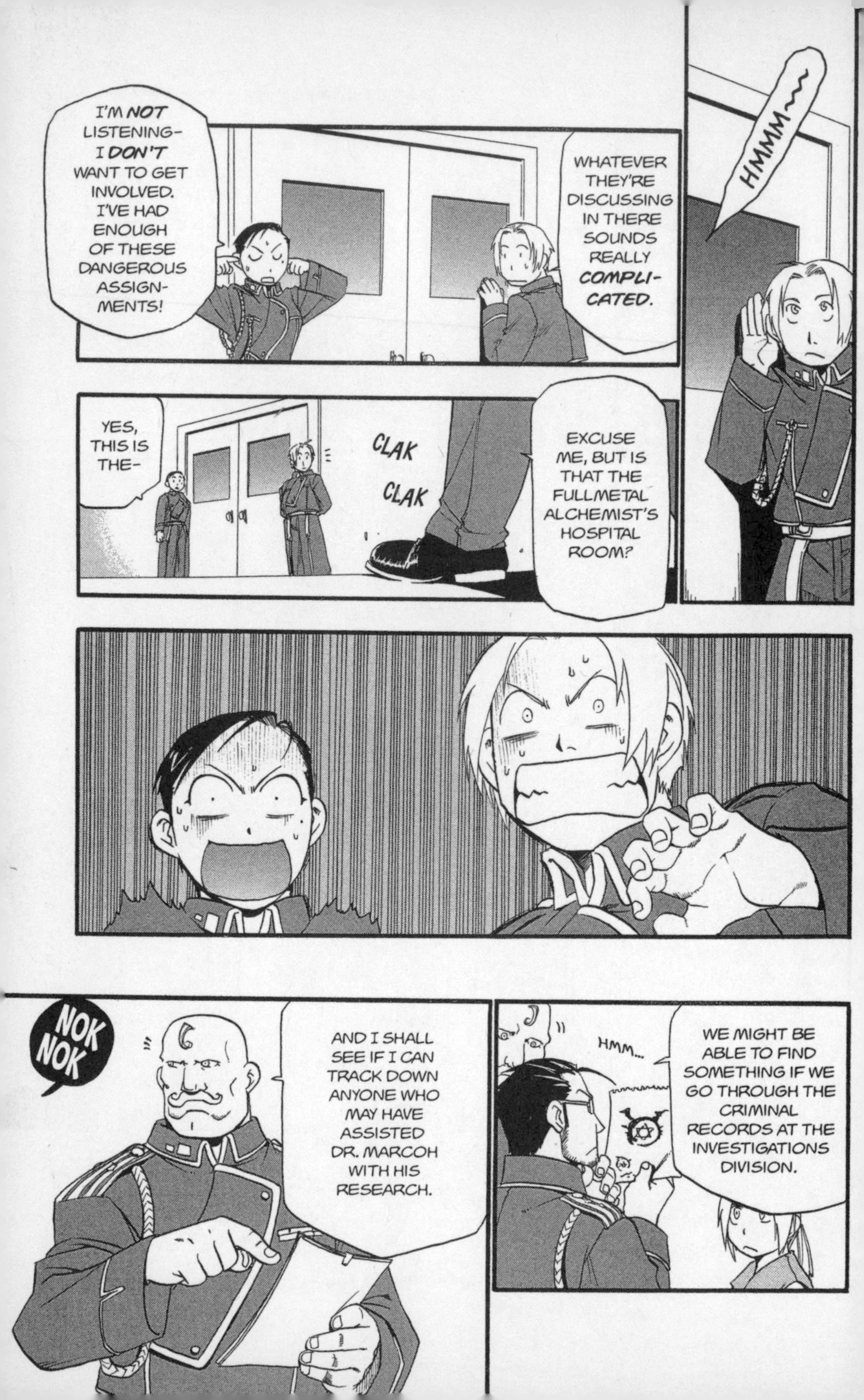
HMMM~~
WHATEVER THEY'RE DISCUSSING IN THERE SOUNDS REALLY *COMPLICATED.*
I'M *NOT* LISTENING- I *DON'T* WANT TO GET INVOLVED. I'VE HAD ENOUGH OF THESE DANGEROUS ASSIGNMENTS!
EXCUSE ME, BUT IS THAT THE FULLMETAL ALCHEMIST'S HOSPITAL ROOM?
CLAK
CLAK
YES, THIS IS THE-
WE MIGHT BE ABLE TO FIND SOMETHING IF WE GO THROUGH THE CRIMINAL RECORDS AT THE INVESTIGATIONS DIVISION.
HMM...
AND I SHALL SEE IF I CAN TRACK DOWN ANYONE WHO MAY HAVE ASSISTED DR. MARCOH WITH HIS RESEARCH.
NOK NOK

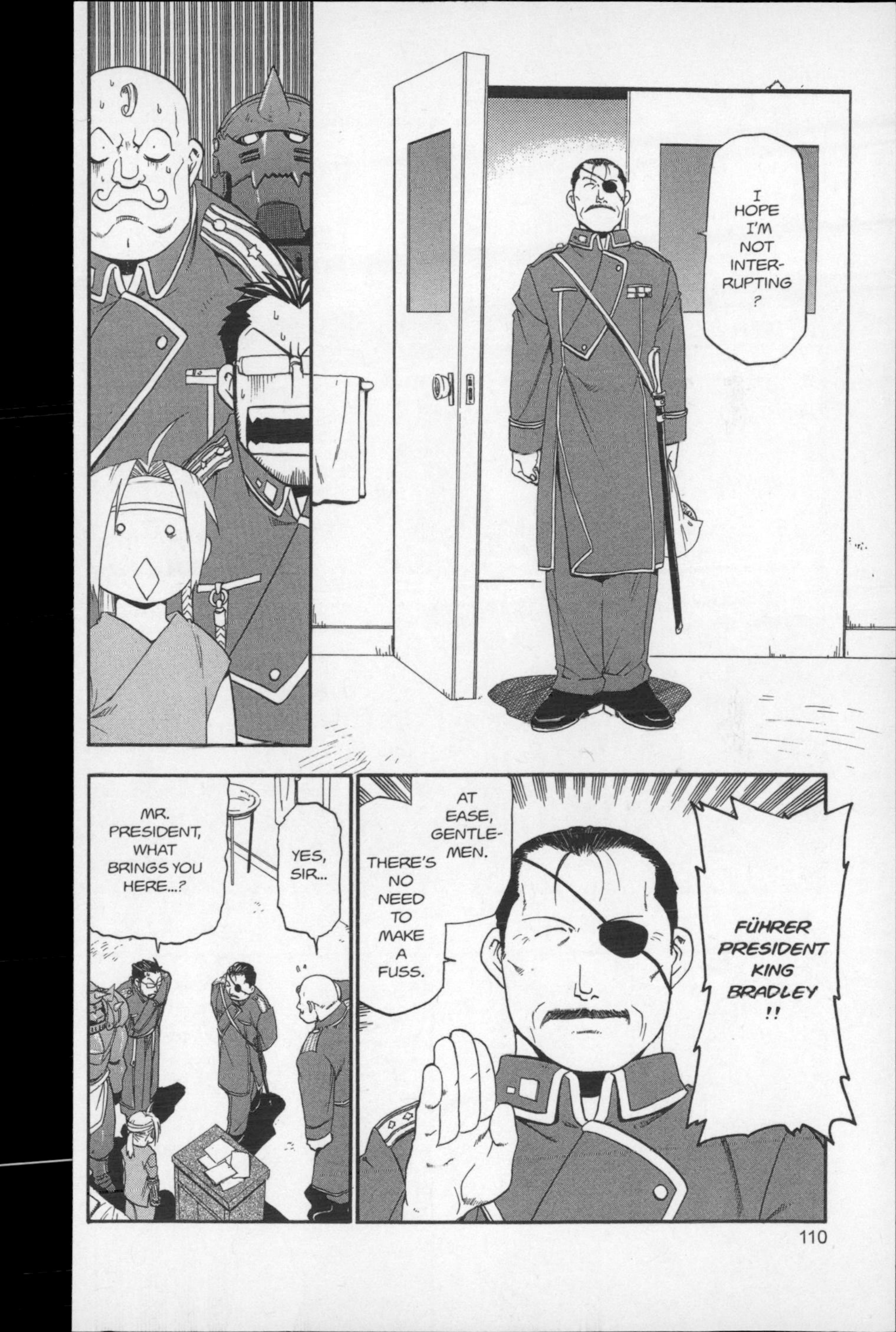
I HOPE I'M NOT INTERRUPTING?
FÜHRER PRESIDENT KING BRADLEY!!
AT EASE, GENTLEMEN.
THERE'S NO NEED TO MAKE A FUSS.
YES, SIR...
MR. PRESIDENT, WHAT BRINGS YOU HERE...?

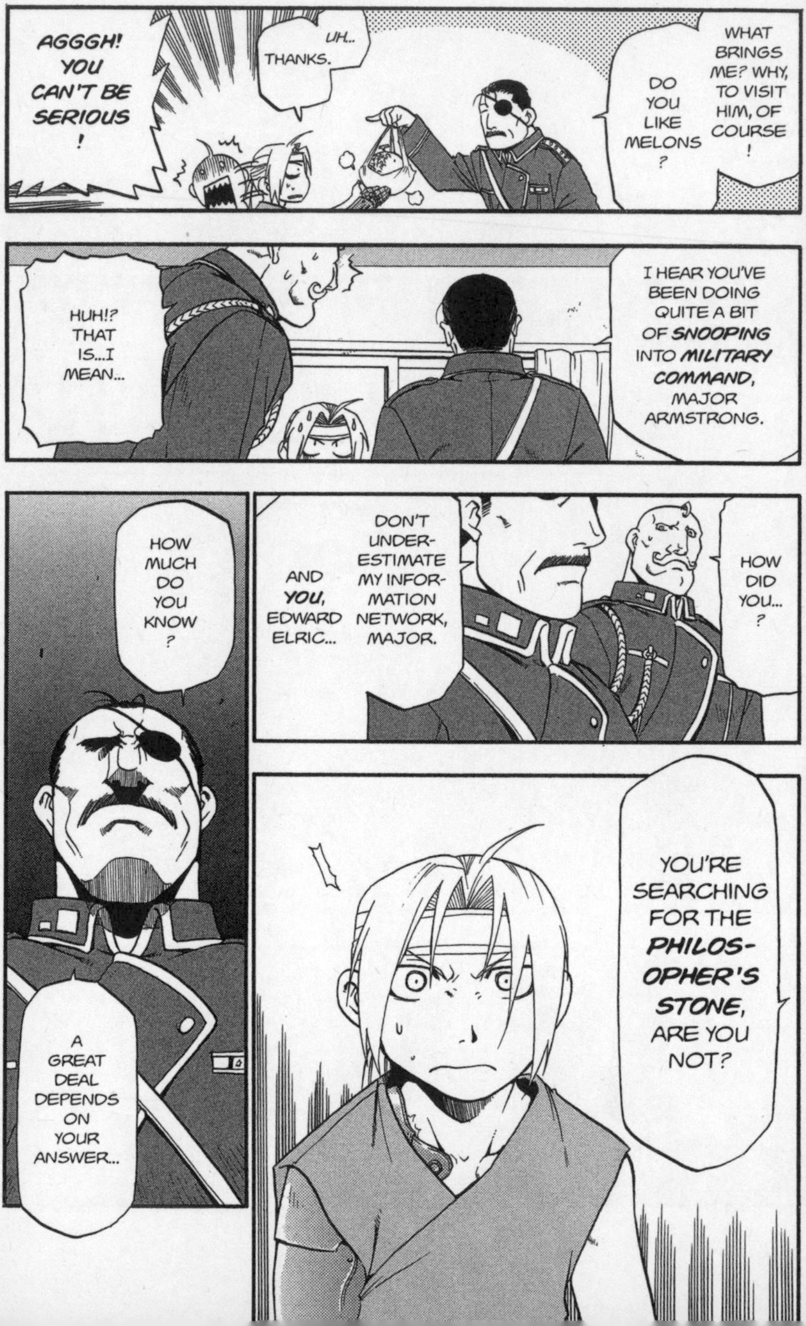
WHAT BRINGS ME? WHY, TO VISIT HIM, OF COURSE!
DO YOU LIKE MELONS?
UH... THANKS.
AGGGH! YOU CAN'T BE SERIOUS!
I HEAR YOU'VE BEEN DOING QUITE A BIT OF SNOOPING INTO MILITARY COMMAND, MAJOR ARMSTRONG.
HUH!? THAT IS...I MEAN...
HOW DID YOU...?
DON'T UNDER-ESTIMATE MY INFOR-MATION NETWORK, MAJOR.
AND YOU, EDWARD ELRIC...
YOU'RE SEARCHING FOR THE PHILOS-OPHER'S STONE, ARE YOU NOT?
HOW MUCH DO YOU KNOW?
A GREAT DEAL DEPENDS ON YOUR ANSWER...

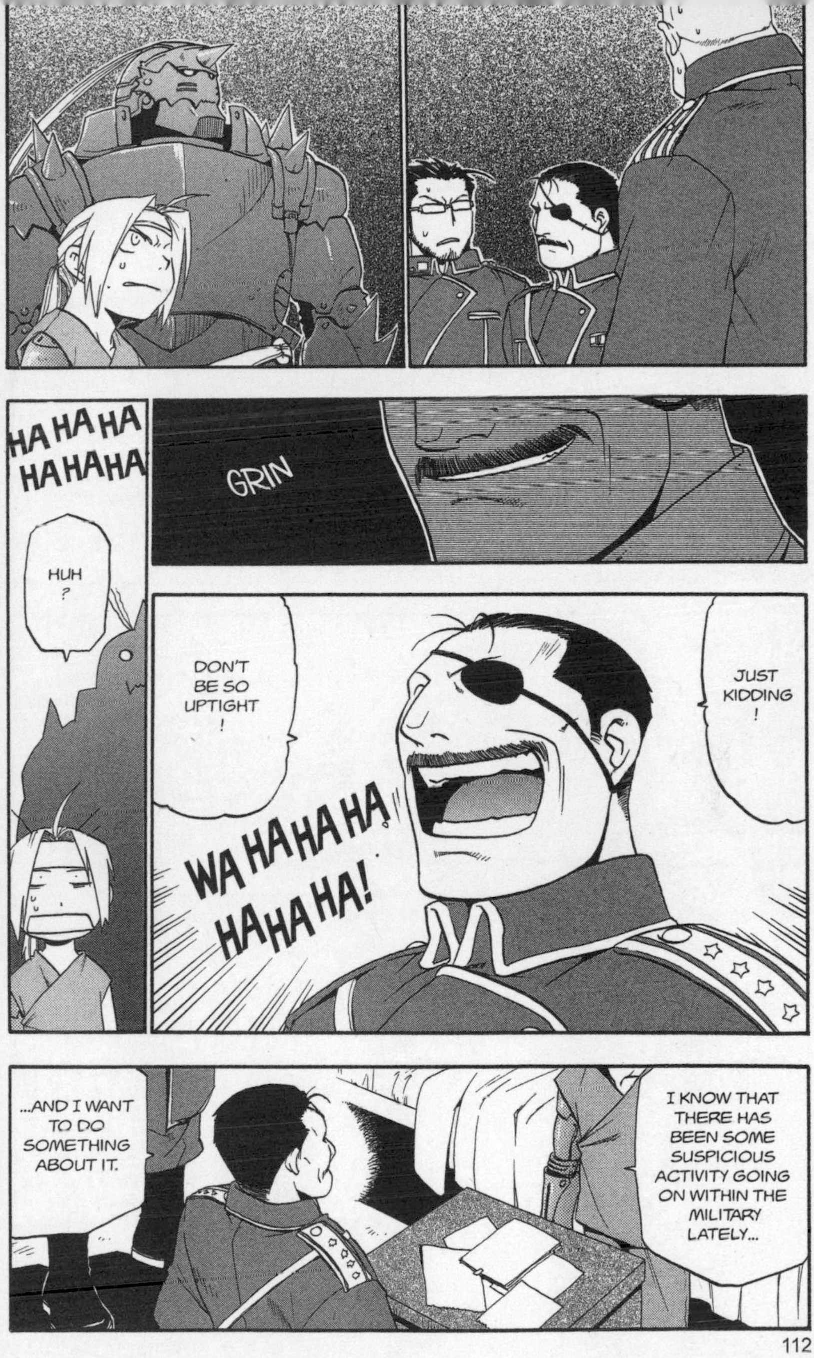
GRIN
JUST KIDDING!
DON'T BE SO UPTIGHT!
WA HA HA HA HA HA HA HA!
HA HA HA HA HA HA
HUH?
I KNOW THAT THERE HAS BEEN SOME SUSPICIOUS ACTIVITY GOING ON WITHIN THE MILITARY LATELY...
...AND I WANT TO DO SOMETHING ABOUT IT.

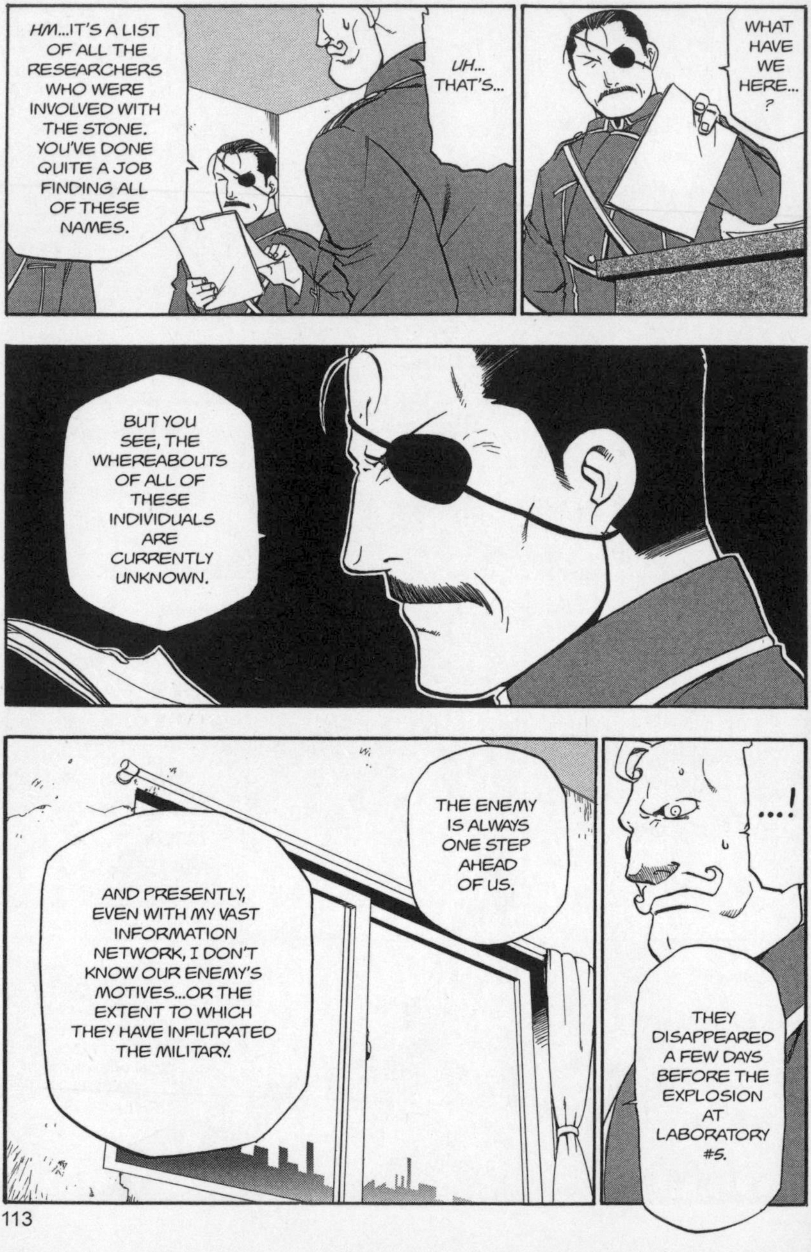
WHAT HAVE WE HERE...?
UH... THAT'S...
HM...IT'S A LIST OF ALL THE RESEARCHERS WHO WERE INVOLVED WITH THE STONE. YOU'VE DONE QUITE A JOB FINDING ALL OF THESE NAMES.
BUT YOU SEE, THE WHEREABOUTS OF ALL OF THESE INDIVIDUALS ARE CURRENTLY UNKNOWN.
...!
THEY DISAPPEARED A FEW DAYS BEFORE THE EXPLOSION AT LABORATORY #5.
THE ENEMY IS ALWAYS ONE STEP AHEAD OF US.
AND PRESENTLY, EVEN WITH MY VAST INFORMATION NETWORK, I DON'T KNOW OUR ENEMY'S MOTIVES...OR THE EXTENT TO WHICH THEY HAVE INFILTRATED THE MILITARY.

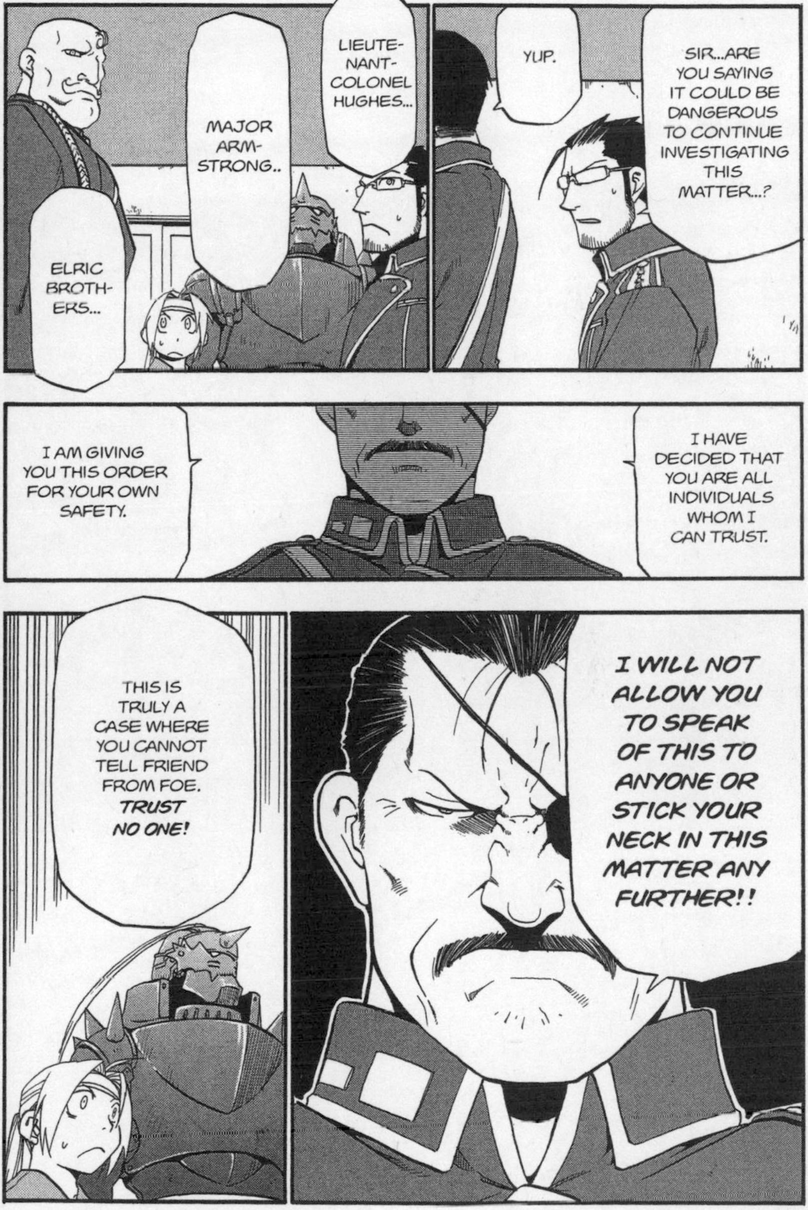
SIR...ARE YOU SAYING IT COULD BE DANGEROUS TO CONTINUE INVESTIGATING THIS MATTER...?
YUP.
LIEUTE-NANT-COLONEL HUGHES...
MAJOR ARM-STRONG..
ELRIC BROTH-ERS...
I HAVE DECIDED THAT YOU ARE ALL INDIVIDUALS WHOM I CAN TRUST.
I AM GIVING YOU THIS ORDER FOR YOUR OWN SAFETY.
I WILL NOT ALLOW YOU TO SPEAK OF THIS TO ANYONE OR STICK YOUR NECK IN THIS MATTER ANY FURTHER!!
THIS IS TRULY A CASE WHERE YOU CANNOT TELL FRIEND FROM FOE. TRUST NO ONE!

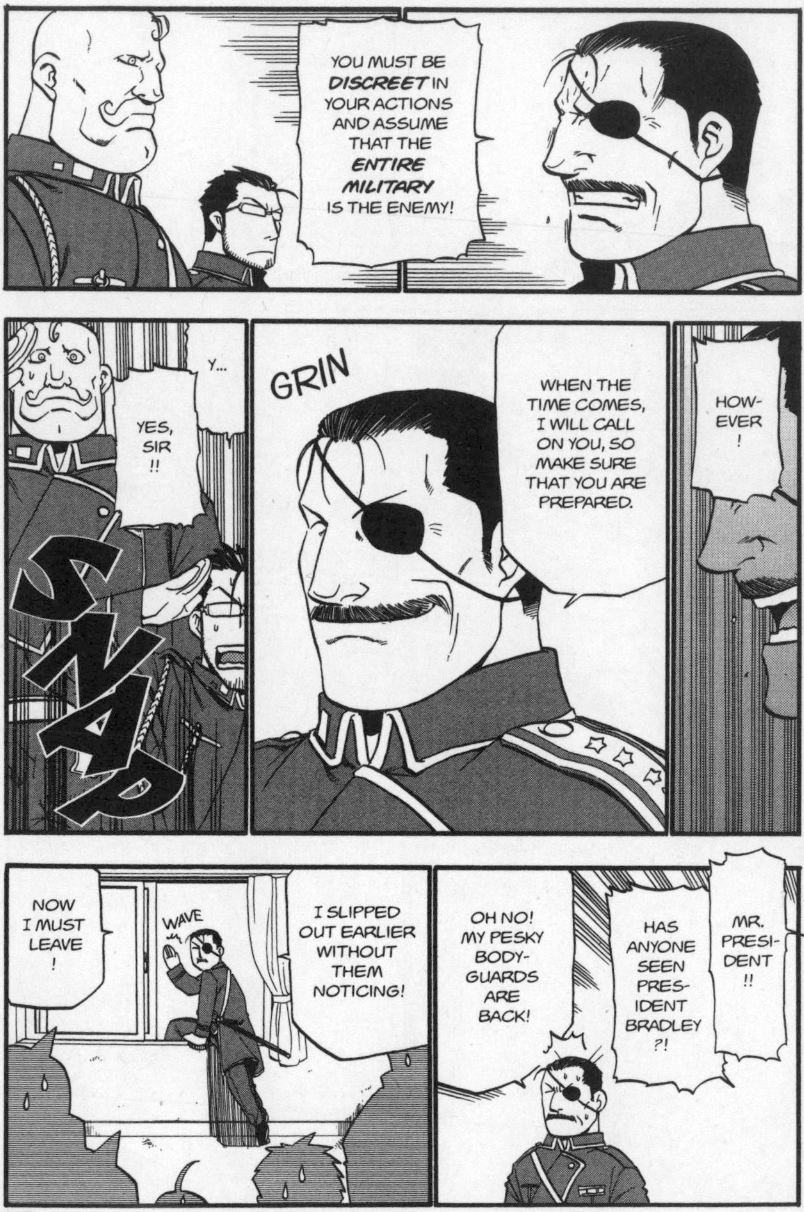
YOU MUST BE DISCREET IN YOUR ACTIONS AND ASSUME THAT THE ENTIRE MILITARY IS THE ENEMY!
HOW-EVER !
GRIN
WHEN THE TIME COMES, I WILL CALL ON YOU, SO MAKE SURE THAT YOU ARE PREPARED.
Y...
YES, SIR !!
SNAP
MR. PRESI-DENT !!
HAS ANYONE SEEN PRES-IDENT BRADLEY ?!
OH NO! MY PESKY BODY-GUARDS ARE BACK!
I SLIPPED OUT EARLIER WITHOUT THEM NOTICING!
WAVE
NOW I MUST LEAVE !

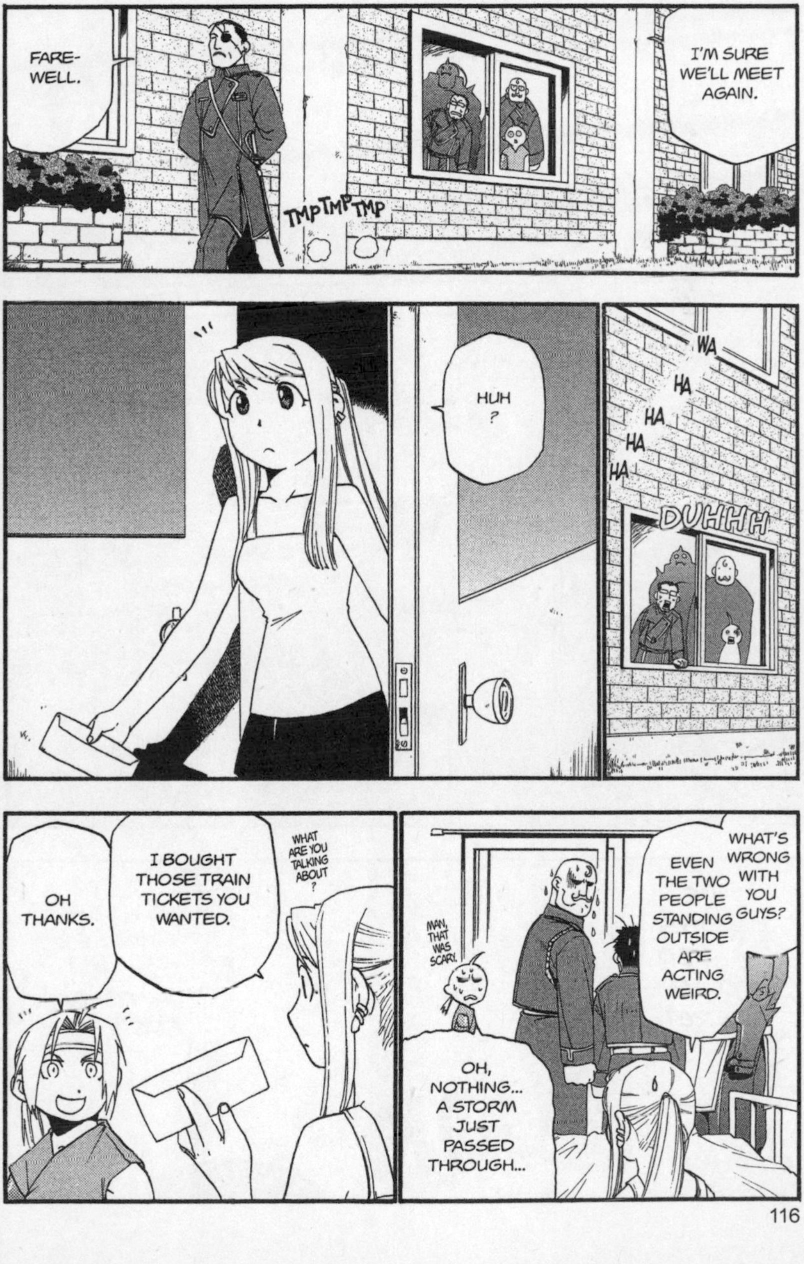
I'M SURE WE'LL MEET AGAIN.
FARE-WELL.
TMP TMP TMP
WA HA HA HA HA
DUHHH
HUH?
WHAT'S WRONG WITH YOU GUYS?
EVEN THE TWO PEOPLE STANDING OUTSIDE ARE ACTING WEIRD.
MAN, THAT WAS SCARY.
OH, NOTHING... A STORM JUST PASSED THROUGH...
WHAT ARE YOU TALKING ABOUT?
I BOUGHT THOSE TRAIN TICKETS YOU WANTED.
OH THANKS.

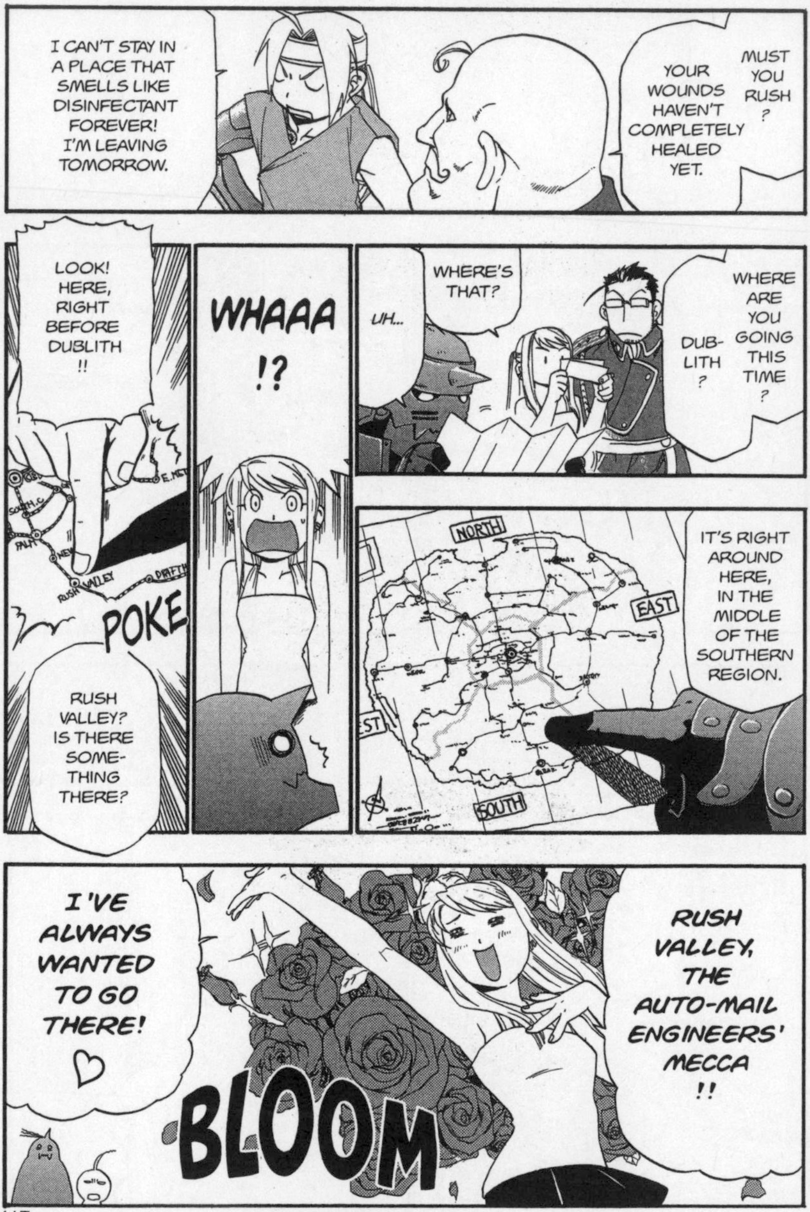
MUST YOU RUSH?
YOUR WOUNDS HAVEN'T COMPLETELY HEALED YET.
I CAN'T STAY IN A PLACE THAT SMELLS LIKE DISINFECTANT FOREVER! I'M LEAVING TOMORROW.
WHERE ARE YOU GOING THIS TIME?
DUBLITH?
UH...
WHERE'S THAT?
NORTH
EAST
SOUTH
IT'S RIGHT AROUND HERE, IN THE MIDDLE OF THE SOUTHERN REGION.
WHAAA !?
LOOK! HERE, RIGHT BEFORE DUBLITH !!
RUSH VALLEY
POKE
RUSH VALLEY? IS THERE SOMETHING THERE?
RUSH VALLEY, THE AUTO-MAIL ENGINEERS' MECCA !!
I'VE ALWAYS WANTED TO GO THERE! ♡
BLOOM

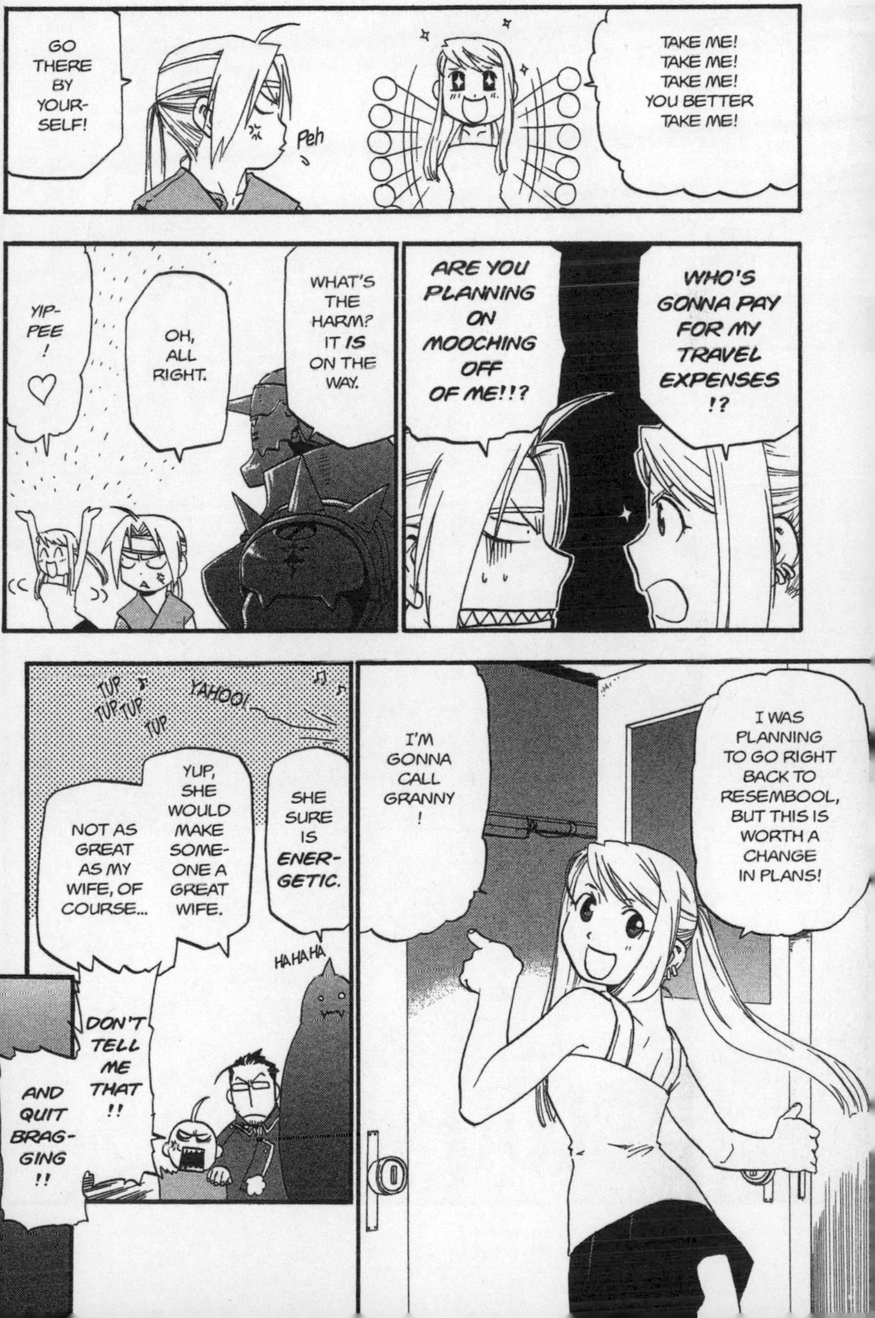
TAKE ME! TAKE ME! TAKE ME! YOU BETTER TAKE ME!
GO THERE BY YOURSELF!
Peh
WHO'S GONNA PAY FOR MY TRAVEL EXPENSES!?
ARE YOU PLANNING ON MOOCHING OFF OF ME!!?
WHAT'S THE HARM? IT IS ON THE WAY.
OH, ALL RIGHT.
YIPPEE! ♡
I WAS PLANNING TO GO RIGHT BACK TO RESEMBOOL, BUT THIS IS WORTH A CHANGE IN PLANS!
I'M GONNA CALL GRANNY!
YAHOO!
TUP TUP TUP TUP
SHE SURE IS ENERGETIC.
YUP, SHE WOULD MAKE SOMEONE A GREAT WIFE.
NOT AS GREAT AS MY WIFE, OF COURSE...
HAHAHA
DON'T TELL ME THAT!!
AND QUIT BRAGGING!!

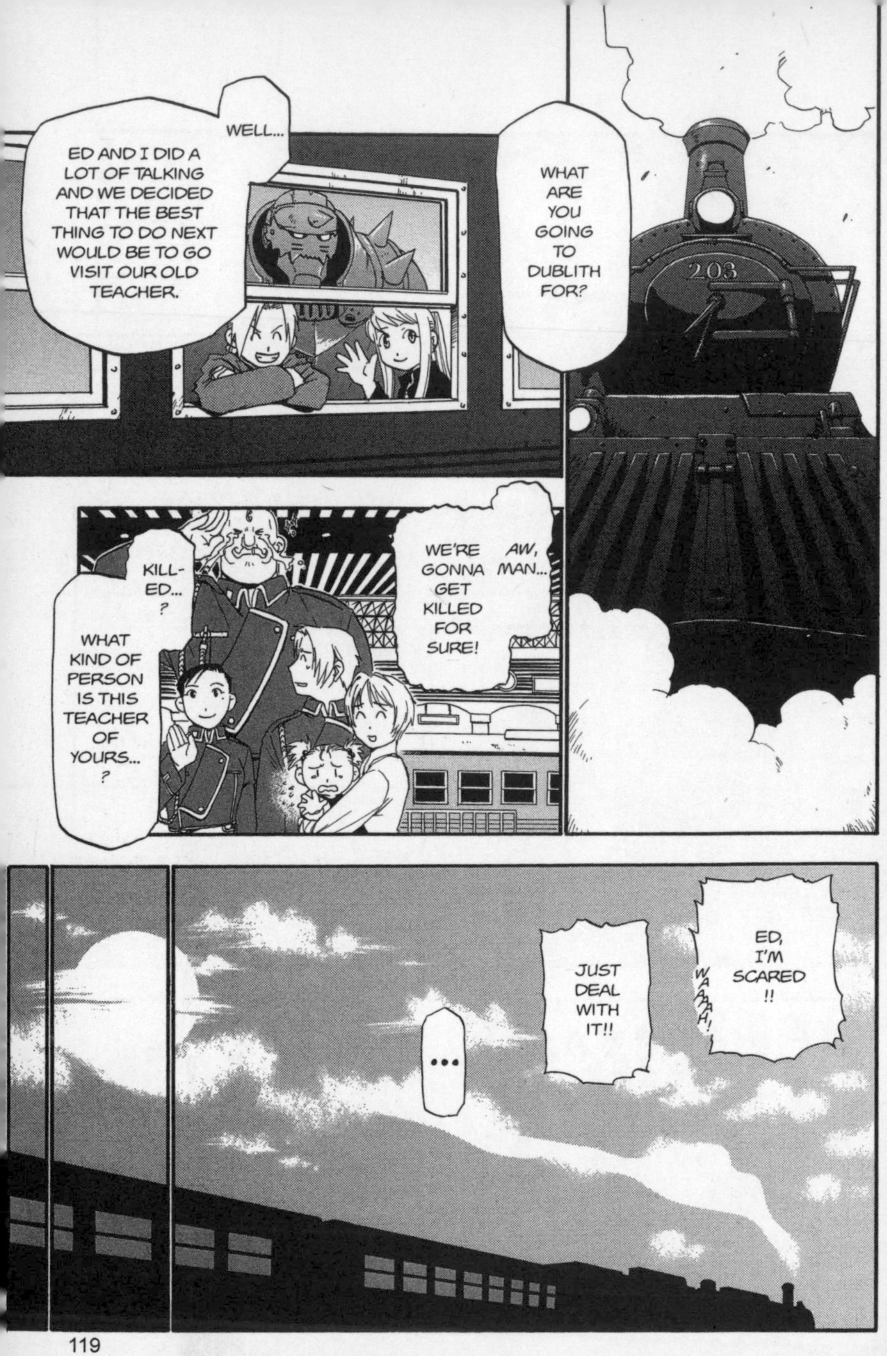
203
WHAT ARE YOU GOING TO DUBLITH FOR?
WELL...
ED AND I DID A LOT OF TALKING AND WE DECIDED THAT THE BEST THING TO DO NEXT WOULD BE TO GO VISIT OUR OLD TEACHER.
AW, MAN...
WE'RE GONNA GET KILLED FOR SURE!
KILL-ED...?
WHAT KIND OF PERSON IS THIS TEACHER OF YOURS...?
ED, I'M SCARED!!
WAAAH!
JUST DEAL WITH IT!!
...

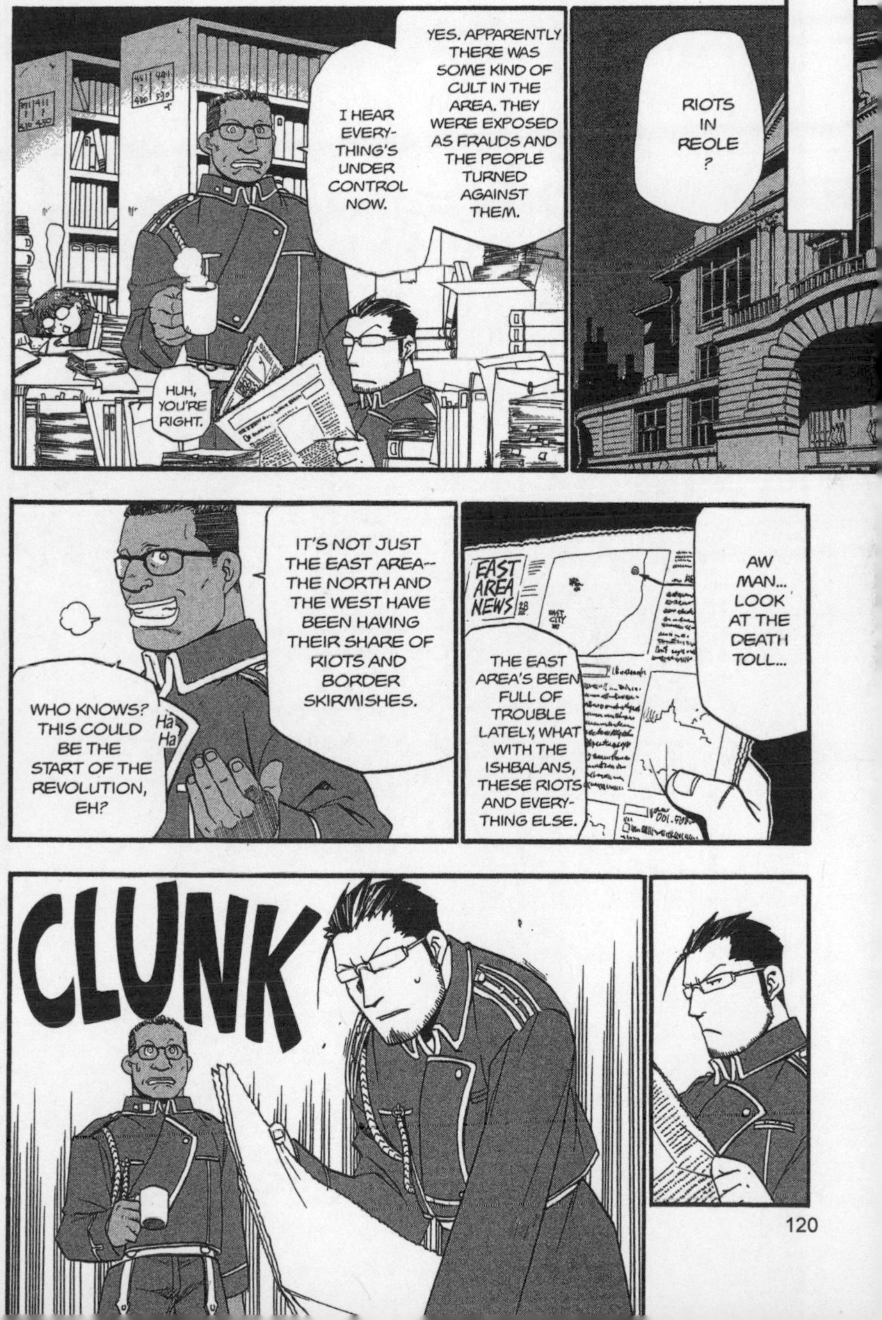

RIOTS IN REOLE?
YES. APPARENTLY THERE WAS SOME KIND OF CULT IN THE AREA. THEY WERE EXPOSED AS FRAUDS AND THE PEOPLE TURNED AGAINST THEM.
I HEAR EVERY-THING'S UNDER CONTROL NOW.
HUH, YOU'RE RIGHT.
AW MAN... LOOK AT THE DEATH TOLL...
EAST AREA NEWS
THE EAST AREA'S BEEN FULL OF TROUBLE LATELY, WHAT WITH THE ISHBALANS, THESE RIOTS AND EVERY-THING ELSE.
IT'S NOT JUST THE EAST AREA-- THE NORTH AND THE WEST HAVE BEEN HAVING THEIR SHARE OF RIOTS AND BORDER SKIRMISHES.
Ha Ha
WHO KNOWS? THIS COULD BE THE START OF THE REVOLUTION, EH?
CLUNK

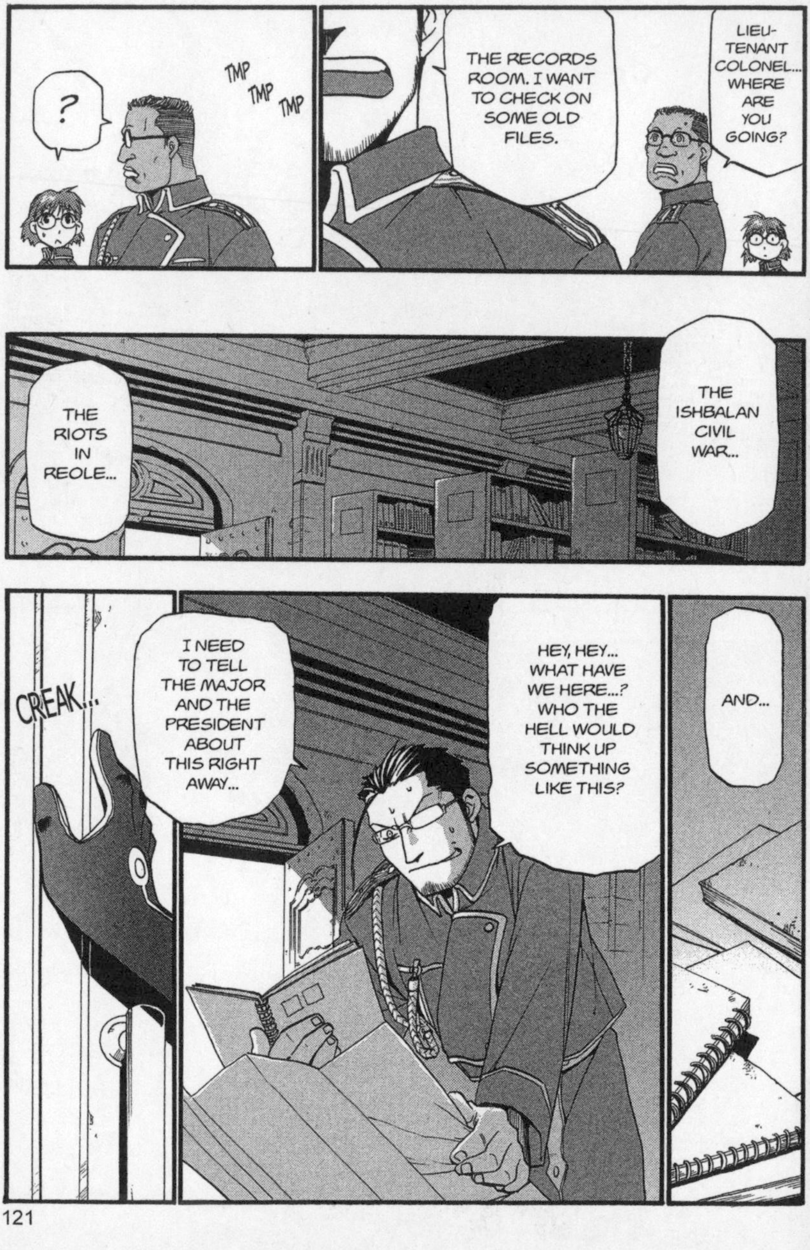
LIEU-TENANT COLONEL... WHERE ARE YOU GOING?
THE RECORDS ROOM. I WANT TO CHECK ON SOME OLD FILES.
TMP TMP TMP
?
THE ISHBALAN CIVIL WAR...
THE RIOTS IN REOLE...
AND...
HEY, HEY... WHAT HAVE WE HERE...? WHO THE HELL WOULD THINK UP SOMETHING LIKE THIS?
I NEED TO TELL THE MAJOR AND THE PRESIDENT ABOUT THIS RIGHT AWAY...
CREAK...

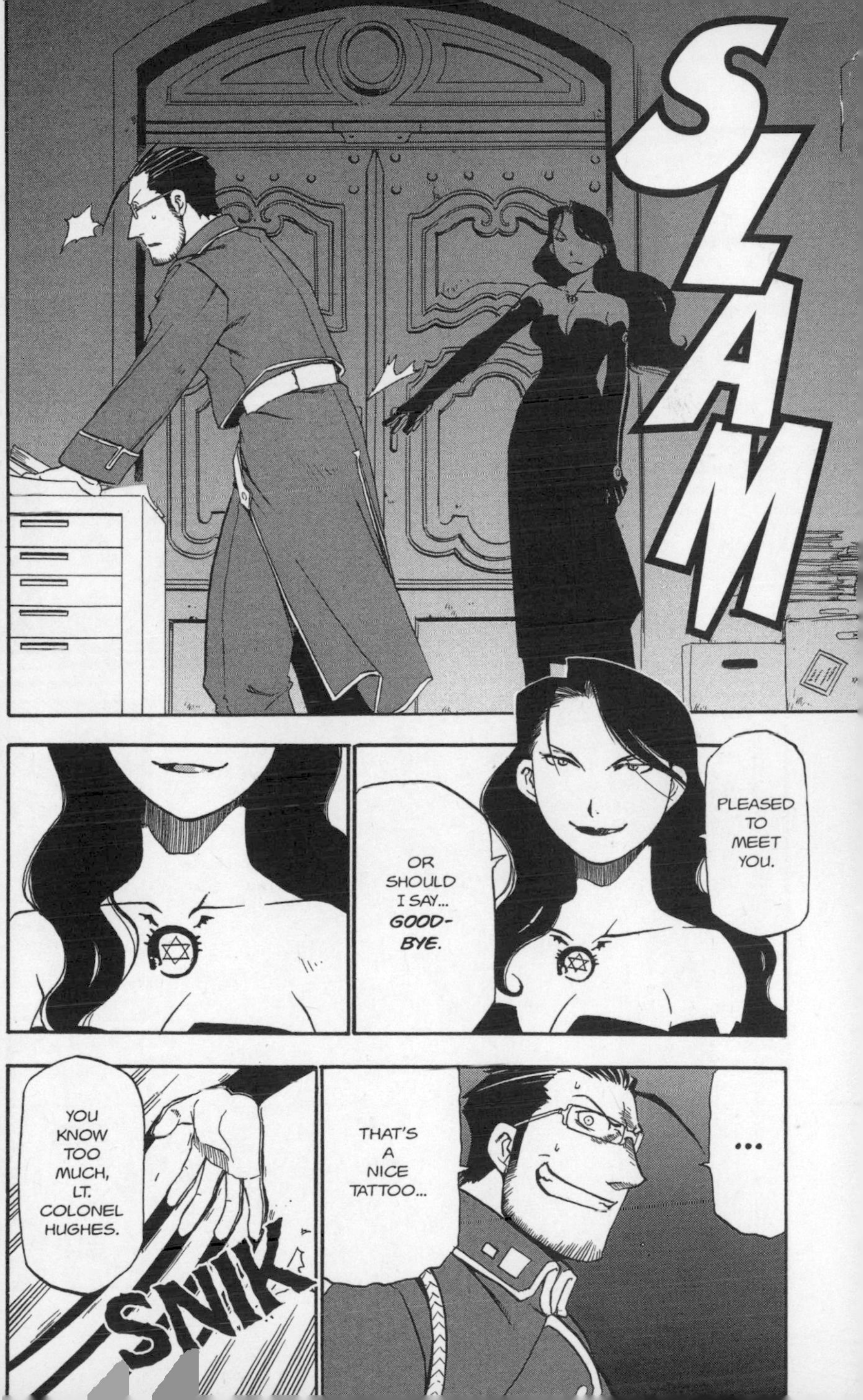
SLAM
PLEASED TO MEET YOU.
OR SHOULD I SAY... GOOD-BYE.
...
THAT'S A NICE TATTOO...
YOU KNOW TOO MUCH, LT. COLONEL HUGHES.
SNIK

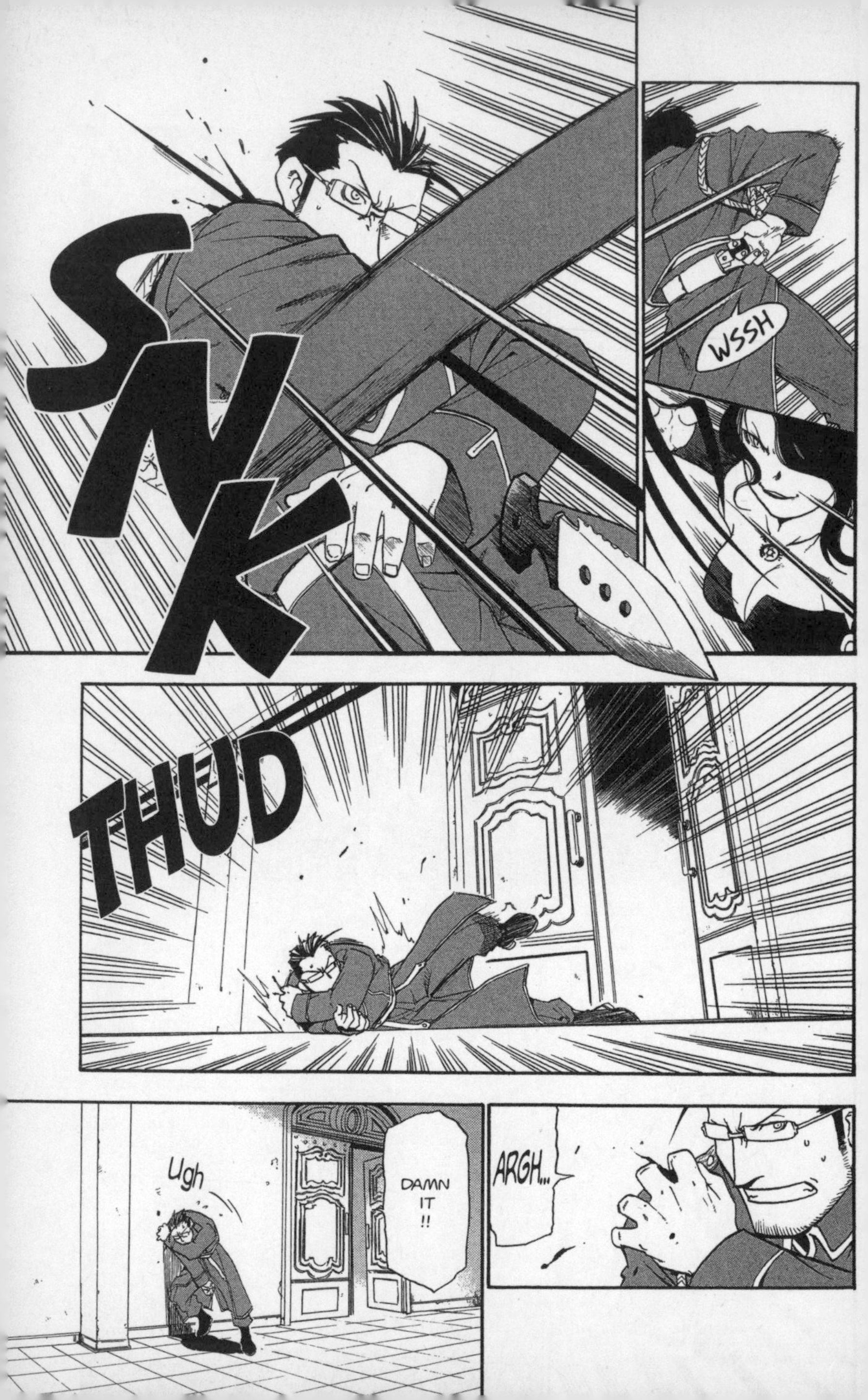
WSSH
SNK
THUD
ARGH...
DAMN IT !!
Ugh

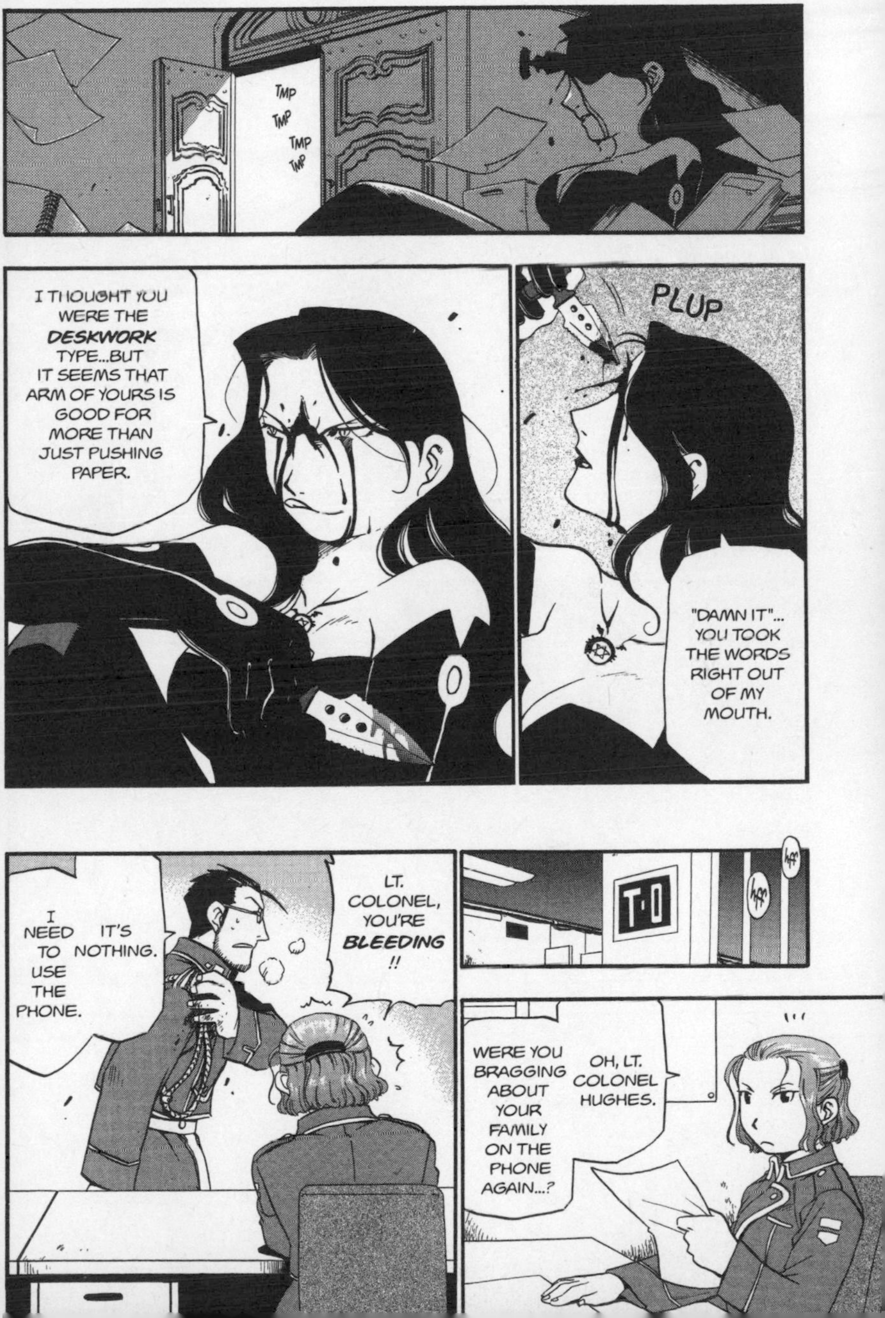
TMP TMP TMP TMP
PLUP
"DAMN IT"... YOU TOOK THE WORDS RIGHT OUT OF MY MOUTH.
I THOUGHT YOU WERE THE **DESKWORK** TYPE...BUT IT SEEMS THAT ARM OF YOURS IS GOOD FOR MORE THAN JUST PUSHING PAPER.
hff
hff
OH, LT. COLONEL HUGHES.
WERE YOU BRAGGING ABOUT YOUR FAMILY ON THE PHONE AGAIN...?
LT. COLONEL, YOU'RE **BLEEDING** !!
IT'S NOTHING.
I NEED TO USE THE PHONE.

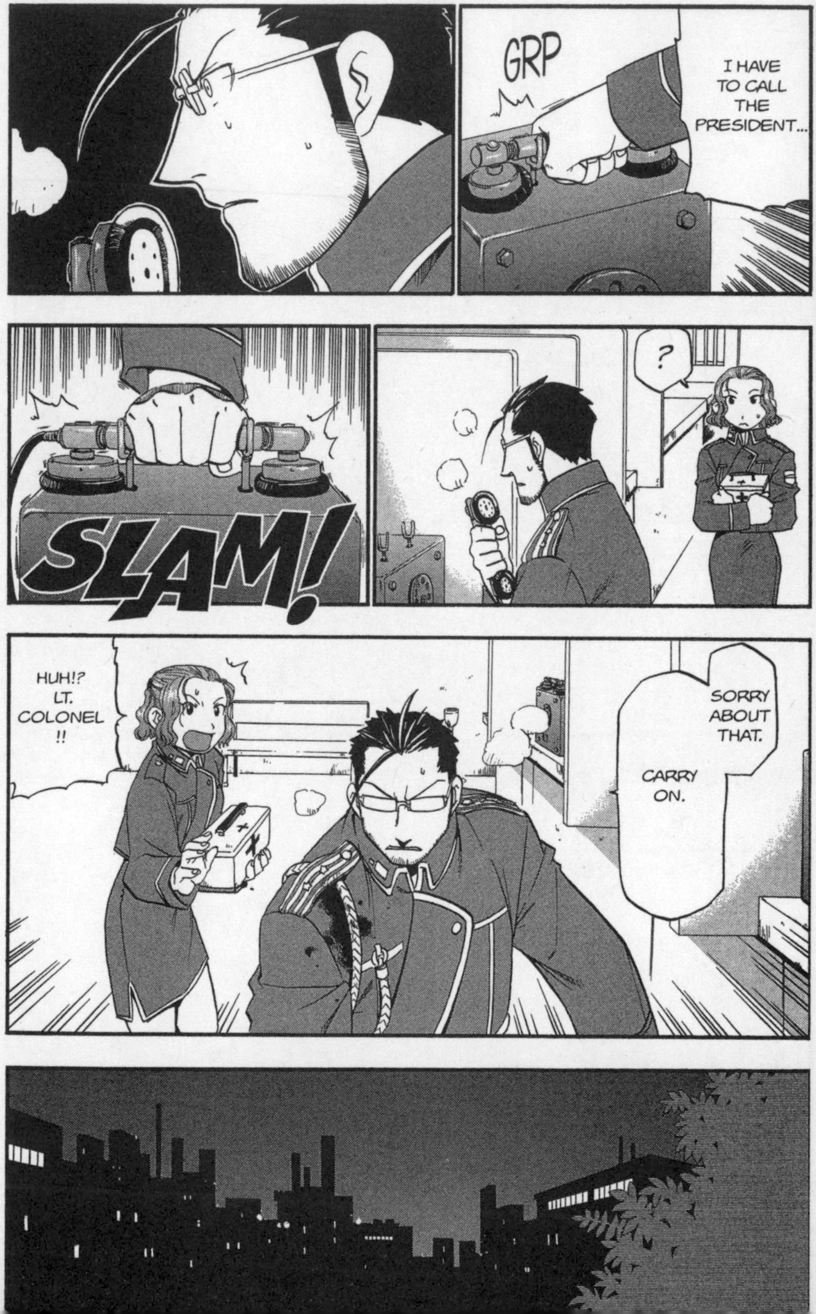
I HAVE TO CALL THE PRESIDENT...
GRP
?
SLAM!
SORRY ABOUT THAT.
CARRY ON.
HUH!? LT. COLONEL !!

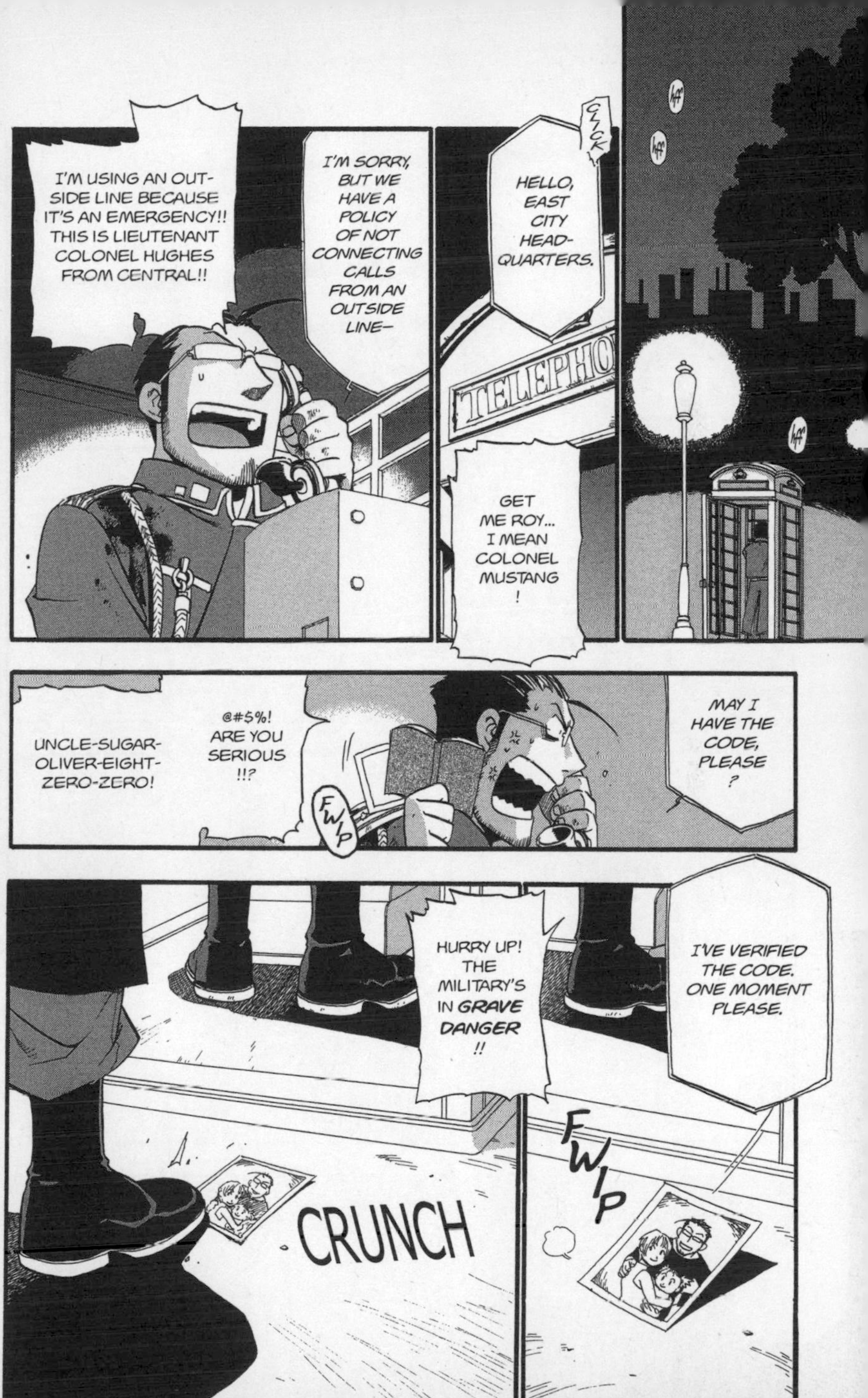
hff
hff
hff
CLICK
HELLO, EAST CITY HEADQUARTERS.
GET ME ROY... I MEAN COLONEL MUSTANG!
I'M SORRY, BUT WE HAVE A POLICY OF NOT CONNECTING CALLS FROM AN OUTSIDE LINE–
I'M USING AN OUTSIDE LINE BECAUSE IT'S AN EMERGENCY!! THIS IS LIEUTENANT COLONEL HUGHES FROM CENTRAL!!
TELEPHO
MAY I HAVE THE CODE, PLEASE?
FWIP
@#$%! ARE YOU SERIOUS!!?
UNCLE-SUGAR-OLIVER-EIGHT-ZERO-ZERO!
I'VE VERIFIED THE CODE. ONE MOMENT PLEASE.
HURRY UP! THE MILITARY'S IN **GRAVE DANGER**!!
FWIP
CRUNCH

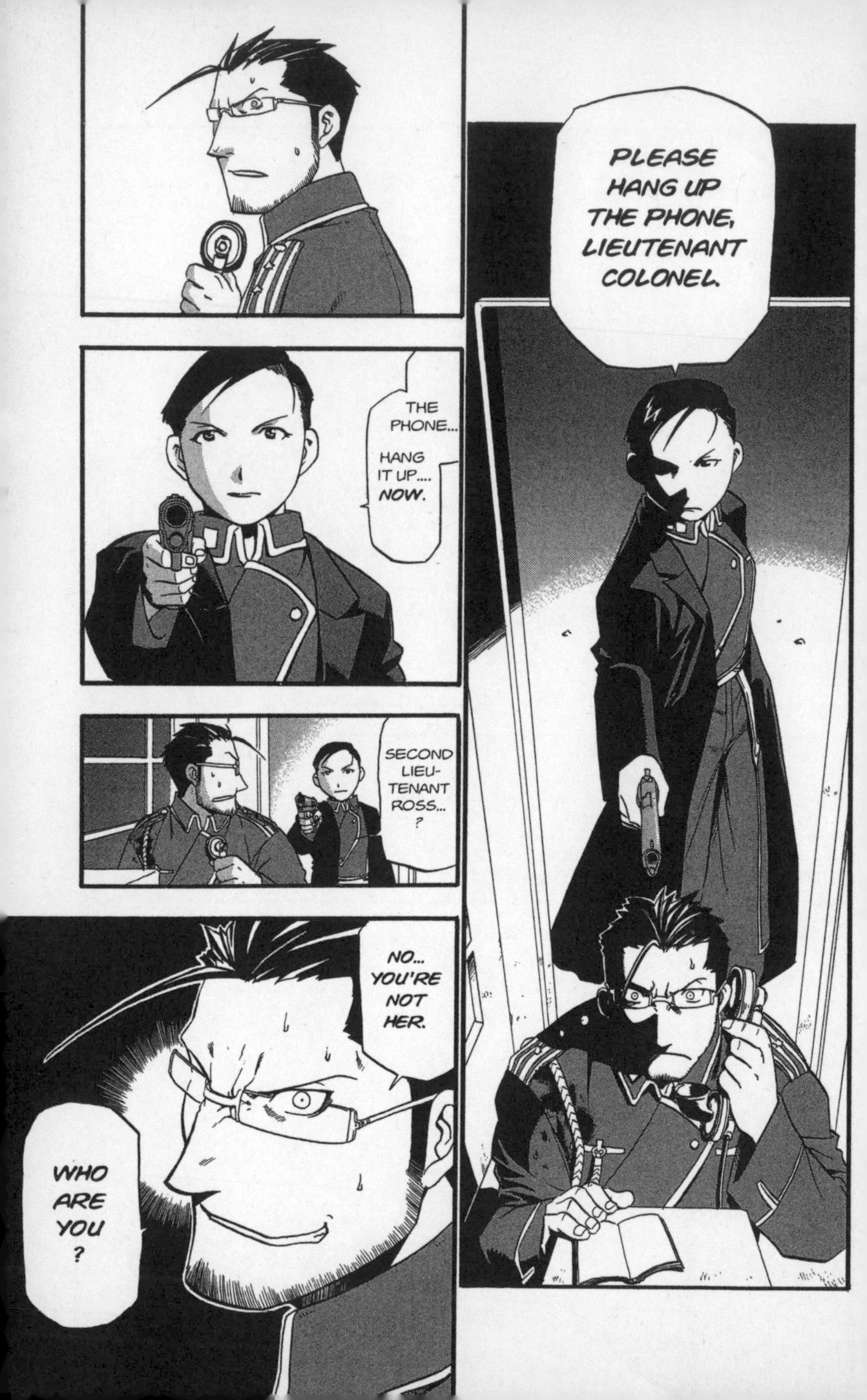

PLEASE HANG UP THE PHONE, LIEUTENANT COLONEL.
THE PHONE...
HANG IT UP.... NOW.
SECOND LIEU-TENANT ROSS... ?
NO... YOU'RE NOT HER.
WHO ARE YOU ?

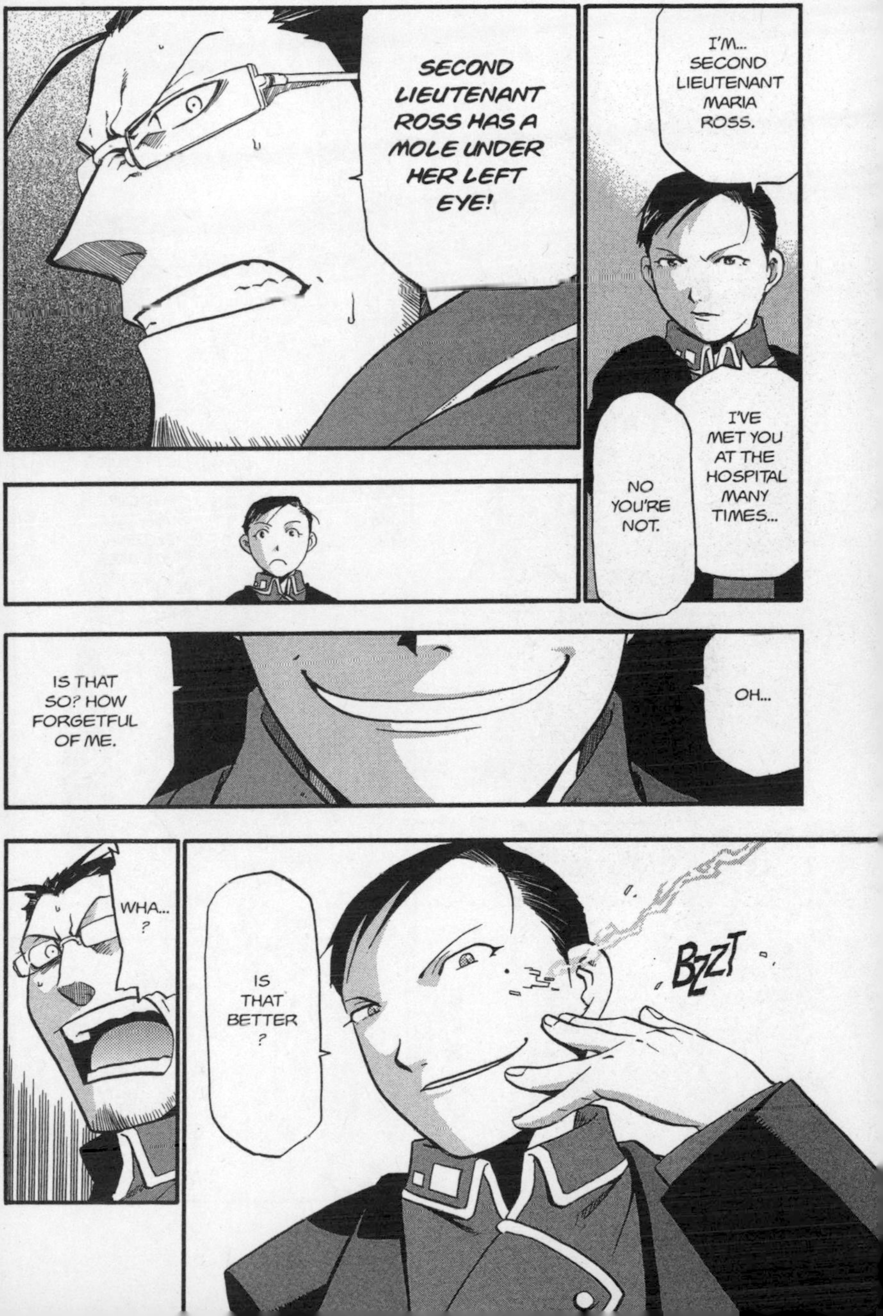
I'M... SECOND LIEUTENANT MARIA ROSS.
I'VE MET YOU AT THE HOSPITAL MANY TIMES...
NO YOU'RE NOT.
SECOND LIEUTENANT ROSS HAS A MOLE UNDER HER LEFT EYE!
OH...
IS THAT SO? HOW FORGETFUL OF ME.
IS THAT BETTER?
BZZT
WHA... ?

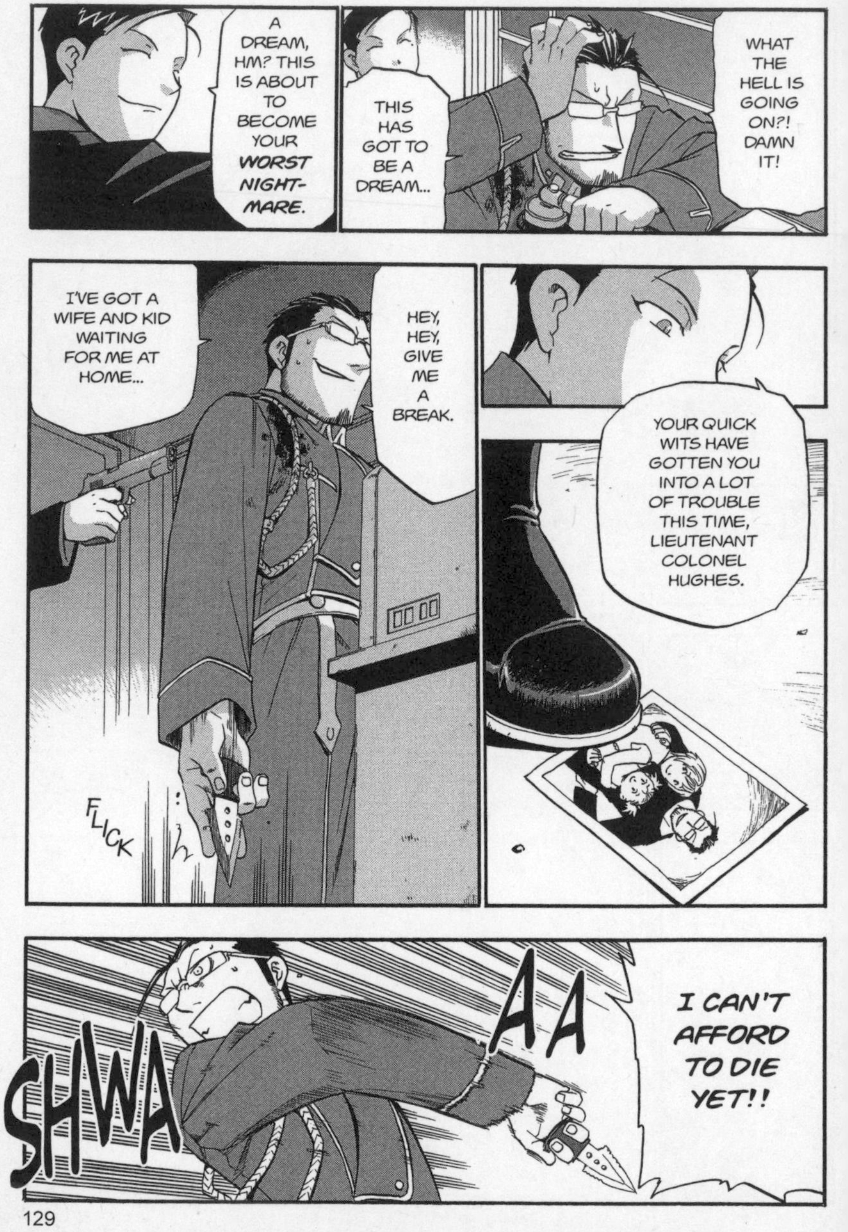
WHAT THE HELL IS GOING ON?! DAMN IT!
THIS HAS GOT TO BE A DREAM...
A DREAM, HM? THIS IS ABOUT TO BECOME YOUR WORST NIGHT-MARE.
YOUR QUICK WITS HAVE GOTTEN YOU INTO A LOT OF TROUBLE THIS TIME, LIEUTENANT COLONEL HUGHES.
HEY, HEY, GIVE ME A BREAK.
I'VE GOT A WIFE AND KID WAITING FOR ME AT HOME...
FLICK
I CAN'T AFFORD TO DIE YET!!
AA
SHWA

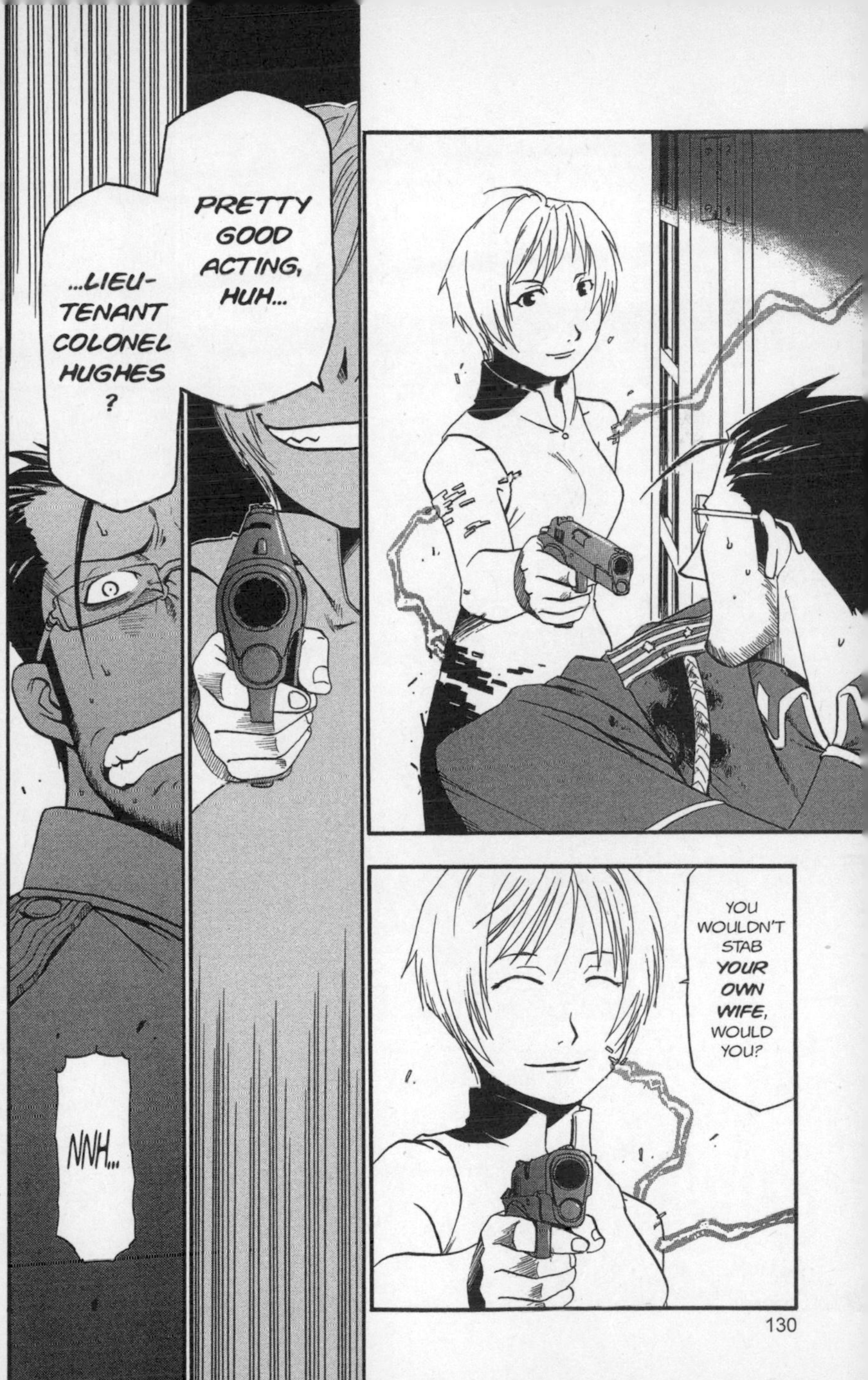
YOU WOULDN'T STAB **YOUR OWN WIFE**, WOULD YOU?
PRETTY GOOD ACTING, HUH...
...LIEU-TENANT COLONEL HUGHES?
NNH...

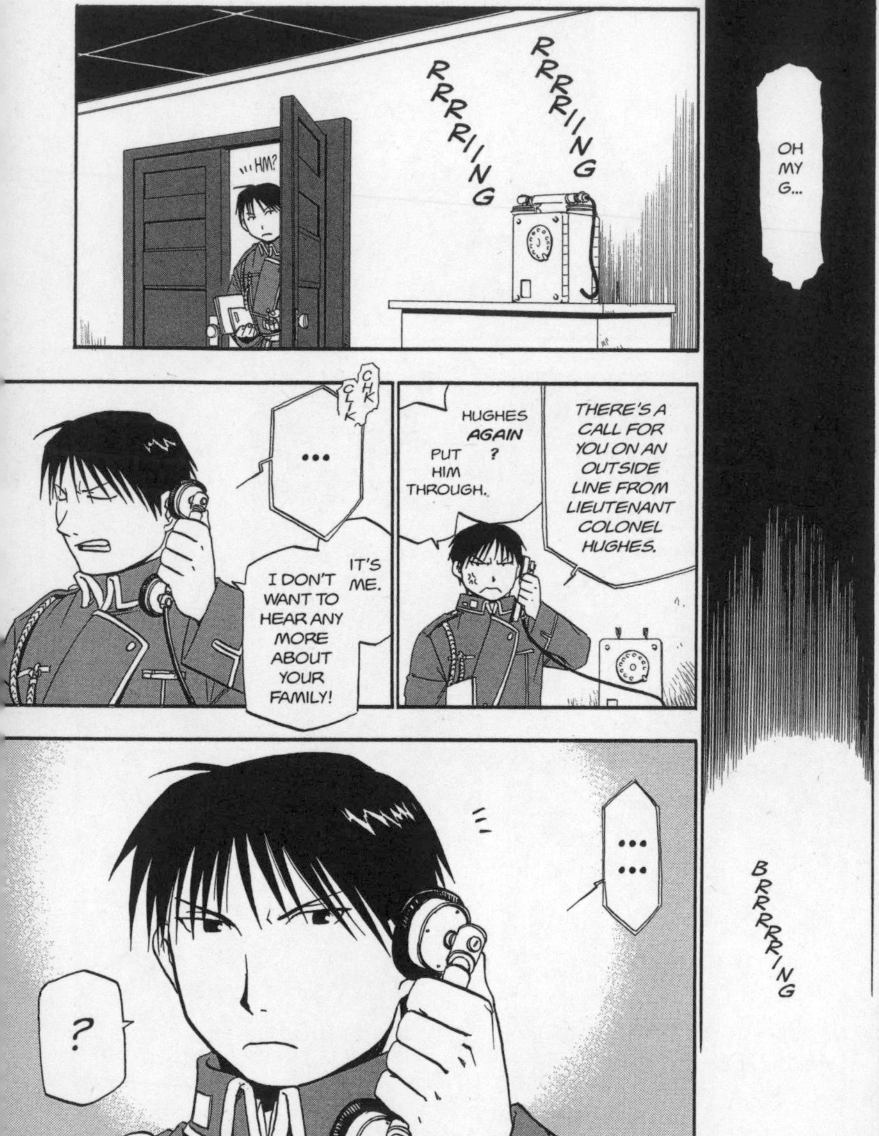

OH MY G...
BRRRRING
RRRRIIING
RRRRIIING
HM?
THERE'S A CALL FOR YOU ON AN OUTSIDE LINE FROM LIEUTENANT COLONEL HUGHES.
HUGHES AGAIN?
PUT HIM THROUGH.
CHK CLIK
...
IT'S ME.
I DON'T WANT TO HEAR ANY MORE ABOUT YOUR FAMILY!
... ...
?

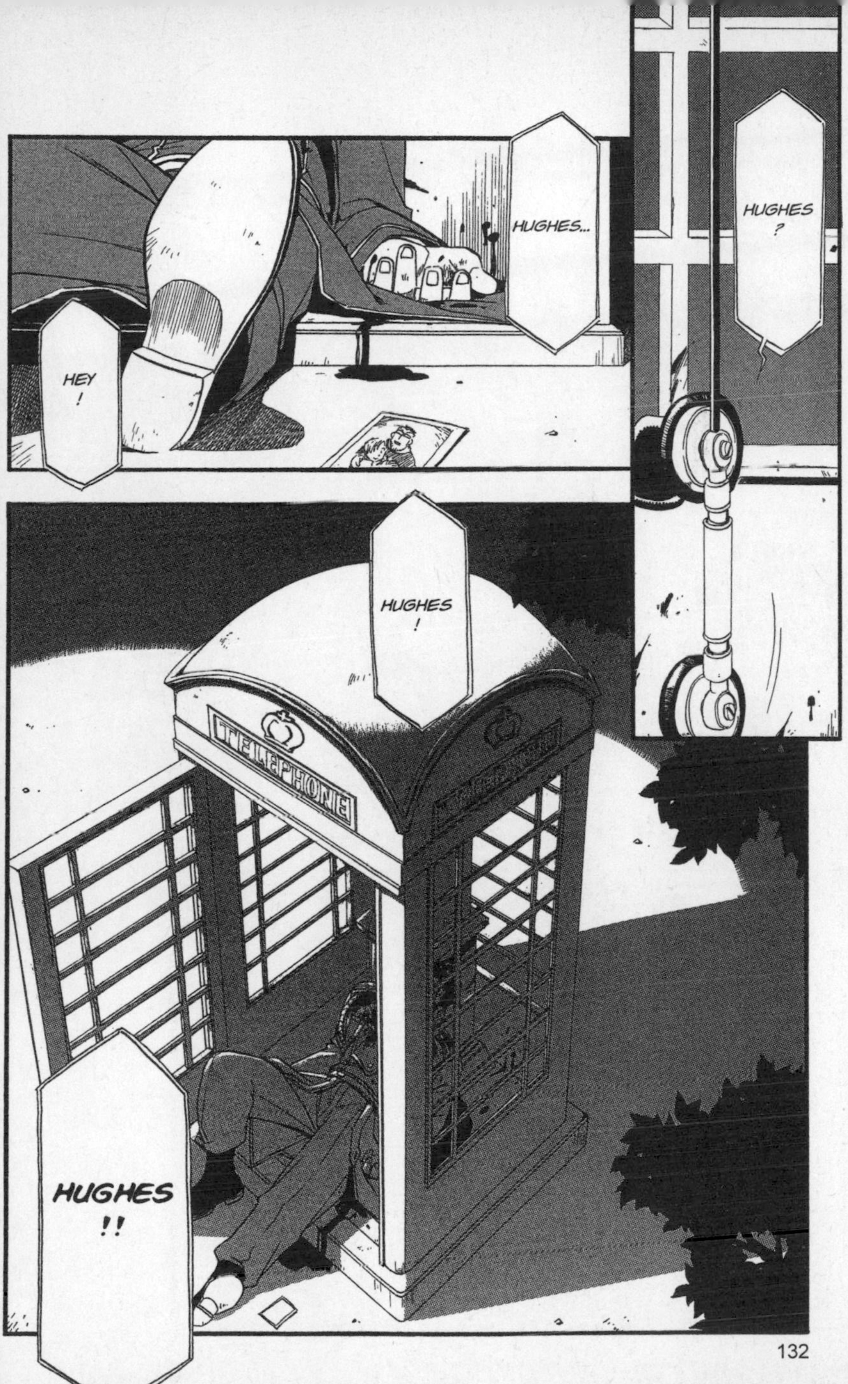
HUGHES ?
HUGHES...
HEY !
HUGHES !
TELEPHONE
HUGHES !!

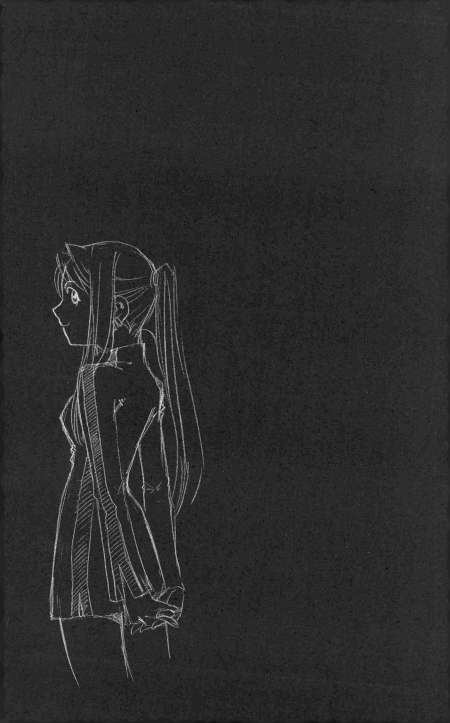

FULLMETAL
ALCHEMIST

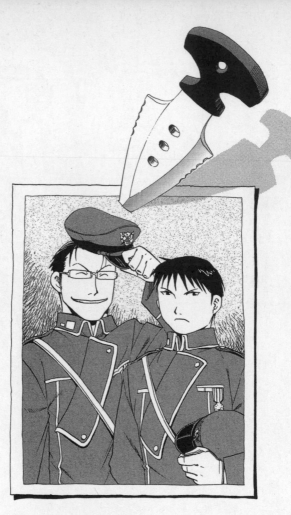

Chapter 16:
Separate Paths

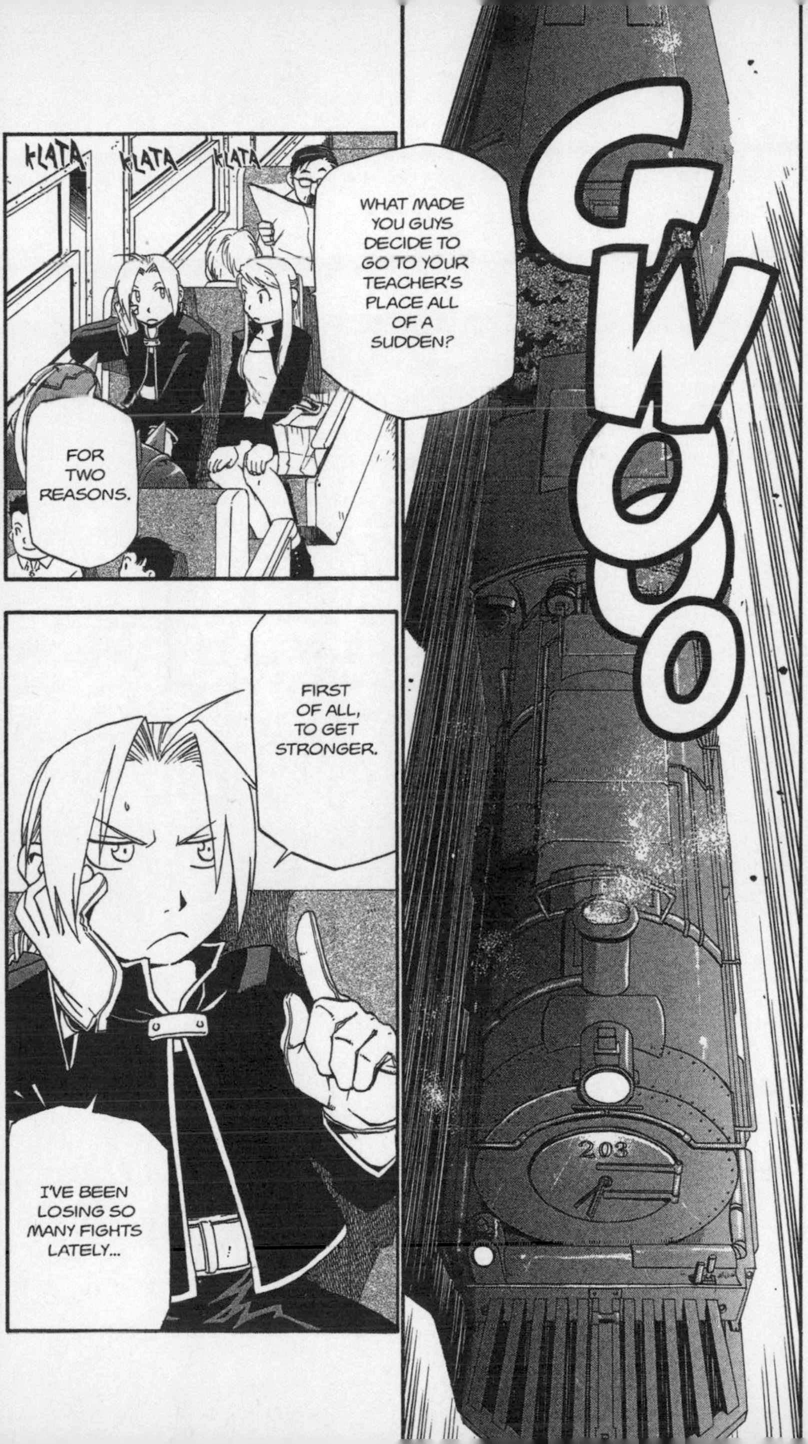
GWOOO
KLATA KLATA KLATA
WHAT MADE YOU GUYS DECIDE TO GO TO YOUR TEACHER'S PLACE ALL OF A SUDDEN?
FOR TWO REASONS.
FIRST OF ALL, TO GET STRONGER.
I'VE BEEN LOSING SO MANY FIGHTS LATELY...

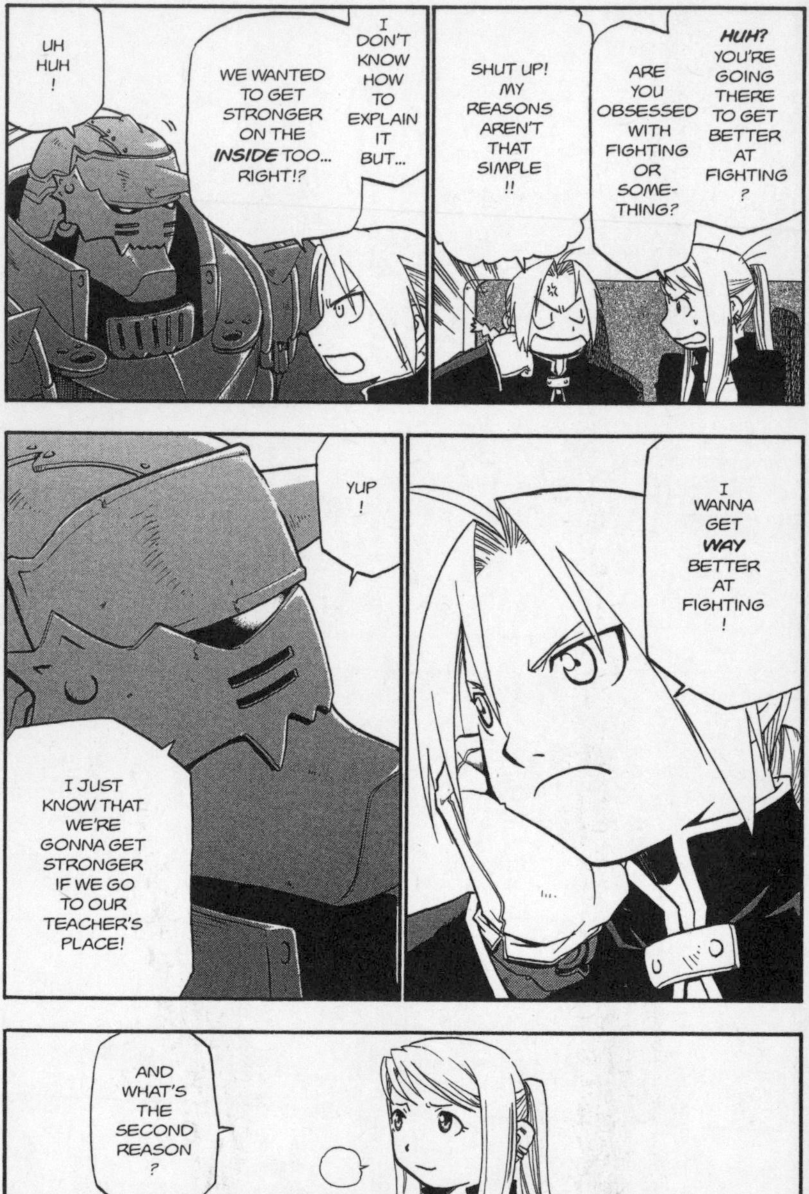
HUH? YOU'RE GOING THERE TO GET BETTER AT FIGHTING?
ARE YOU OBSESSED WITH FIGHTING OR SOME-THING?
SHUT UP! MY REASONS AREN'T THAT SIMPLE!!
I DON'T KNOW HOW TO EXPLAIN IT BUT...
WE WANTED TO GET STRONGER ON THE INSIDE TOO... RIGHT!?
UH HUH!
I WANNA GET WAY BETTER AT FIGHTING!
YUP!
I JUST KNOW THAT WE'RE GONNA GET STRONGER IF WE GO TO OUR TEACHER'S PLACE!
AND WHAT'S THE SECOND REASON?

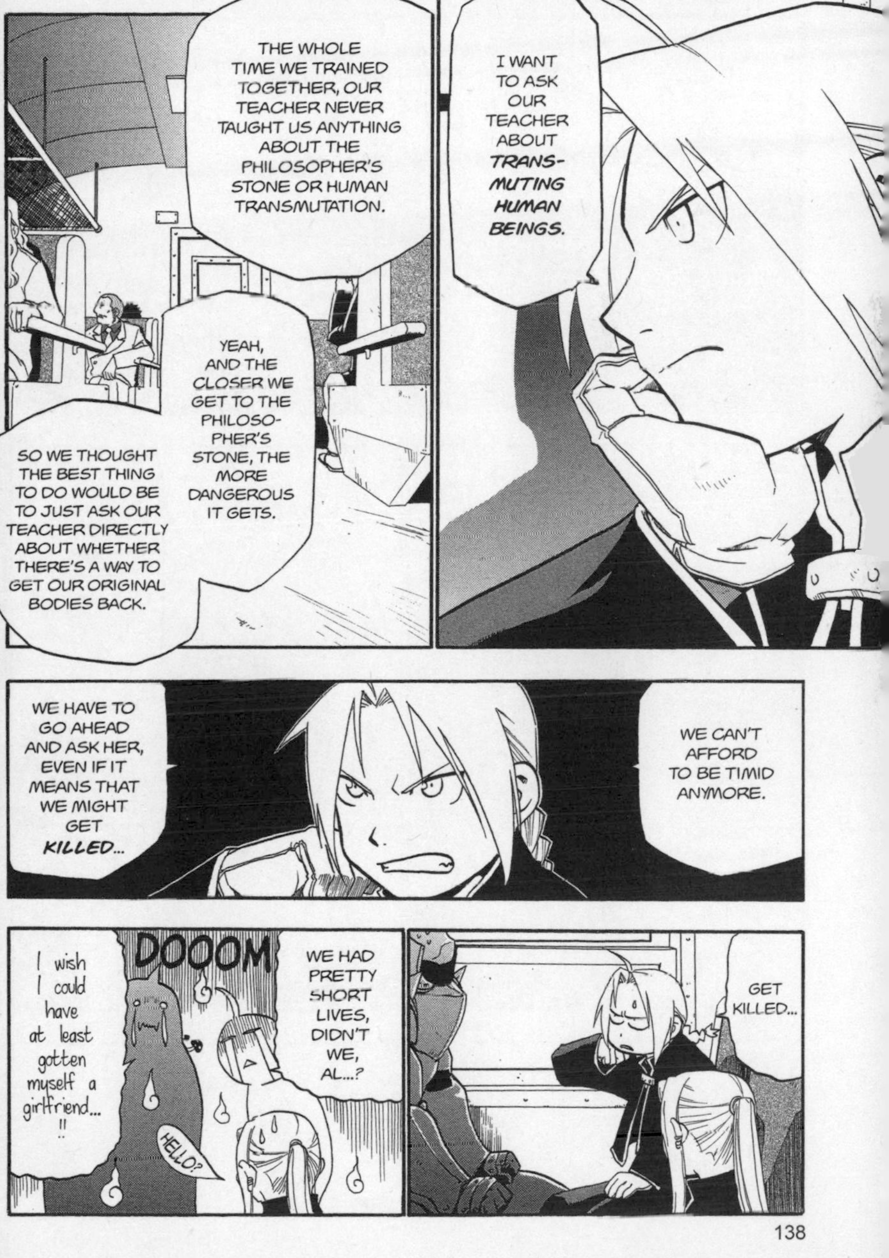
I WANT TO ASK OUR TEACHER ABOUT ***TRANS-MUTING HUMAN BEINGS.***
THE WHOLE TIME WE TRAINED TOGETHER, OUR TEACHER NEVER TAUGHT US ANYTHING ABOUT THE PHILOSOPHER'S STONE OR HUMAN TRANSMUTATION.
YEAH, AND THE CLOSER WE GET TO THE PHILOSO-PHER'S STONE, THE MORE DANGEROUS IT GETS.
SO WE THOUGHT THE BEST THING TO DO WOULD BE TO JUST ASK OUR TEACHER DIRECTLY ABOUT WHETHER THERE'S A WAY TO GET OUR ORIGINAL BODIES BACK.
WE CAN'T AFFORD TO BE TIMID ANYMORE.
WE HAVE TO GO AHEAD AND ASK HER, EVEN IF IT MEANS THAT WE MIGHT GET ***KILLED...***
GET KILLED...
DOOOM
WE HAD PRETTY SHORT LIVES, DIDN'T WE, AL...?
I wish I could have at least gotten myself a girlfriend...!!
HELLO?

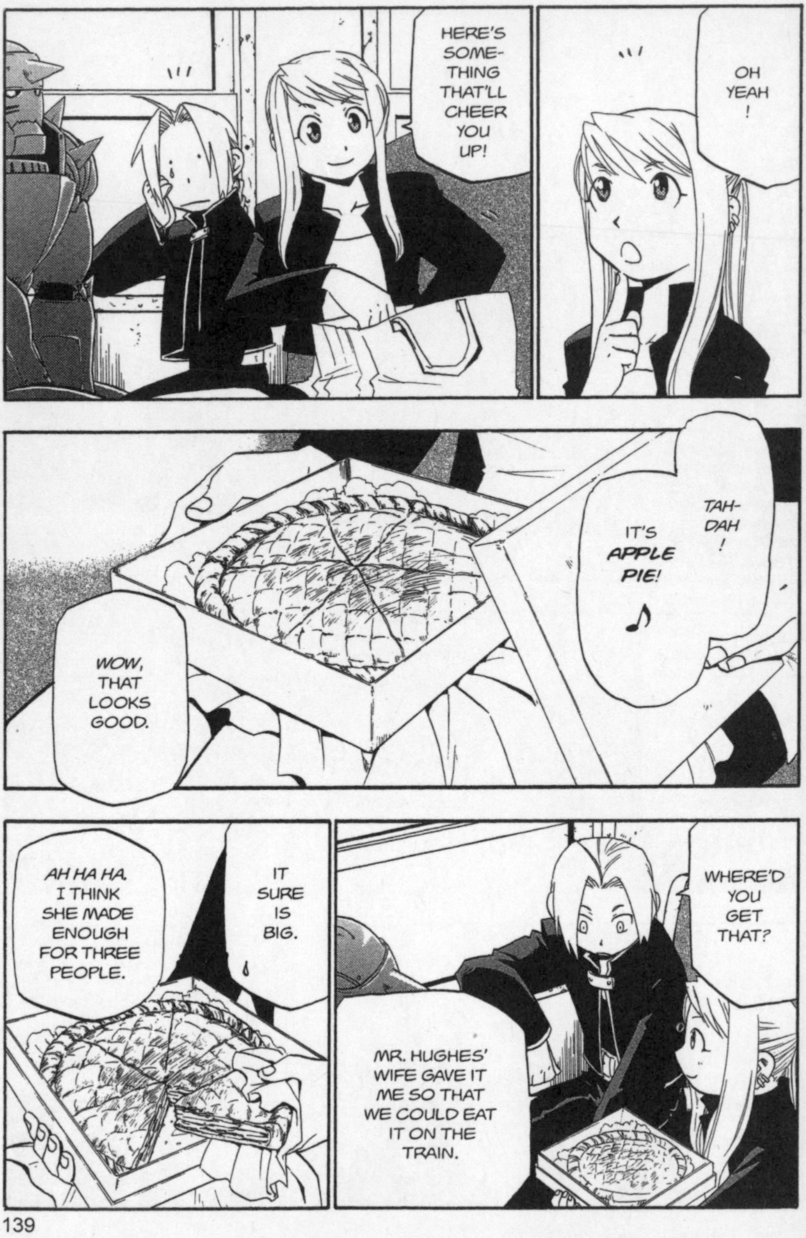
OH YEAH!
HERE'S SOMETHING THAT'LL CHEER YOU UP!
TAH-DAH!
IT'S *APPLE PIE!* ♪
WOW, THAT LOOKS GOOD.
WHERE'D YOU GET THAT?
MR. HUGHES' WIFE GAVE IT ME SO THAT WE COULD EAT IT ON THE TRAIN.
IT SURE IS BIG.
AH HA HA. I THINK SHE MADE ENOUGH FOR THREE PEOPLE.

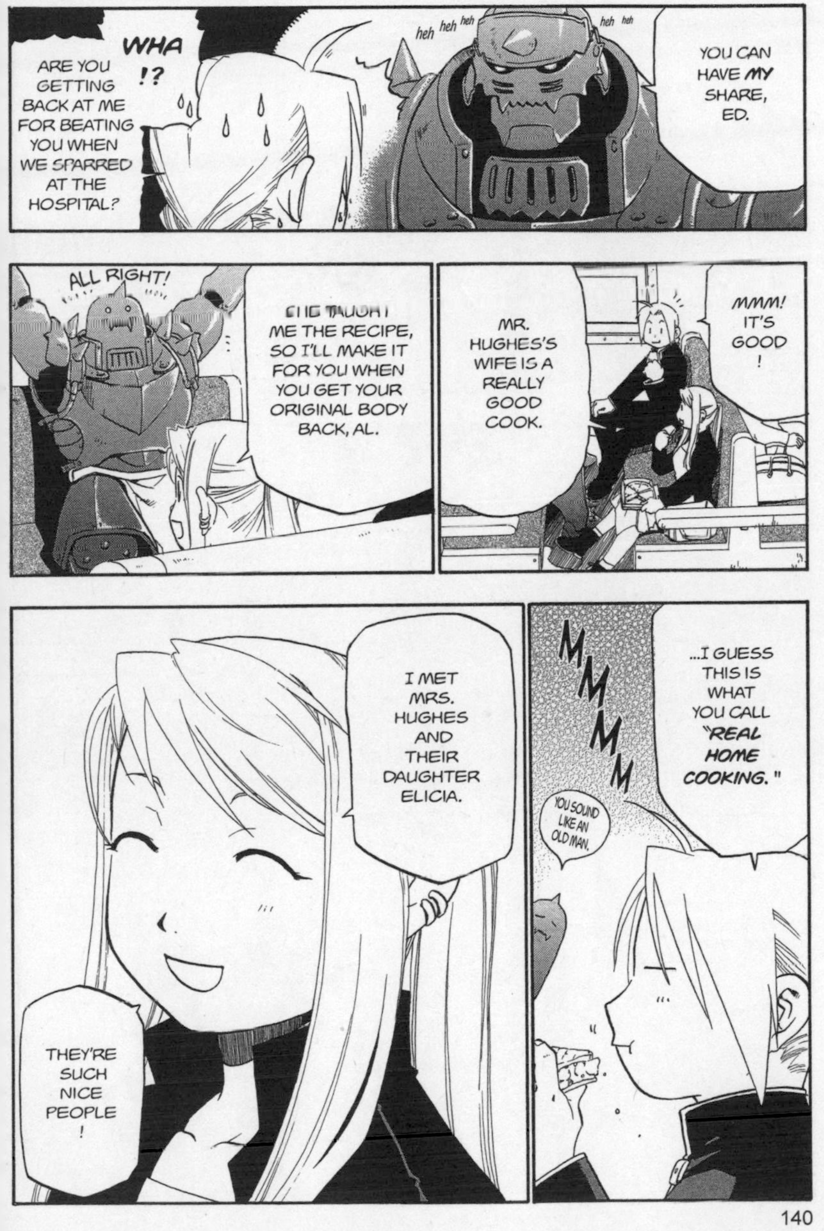
YOU CAN HAVE MY SHARE, ED.
heh heh heh
heh heh
WHA !?
ARE YOU GETTING BACK AT ME FOR BEATING YOU WHEN WE SPARRED AT THE HOSPITAL?
MMM! IT'S GOOD !
MR. HUGHES'S WIFE IS A REALLY GOOD COOK.
SHE TAUGHT ME THE RECIPE, SO I'LL MAKE IT FOR YOU WHEN YOU GET YOUR ORIGINAL BODY BACK, AL.
ALL RIGHT!
...I GUESS THIS IS WHAT YOU CALL "REAL HOME COOKING."
MMMM
YOU SOUND LIKE AN OLD MAN.
I MET MRS. HUGHES AND THEIR DAUGHTER ELICIA.
THEY'RE SUCH NICE PEOPLE !

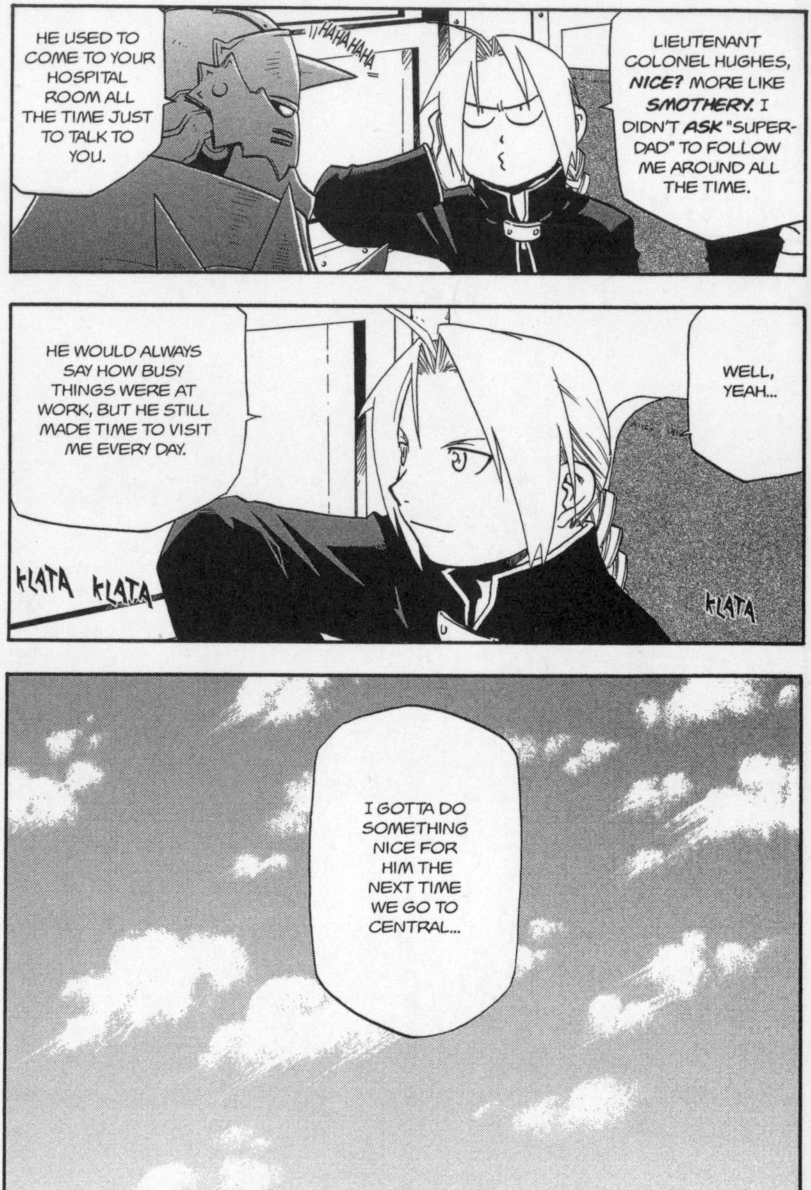

LIEUTENANT COLONEL HUGHES, **NICE?** MORE LIKE **SMOTHERY.** I DIDN'T **ASK** "SUPER-DAD" TO FOLLOW ME AROUND ALL THE TIME.
HAHAHAHA
HE USED TO COME TO YOUR HOSPITAL ROOM ALL THE TIME JUST TO TALK TO YOU.
WELL, YEAH...
HE WOULD ALWAYS SAY HOW BUSY THINGS WERE AT WORK, BUT HE STILL MADE TIME TO VISIT ME EVERY DAY.
KLATA
KLATA KLATA
I GOTTA DO SOMETHING NICE FOR HIM THE NEXT TIME WE GO TO CENTRAL...

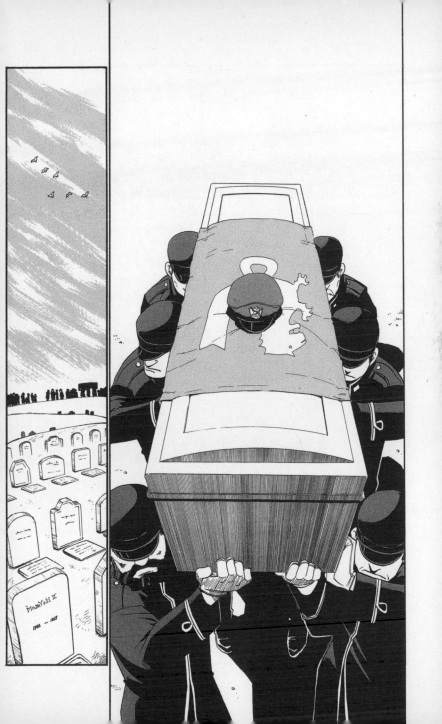

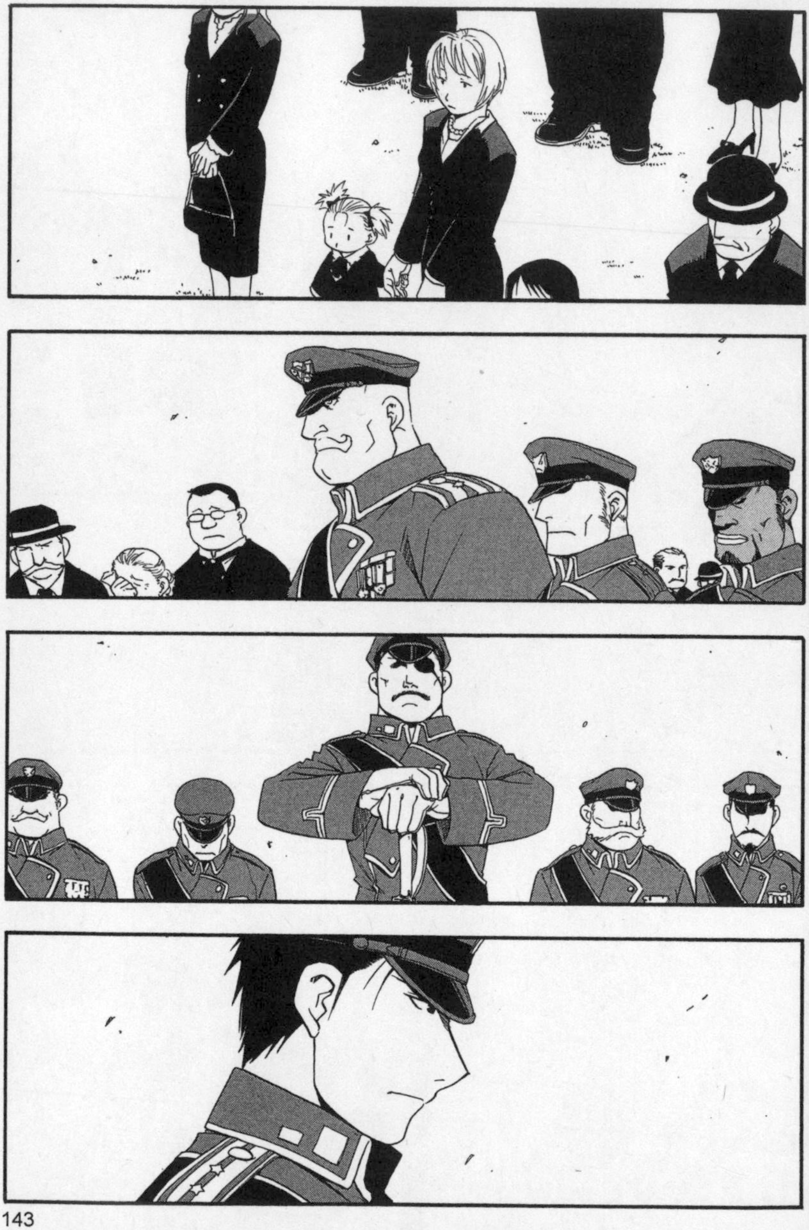

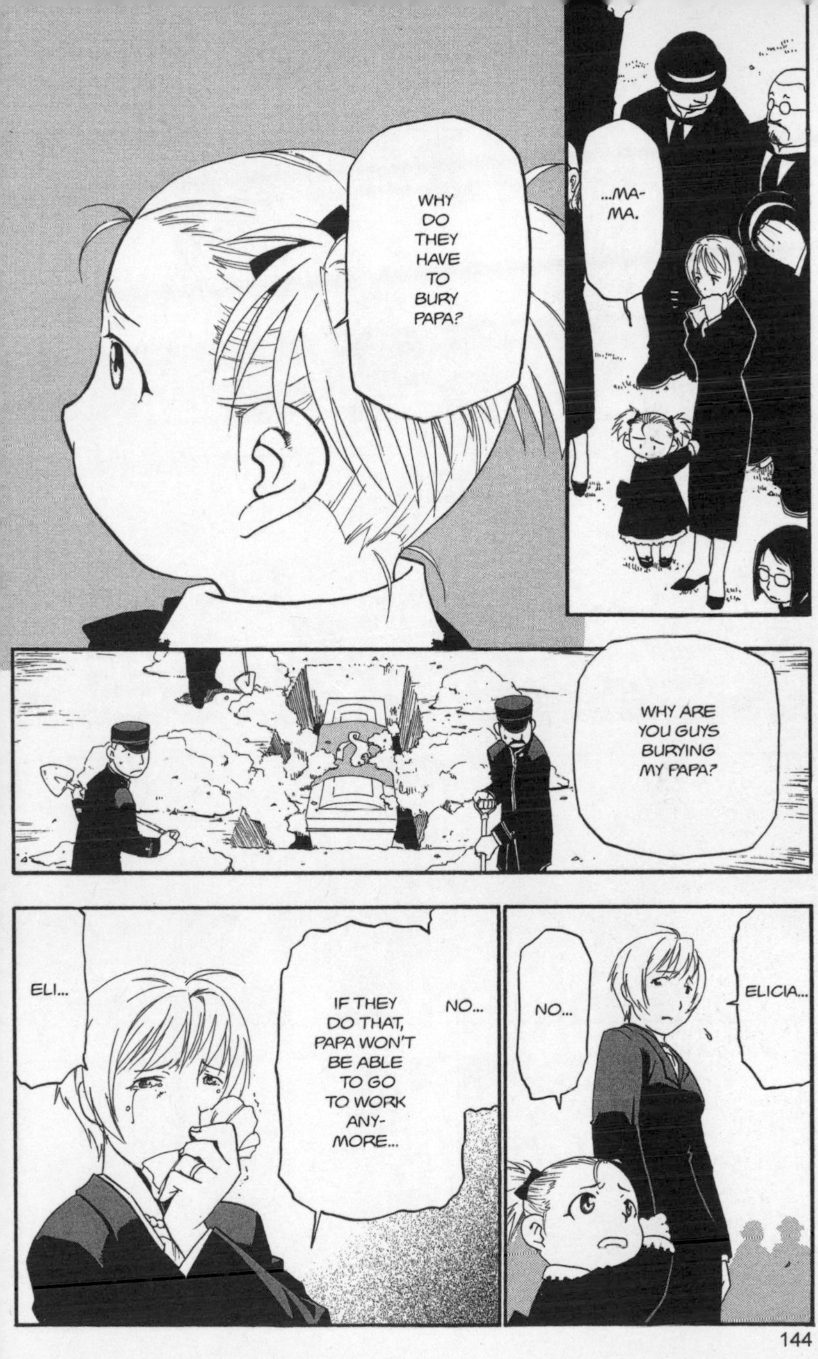
...MA-MA.
WHY DO THEY HAVE TO BURY PAPA?
WHY ARE YOU GUYS BURYING MY PAPA?
ELICIA...
NO...
NO...
IF THEY DO THAT, PAPA WON'T BE ABLE TO GO TO WORK ANY-MORE...
ELI...

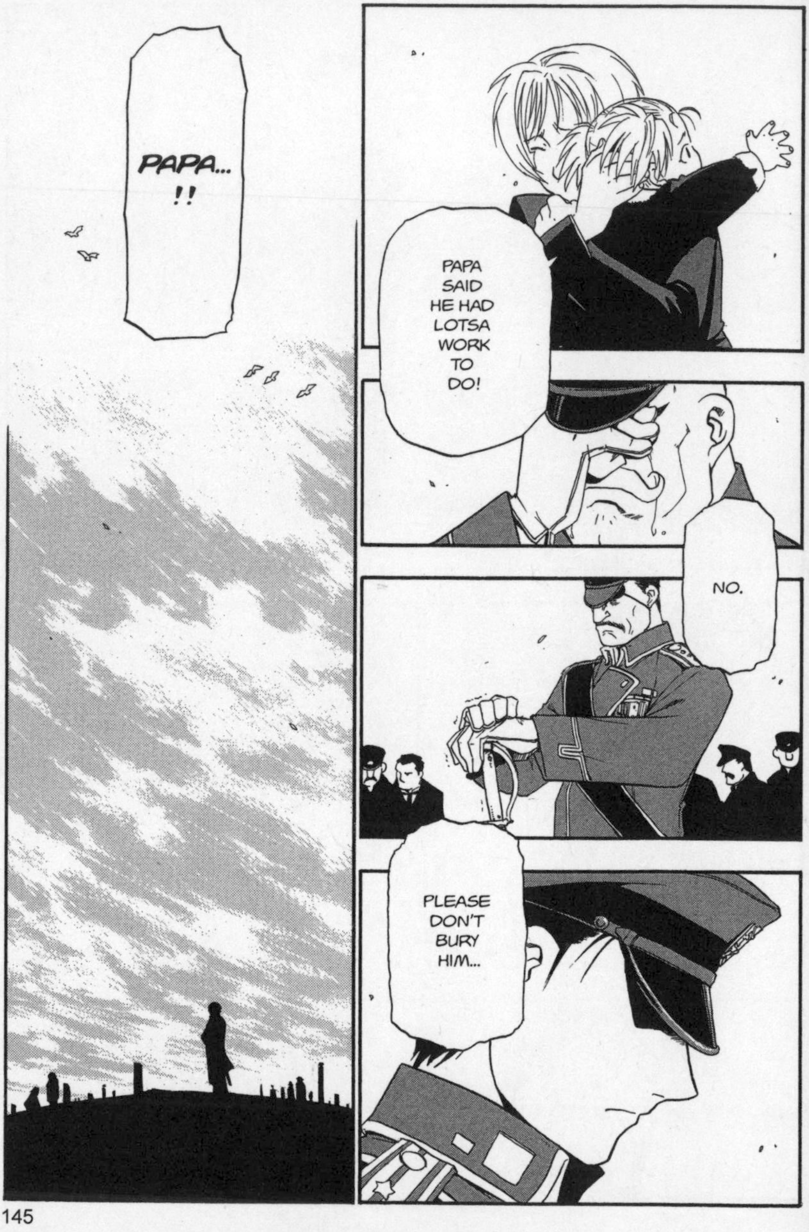
PAPA SAID HE HAD LOTSA WORK TO DO!
NO.
PLEASE DON'T BURY HIM...
PAPA... !!

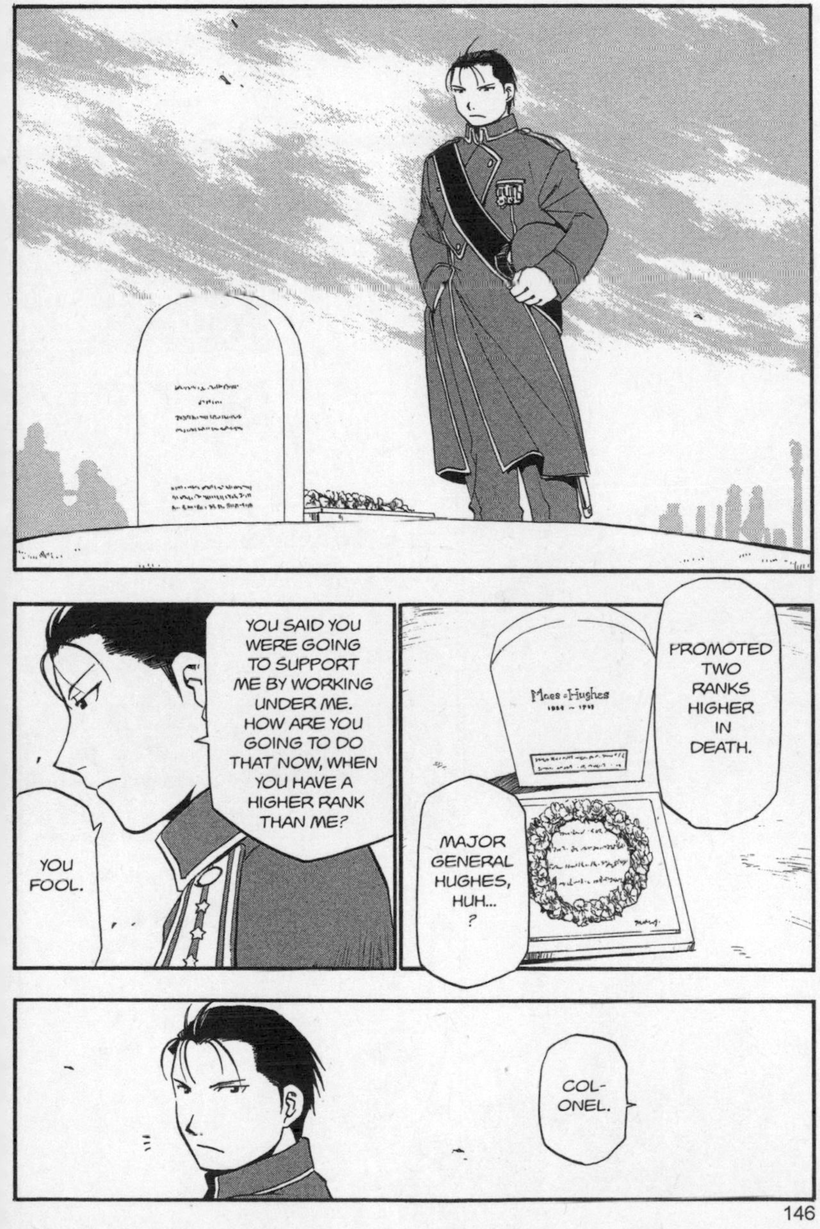
PROMOTED TWO RANKS HIGHER IN DEATH.
MAJOR GENERAL HUGHES, HUH...?
YOU SAID YOU WERE GOING TO SUPPORT ME BY WORKING UNDER ME. HOW ARE YOU GOING TO DO THAT NOW, WHEN YOU HAVE A HIGHER RANK THAN ME?
YOU FOOL.
COL-ONEL.

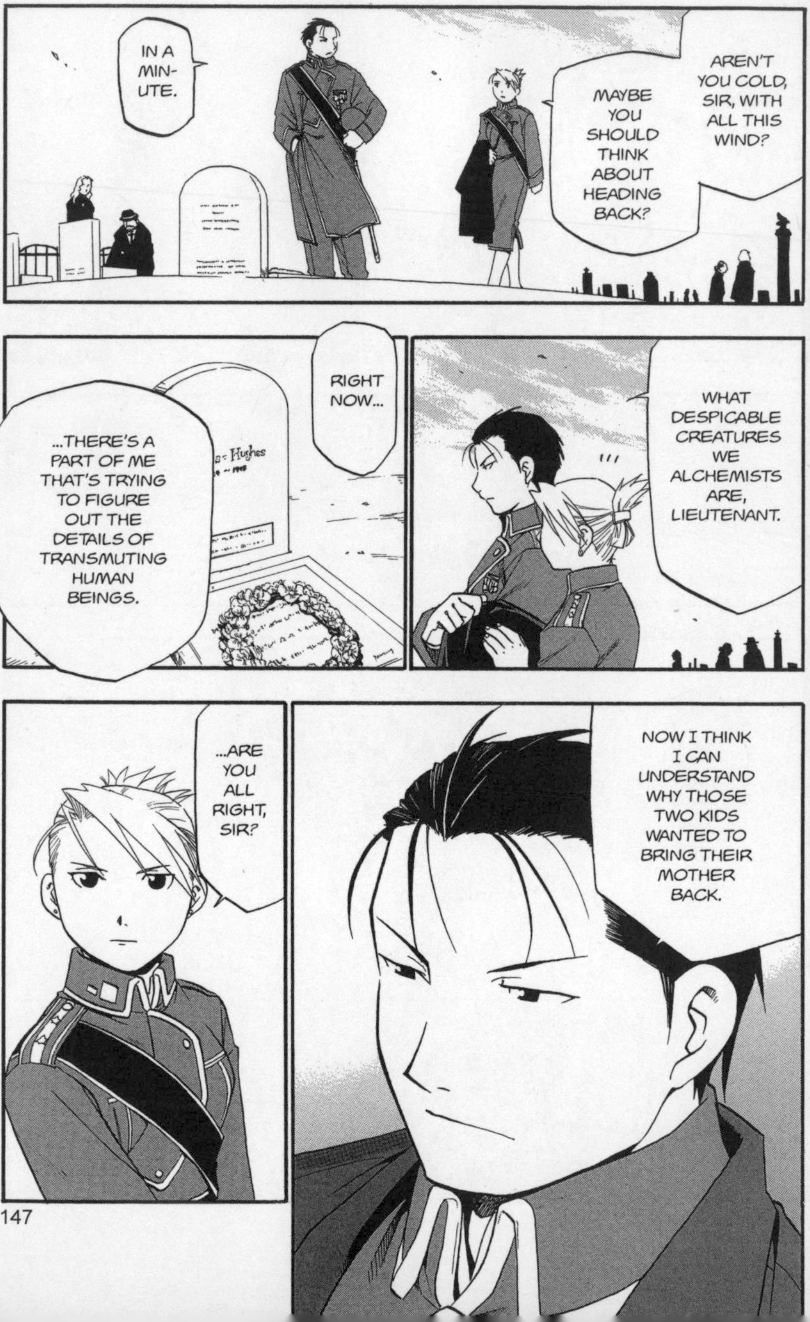
AREN'T YOU COLD, SIR, WITH ALL THIS WIND?
MAYBE YOU SHOULD THINK ABOUT HEADING BACK?
IN A MIN-UTE.
WHAT DESPICABLE CREATURES WE ALCHEMISTS ARE, LIEUTENANT.
RIGHT NOW...
...THERE'S A PART OF ME THAT'S TRYING TO FIGURE OUT THE DETAILS OF TRANSMUTING HUMAN BEINGS.
NOW I THINK I CAN UNDERSTAND WHY THOSE TWO KIDS WANTED TO BRING THEIR MOTHER BACK.
...ARE YOU ALL RIGHT, SIR?

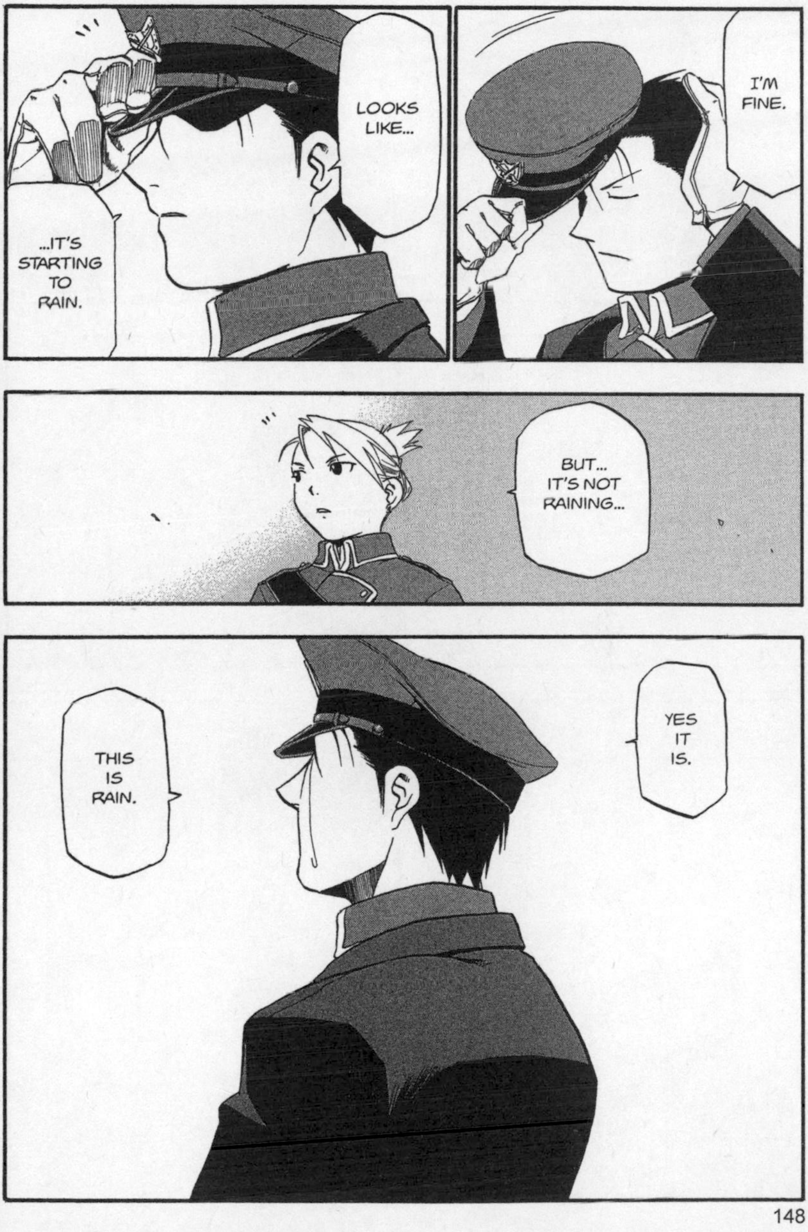
I'M FINE.
LOOKS LIKE...
...IT'S STARTING TO RAIN.
BUT... IT'S NOT RAINING...
YES IT IS.
THIS IS RAIN.

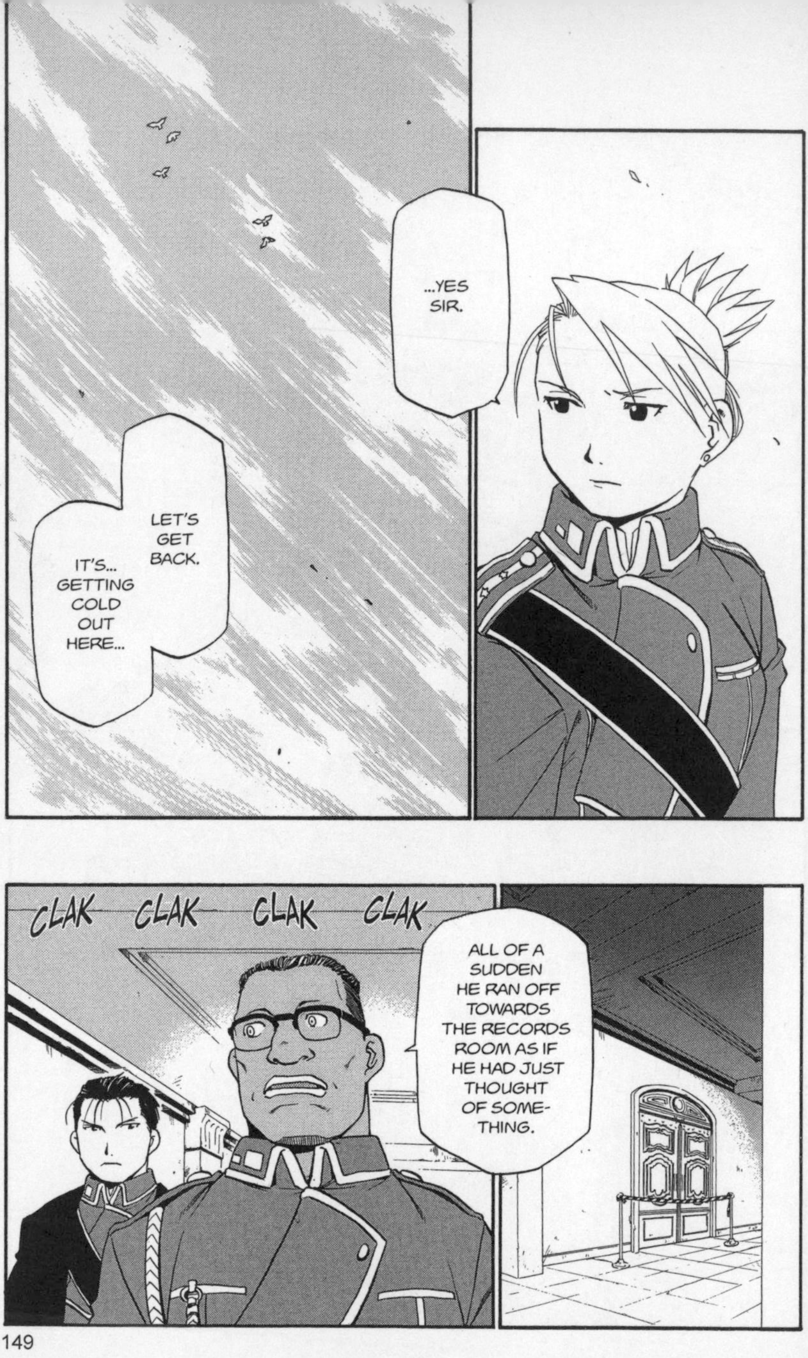
IT'S... GETTING COLD OUT HERE...
LET'S GET BACK.
...YES SIR.
CLAK CLAK CLAK CLAK
ALL OF A SUDDEN HE RAN OFF TOWARDS THE RECORDS ROOM AS IF HE HAD JUST THOUGHT OF SOME-THING.

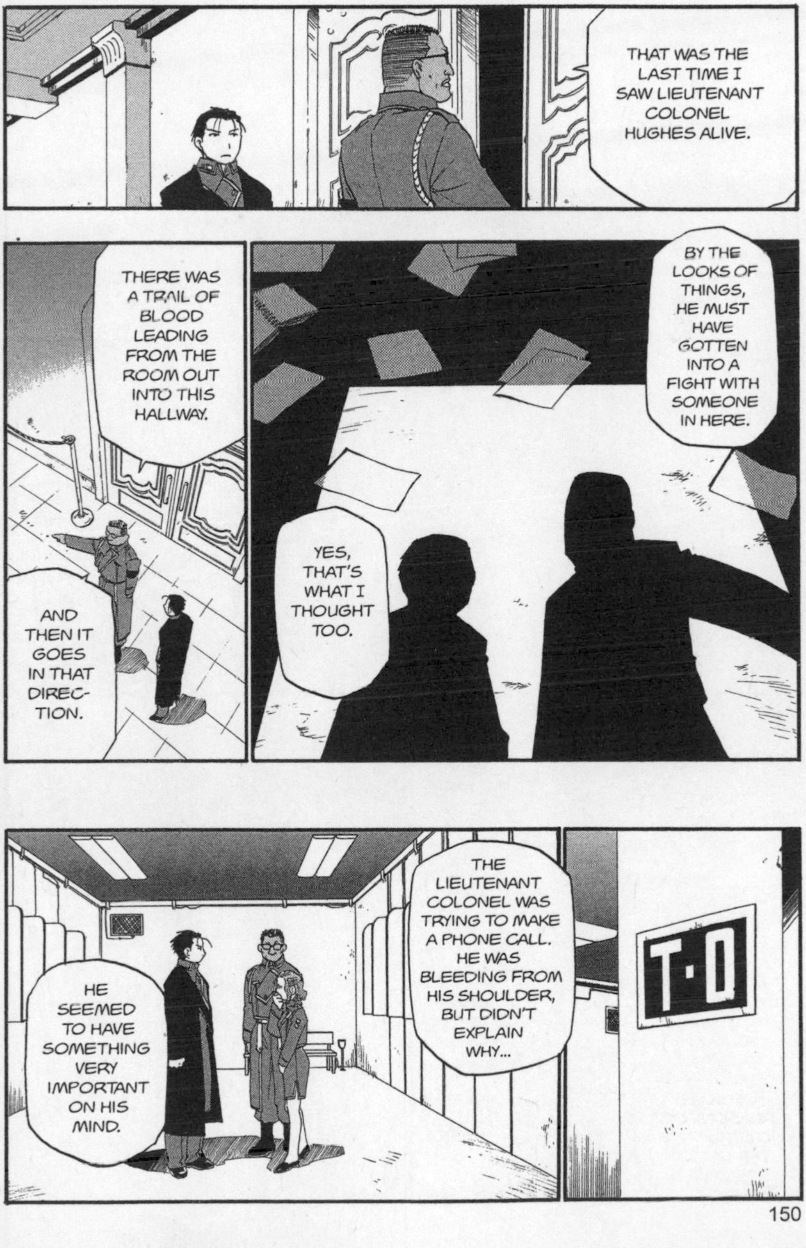
THAT WAS THE LAST TIME I SAW LIEUTENANT COLONEL HUGHES ALIVE.
BY THE LOOKS OF THINGS, HE MUST HAVE GOTTEN INTO A FIGHT WITH SOMEONE IN HERE.
YES, THAT'S WHAT I THOUGHT TOO.
THERE WAS A TRAIL OF BLOOD LEADING FROM THE ROOM OUT INTO THIS HALLWAY.
AND THEN IT GOES IN THAT DIREC-TION.
T·O
THE LIEUTENANT COLONEL WAS TRYING TO MAKE A PHONE CALL. HE WAS BLEEDING FROM HIS SHOULDER, BUT DIDN'T EXPLAIN WHY...
HE SEEMED TO HAVE SOMETHING VERY IMPORTANT ON HIS MIND.

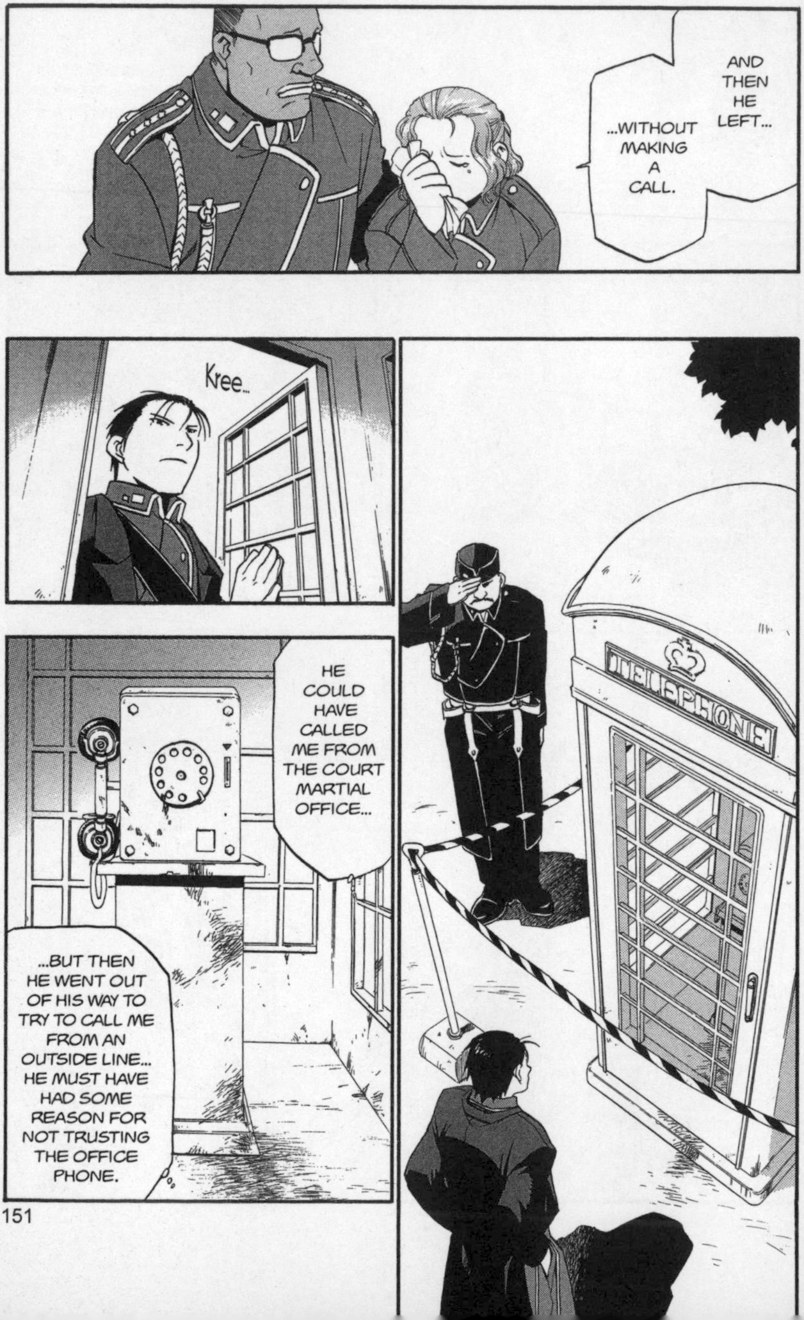
AND THEN HE LEFT...
...WITHOUT MAKING A CALL.
Kree...
HE COULD HAVE CALLED ME FROM THE COURT MARTIAL OFFICE...
...BUT THEN HE WENT OUT OF HIS WAY TO TRY TO CALL ME FROM AN OUTSIDE LINE... HE MUST HAVE HAD SOME REASON FOR NOT TRUSTING THE OFFICE PHONE.

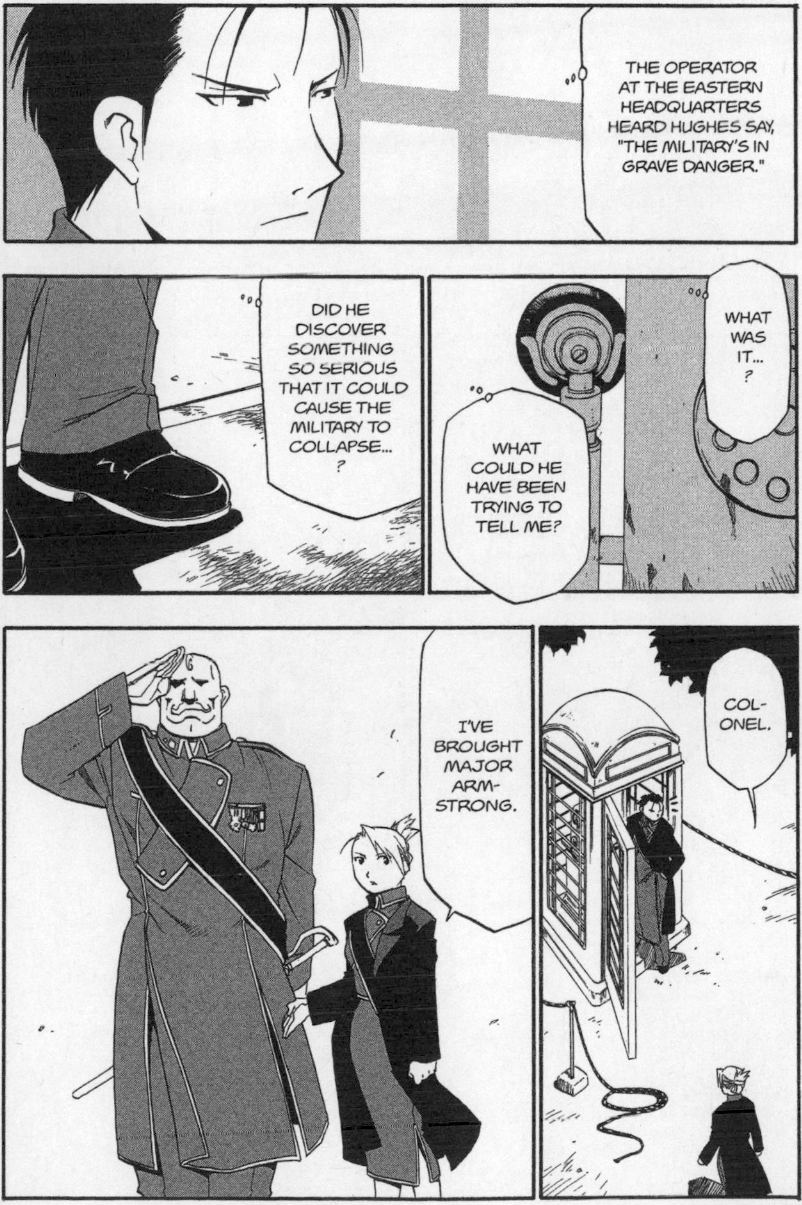
THE OPERATOR AT THE EASTERN HEADQUARTERS HEARD HUGHES SAY, "THE MILITARY'S IN GRAVE DANGER."
WHAT WAS IT... ?
WHAT COULD HE HAVE BEEN TRYING TO TELL ME?
DID HE DISCOVER SOMETHING SO SERIOUS THAT IT COULD CAUSE THE MILITARY TO COLLAPSE... ?
COL-ONEL.
I'VE BROUGHT MAJOR ARM-STRONG.

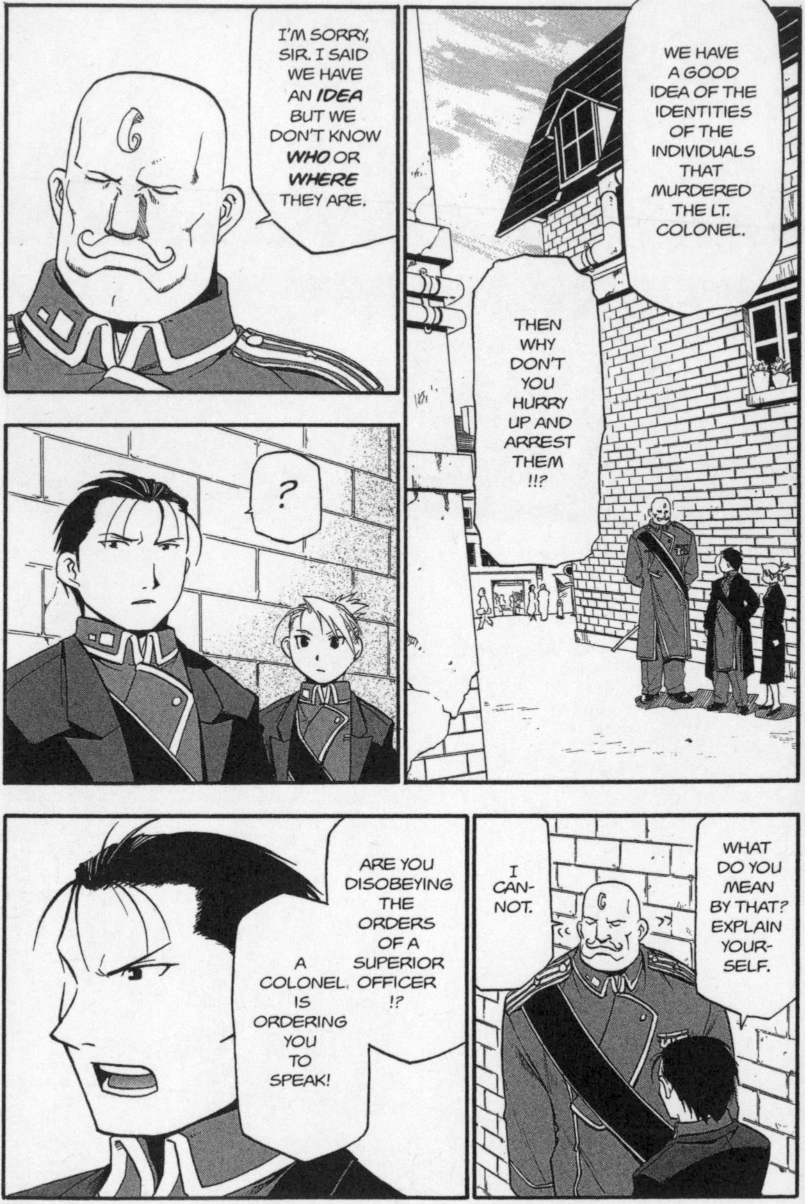
WE HAVE A GOOD IDEA OF THE IDENTITIES OF THE INDIVIDUALS THAT MURDERED THE LT. COLONEL.
THEN WHY DON'T YOU HURRY UP AND ARREST THEM!!?
I'M SORRY, SIR. I SAID WE HAVE AN **IDEA** BUT WE DON'T KNOW **WHO** OR **WHERE** THEY ARE.
?
WHAT DO YOU MEAN BY THAT? EXPLAIN YOURSELF.
I CAN-NOT.
ARE YOU DISOBEYING THE ORDERS OF A SUPERIOR OFFICER!?
A COLONEL IS ORDERING YOU TO SPEAK!

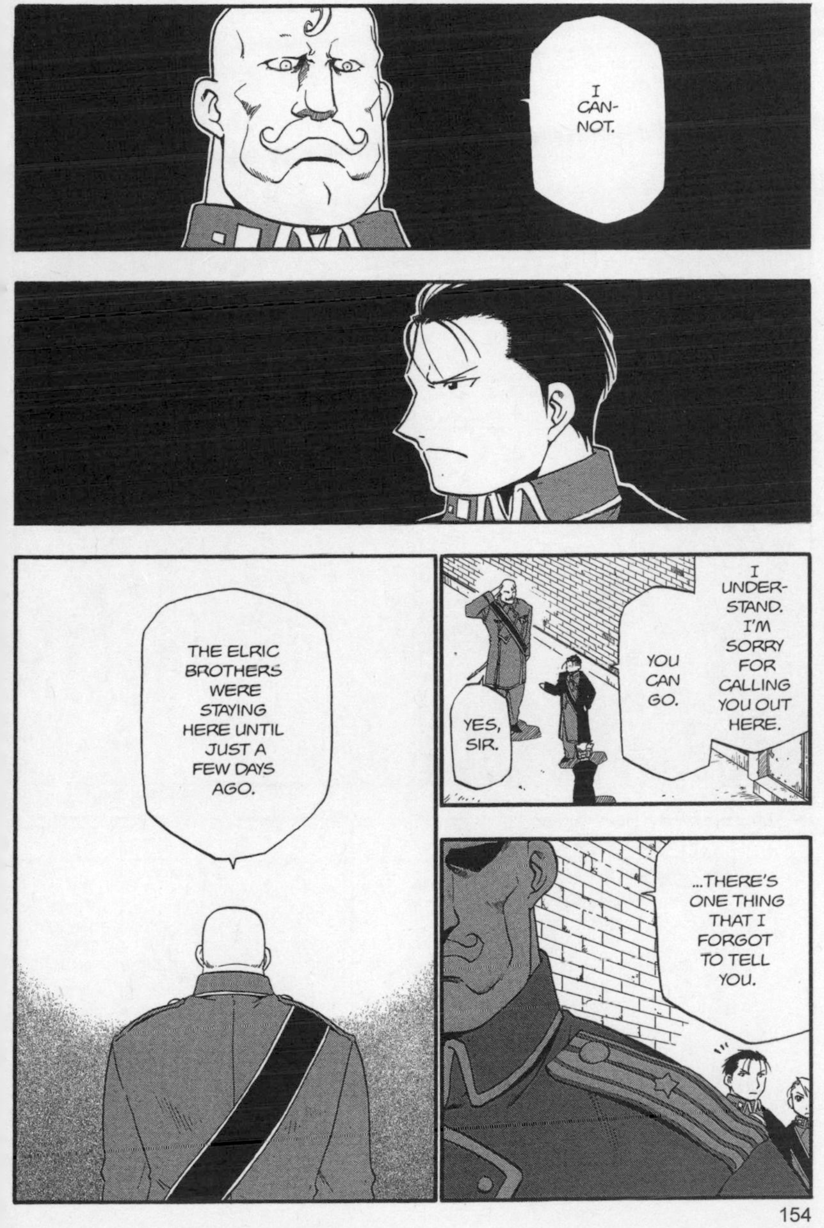
I CAN-NOT.
I UNDER-STAND. I'M SORRY FOR CALLING YOU OUT HERE.
YOU CAN GO.
YES, SIR.
...THERE'S ONE THING THAT I FORGOT TO TELL YOU.
THE ELRIC BROTHERS WERE STAYING HERE UNTIL JUST A FEW DAYS AGO.

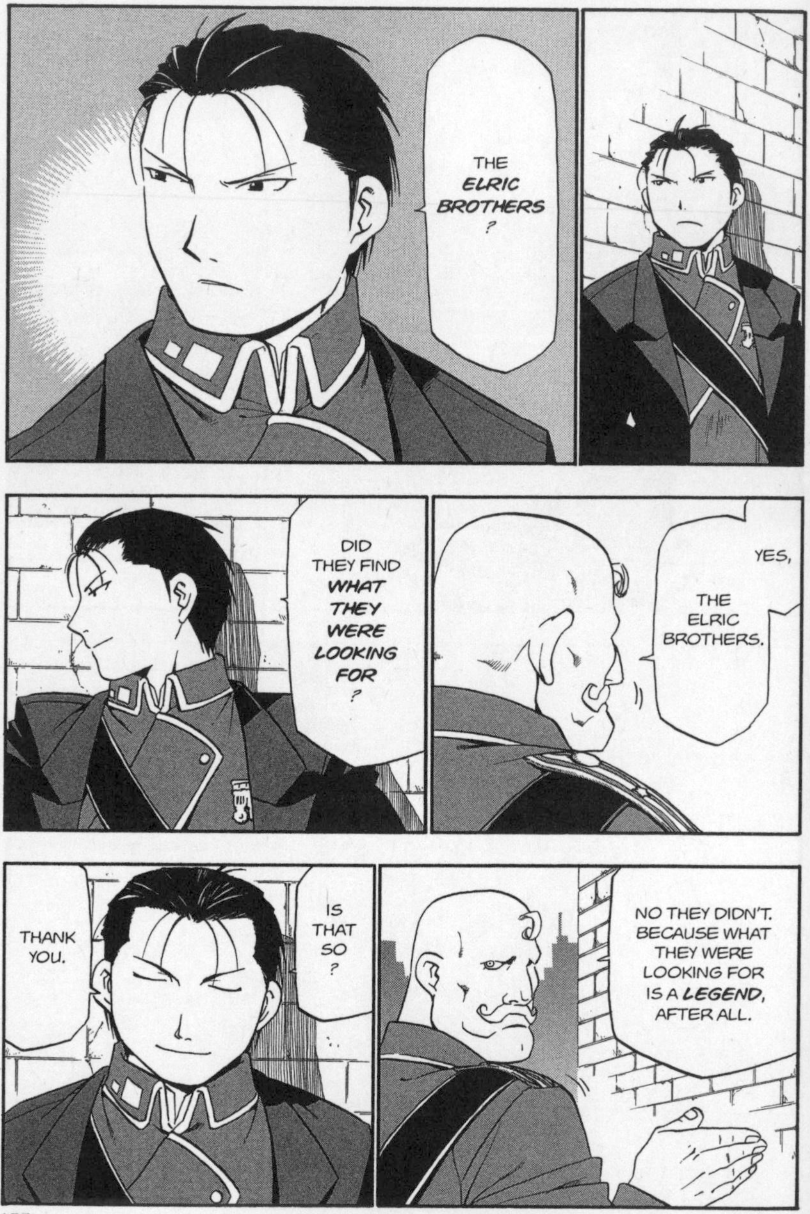
THE ELRIC BROTHERS?
YES,
THE ELRIC BROTHERS.
DID THEY FIND WHAT THEY WERE LOOKING FOR?
NO THEY DIDN'T. BECAUSE WHAT THEY WERE LOOKING FOR IS A LEGEND, AFTER ALL.
IS THAT SO?
THANK YOU.

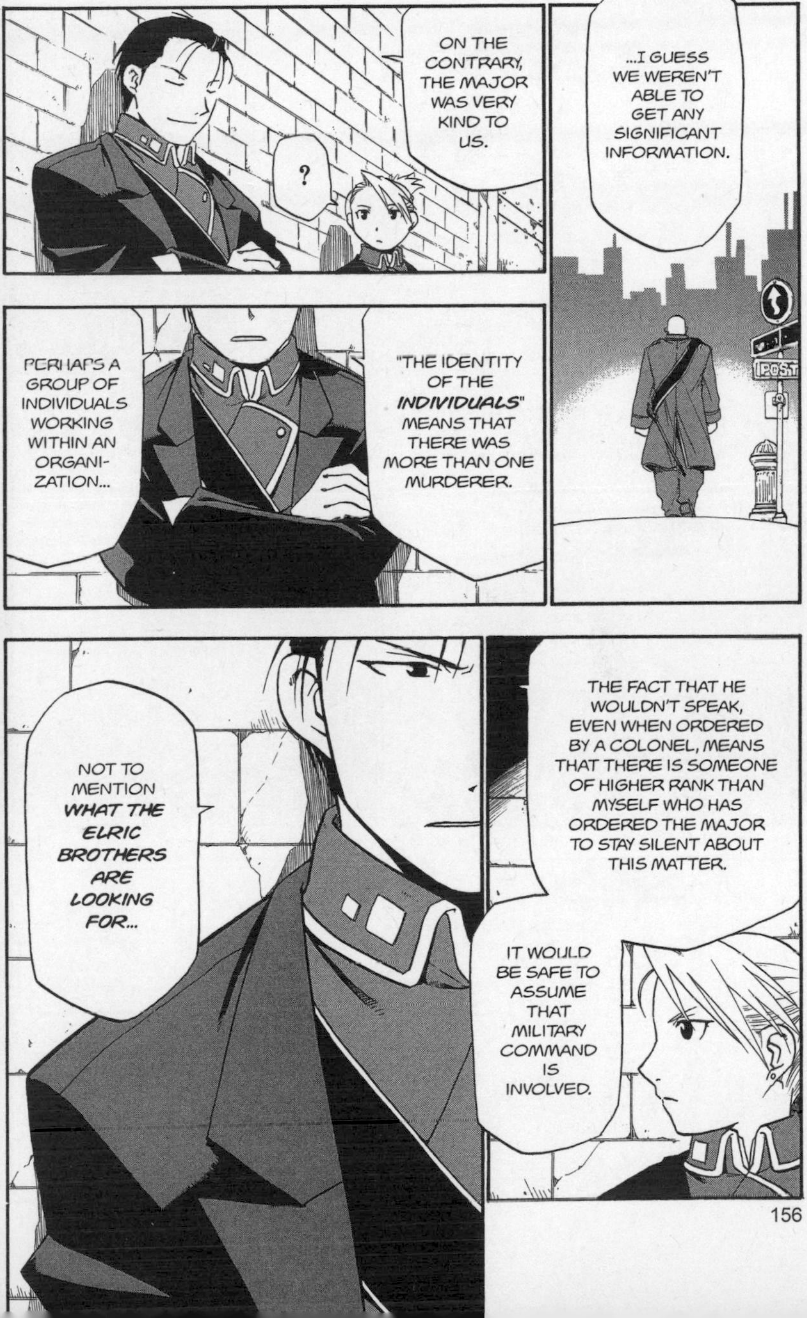

...I GUESS WE WEREN'T ABLE TO GET ANY SIGNIFICANT INFORMATION.
ON THE CONTRARY, THE MAJOR WAS VERY KIND TO US.
?
"THE IDENTITY OF THE *INDIVIDUALS*" MEANS THAT THERE WAS MORE THAN ONE MURDERER.
PERHAPS A GROUP OF INDIVIDUALS WORKING WITHIN AN ORGANI-ZATION...
THE FACT THAT HE WOULDN'T SPEAK, EVEN WHEN ORDERED BY A COLONEL, MEANS THAT THERE IS SOMEONE OF HIGHER RANK THAN MYSELF WHO HAS ORDERED THE MAJOR TO STAY SILENT ABOUT THIS MATTER.
IT WOULD BE SAFE TO ASSUME THAT MILITARY COMMAND IS INVOLVED.
NOT TO MENTION *WHAT THE ELRIC BROTHERS ARE LOOKING FOR...*

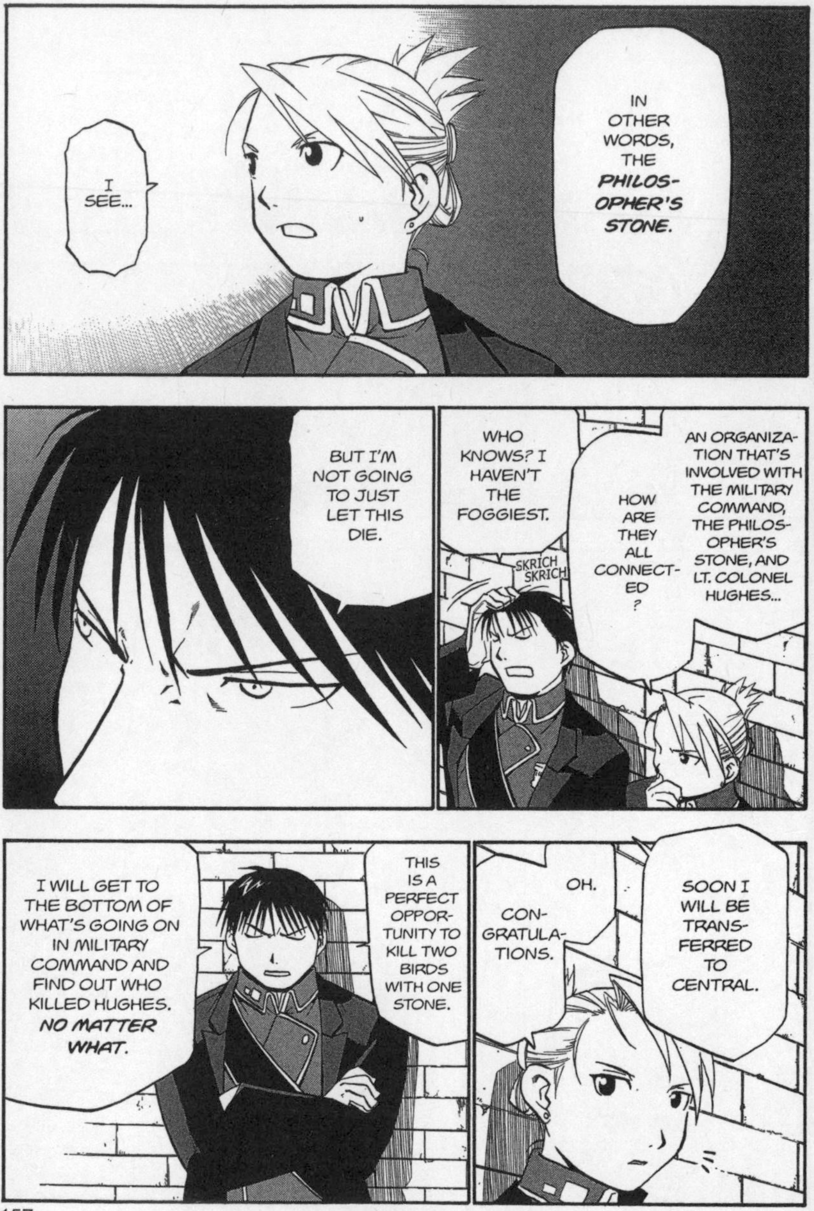
IN OTHER WORDS, THE *PHILOSOPHER'S STONE.*
I SEE...
AN ORGANIZATION THAT'S INVOLVED WITH THE MILITARY COMMAND, THE PHILOSOPHER'S STONE, AND LT. COLONEL HUGHES...
HOW ARE THEY ALL CONNECTED?
WHO KNOWS? I HAVEN'T THE FOGGIEST.
SKRICH SKRICH
BUT I'M NOT GOING TO JUST LET THIS DIE.
SOON I WILL BE TRANSFERRED TO CENTRAL.
OH.
CONGRATULATIONS.
THIS IS A PERFECT OPPORTUNITY TO KILL TWO BIRDS WITH ONE STONE.
I WILL GET TO THE BOTTOM OF WHAT'S GOING ON IN MILITARY COMMAND AND FIND OUT WHO KILLED HUGHES. *NO MATTER WHAT.*

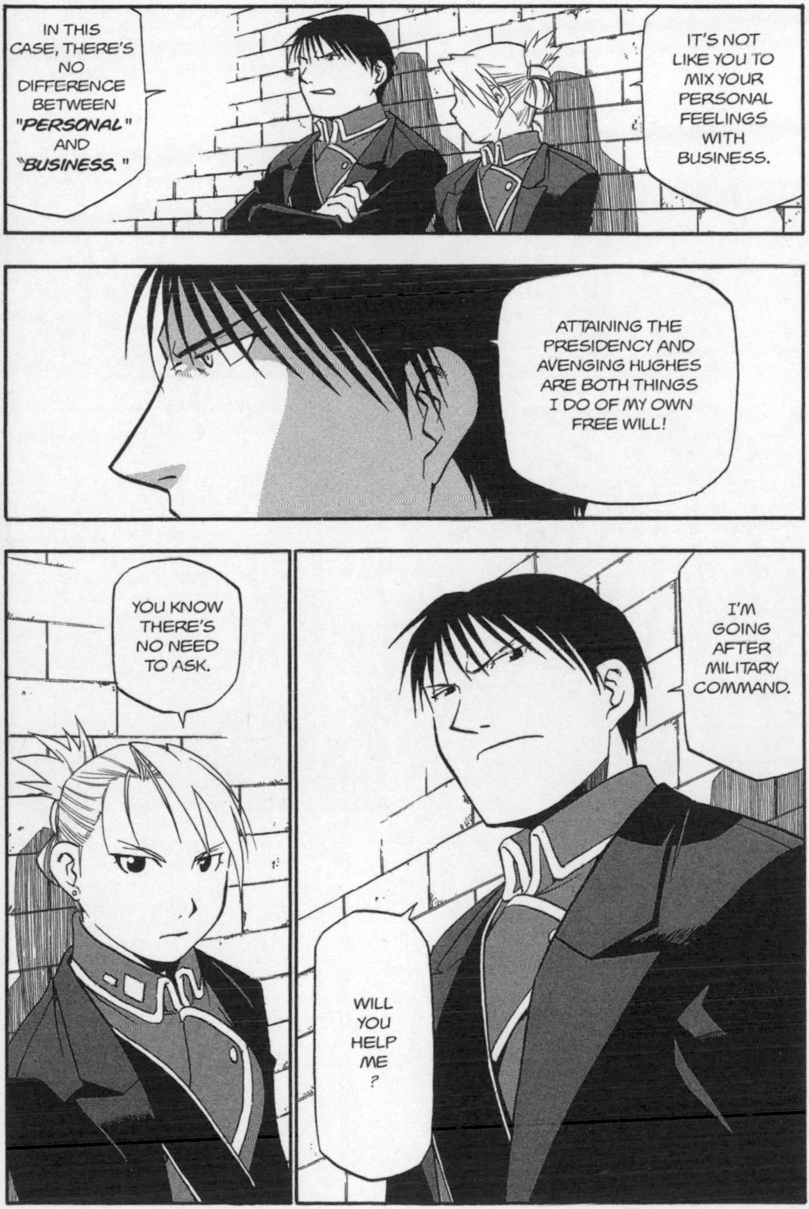
IT'S NOT LIKE YOU TO MIX YOUR PERSONAL FEELINGS WITH BUSINESS.
IN THIS CASE, THERE'S NO DIFFERENCE BETWEEN "PERSONAL" AND "BUSINESS."
ATTAINING THE PRESIDENCY AND AVENGING HUGHES ARE BOTH THINGS I DO OF MY OWN FREE WILL!
I'M GOING AFTER MILITARY COMMAND.
WILL YOU HELP ME?
YOU KNOW THERE'S NO NEED TO ASK.

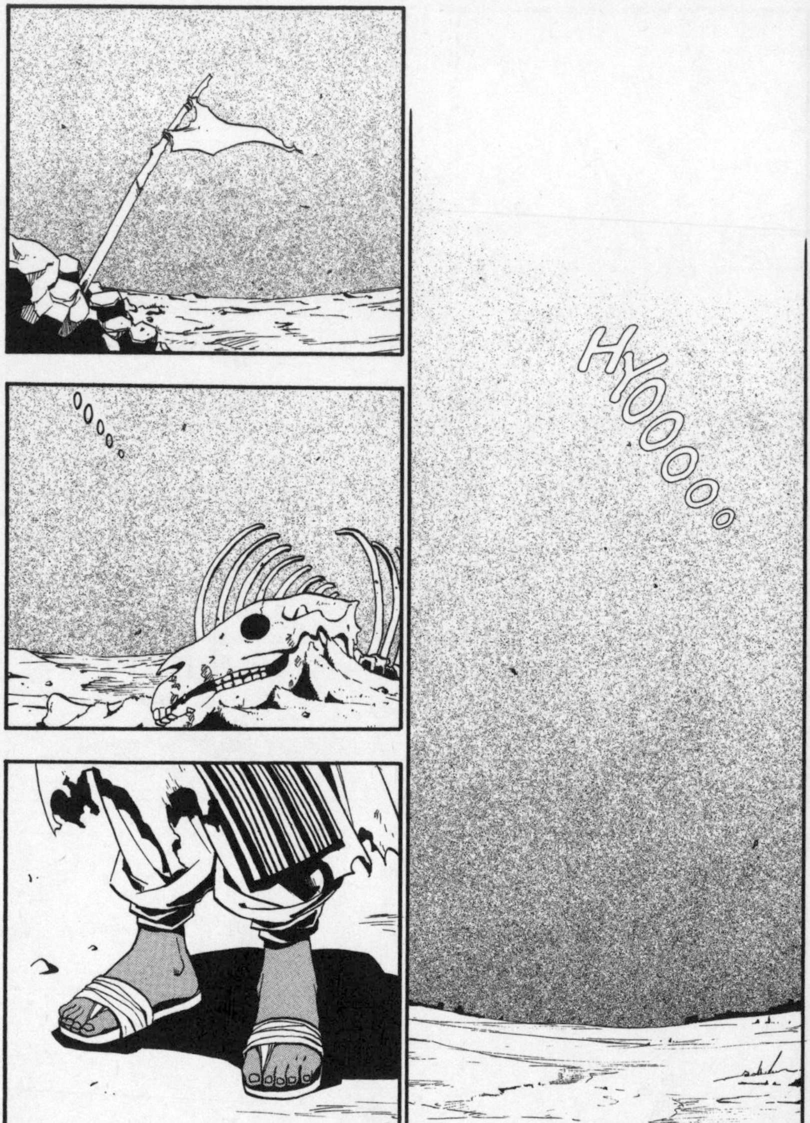
HYOOOOO
OOOOO

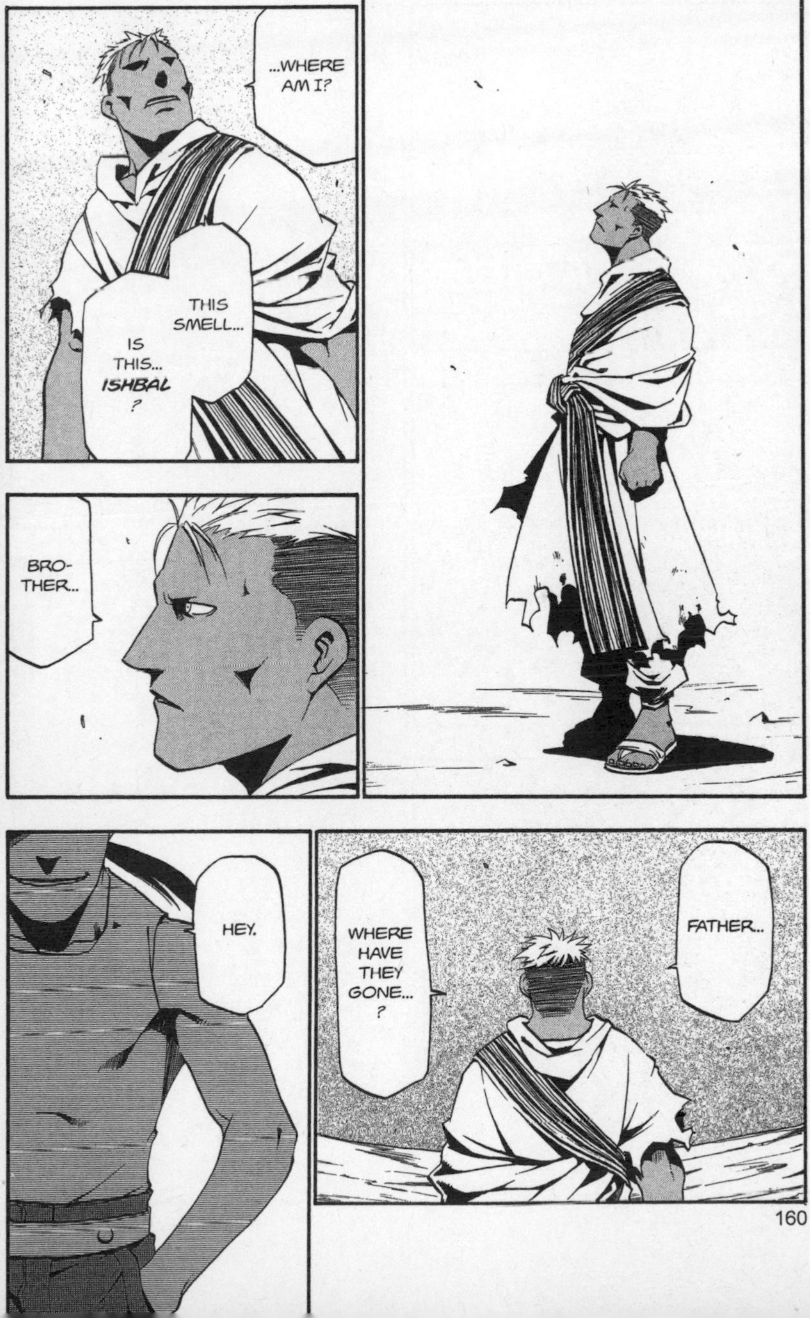
...WHERE AM I?
THIS SMELL...
IS THIS... ISHBAL?
BRO-THER...
FATHER...
WHERE HAVE THEY GONE...?
HEY.

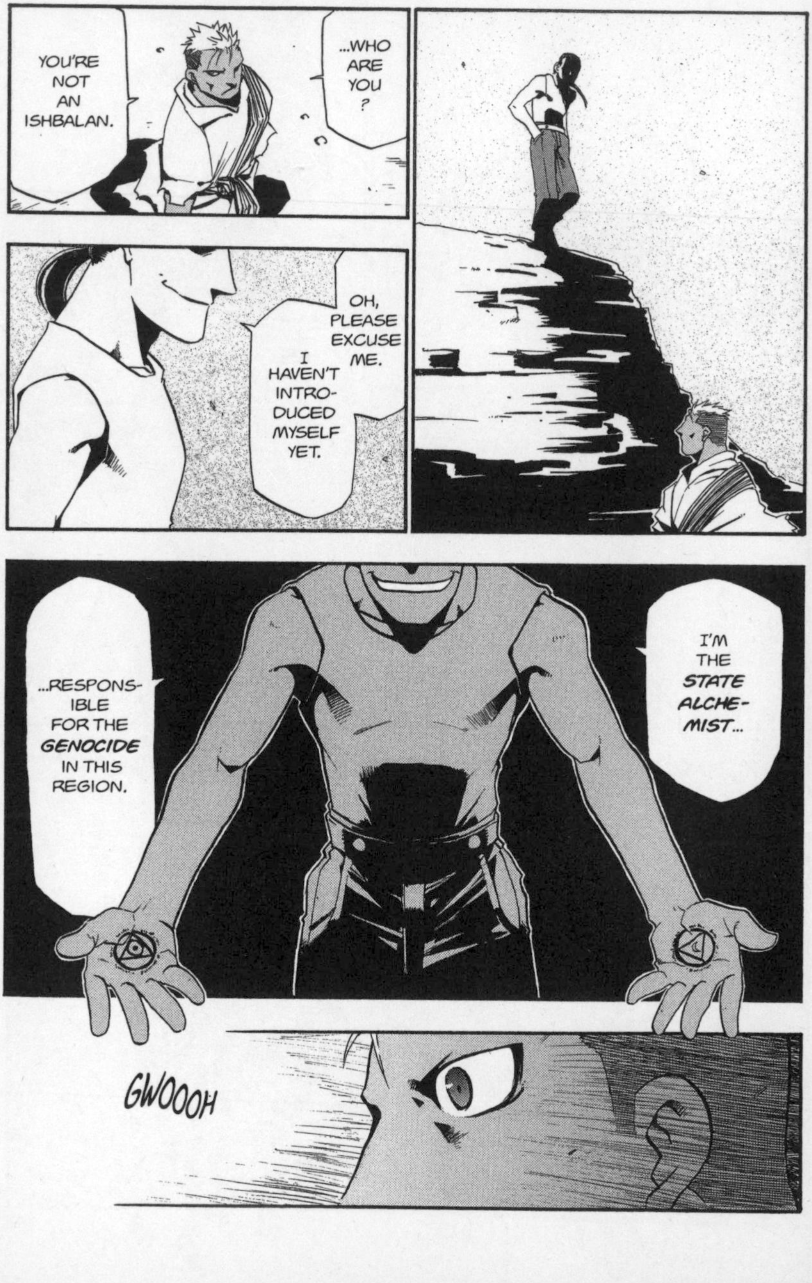
...WHO ARE YOU ?
YOU'RE NOT AN ISHBALAN.
OH, PLEASE EXCUSE ME.
I HAVEN'T INTRODUCED MYSELF YET.
I'M THE *STATE ALCHEMIST*...
...RESPONSIBLE FOR THE *GENOCIDE* IN THIS REGION.
GWOOOH

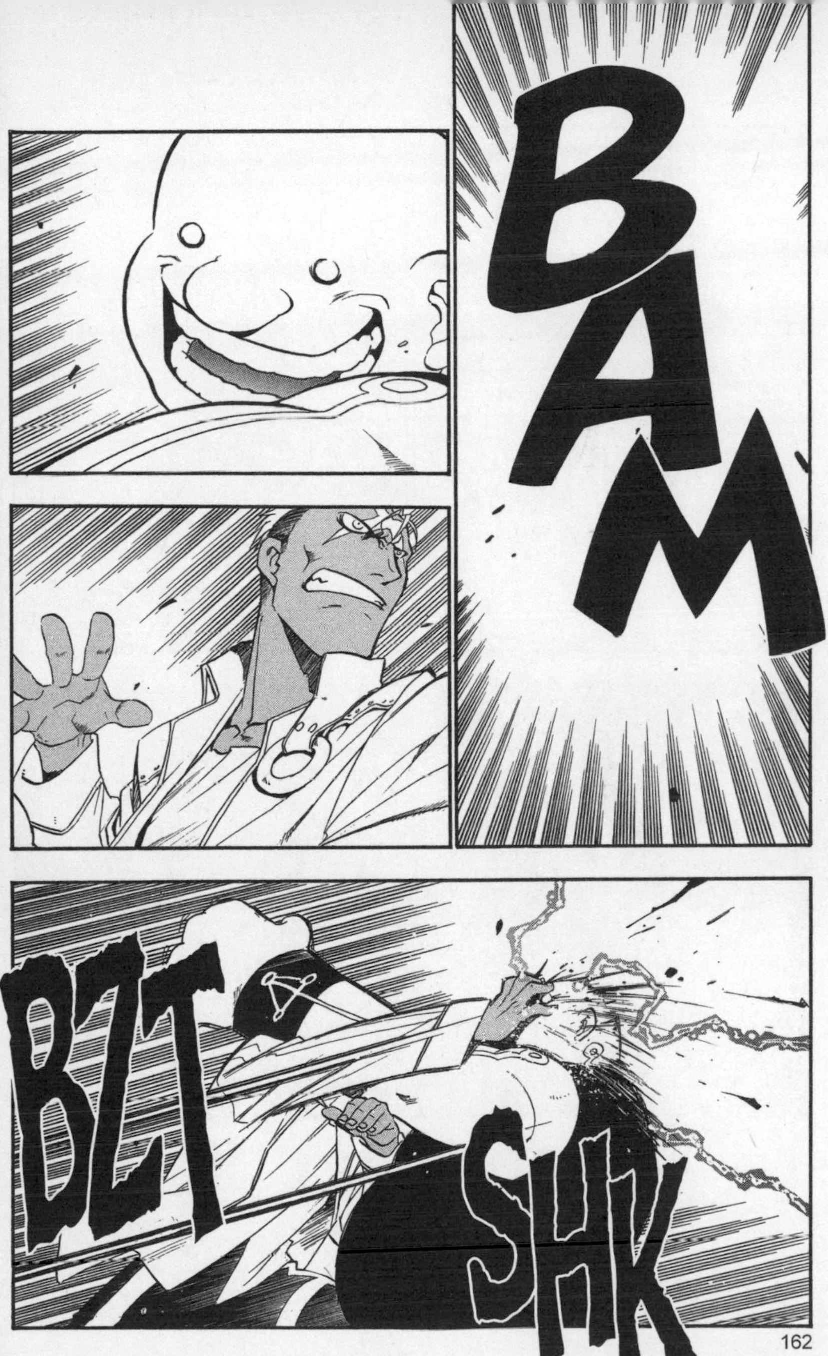
BAM
SHK
BZT

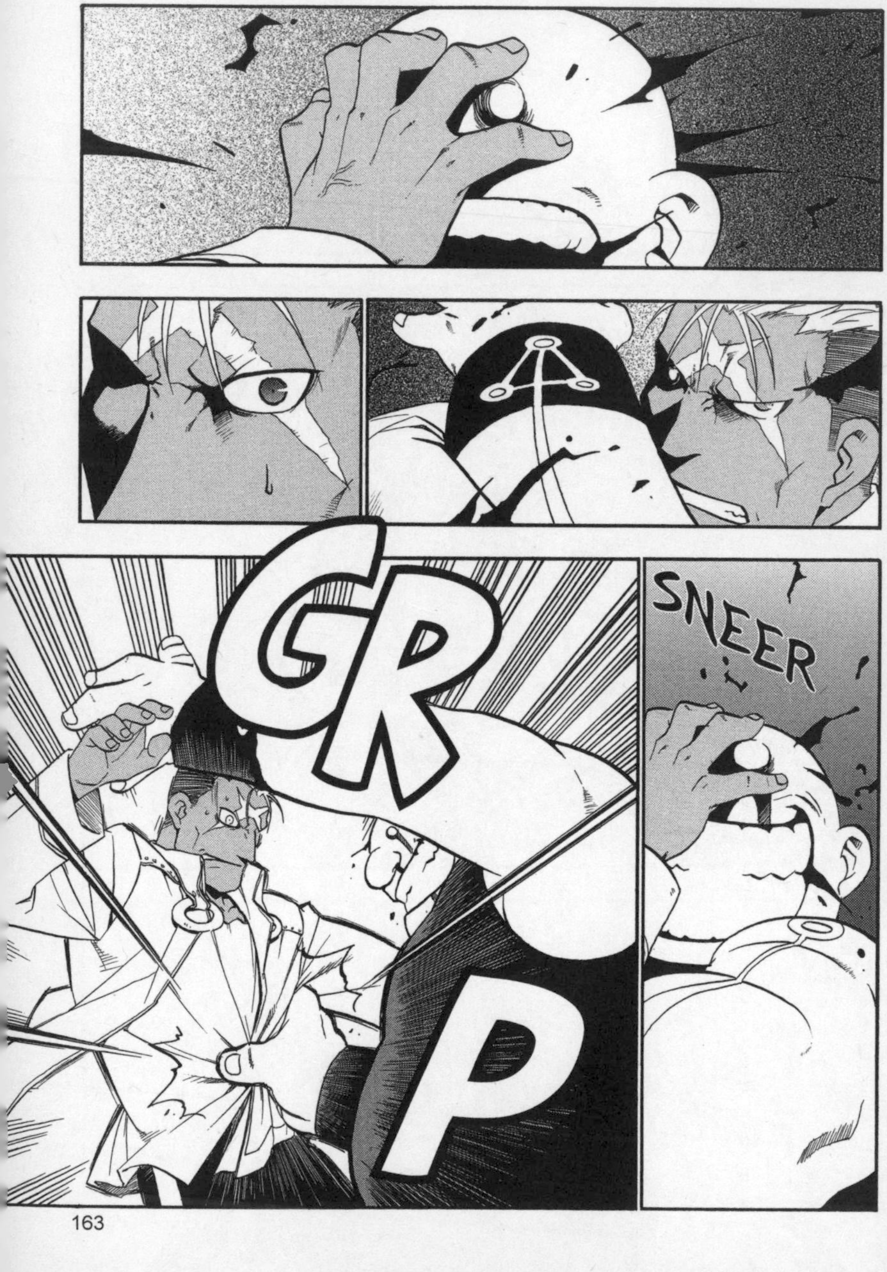
SNEER
GRP

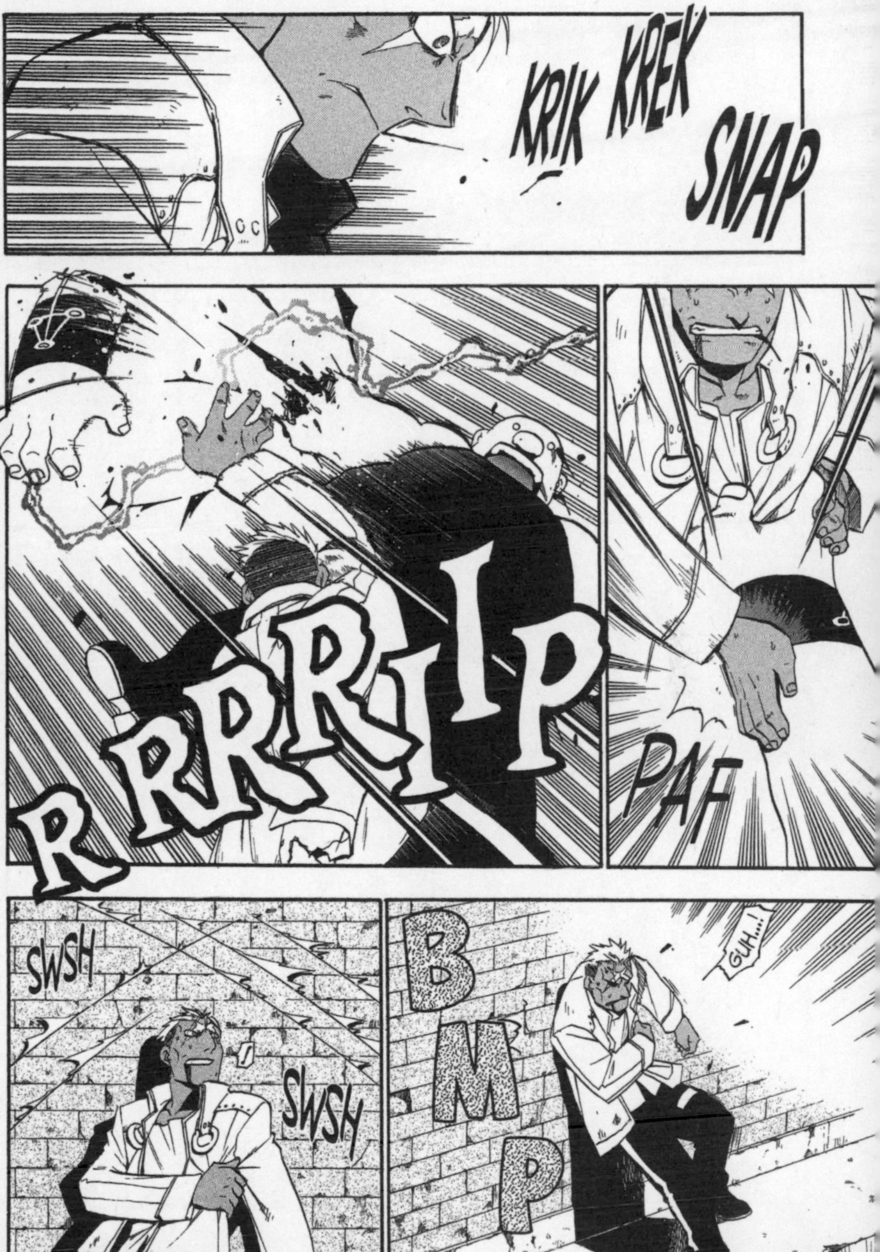
KRIK KREK
SNAP
PAF
RRRRIP
BMP
GUH...!
SWSH
SWSH

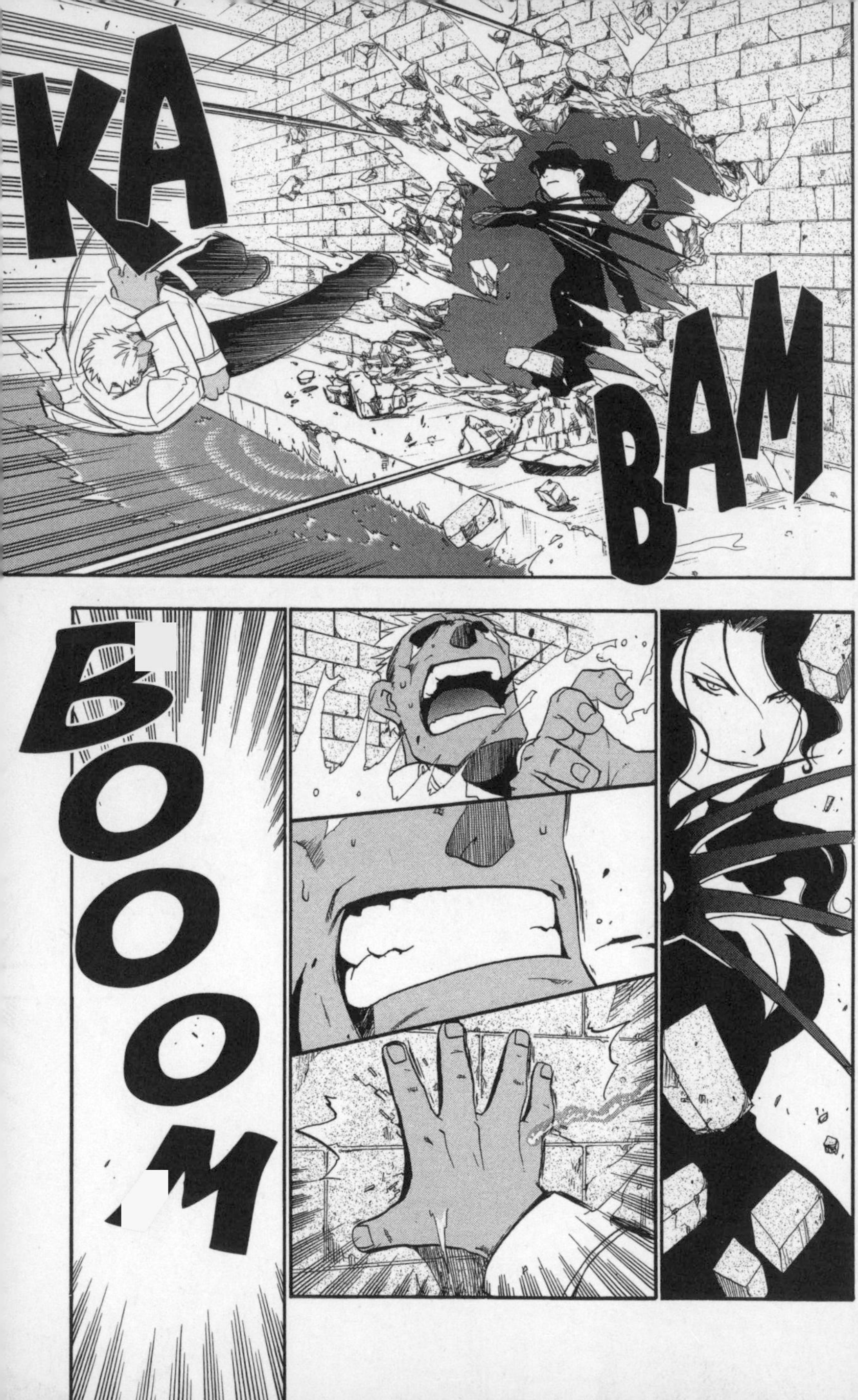
KA
BAM
BOOOM

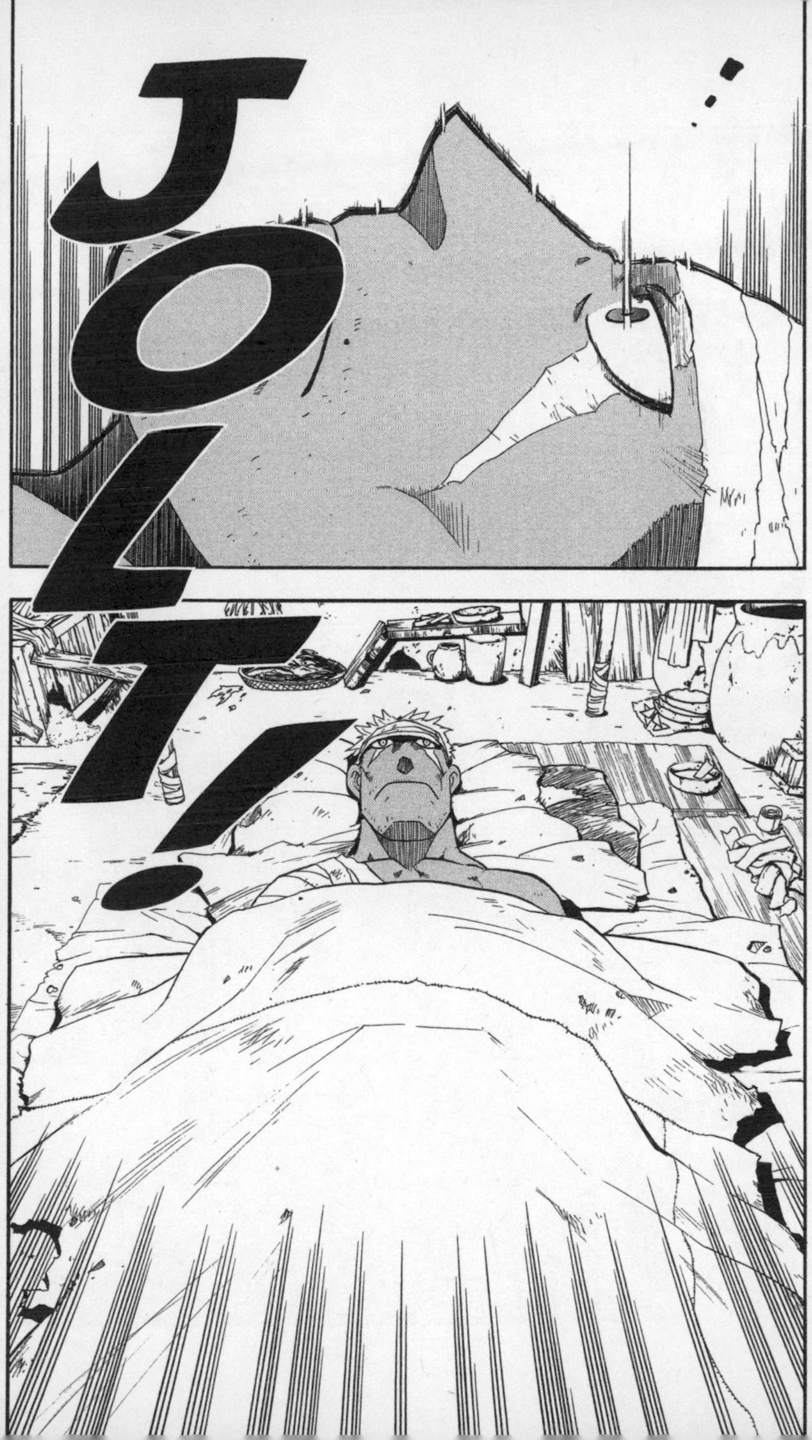
JOLT!

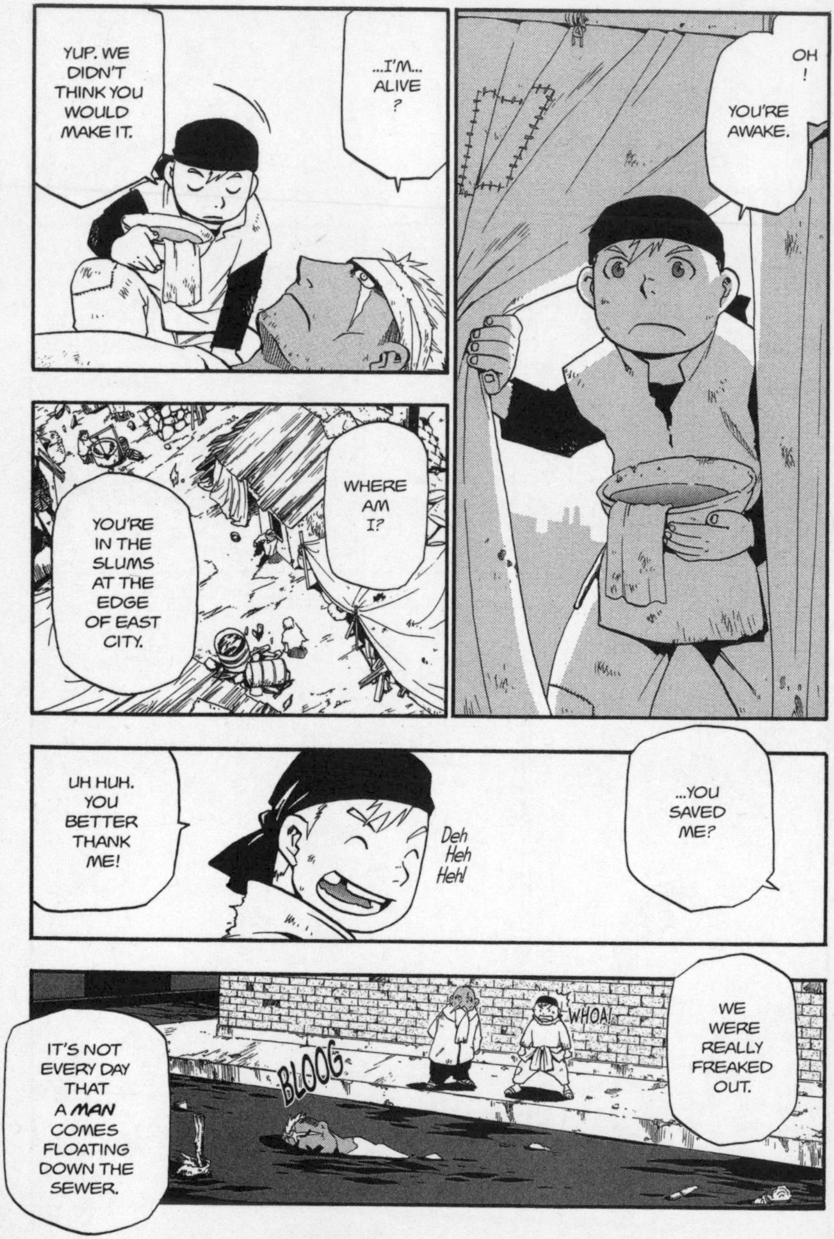
OH! YOU'RE AWAKE.
...I'M... ALIVE?
YUP. WE DIDN'T THINK YOU WOULD MAKE IT.
WHERE AM I?
YOU'RE IN THE SLUMS AT THE EDGE OF EAST CITY.
...YOU SAVED ME?
Deh Heh Heh!
UH HUH. YOU BETTER THANK ME!
WE WERE REALLY FREAKED OUT.
WHOA!
BLOOG
IT'S NOT EVERY DAY THAT A **MAN** COMES FLOATING DOWN THE SEWER.

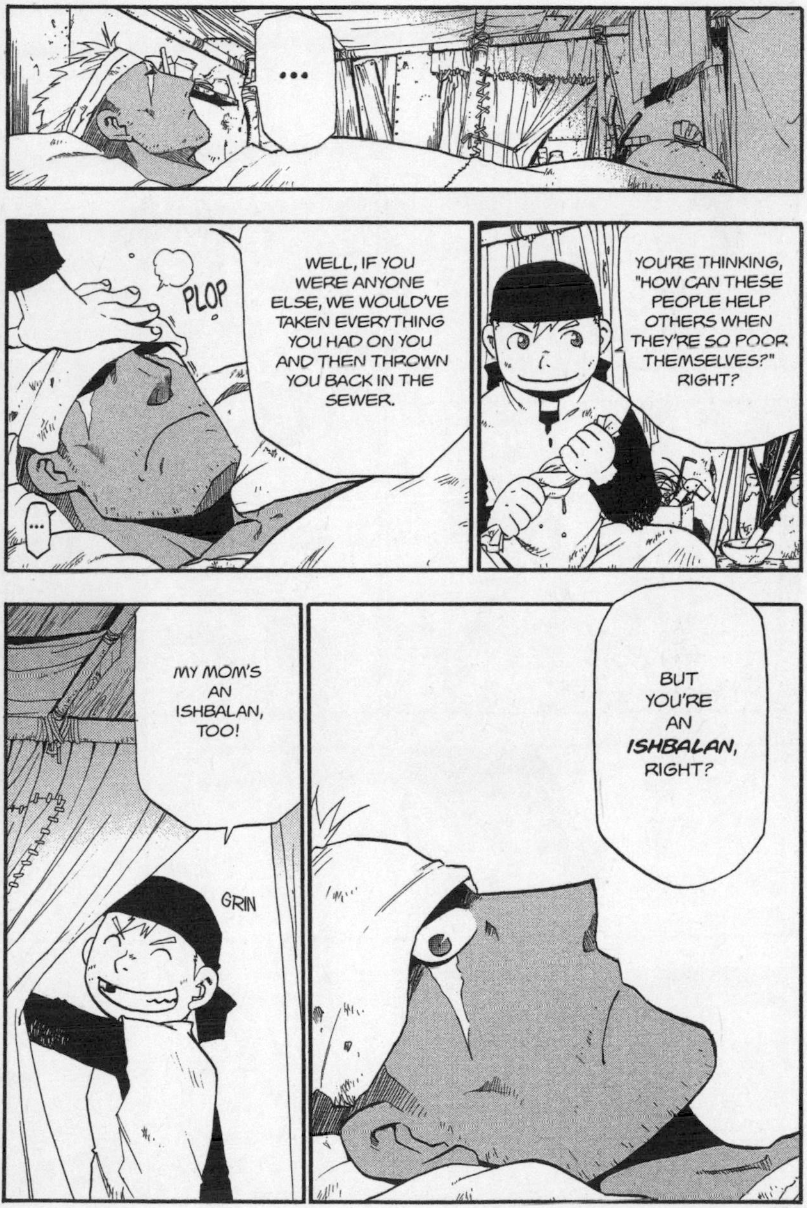

...
YOU'RE THINKING, "HOW CAN THESE PEOPLE HELP OTHERS WHEN THEY'RE SO POOR THEMSELVES?" RIGHT?
WELL, IF YOU WERE ANYONE ELSE, WE WOULD'VE TAKEN EVERYTHING YOU HAD ON YOU AND THEN THROWN YOU BACK IN THE SEWER.
PLOP
...
BUT YOU'RE AN ISHBALAN, RIGHT?
MY MOM'S AN ISHBALAN, TOO!
GRIN

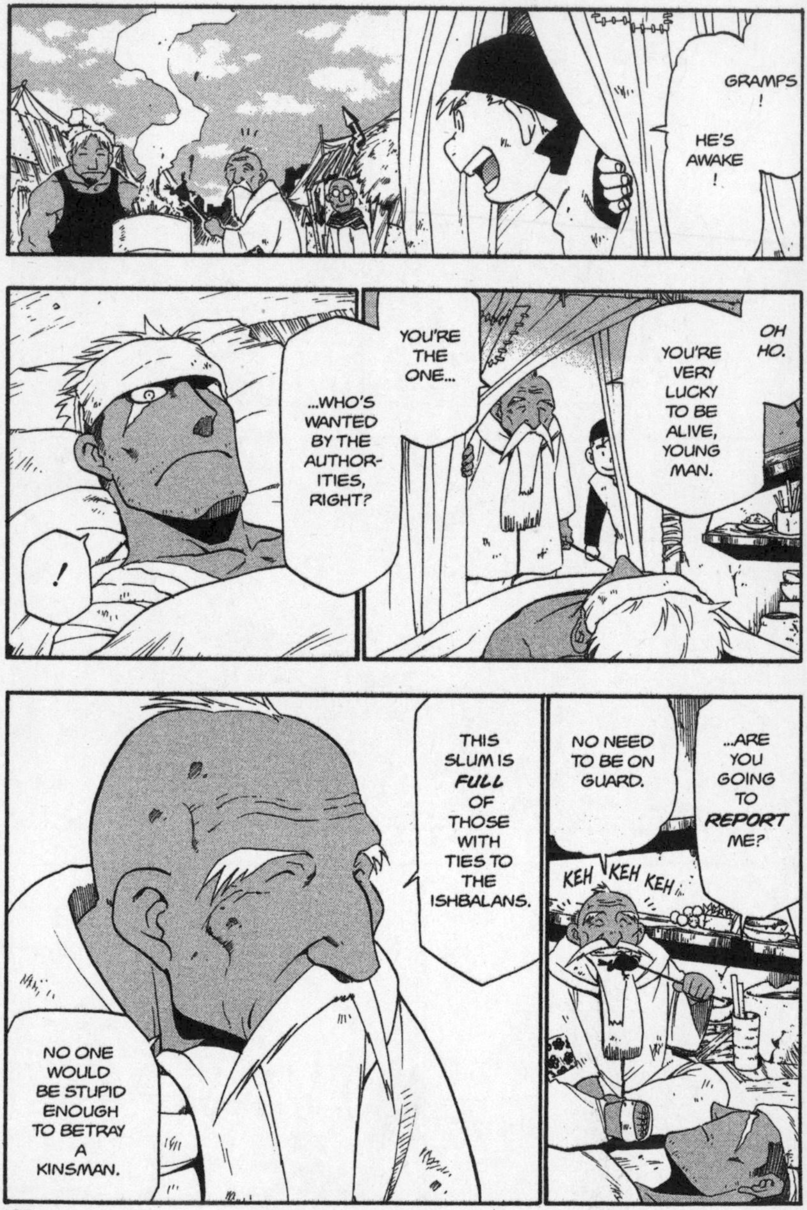
GRAMPS!
HE'S AWAKE!
OH HO.
YOU'RE VERY LUCKY TO BE ALIVE, YOUNG MAN.
YOU'RE THE ONE...
...WHO'S WANTED BY THE AUTHOR-ITIES, RIGHT?
!
...ARE YOU GOING TO REPORT ME?
KEH KEH KEH
NO NEED TO BE ON GUARD.
THIS SLUM IS FULL OF THOSE WITH TIES TO THE ISHBALANS.
NO ONE WOULD BE STUPID ENOUGH TO BETRAY A KINSMAN.

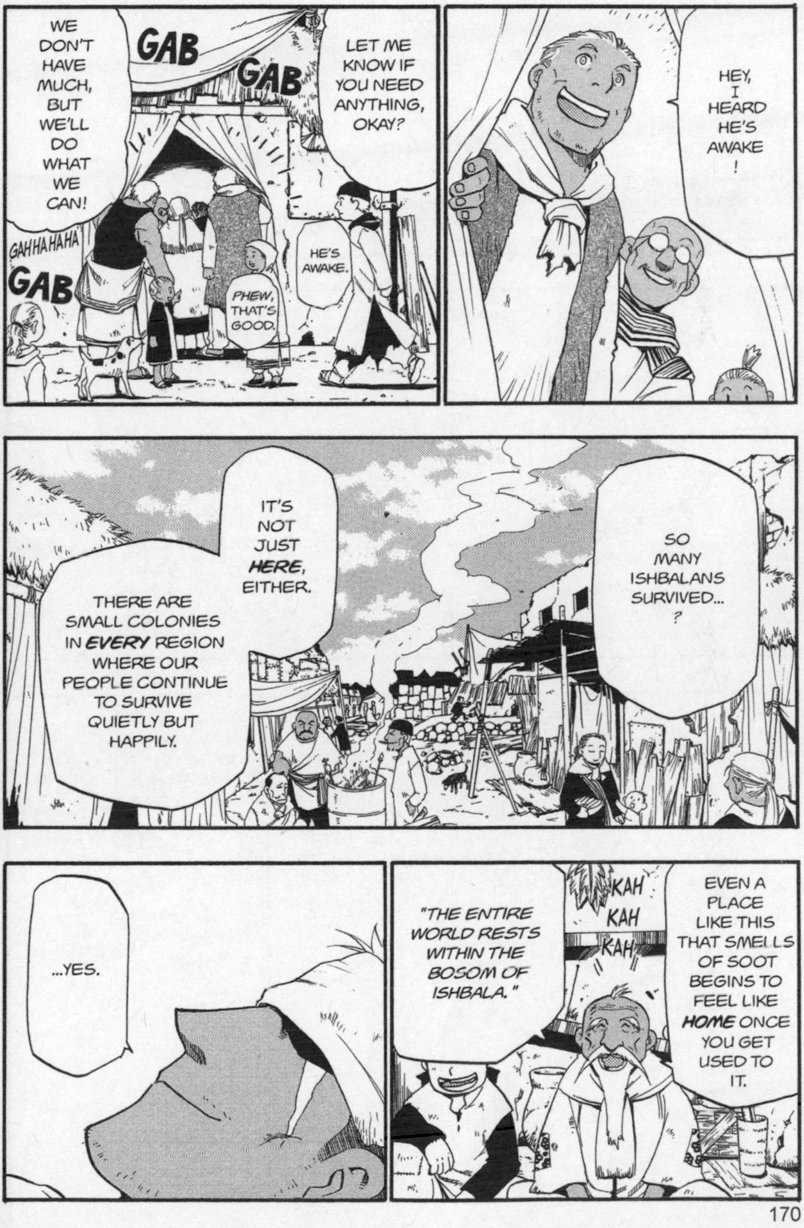
HEY, I HEARD HE'S AWAKE!
LET ME KNOW IF YOU NEED ANYTHING, OKAY?
GAB GAB
WE DON'T HAVE MUCH, BUT WE'LL DO WHAT WE CAN!
HE'S AWAKE.
PHEW, THAT'S GOOD.
GAHHAHAHA
GAB
SO MANY ISHBALANS SURVIVED...?
IT'S NOT JUST HERE, EITHER.
THERE ARE SMALL COLONIES IN EVERY REGION WHERE OUR PEOPLE CONTINUE TO SURVIVE QUIETLY BUT HAPPILY.
EVEN A PLACE LIKE THIS THAT SMELLS OF SOOT BEGINS TO FEEL LIKE HOME ONCE YOU GET USED TO IT.
KAH KAH KAH
"THE ENTIRE WORLD RESTS WITHIN THE BOSOM OF ISHBALA."
...YES.

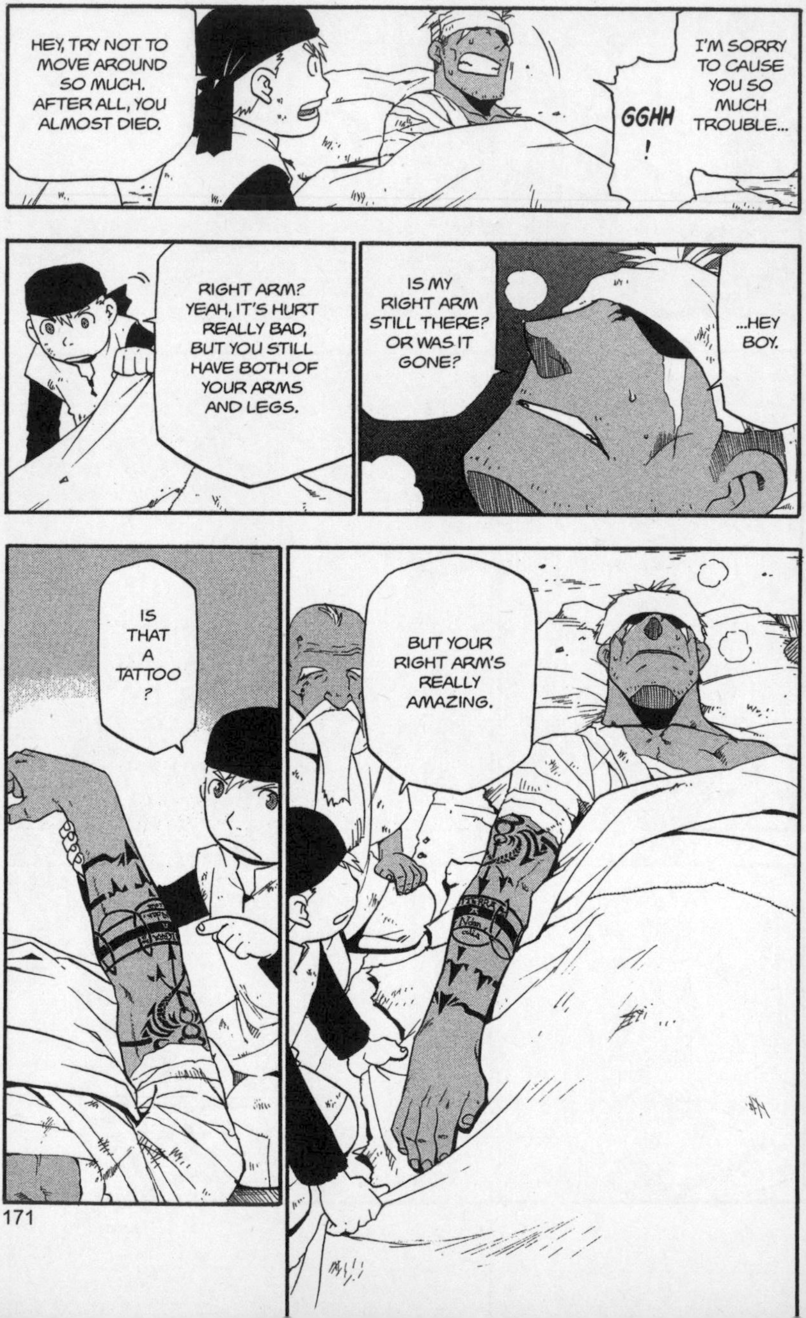

I'M SORRY TO CAUSE YOU SO MUCH TROUBLE...
GGHH!
HEY, TRY NOT TO MOVE AROUND SO MUCH. AFTER ALL, YOU ALMOST DIED.
...HEY BOY.
IS MY RIGHT ARM STILL THERE? OR WAS IT GONE?
RIGHT ARM? YEAH, IT'S HURT REALLY BAD, BUT YOU STILL HAVE BOTH OF YOUR ARMS AND LEGS.
BUT YOUR RIGHT ARM'S REALLY AMAZING.
IS THAT A TATTOO?

THIS MANGA WAS ORIGINALLY PRINTED IN MONTHLY
SHONEN GANGAN*, AUGUST 2002 THROUGH NOVEMBER 2002.*

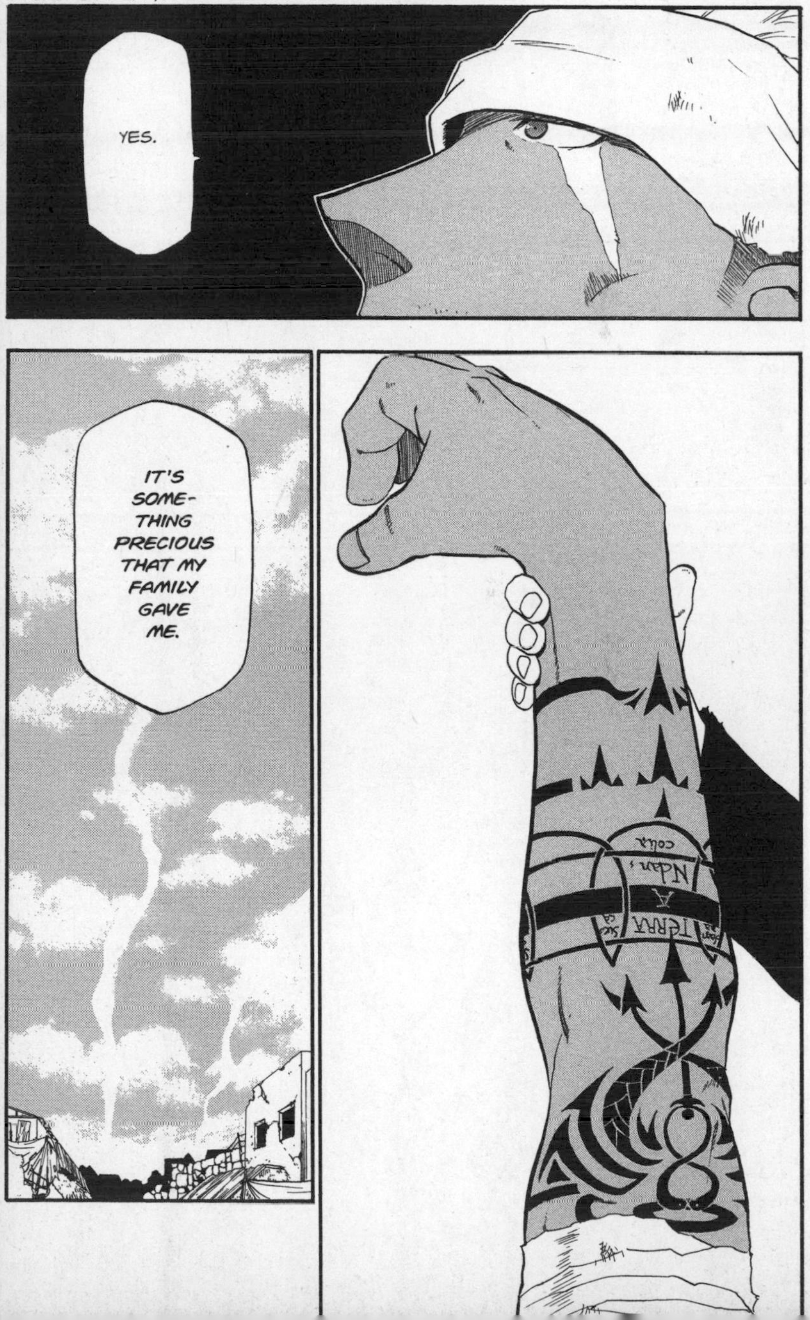
YES.
IT'S SOME-THING PRECIOUS THAT MY FAMILY GAVE ME.

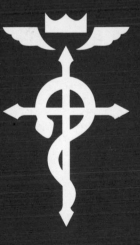

FULLMETAL
ALCHEMIST

Side Story: Dog of the Military?

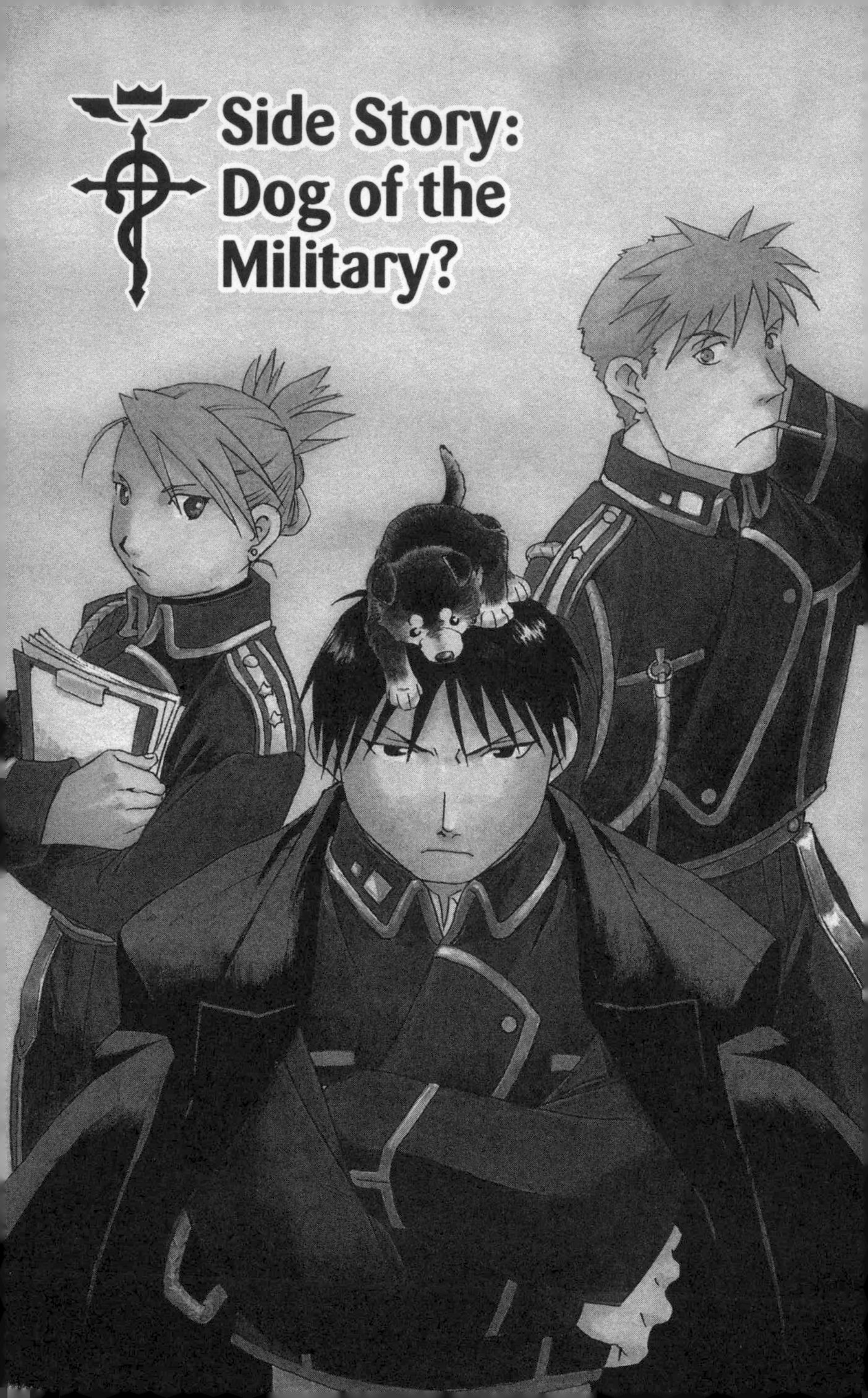

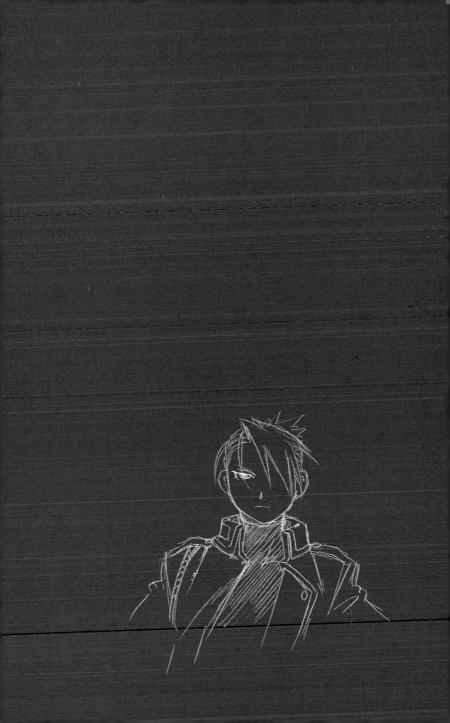

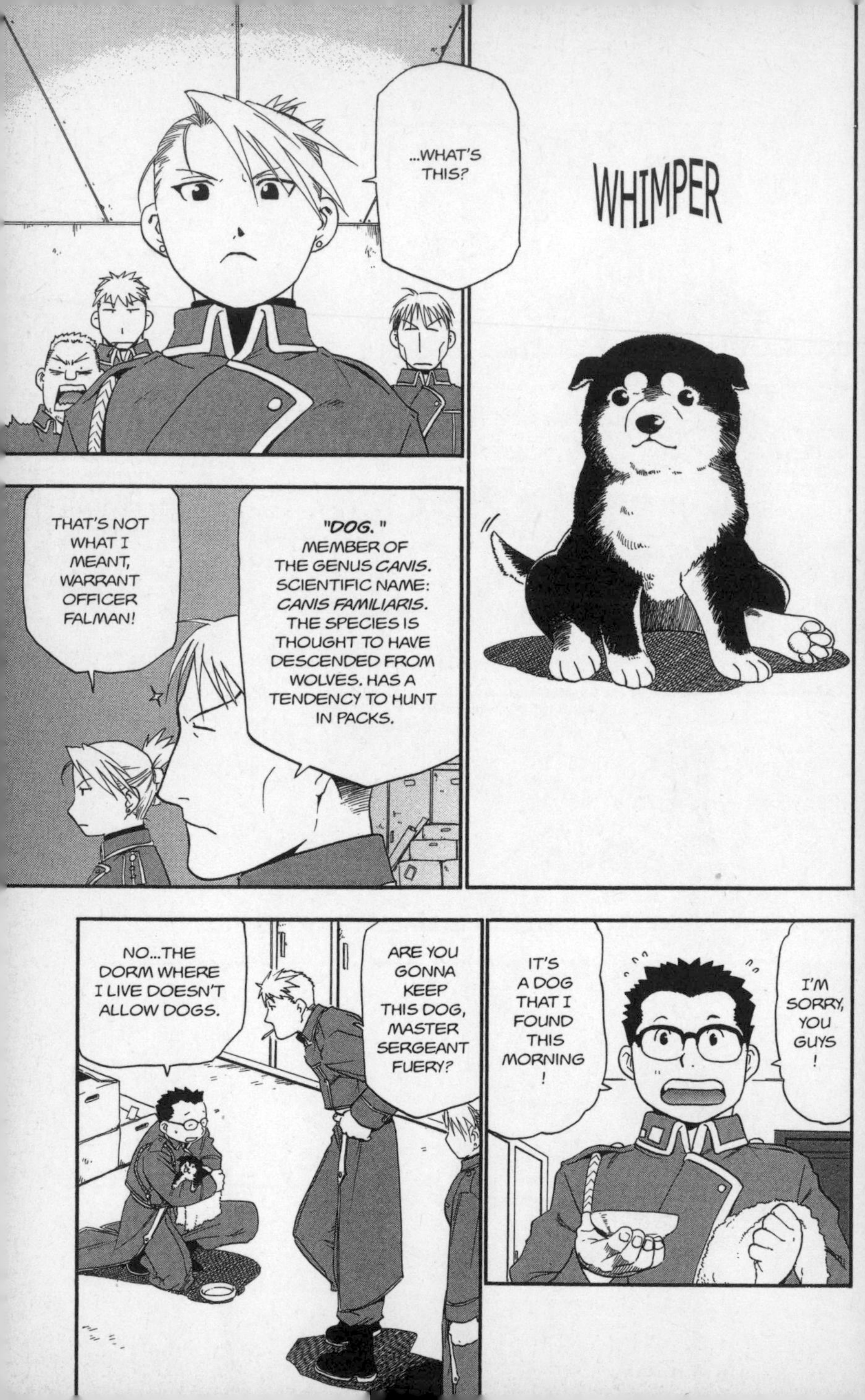
WHIMPER
...WHAT'S THIS?
"DOG." MEMBER OF THE GENUS CANIS. SCIENTIFIC NAME: CANIS FAMILIARIS. THE SPECIES IS THOUGHT TO HAVE DESCENDED FROM WOLVES. HAS A TENDENCY TO HUNT IN PACKS.
THAT'S NOT WHAT I MEANT, WARRANT OFFICER FALMAN!
I'M SORRY, YOU GUYS!
IT'S A DOG THAT I FOUND THIS MORNING!
ARE YOU GONNA KEEP THIS DOG, MASTER SERGEANT FUERY?
NO...THE DORM WHERE I LIVE DOESN'T ALLOW DOGS.

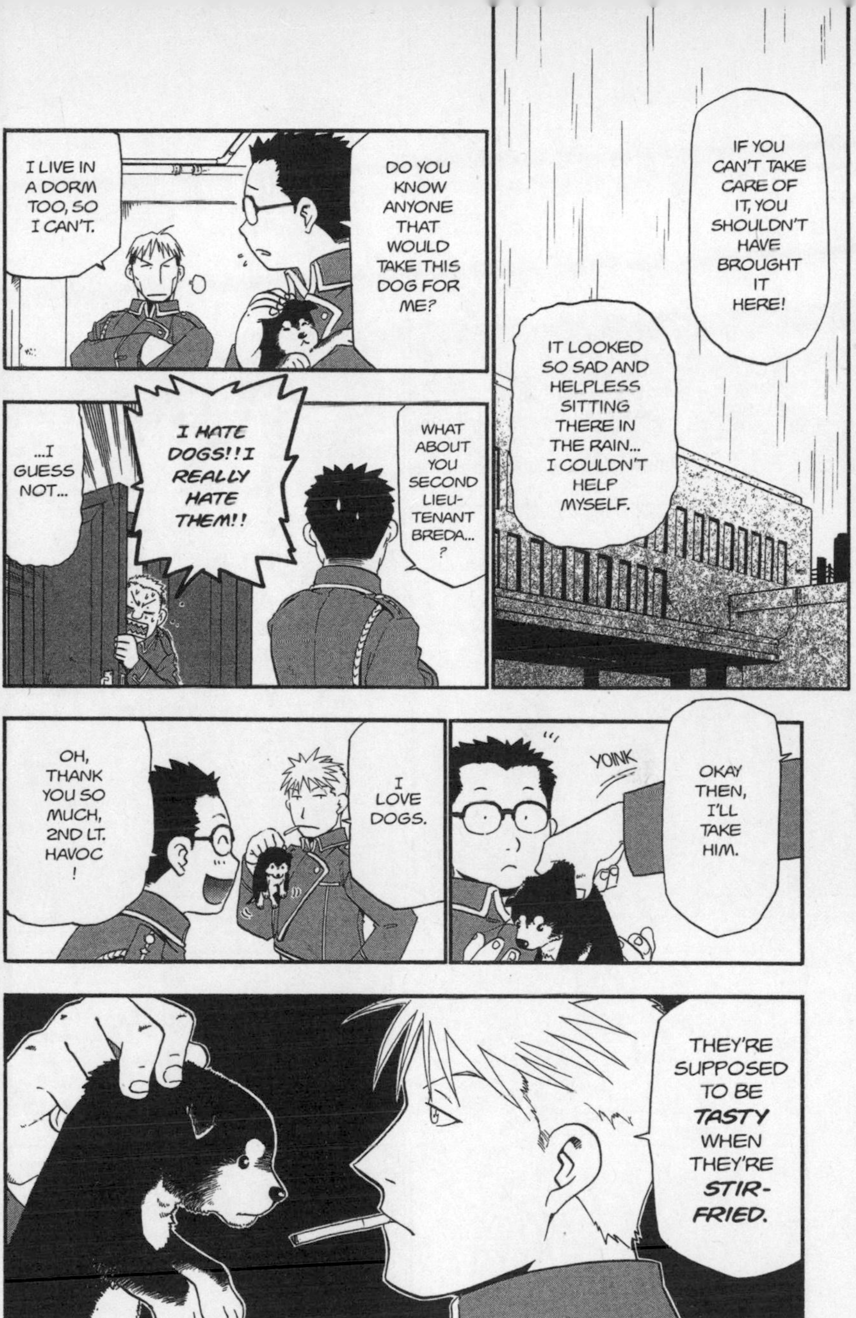
IF YOU CAN'T TAKE CARE OF IT, YOU SHOULDN'T HAVE BROUGHT IT HERE!
IT LOOKED SO SAD AND HELPLESS SITTING THERE IN THE RAIN... I COULDN'T HELP MYSELF.
DO YOU KNOW ANYONE THAT WOULD TAKE THIS DOG FOR ME?
I LIVE IN A DORM TOO, SO I CAN'T.
WHAT ABOUT YOU SECOND LIEU-TENANT BREDA...?
I HATE DOGS!! I REALLY HATE THEM!!
...I GUESS NOT...
OKAY THEN, I'LL TAKE HIM.
YOINK
I LOVE DOGS.
OH, THANK YOU SO MUCH, 2ND LT. HAVOC!
THEY'RE SUPPOSED TO BE TASTY WHEN THEY'RE STIR-FRIED.

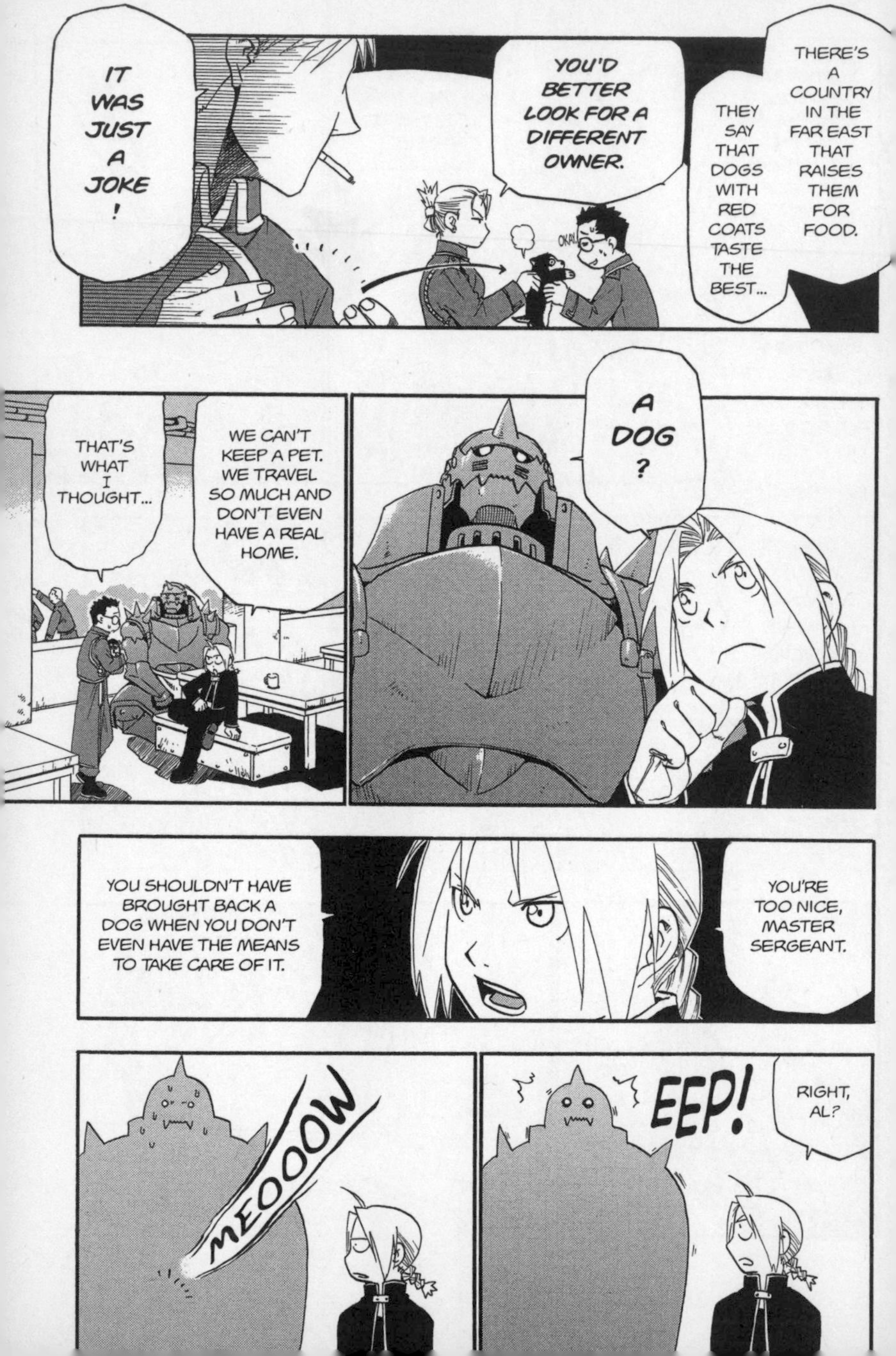
THERE'S A COUNTRY IN THE FAR EAST THAT RAISES THEM FOR FOOD.
THEY SAY THAT DOGS WITH RED COATS TASTE THE BEST...
YOU'D BETTER LOOK FOR A DIFFERENT OWNER.
OKAY!
IT WAS JUST A JOKE!
A DOG?
WE CAN'T KEEP A PET. WE TRAVEL SO MUCH AND DON'T EVEN HAVE A REAL HOME.
THAT'S WHAT I THOUGHT...
YOU'RE TOO NICE, MASTER SERGEANT.
YOU SHOULDN'T HAVE BROUGHT BACK A DOG WHEN YOU DON'T EVEN HAVE THE MEANS TO TAKE CARE OF IT.
RIGHT, AL?
EEP!
MEOOOW

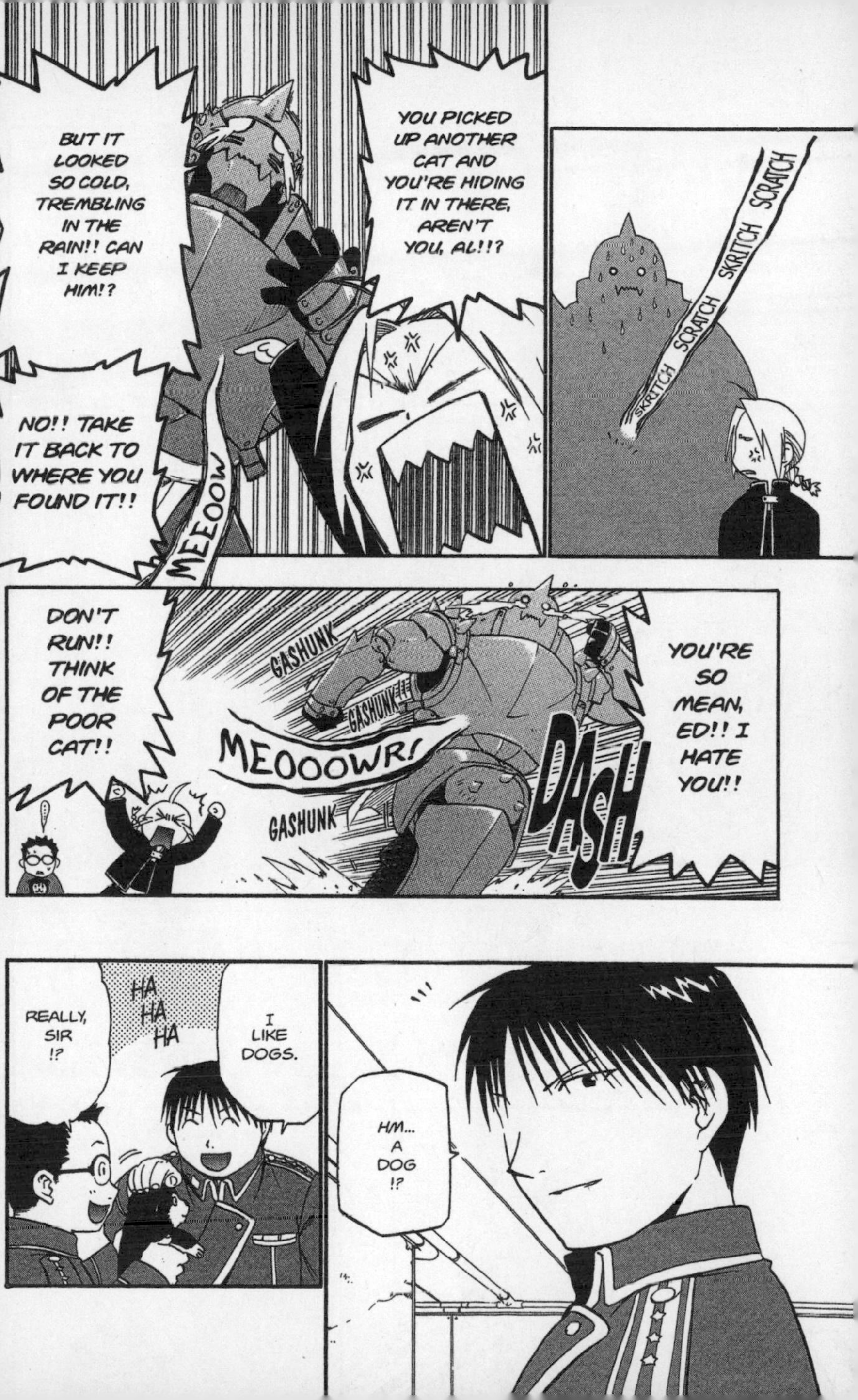
SKRITCH SCRATCH SKRITCH SCRATCH
YOU PICKED UP ANOTHER CAT AND YOU'RE HIDING IT IN THERE, AREN'T YOU, AL!!?
BUT IT LOOKED SO COLD, TREMBLING IN THE RAIN!! CAN I KEEP HIM!?
NO!! TAKE IT BACK TO WHERE YOU FOUND IT!!
MEEEOOW
YOU'RE SO MEAN, ED!! I HATE YOU!!
DASH
GASHUNK
GASHUNK!!
GASHUNK
MEOOOOWR!
DON'T RUN!! THINK OF THE POOR CAT!!
HM... A DOG !?
I LIKE DOGS.
HA HA HA
REALLY, SIR !?

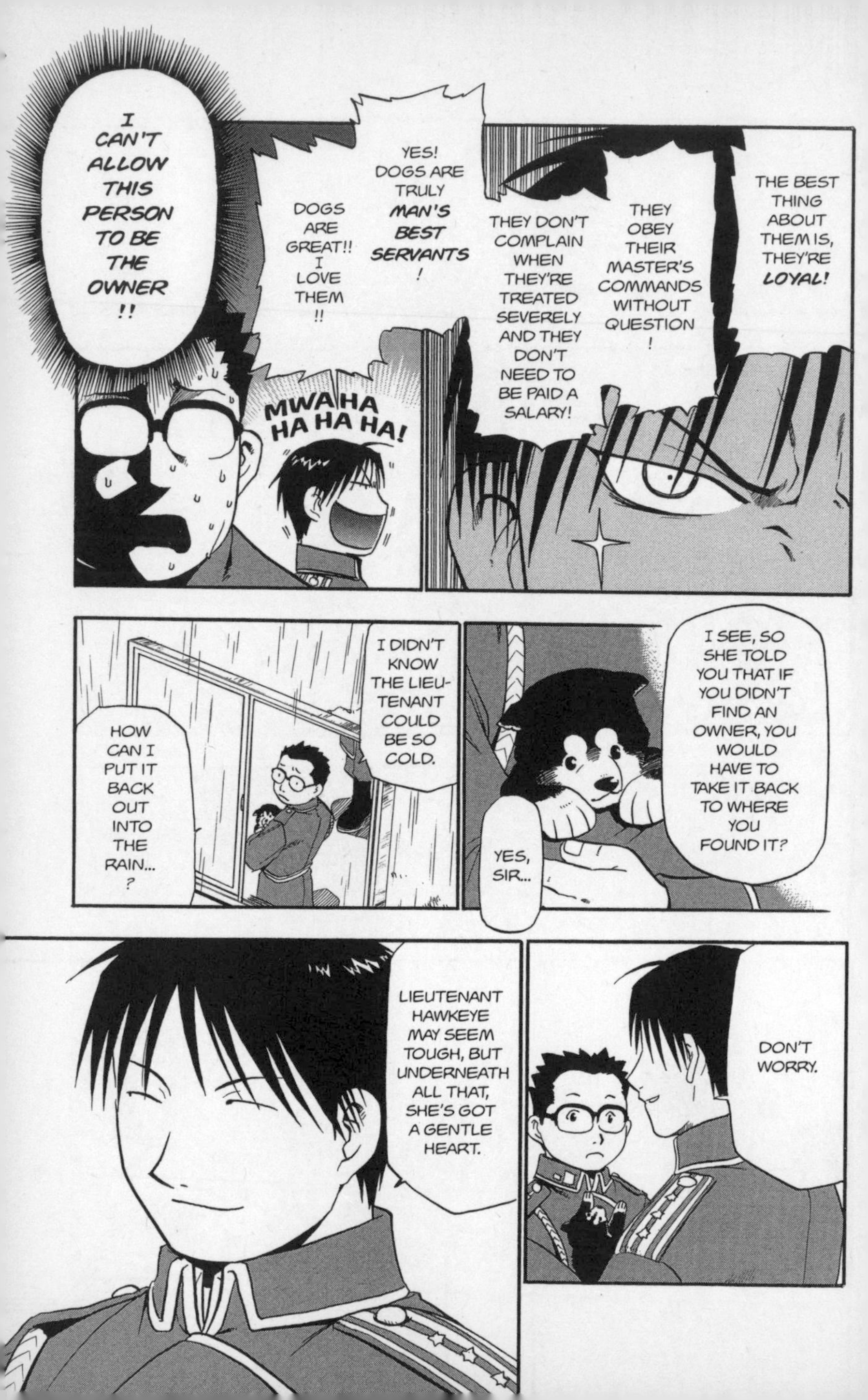
THE BEST THING ABOUT THEM IS, THEY'RE LOYAL!
THEY OBEY THEIR MASTER'S COMMANDS WITHOUT QUESTION!
THEY DON'T COMPLAIN WHEN THEY'RE TREATED SEVERELY AND THEY DON'T NEED TO BE PAID A SALARY!
YES! DOGS ARE TRULY MAN'S BEST SERVANTS!
DOGS ARE GREAT!! I LOVE THEM!!
MWAHA HA HA HA!
I CAN'T ALLOW THIS PERSON TO BE THE OWNER!!
I SEE, SO SHE TOLD YOU THAT IF YOU DIDN'T FIND AN OWNER, YOU WOULD HAVE TO TAKE IT BACK TO WHERE YOU FOUND IT?
YES, SIR...
I DIDN'T KNOW THE LIEUTENANT COULD BE SO COLD.
HOW CAN I PUT IT BACK OUT INTO THE RAIN...?
DON'T WORRY.
LIEUTENANT HAWKEYE MAY SEEM TOUGH, BUT UNDERNEATH ALL THAT, SHE'S GOT A GENTLE HEART.

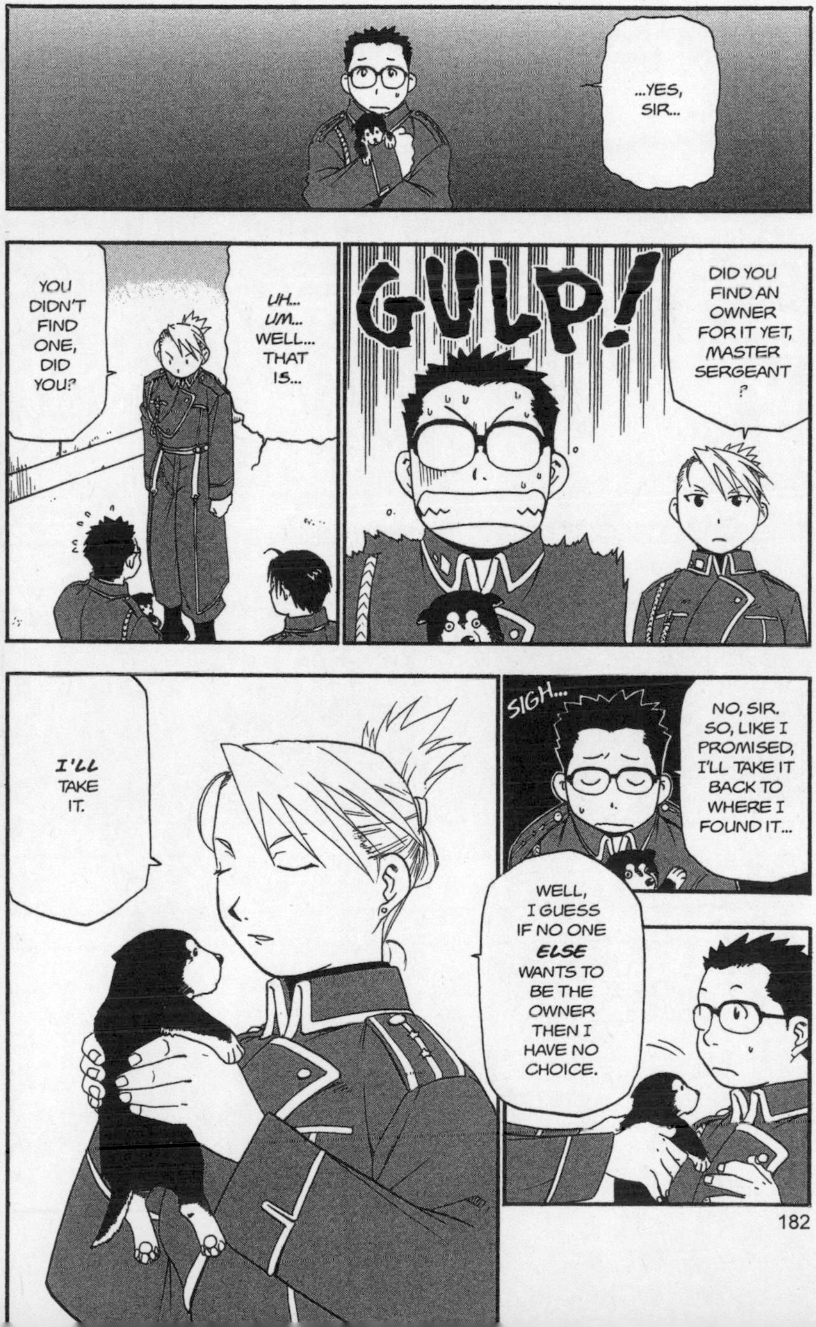
...YES, SIR...
GULP!
DID YOU FIND AN OWNER FOR IT YET, MASTER SERGEANT?
UH... UM... WELL... THAT IS...
YOU DIDN'T FIND ONE, DID YOU?
SIGH...
NO, SIR. SO, LIKE I PROMISED, I'LL TAKE IT BACK TO WHERE I FOUND IT...
WELL, I GUESS IF NO ONE *ELSE* WANTS TO BE THE OWNER THEN I HAVE NO CHOICE.
I'LL TAKE IT.

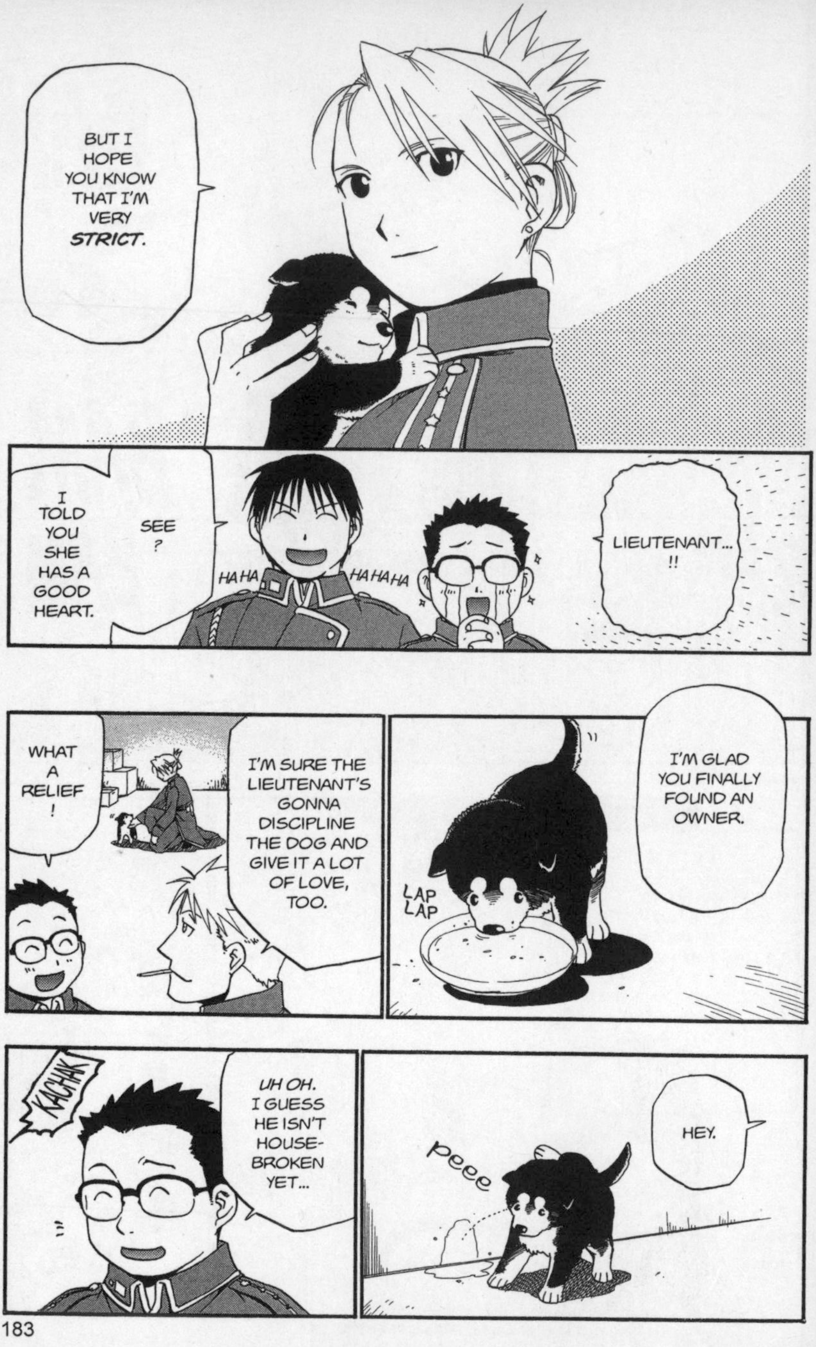
BUT I HOPE YOU KNOW THAT I'M VERY **STRICT**.
LIEUTENANT... !!
HA HA HA
HA HA
SEE?
I TOLD YOU SHE HAS A GOOD HEART.
I'M GLAD YOU FINALLY FOUND AN OWNER.
LAP LAP
I'M SURE THE LIEUTENANT'S GONNA DISCIPLINE THE DOG AND GIVE IT A LOT OF LOVE, TOO.
WHAT A RELIEF!
HEY.
peee
UH OH. I GUESS HE ISN'T HOUSE-BROKEN YET...
KACHAK

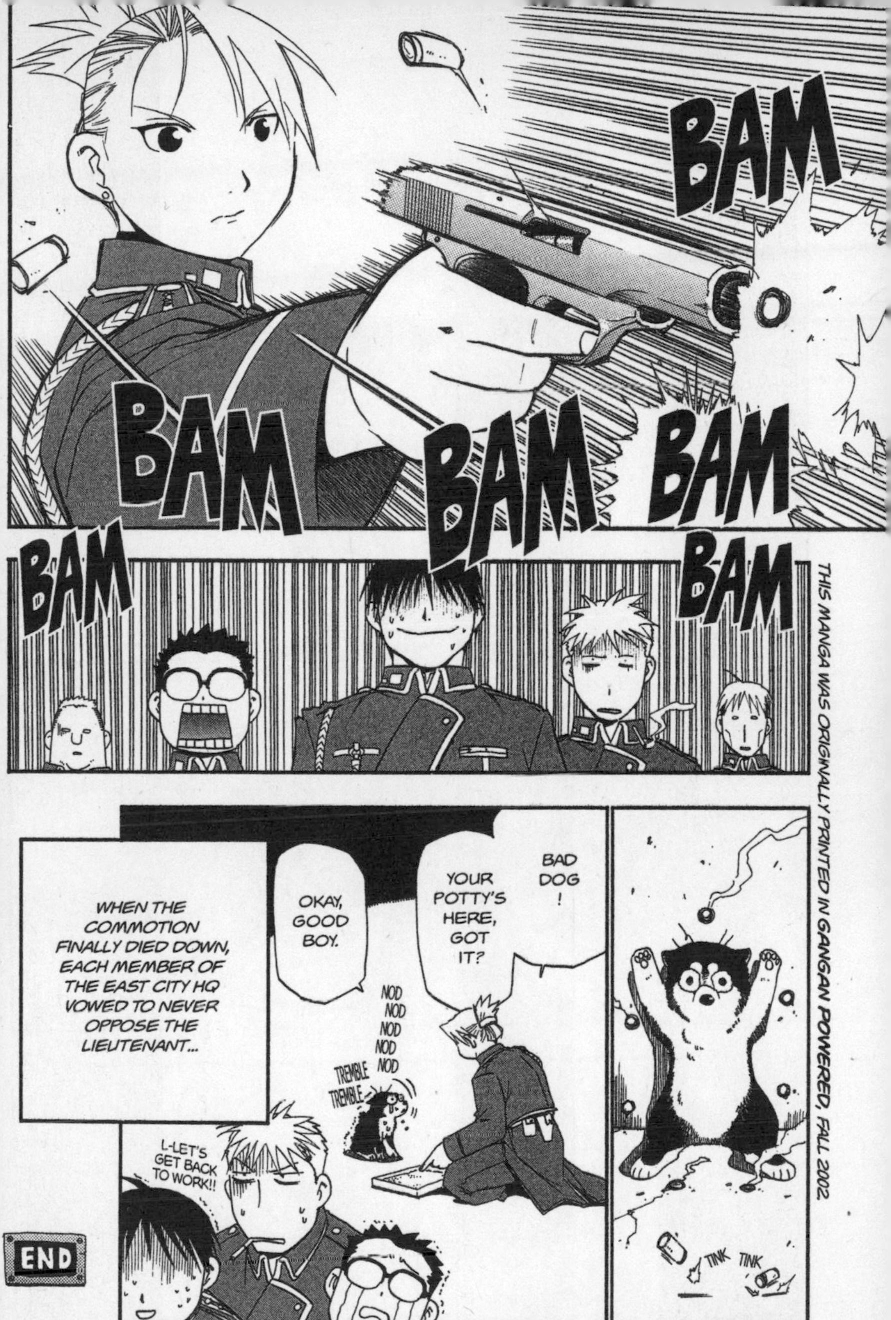
BAM
BAM
BAM
BAM
BAM
BAM
TINK
TINK
BAD DOG!
YOUR POTTY'S HERE, GOT IT?
OKAY, GOOD BOY.
NOD NOD NOD NOD NOD
TREMBLE TREMBLE
WHEN THE COMMOTION FINALLY DIED DOWN, EACH MEMBER OF THE EAST CITY HQ VOWED TO NEVER OPPOSE THE LIEUTENANT...
L-LET'S GET BACK TO WORK!!
END

THIS MANGA WAS ORIGINALLY PRINTED IN GANGAN POWERED, FALL 2002

TO BE CONTINUED IN FULLMETAL ALCHEMIST VOL. 5!

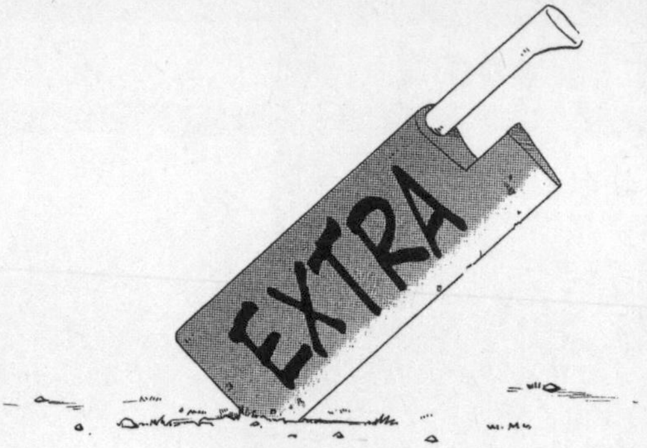
EXTRA

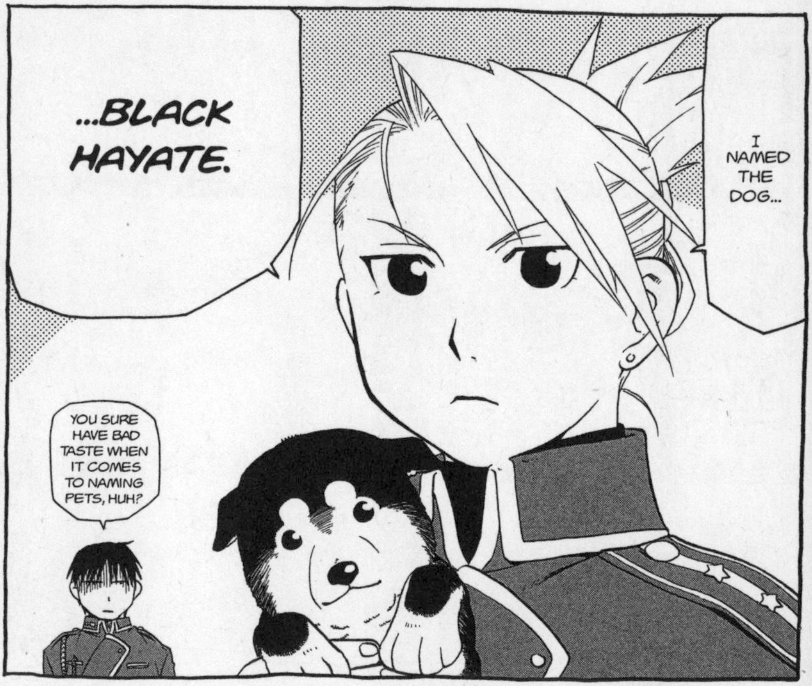
I NAMED THE DOG...
...BLACK HAYATE.
YOU SURE HAVE BAD TASTE WHEN IT COMES TO NAMING PETS, HUH?

Cat

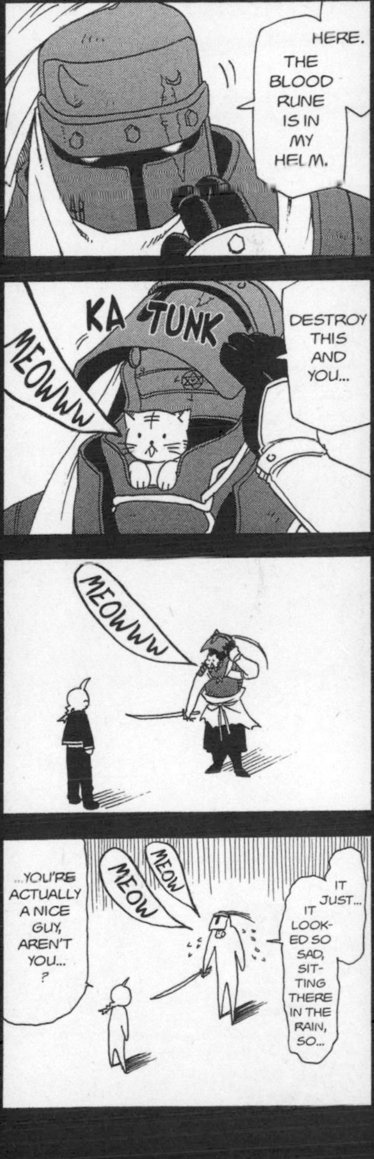
HERE. THE BLOOD RUNE IS IN MY HELM.
KA TUNK
DESTROY THIS AND YOU...
MEOWWW
MEOWWW
MEOW
MEOW
...YOU'RE ACTUALLY A NICE GUY, AREN'T YOU...?
IT JUST... IT LOOKED SO SAD, SITTING THERE IN THE RAIN, SO...

Cat: Episode 2

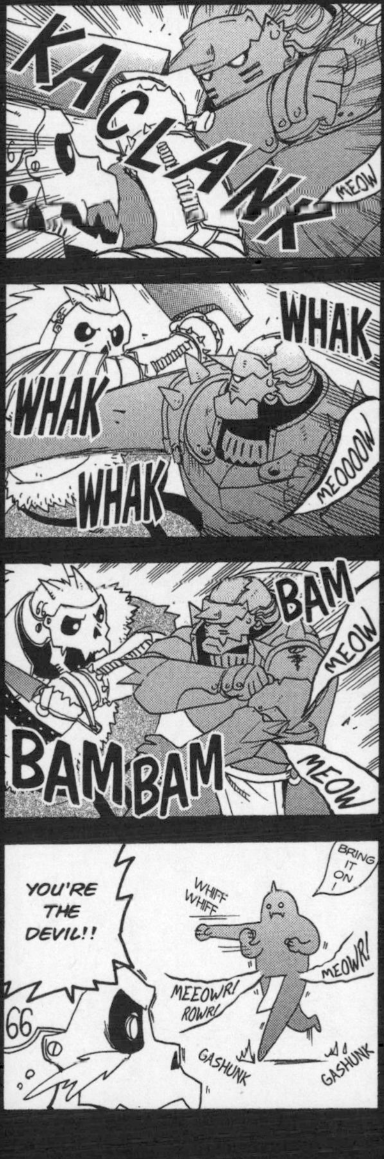
KACLANK
MEOW
WHAK
WHAK
WHAK
MEOOOOW
BAM
MEOW
BAM BAM
MEOW
BRING IT ON!
WHIFF WHIFF
YOU'RE THE DEVIL!!
MEOWR!
MEEOWR! ROWR!
GASHUNK
GASHUNK

Somebody Stop Them

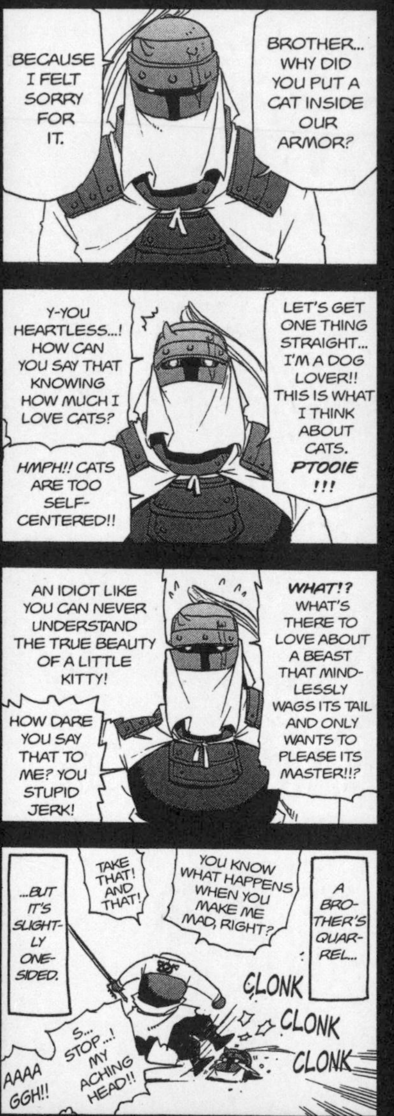
BROTHER... WHY DID YOU PUT A CAT INSIDE OUR ARMOR?
BECAUSE I FELT SORRY FOR IT.
LET'S GET ONE THING STRAIGHT... I'M A DOG LOVER!! THIS IS WHAT I THINK ABOUT CATS. PTOOIE!!!
Y-YOU HEARTLESS...! HOW CAN YOU SAY THAT KNOWING HOW MUCH I LOVE CATS?
HMPH!! CATS ARE TOO SELF-CENTERED!!
WHAT!? WHAT'S THERE TO LOVE ABOUT A BEAST THAT MINDLESSLY WAGS ITS TAIL AND ONLY WANTS TO PLEASE ITS MASTER!!?
AN IDIOT LIKE YOU CAN NEVER UNDERSTAND THE TRUE BEAUTY OF A LITTLE KITTY!
HOW DARE YOU SAY THAT TO ME? YOU STUPID JERK!
A BROTHER'S QUARREL...
YOU KNOW WHAT HAPPENS WHEN YOU MAKE ME MAD, RIGHT?
TAKE THAT! AND THAT!
...BUT IT'S SLIGHTLY ONE-SIDED.
CLONK
CLONK
CLONK
S... STOP...! MY ACHING HEAD!!
AAAAGGH!!

Miracle Hair

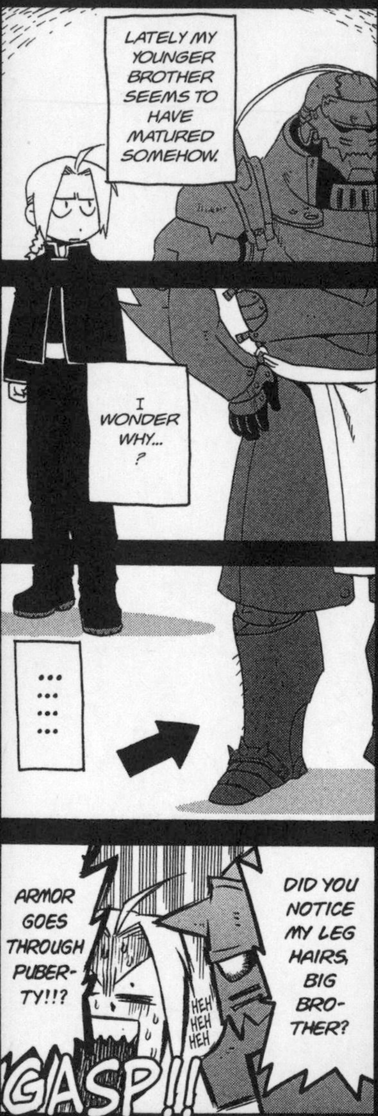
LATELY MY YOUNGER BROTHER SEEMS TO HAVE MATURED SOMEHOW.
I WONDER WHY...?
... ...
DID YOU NOTICE MY LEG HAIRS, BIG BROTHER?
ARMOR GOES THROUGH PUBERTY!!?
HEH HEH HEH
GASP!!

The Ambitious Alchemist: Part 2

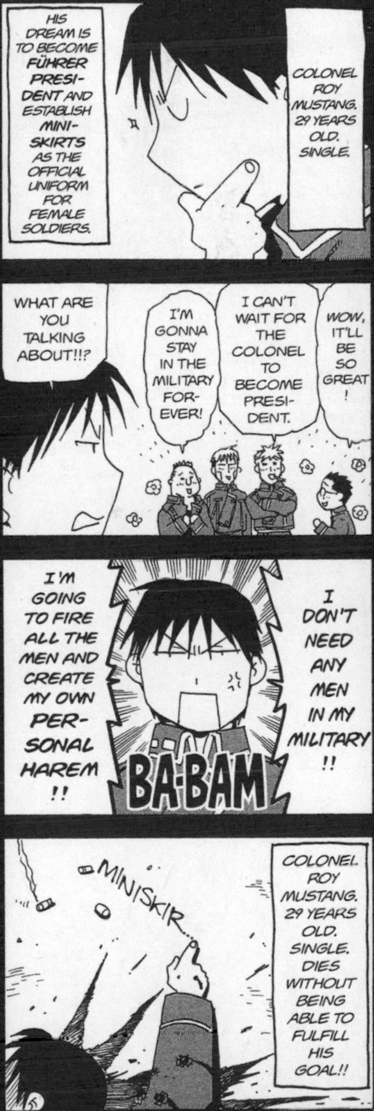
COLONEL ROY MUSTANG. 29 YEARS OLD. SINGLE.
HIS DREAM IS TO BECOME FÜHRER PRESIDENT AND ESTABLISH MINI-SKIRTS AS THE OFFICIAL UNIFORM FOR FEMALE SOLDIERS.
WOW, IT'LL BE SO GREAT!
I CAN'T WAIT FOR THE COLONEL TO BECOME PRESIDENT.
I'M GONNA STAY IN THE MILITARY FOREVER!
WHAT ARE YOU TALKING ABOUT!!?
I DON'T NEED ANY MEN IN MY MILITARY!!
I'M GOING TO FIRE ALL THE MEN AND CREATE MY OWN PERSONAL HAREM!!
BA-BAM
COLONEL ROY MUSTANG. 29 YEARS OLD. SINGLE. DIES WITHOUT BEING ABLE TO FULFILL HIS GOAL!!
MINISKIR...

A Man's Dignity

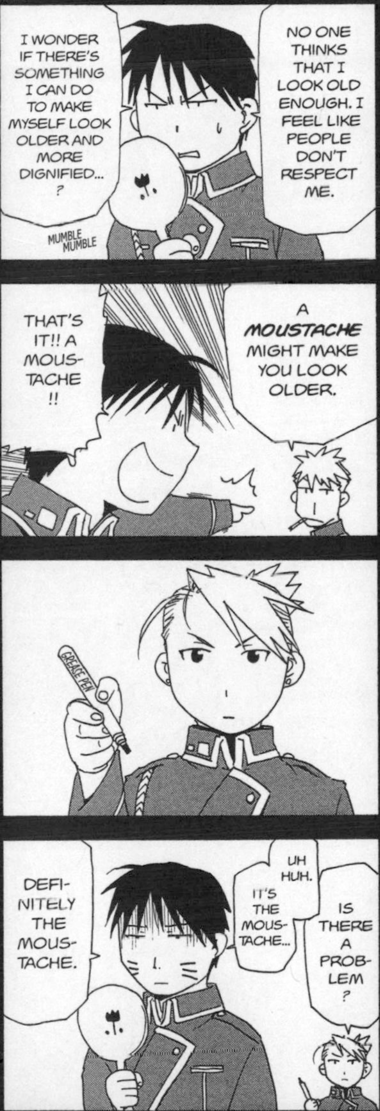
NO ONE THINKS THAT I LOOK OLD ENOUGH. I FEEL LIKE PEOPLE DON'T RESPECT ME.
I WONDER IF THERE'S SOMETHING I CAN DO TO MAKE MYSELF LOOK OLDER AND MORE DIGNIFIED...?
MUMBLE MUMBLE
A MOUSTACHE MIGHT MAKE YOU LOOK OLDER.
THAT'S IT!! A MOUSTACHE!!
GREASE PEN
UH HUH.
IS THERE A PROBLEM?
IT'S THE MOUSTACHE...
DEFINITELY THE MOUSTACHE.

Maybe The Loincloth Is The Problem?

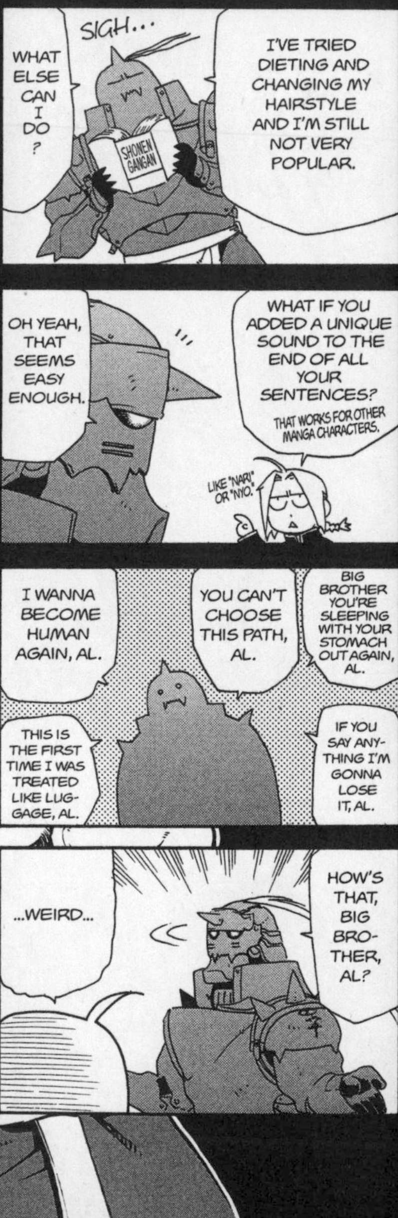
I'VE TRIED DIETING AND CHANGING MY HAIRSTYLE AND I'M STILL NOT VERY POPULAR.
SIGH...
WHAT ELSE CAN I DO ?
SHONEN GANGAN
WHAT IF YOU ADDED A UNIQUE SOUND TO THE END OF ALL YOUR SENTENCES?
THAT WORKS FOR OTHER MANGA CHARACTERS.
LIKE "NARI" OR "NYO."
OH YEAH, THAT SEEMS EASY ENOUGH.
BIG BROTHER YOU'RE SLEEPING WITH YOUR STOMACH OUT AGAIN, AL.
YOU CAN'T CHOOSE THIS PATH, AL.
I WANNA BECOME HUMAN AGAIN, AL.
IF YOU SAY ANY-THING I'M GONNA LOSE IT, AL.
THIS IS THE FIRST TIME I WAS TREATED LIKE LUG-GAGE, AL.
HOW'S THAT, BIG BRO-THER, AL?
...WEIRD...

FULLMETAL ALCHEMIST 4

SPECIAL THANKS TO...

KEISUI TAKAEDA-SAN

SANKICHI HINODEYA-CHAN

JUN MORIYASU-SAN

MASANORI-SAN

JUNSHI BABA-SAN

YUICHI SHIMOMURA-SHI (MANAGER)

AND YOU!!

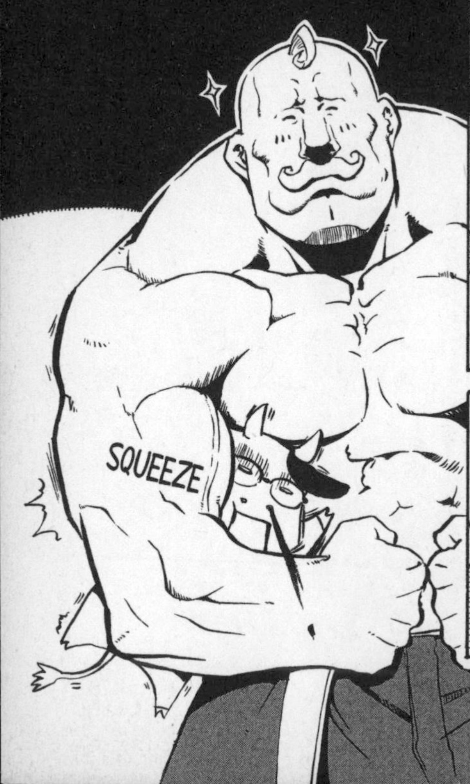
SQUEEZE

TWO YOUNG BROTHERS WANT TO BECOME STRONGER... BUT HOW FAR MUST THEY GO TO REACH THEIR GOAL!?

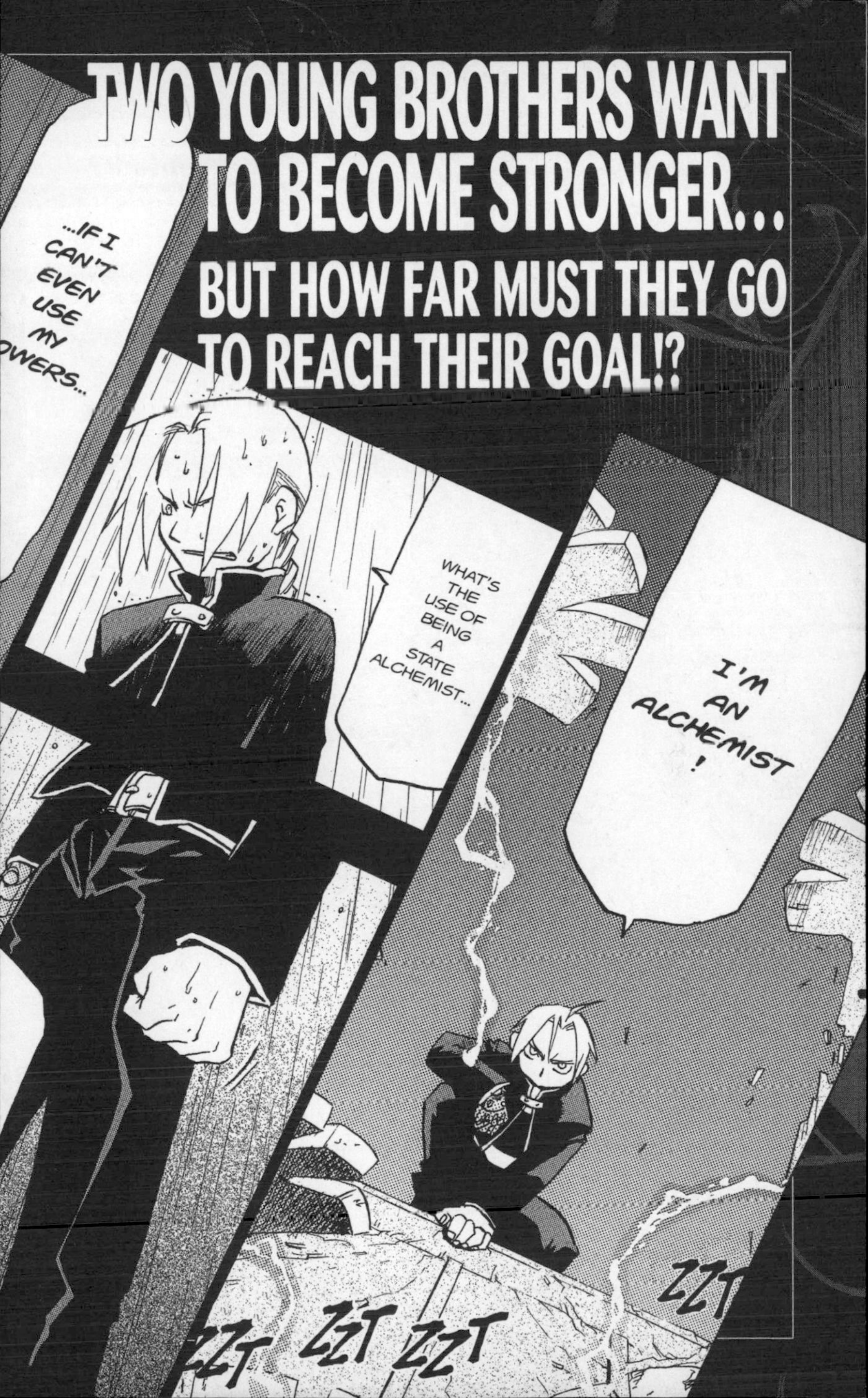

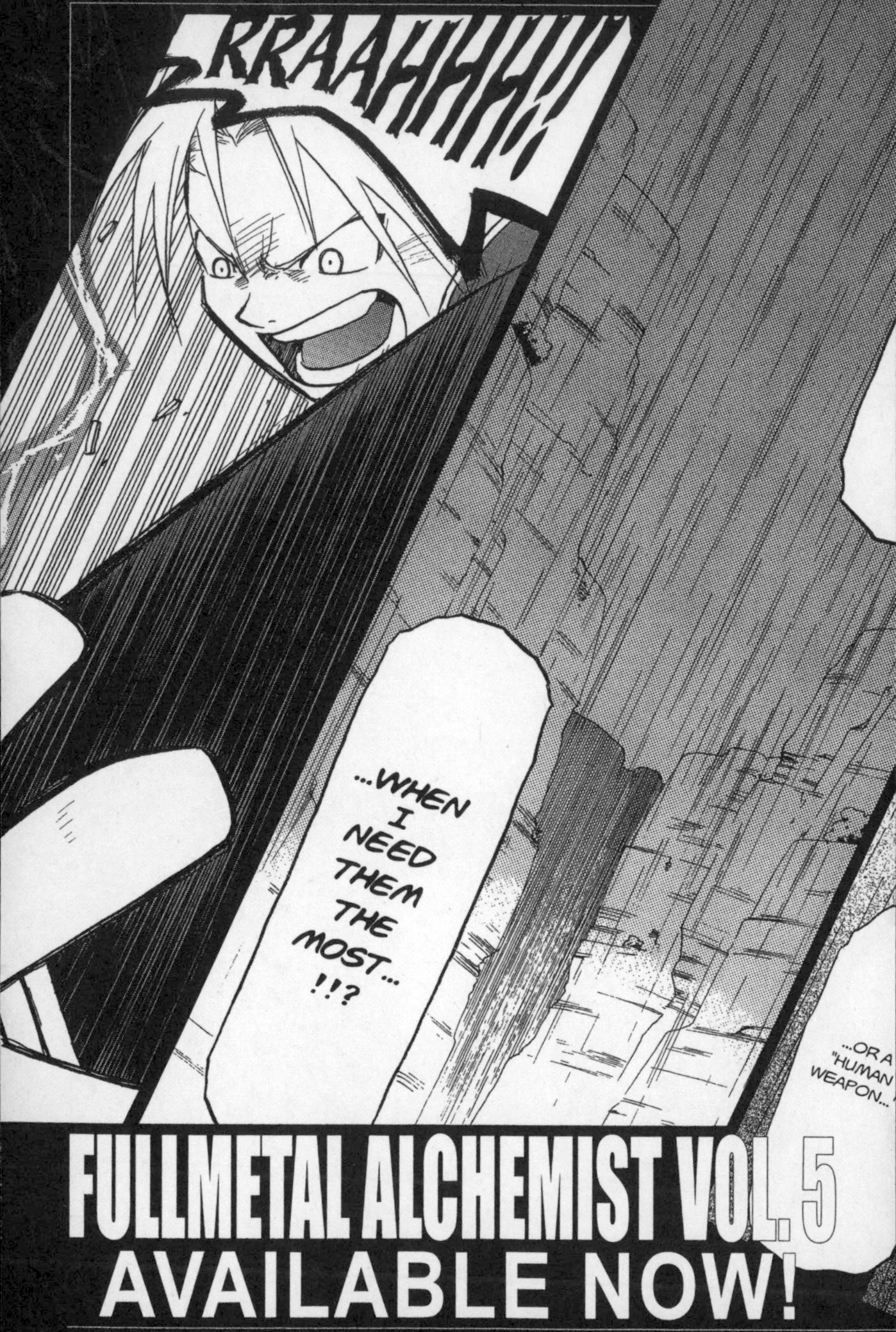
...OR A "HUMAN WEAPON...
KRAAHHHH!!
...WHEN I NEED THEM THE MOST... !!?
FULLMETAL ALCHEMIST VOL. 5
AVAILABLE NOW!

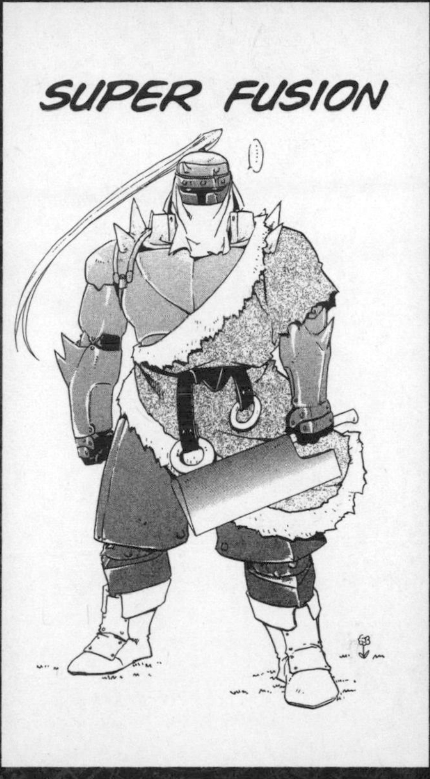
SUPER FUSION

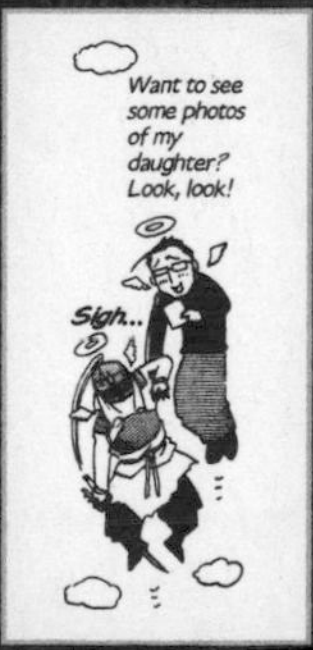
Want to see some photos of my daughter? Look, look!
Sigh...

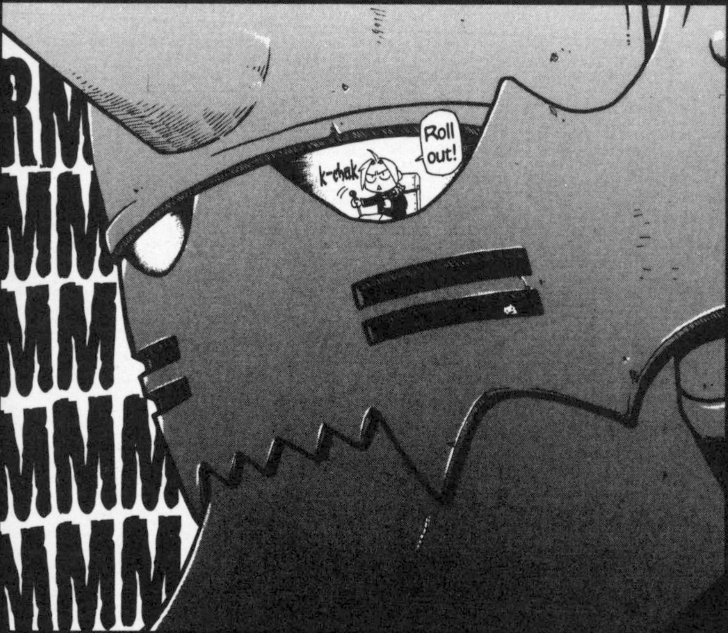
Roll out!
k-chak
RMMMMMMMMMMMM

Tegami Bachi
LETTER·BEE

a BEACON of hope for a world trapped in DARKNESS

STORY AND ART BY

HIROYUKI ASADA

— Manga on sale now! —

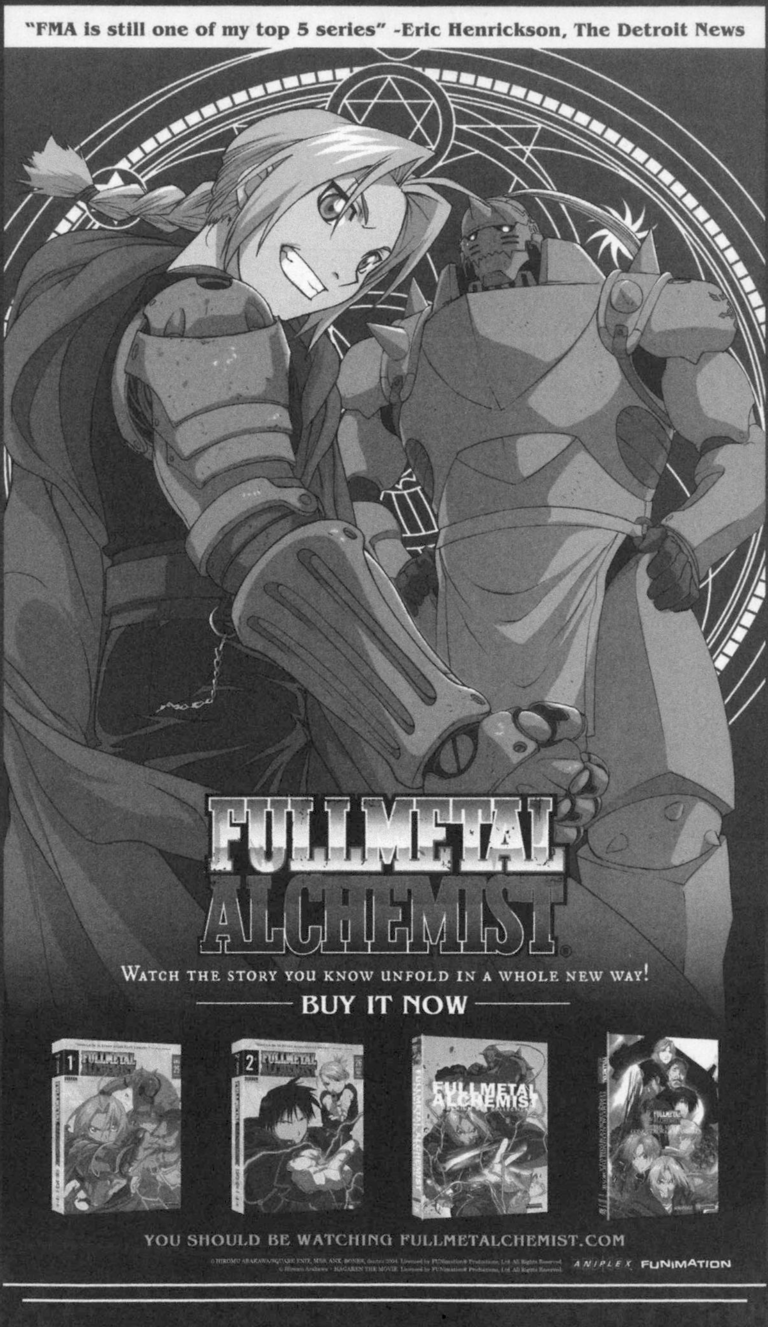

"FMA is still one of my top 5 series" -Eric Henrickson, The Detroit News
FULLMETAL ALCHEMIST®
WATCH THE STORY YOU KNOW UNFOLD IN A WHOLE NEW WAY!
BUY IT NOW
YOU SHOULD BE WATCHING FULLMETALCHEMIST.COM
ANIPLEX
FUNIMATION

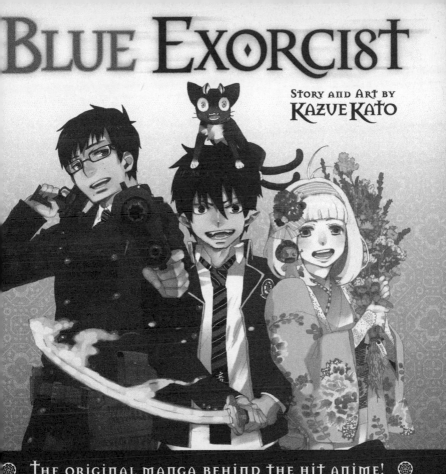
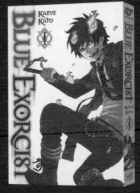

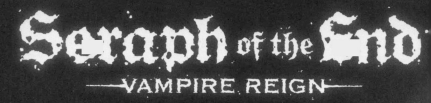

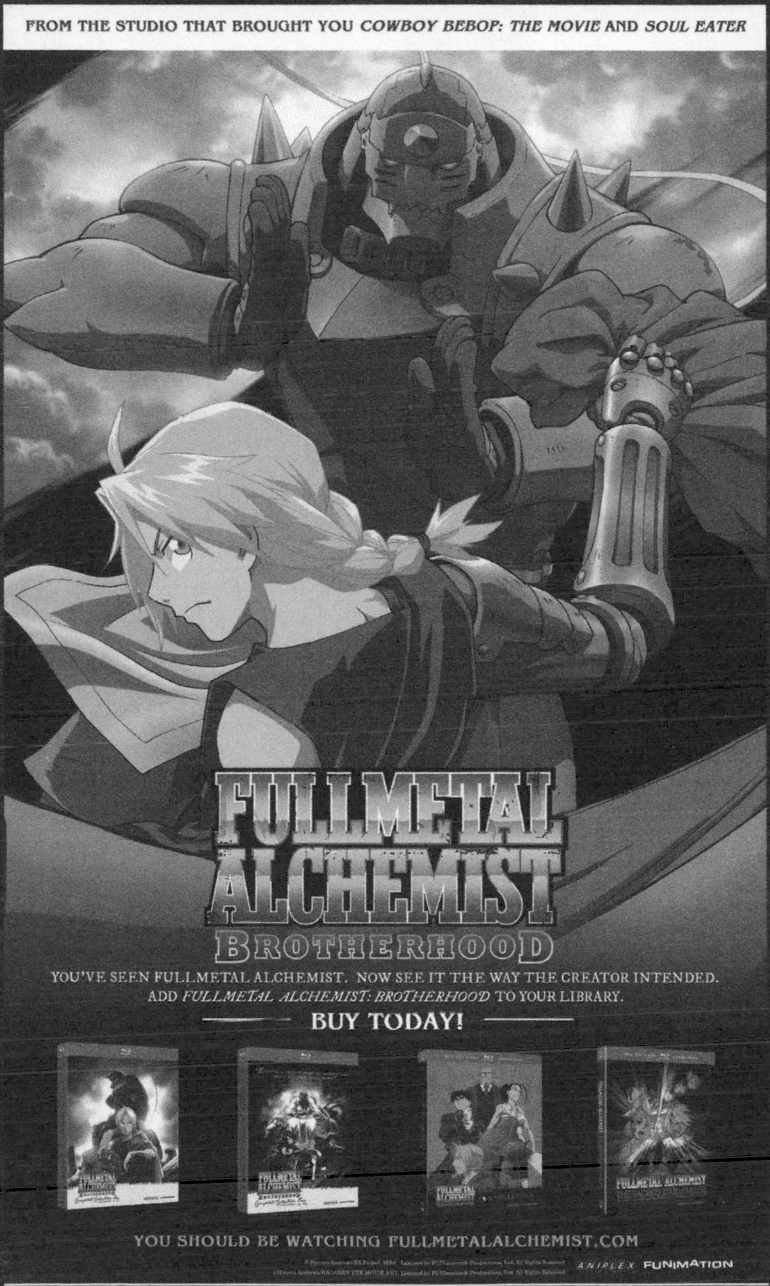
FROM THE STUDIO THAT BROUGHT YOU COWBOY BEBOP: THE MOVIE AND SOUL EATER
FULLMETAL ALCHEMIST
BROTHERHOOD
YOU'VE SEEN FULLMETAL ALCHEMIST. NOW SEE IT THE WAY THE CREATOR INTENDED.
ADD FULLMETAL ALCHEMIST: BROTHERHOOD TO YOUR LIBRARY.
BUY TODAY!
YOU SHOULD BE WATCHING FULLMETALALCHEMIST.COM
ANIPLEX
FUNIMATION

Hey! You're Reading in the Wrong Direction!

This is the **end** of this graphic novel!

To properly enjoy this VIZ graphic novel, please turn it around and begin reading from **right to left.** Unlike English, Japanese is read right to left, so Japanese comics are read in reverse order from the way English comics are typically read.

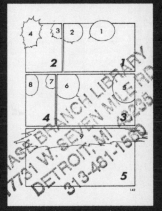

Follow the action this way

This book has been printed in the original Japanese format in order to preserve the orientation of the original artwork. Have fun with it!